Toward a General Theory of Action

Social Science Classics

Toward a General Theory of Action

Theoretical Foundations for the Social Sciences

Talcott Parsons & Edward A. Shils

With a new introduction by
Neil J. Smelser

Transaction Publishers
New Brunswick (U.S.A.) and London (U.K.)

New material in this abridged edition copyright © 2001 by Transaction Publishers, New Brunswick, New Jersey. Originally published in 1951, 1953 by Harvard University Press.

This book is printed on acid-free paper that meets the American National Standard for Permanence of Paper for Printed Library Materials.

Library of Congress Catalog Number: 00-055200
ISBN: 0-7658-0718-1
Printed in the United States of America

Library of Congress Cataloging-in-Publication Data

Toward a general theory of action: theoretical foundations for the social sciences / Talcott Parsons and Edward A. Shils, editors; with a new introduction by Neil J. Smelser.—Abridged ed.
        p.cm.—(Social science classics series)
    Includes bibliographical references (p.) and index.
    ISBN: 0-7658-0718-1 (pbk.: alk. paper)
        1. Functionalism (Social sciences) 2. Social systems. I. Parsons, Talcott, 1902- II. Shils, Edward, 1910-1995. III. Smelser, Neil J. IV. Series.

HM484 . T68 2000
301—dc21

                                                                        00-055200

Contents

PART 1   The General Theory of Action

**Talcott Parsons, Edward A Shils, Gordon W. Allport, Clyde
Kluckhohn, Henry A. Murray, Robert R. Sears, Richard C.
Sheldon, Samuel A. Stouffer, Edward C. Tolman**

(1) Introduction. (2) The frame of reference of the theory of action. (3)
Some fundamentals of behaviour psychology. (4) Interaction and the
development of personality. (5) Cultural aspects of action systems. (6)
The social system. A note on the place of economic theory and political
theory in the general theory of action.

Richard C. Sheldon

PART 2   Values, Motives, and Systems of Action

Talcott Parsons, Edward A. Shils, with the assistance of James Olds

Action and its orientation. Components of the frame of reference
of the theory of action. Commentary on the frame of reference.
Classification of objects. Orientation to the situation. Dilemmas of
orientation and the pattern variables. The definition of pattern
variables. The interrelations of the pattern variables. Classification
of need-dispositions and role-expectations. Classification of components of the object situation. The basic structure of the interac
tive relationship. The concept of system and the classification of
types of systems.

Motivational concepts. Need-dispositions. Functional prerequisites
of the personality system. Learning processes and performance
processes. The mechanisms. Subintegrations in the personality system. The articulation of personality and social systems. Need-dis-
postions and role-expectations. Individuality. Deviance.

Introduction to the Transaction Edition

One spring day in 1951, I was sitting quietly in the hallway of Emerson Hall in Harvard Yard, waiting to meet with a faculty member of the Department of Social Relations in whose course I was enrolled. I was an undergraduate, a junior, at the time. Suddenly and unexpectedly the door of Talcott Parsons' office flew open, and Parsons emerged, waving a brownish-yellow volume in the air. It was a prepublication copy of the heralded *Toward a General Theory of Action.* Parsons proceeded to run around the hallway, displaying the book to all in sight—including me, whom I believe he barely knew at the time—and talking excitedly about "his baby."

The incident had its comical side, and still does, but at the same time it symbolized rather accurately the contemporary fervor felt about the scientific and intellectual mission of the Social Relations enterprise by most faculty and students associated with it, and the excitement about this particular volume, conceived—certainly by Parsons, but by some others as well—as something of a manifesto of that enterprise.

As an undergraduate concentrator in Social Relations, I was sufficiently moved by Parsons' enthusiasm to go out and buy that book at the earliest opportunity, and to read it. I have had occasion to go back to the book on a number of occasions over the years, and now I have read it in full again, nearly a half century after its appearance, in order to re-introduce it to the contemporary behavioral- and social-science world.

THE REPUBLICATION

The republication of the conceptual and theoretical core of *Toward a General Theory of Action* (Parsons and Shils, 1951) is a deserved and welcome event. This work stands as one of the most important theoretical statements in twentieth-century sociology. It marked a peak, if not the high point, in the development of that tradition of sociology known as structural-functional analysis. More than any single publication, it symbolized the brave and important— if impermanent—visionary effort to synthesize the behavioral and social sciences that was embodied in the Department of Social Relations at Harvard. Perhaps most important, almost all of the analytic categories, theoretical issues, and substantive assertions found in *Toward a General Theory of Action* survive in the theoretical discourse and empirical research in the behavioral and social sciences at end of century.

Transactions Publishers has decided—and as informal advisor in the process, I concur completely—to publish only four parts of the original volume:

- Preface, written by Talcott Parsons, explaining the Social Relations background of the collaborative project that produced the volume (pp. v-viii of the original).

- Chapter 1 of Part 1, "Some Fundamental Categories of the Theory of Action: A General Statement." This was the consensus statement of all those who were participating in the collaborative project—Parsons and Shils, Gordon W. Allport, Clyde Kluckhohn, Henry A. Murray, Robert R. Sears, Richard C. Sheldon, Samuel A. Stouffer, Edward C. Tolman. Three of these—Parsons, Allport, and Kluckhohn—were among the founders of the Department of Social Relations—and Stouffer and Murray were members of it (pp. 3-29 of the original).

- Chapter 2 of Part 1, "Some Observations on Theory in the Social Sciences," by Sheldon. This is a perceptive methodological and philosophy-of-science commentary on the status of the "general theory of action" (pp. 30-44 of the original).

- Part 2, "Values, Motives, and Systems of Action," by Parsons and Shils, with the assistance of James Olds. This is the theoretical heart of the project, which has commanded most of the critical attention of the various behavioral- and social-science audiences of the volume since its publication (pp. 45-275 of the original).

The remaining 200 pages of *Toward a General Theory of Action* consist of separate chapters by Tolman, Allport, Kluckhohn, Murray, Sears and Stouffer. Tolman's monograph (pp. 279-362) is a notable, virtuoso creation of a psychological model consistent with the theory of action, and the other essays are briefer elaborations of selected concepts and issues specific to the interests of the several authors. These are not included in this republication, largely because none of them excited the interest or had the staying-power of Parsons' and Shils' general theoretical statement.

INSTITUTIONAL, INTELLECTUAL, AND PERSONAL BACKGROUND

The story of *Toward a General Theory of Action* cannot be told without reference to the story of the Department of Social Relations, and both those stories are inseparable from the biographies of the main actors in each.

In the early 1940s Harvard had Economics, Government, Psychology, Anthropology, and Sociology as established academic departments. The latter three shared one major common characteristic: extreme division along academic/ political lines, and a correspondingly extreme disaffection on the part of a minority of eminent scholars in each. To oversimplify the picture somewhat, Psychology was controlled by a group with biological/experimental interests (Edwin G. Boring, Karl Lashley, and John Beebe-Center) with a significant but outnumbered minority of personality/developmental psychologists (Gordon W. Allport, Henry Murray, and Robert White). Clyde Kluckhohn was the only social/cultural anthropologist in a department dominated by physical anthropologists and archaeologists who found little of interest and value in Kluckhohn's work. Sociology was a very small department chaired by Pitirim A. Sorokin, under whose dictatorial style Talcott Parsons had chafed for a number of years. These respective minorities shared a number of positive intellectual interests in common (Freudian psychoanalysis, for example) and were above all committed to the independent significance of personality, social structure, and culture as salient aspects *and* determinants in human life.

The idea of forming a new, interdisciplinary department crystallized among this group late in the war years, and with the active help of Harvard's provost, Paul Buck, they created a separate Department of Social Relations, with both graduate and undergraduate programs, in 1946. The event marked the splitting-off of some of its members from the Psychology and Anthropology departments, and the overthrow of Sorokin in Sociology. The birth was thus simultaneously a banner-carrying, entrepreneurial mission *and* an assemblage of scholars moving out of their troubled departmental environments (for a general account, see Johnston, 1995, Ch. 5). Parsons became the first chair of Social Relations, and served in that position for ten years. The Government and Economics departments were not involved in the birth, so it was something less than a completely interdisciplinary invention. The editors of *Toward a General Theory of Action* included a brief "note" on the place of political science and economics in the general theory of action (pp. 28-29). This note should be assessed in its own right, but it also stands as a symbolic confirmation that the faculty from these two disciplines were not players in the interdisciplinary enterprise of Social Relations.

We can carry this thought one step further. Any reader of the material between these covers will recognize the centrality of the concepts of personality system, social system, and cultural system as building blocks for the framework of action, as well as other concepts associated with these systems—motivation, learning, imitation, identification, role, social structure, and values. Again, the theory of action should be assessed in the first instance as an intellectual synthesis in its own right. At the same time it can be regarded as a kind of political statement, an act of inclusion of the central preoccupations of the those minority members of the three departments involved—Psychology (personality), Anthropology (culture) and Sociology (social system), respectively.

The special backgrounds of Parsons and some other pioneers of Social Relations must also be acknowledged. Parsons had taken major steps toward formulating a concept of "action" in his 1937 opus, *The Structure of Social Action*, but compared with what was to come later, that was theoretically sketchy, and only a part of a more general effort to demonstrate that a number of apparently diverse social theorists (Alfred Marshall, Vilfredo Pareto, Émile Durkheim, and Max Weber) had converged on a theoretical focus that could be called a voluntaristic notion of motivated and normatively regulated "action" as contrasted with "behavior."

It was also in *The Structure of Social Action* that Parsons began his theoretical work on the pattern-variables, which are so central in the 1951 synthesis. In particular, Parsons was dissatisfied with the Ferdinand Toennies' global distinction between *gemeinschaft* and *gesellschaft* (Toennies, 1963 [1935]). In a famous "note" on this distinction (Parsons, 1937, pp. 686-94), he began to disaggregate it into ascription vs. achievement, universalism vs. particularism and affectivity vs. affective neutrality. These dimensions figured prominently in the "empirical" phase of Parsons' career (1937-48) in which he wrote essays on professional roles, the American family, and American, German, and Japanese social structure (Parsons, 1954, Chs. II, III, V, VI, IX, XIII). The formulations in *Toward a General Theory of Action* raised these pattern-variables to a more abstract theoretical level, at which Parsons and his colleagues treated them not only as a system of universal and exhaustive "choices" involved in the structuring of social action, but also as logically derived from the basic categories of the framework of the theory of action.

Toward a General Theory of Action, then, is a product of many stories. It is in large part a creation of Talcott Parsons (with Edward Shils' important collaboration) which, however, also incorporated the major working variables of academic psychology, anthropology, and sociology of the day, as well as special interests of individual collaborators—for example, Murray on needs and need-dispositions, Kluckhohn on explicit vs. implicit culture, and Allport on the "functional autonomy" of motives. It is certainly a collective expression of the Department of Social Relations, though some members of the Department, notably George Homans, violently rejected that idea (Homans, 1984). And above all, both Social Relations and *Toward a General Theory of Action* were expressions of the remarkable optimism abroad in the postwar years about the scientific and practical promise of the behavioral and social sciences (see Chase, 1948). One ingredient of this optimism, moreover, was the vision, faith, and hope for a unity of science—voiced both before and after mid-century but certainly salient at that moment. This impulse was found in the work and labors of Parsons himself and some of his students (for example, Levy, 1952); in the general systems theory (Boulding, 1956; Buckley, 1967); in specific theories such as cybernetics (Wiener, 1948), and in the philosophy of science of the day (Carnap, 1934, 1966; Toulmin, 1953; Kaplan, 1964).

As formidable a statement as *Toward a General Theory of Action* is, that particular expression of the theory of action turned out to be very short-lived. Already in 1952 Parsons was beginning his collaboration with the psychologist, Robert F. Bales, whose pioneering research focused on group processes as they related to group performance and solidarity (Bales, 1949). Within another year (Parsons, Bales, and Shils, 1953), the pattern-variables had formally been incorporated into a new version of action—that of the functional system-problems—that was to remain the theoretical centerpiece of Parsons' work during the last quarter-century of his career.

THE INGREDIENTS OF THE GENERAL THEORY OF ACTION

In "Values, Motives, and Systems of Action," Parsons and Shils first make an effort to establish the scientific status of "the general theory of action." They list four types of systematization of knowledge, moving in ascending levels—from primitiveness to completeness—with respect to the goals of scientific explanation:

1. *ad hoc* classificatory systems, a group of "more or less arbitrary classes for the sake of making . . . statements about the subject-matter" (p. 50). "Flesh, fish, or fowl" is an example.

2. categorical systems, which involves the statement of logical *relationships* among classes—relationships of priority, interdependence, etc.

3. theoretical systems, which contain statements of abstract *laws* or expected outcomes which are derived from the logical relationships.

4. empirical-theoretical systems, which involves the specification and explanation of empirical regularities found in the observed world.

Parsons and Shils acknowledge that the range of theory they present in the volume "has not yet reached far enough to justify calling ours a theoretical system" (p. 51). From the beginning, then, according to the authors' own assessment, the theory of action should be regarded mainly as a categorical system.

What, then, are the major categories of "action"? Parsons and Shils list four:

(1) Behavior is oriented to the attainment of ends or goals or other anticipated states of affairs. (2) It takes place in situations. (3) It is normatively regulated. (4) It involves expenditure or effort in "motivation" . . . (p. 53).

The objects (both nonsocial [physical and cultural] and social [other persons and groups]) in actors' situations may be goals of action, means of action, obstacles, or symbols. Moreover, action of human beings is organized into *systems*, the simplest of which can be represented in Figure 1.

The orientation of action to objects involves cognition, or knowing about the objects; cathexis, or positive or negative attachment to objects; and evaluation, or the selection among different objects in terms of standards important to the actor.

In keeping with the principle that action is organized into systems, Parsons and his collaborators identified three fundamental system-levels:

1. The personality system, the organizing principle of which is need-dispositions; the fundamental units of analysis are needs, drives, sentiments, beliefs, and skills.

2. The social system, which is composed of two or more actors in a situation, as Figure 1 shows. The basic units of analysis are clusters of activities, roles, and collectivities.

3. The cultural system, which is made up of values, belief-systems, ideologies, expressive symbols, and cognitive productions.

Figure 1

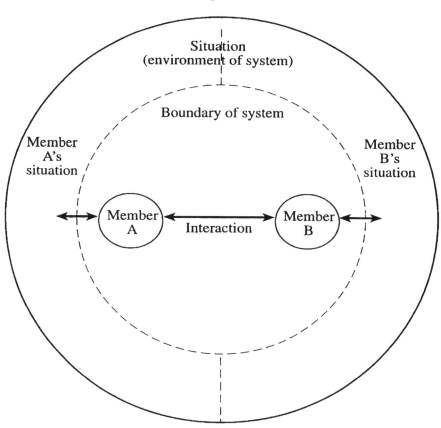

Throughout the authors insist that the three system-levels are conceptual constructs—ways of regarding the empirical reality from which they are extracted. Each is logically independent from and non-reducible to the others. However, the three systems interpenetrate–for example, through the infusion of culture into the personality system in the process of internalization, and through the infusion of culture into the social system in the process of institutionalization.

By being organized into three distinct levels or systems, action takes on a measure of *structure* (the ideas of structure and structuring are recurrent if not omnipresent in the Parsons-Shils monograph). An additional way in which action is structured is found in the pattern-variables. This somewhat oddly-named complex refers to certain "dilemmas of orientation", which must be addressed if action is to take place at all. Parsons and Shils characterize them as "dichotomies, one side of which must be chosen by an actor before the meaning of a situation is determinate for him, and thus before he can act with respect to that situation" (p. 77). Parsons and Shils assert that these are derived from the definitional framework of action itself. The pattern-variables are five in number and can be summarized in the following way:

1. Does the actor react to an object in terms of its *qualities* (which are relatively independent of present or expected performances) or does the actor give primacy to present or expected *performances?* This is the essence of the pattern-variable of *ascription-achievement.* An example of ascription is confirmation into a church, which occurs at a specified age; an example of achievement is graduation from college, which depends on an individual's performances.

2. How broad is the scope of significance of the object for the actor? An example of a narrow scope is a physician's interest in a patient's symptoms, which usually excludes an interest in matters other than health. An example of a broad scope is the relationship between spouses or intimate partners, in which most aspects of the relationship are legitimate matters of concern. This distinction yields the pattern-variable of *functional specificity-functional diffuseness.*

3. Can impulses be gratified or is some kind of inhibition or postponement involved? The child, in his or her relationship to a parent, is permitted a wide range of expression of emotion. The physician, in relation to a patient, is expected to withhold emotional reactions, even in the face of situations that would seem to call for them. This distinction yields the pattern-variable of *affectivity-affective neutrality.*

4. Does the actor relate to the object in terms of some specific relationship he or she has with the object, or in terms of some general rule? An example of the former is forgiving a library fine because the offender is the librarian's brother; an example of the latter is collecting the fine because a library rule has been violated. This distinction yields the pattern-variable of *universalism-particularism.*

5. Is the actor permitted to be "out for himself" or should the actor be guided more by moral considerations, that is, the interests of a higher collectivity? The institutionalization of the business role in American society allows for a high level of self-interest; the institutionalization of most religious roles calls for helping of others. This distinction yields the pattern-variable of *self-interest—collectivity-interest.*

These pattern-variables are exhaustive in that they "[cover] all the fundamental alternatives which can arise directly out to the frame of reference for the theory of action" (p. 88). They are universal in that they constitute the bases on which personality systems, social systems, and cultural systems are structured. All of these systems can be characterized according to how they have "chosen" in relation to these dilemmas, or alternatively, how they have "solved" them.

The Parsons-Shils monograph consists of an elaborate development of action and its attributes, and incorporates, along the way, a multiplicity of phenomena and issues familiar to behavioral and social sciences—the blend of genetic influences and learning in the determination of motivational needs, plasticity of action, role theory, social structure, deviance, and, above all, the balances between integration and breakdown and between stability and change in systems of action.

UNSOLVED PROBLEMS, AMBIVALENCES, DILEMMAS, AND RIDDLES

It remains to address some of the limitations of theoretical enterprise that appears in *Toward a General Theory of Action*. In doing this I will not evoke broadside criticisms such as "this is the wrong approach to social science," but will focus, rather, on problems that emerge from the internal logic of the general theory of action and in its exposition.

A THEORY OR A FRAMEWORK?

The title of the work contains the words "general theory," but the same title expresses a hesitation, embodied in the words "toward a," clearly implying that the journey to a theory is not complete. The words "theory of action" recur repeatedly throughout the text, implying that it is a theory, but at the same time the reader is repeatedly assured that it is a framework, a "conceptual scheme" (p. 235) and a classificatory system, and that it falls short of a developed theory. The main import of Sheldon's essay is that the theory of action "does not purport to be a final, fully worked out theory. In large measure it is a statement of the categories, or variables, which are *to make up* a complete general theory for the social sciences" (p. 42, italics added). What it lacks, he adds, is operational definitions, or ways in which the categories "are to be connected to sense data," and "principles . . . whereby relationships subject to empirical test can be derived" (p. 43). The whole of the exposition of "Values, Motives, and Systems of Action" occupies some middle ground of ambivalence between grandiosity and modesty with respect to theoretical claims. I record this ambivalence both because it stands out in the exposition, and because of the recurrent criticism of Parsons' work in general: that it was a proliferation of abstract categories devoid of concrete or testable hypotheses.

THREE SYSTEMS?

The triad of the personality system, social system, and cultural system is one of the principal elements of the theory of action. At the outset of the "general statement" the authors announce that "[in] the formation of systems made up of human actions or the components of human action, this elaboration occurs in three configurations . . . personality system, social system, and cultural system" (p. 7), analytically independent from one another but interrelated and interpenetrating. However, an asymmetry appears immediately. Personality and social systems are described as "concrete systems of action," and culture is "not in itself organized as a system of action" and thus lies on a "different plane" (ibid.). In a later footnote, it is acknowledged that "cultural systems are *symbolic* systems in which the components have logical rather than functional relationships with one another," and that "[in] cultural systems the systemic feature is *coherence*; the components of the cultural system are either *logically consistent* or meaningfully *congruous*" (p. 173, italics in original).

Given these acknowledgments, one wonders why culture is to be represented as a "system of action," as it is in the title, "Values, Motives, and Systems of Action." Culture as a system has neither actors nor action; its principles of "systemness" are qualitatively different from the other two; and the mechanisms involved in maintaining a degree of cultural integrity or equilibrium, in culture conflict, and in culture change seem qualitatively so different from those involved in personality and social processes as to resist comparisons with one another. Throughout his scholarly career Parsons insisted on the "systemness" of culture, but the conceptual uneasiness about what that actually entails—an uneasiness expressed in *Toward a General Theory of Action*—always persisted.

CULTURE AS COMMON AND COHERENT?

Two constants in Parsons' sociology are the postulates that societies must have consensus on common values and that cultures must have a degree of integration if they are to survive. These threads appear in *Toward a General Theory of Action*. With respect to commonness, the matter is stated as something of a postulate:

> Value-orientations . . . possess . . . the potentiality of becoming the common values of the members of a collectivity. Concretely, value-orientations are overwhelmingly involved in processes of social interaction. For this reason consistency of normative orientation cannot be confined to one actor in his action in different situations and at different times; there must also be integration on an inter-individual level. Rules, that is, must be generalized in a manner to apply to all actors in the relevant situations in the interaction system. This is an elementary prerequisite of social order (p. 173).

The degree of coherence of culture and cultures is a long-standing preoccupation and debate in the social sciences. The issue arises in the formulations of early social and cultural anthropologists, in the literature on subcultures and countercultures, and not least in the post-modernist literature (see Smelser, 1992). In almost all of the secondary literature on the sociology of Talcott Parsons, he is regarded as occupying one theoretical extreme, insisting on the need for coherence or integration of culture.

Evidence on the issue of cultural coherence appears in *Toward a General Theory of Action*. In the "General Statement" it is asserted, cultural patterns tend to become organized into systems. The peculiar feature of this systematization is a type of integration which we may call *consistency of pattern*. Whether it be the logical consistency of a belief system, the stylistic harmony of an art form, or the rational compatibility of a body of moral rules, the internal coherence of a body of cultural patterns is always a crucial problem for the student of culture (p. 21; italics in original).

Why this is a "crucial problem" is never really explained, though reasons might be imagined—for example, the impossibility for action to occur in a completely unstructured environment, or, as indicated in the quotation below, the need to minimize conflict.

Another point of incompleteness in the treatment of cultural coherence concerns the degree to which it is observed in actual cultures or how much might be functionally required for it to qualify as a culture. On this score we receive nothing more than an equivocation:

> [All patterns of moral standards] . . . will, as systems, inevitably fall short of "perfect integration" *which in the case of culture pattern systems must be interpreted to mean consistency of pattern.* At the same time the imperative of approximating the consistency of pattern arising from the need to minimize the strain of conflict within a system of action is so strong that it is improbable that the actual ranges of variation of systems of moral standards will coincide with the range of possible combinations of orientations to different classes of objects (p. 171; italics in original).

From this we may conclude that the issue of coherence is certainly paramount in the minds of the authors, and that cultural coherence is more than random and less than complete. The text is silent, however, on criteria for ascertaining the degree of actual or optimal coherence of a culture.

THREE PUZZLES CONCERNING THE PATTERN-VARIABLES

(1) *Derived?* This puzzle concerns their logical status. The authors say that pattern-variables are "the most important thread of continuity running through ['Values, Motives, and Systems of Action']" (p. 48), and refer to them as a "highly important, derived, classificatory system" (p. 76). By "derived" they mean that they follow logically from the categories of the framework of action—the idea of action itself, ends or goals, motivation, and normative regulation. Several examples of such derivation follow:

a. Affectivity-affective neutrality: "the actor must choose whether to accept gratification from the immediately cognized and cathected object or to evaluate such gratification in terms of its consequences for other aspects of the action system" (p. 77).

b. Self-orientation—collectivity-orientation: "if the actor decides to evaluate, he must choose whether or not to give primacy to the moral standards of the social system or subsystem" (ibid.)

c. Universalism-particularism: "whether or not he decides togrant primacy to such moral standards, he must choose whether cognitive or appreciative standards are to be dominant, the one set with relation to the other. If cognitive standards are dominant over appreciative standards, the actor will tend to locate objects in terms of their relation to some generalized frame of reference [universalism]; if appreciative standards are dominant over cognitive, the actor will tend to locate objects in terms of their relation to himself, or to his motives [particularism]" (ibid.)

One can raise detailed critical questions about these definitions—for example, whether the logic of universalism as elsewhere used is equivalent to cognitive primacy and whether the logic of particularism as elsewhere used is equivalent to cathective primacy. More generally, however, it is difficult to understand in what exact sense the pattern-variables are derived, as a matter of logical entailment, from the categories of the framework of action—actor, object, situation, and cognition-cathexis-evaluation. Certainly the pattern variables are *described* in terms of those categories, and, as far as can be determined, they are by and large *consistent* with their usage. But to proclaim logical derivation is, I suspect, an instance of an over-claiming of scientific precision and formality.

(2) *Dichotomous?* In characterizing the pattern-variables, the authors assert that "the actor must make five specific dichotomous choices before any situation will have a determinate meaning" (p. 76). And throughout the Parsons-Shils monographs the pattern-variables are characterized as dichotomies, that is, two-value or either-or variables. Yet the logic-in-use of these distinction reveals something different than either-or. For example, specificity-diffuseness refers to a *range* or *scope* or *numbers* of ways in which a situation is relevant to or makes demands on an actor. Surely this is a continuum, not reducible to exclusively "broad" or "narrow." The distinction between self-orientation and collectivity-orientation also seems more complex than a dichotomy; surely action can be characterized by complex mixes of self-interest and interest for superordinate group memberships, rather than exclusive choices between the two. It seems conceivable, furthermore, that dedication to the cause of some higher collectivity can at the same time be self-interested. It appears to me that the authors did not have any particular analytic need to characterize the pattern-variables as dichotomous, and to have done so involves them in some inconsistencies. My own view is that they should have advertised the pattern-variables for what they were—very general dimensions involved in the structuring of social action, and valuable as such in the comparative analysis of social structure. I think, furthermore, that in coating them with an unwarranted scientific precision, they did both the pattern-variables and themselves a disservice.

(3) *Choices?* The definitional statement "the actor must make . . . choices before any situation will have a determinate meaning," must be assigned a metaphorical meaning. If it implies deliberate choice, it carries both individualistic and free-will biases inconsistent with Parsons' and Shils' general views on the determination of action. In addition, the institutionalization of the pattern-variables at the cultural and social-system levels are surely not actors' "choices," but rather aspects of the situation that are presented to and determined for the

actor. Throughout the manuscript the term "choice" is used more or less interchangeably with the term "selection"; this seems to reveal the ambiguity of using "choosing" to refer to the pattern-variables.

As a theorist Parsons has been regarded widely if not universally as a theorist of stability—assuming that societies are "going concerns," or, if they experience strains, will activate restorative mechanisms that tend to re-equilibrate. That view emerges in part in the pages of *Toward a General Theory of Action*, but it conforms only partially to the received view. It is appropriate to remind ourselves of that imagery.

As indicated above, Parsons and Shils take the view that any system—personality, social, or cultural—is neither perfectly integrated nor completely random. Thus inconsistency and the potentiality for strain appear to be inevitable in any system. In addition, the authors assume that the exigencies of each system are different and sometimes incompatible with one another, and this constitutes another source of tension and strain.

The main mechanisms for maintaining equilibrium in social systems are *socialization* and *social control*. Socialization is the inculcation, through learning, of dispositions to conform to the role-expectations of the social system (p. 227). Socialization is best regarded as the first line of defense against deviance. However, "[failure] of the mechanisms of socialization to motivate conformity with expectations creates tendencies to deviant behavior which, beyond certain critical points, would be disruptive of the social order or equilibrium" (p. 228). The response of the social system is to activate various mechanisms of social control, which include imposition of sanctions (rewards and deprivations), insulation and segregation, and contingent reintegration (p. 230). Yet even these do not assure equilibrium:

> The loopholes in the institutional system are one of the main channels through which [shifts in the balance between . . . institutionalized patterns] often take place. Hence, in the combination of the inherent tendencies to deviation and the imperfections of the integration of value-orientations, there are in every social system inherent possibilities (p. 231).

The potential for social change in social systems is omnipresent, but the theory, as sketched, treats social change as something of a "last resort" phenomenon, resulting from the failure of equilibrating mechanisms. It is also a relatively narrow theoretical statement, not including possibilities of institutionalized sources of change, for example, which Parsons himself stressed in noting dynamic tendencies inherent in American cultural values of instrumental activism and mastery.

A Concluding Remark

At century's end *Toward a General Theory of Action* remains one of the most important, highly formalized, bold and heroic, yet incomplete efforts at general theoretical syntheses of the century. Perhaps the most lasting assessment may be

found in the words of Parsons and Shils themselves. They did not claim originality in content; "nearly all the concepts which have here been brought together
have been current in various forms and on various levels of concreteness in the
social sciences in the twentieth century" (p. 238). Any originality that is found is
"in the way in which the concepts have been related to one another" (ibid.).
However, they argued that "it might be fairly claimed that the present scheme
offers the basis of an important advance toward the construction of a unified
theory of science" (ibid.)

Yet neither Parsons nor his collaborators pushed this particular project further toward "a unified theory of science." Nor did others. In the past half-
century, American behavioral and social scientists have come to shun such efforts at such general social theorizing, and have chosen more modest, though
not necessarily more successful, ways to advance their sciences.

NEIL J. SMELSER

REFERENCES

Bales, Robert F. 1949. *Interaction Process Analysis.* Cambridge, MA: Addison-Wesley
    Press.
Boulding, Kenneth. 1956. *The Image.* Ann Arbor: University of Michigan Press.
Buckley, Walter. 1967. *Sociology and Modern Systems Theory.* Englewood Cliffs, NJ:
    Prentice-Hall.
Carnap, Rudolf. 1934. *The Unity of Science.* London: Kegan Paul, Trench, Trubner & Co.
Carnap, Rudolf. 1966. *Philosoophical Foundations of Physics.* New York: Basic Books.
Chase, Stuart. 1948. *The Proper Study of Mankind.* New York: Harper.
Homans, George C. 1984. *Coming to My Senses.* New Brunswick, NJ: Transaction Publish-
    ers.
Johnston, Barry V. 1995. *Pitirim A. Sorokin: An Intellectual Biography.* Lawrence: Univer-
    sity of Kansas Press.
Kaplan, Abraham. 1964. *The Conduct of Inquiry.* San Francisco, CA: Chandler.
Parsons, Talcott. 1937. *The Structure of Social Action.* New York: McGraw-Hill.
_____. 1954. *Essays in Sociological Theory* (revised edition). Glencoe, IL: The
    Free Press.
Parsons, Talcott and Edward A Shils, eds. 1951. *Toward a General Theory of Action.*
    Cambridge, MA: Harvard University Press.
Parsons, Talcott, Robert F. Bales, and Edward A. Shils. 1953. *Working Papers in the Theory
    of Action.* Glencoe, IL.: The Free Press
Smelser, Neil J. 1992. "Culture: Coherent or Incoherent," in *Theory of Culture,* edited
    by Richard Münch and Neil J. Smelser. Berkeley: University of California Press, pp.
    3-28.
Toennies, Ferdinand. 1963. *Gemeinschaft und Gesellschaft.* Darmstadt: Wissenschaftliche
    [1935] Buchgesellschaft.
Toulmin, Stephen E. 1953. *The Philosophy of Science.* London: Hutchinson's University
    Library.
Wiener, Norbert. 1948. *Cybernetics.* New York: John Wiley and Sons.

Preface

In the fall of 1948 some members of the Department of Social Relations of Harvard University had an informal discussion with the officers of the Carnegie Corporation of New York about the possibility of a "stocktaking" of the theoretical resources of the field of Social Relations. It seemed to both groups that a careful analysis of the theoretical foundations underlying the synthesis which had been worked out on the organizational level through the foundation of the Department of Social Relations two years before might be useful not only in the Department itself but for the development of the social sciences generally. Within the Department it seemed likely to help greatly in clarifying the problems we faced individually in our teaching and research as well as in our corporate capacity as a department.

After some exploration of the feasibility of the project, the Carnegie Corporation kindly placed a grant at the disposal of the Department. This grant was supplemented by funds from the Laboratory of Social Relations at Harvard. Through the coöperation of Provost Paul H. Buck of Harvard, I was relieved of teaching and administrative duties for the fall term of 1949–50, and two distinguished scholars, Professor Edward C. Tolman of the University of California and Professor Edward A. Shils of the University of Chicago, were invited to come to Harvard for the term to collaborate in the project. In addition, the services of Richard C. Sheldon, Fellow of the Russian Research Center and a social anthropologist, were made available on a full-time basis. The four of us constituted the staff of the project.

In addition to the direct work of the staff, we decided to hold a series of discussions with each of two groups, out of which it was hoped that clear lines of thinking would emerge. Because of the great advantages of discussion in a small group, especially when such subtle questions are at issue, one such group was organized. This, besides the four staff members, consisted in the five who have collaborated with the staff in the present volume. However, this policy, if adhered to alone, would have meant going without the extremely valuable contributions of many other, especially the younger, members of the Department. Hence all interested members of the Department were invited to participate with the staff in a second discussion group on theoretical problems. Many of the more important ideas published here owe much to this larger, and younger, group.

Both of these groups met weekly from late September 1949 through January 1950. A highly informal procedure was followed. There had previously been circulated within the Department some three versions of a document

entitled "Assumptions of Basic Social Science," which had been formulated
in connection with the departmental proseminar on Problems and Concepts
of Social Relations.* This document was taken as the point of departure, and
various attempts to begin a revision of it were made. Some members of the
group also drafted memoranda on particular theoretical problem areas.
In November we reached agreement that the general theoretical scheme in
which we were interested could be couched within what we agreed (in the
smaller group) to call the "action" frame of reference. Shortly after that, stimulated especially by Clyde Kluckhohn's presentation, before the smaller group,
of his approach to the analysis of values, the staff evolved a number of new
theoretical insights and developments. All of the subsequent meetings were devoted to discussion of various aspects of these developments and their possible
implications.

Work was not, however, limited to the weekly meetings; we had many personal discussions and applied ourselves to writing as well. After many long
discussions with Edward Shils, I undertook the first draft of what appears in
this volume as Part II, "Values, Motives, and Systems of Action"; Professor
Shils took the lead in the draft's extensive revision. Professor Tolman began
work on his "Psychological Model," which forms Part III of this book. Mr.
Sheldon's contribution, "Some Observations on Theory in Social Science,"
appears as Chapter II of Part I.†

The question of exactly what the material outcome of the project would be
had to be left in abeyance until we could explore the implications of some of
the new developments. It finally was agreed to prepare the present volume for
publication and to include contributions from the staff and also papers from
the other participants in the smaller discussion group. It was decided that
the non-staff collaborators would write on a subject of particular personal interest which would be relevant to the general theoretical field of the project.
These papers make up Part IV of this volume. This made such a large book
that, unfortunately, contributions from members of the larger discussion
group were precluded; hence, as noted, the book fails to do justice to their
important part in the project.

It gradually became clear that what originally had been drafted as an
introductory chapter of Part II contained the basis of an agreed statement
of general principle. Though this draft, which in turn was based on many
discussions, provided the starting point, it was subjected to several severe
— indeed radical — revisions before it emerged as the "General Statement"
which forms the first chapter of Part I. All members of the group contributed
careful and detailed critical comments on several of the drafts, so that as far

---

* The principal authors were Professors Kluckhohn and Murray.

† Mr. Sheldon also carried the heavy burden of supervising the production of a record
of the weekly meetings; this unfortunately limited the time he could devote to theoretical
work as such.

as humanly possible, the statement represents both a carefully considered and a collaborative product. To be sure that no member of the group was having views attributed to him which he did not really share, we agreed that each one should have the privilege of including over his own initials notes of explication or dissent on particular points. The fact that only two members have availed themselves of this privilege, one of them mainly for clarification, is, we feel, an index of the fullness of the measure of agreement we have been able to attain.

This volume thus is the product of nine individual social scientists. The whole character of the enterprise, however, and the constitution of the group, which included four psychologists, three sociologists, and two anthropologists, make its relation to current movements of thought in the field of some interest. Many influences and sources are discernible in the material here set forth. Perhaps the two most important sources in the field of psychology are the study of human personality and the study of animal behavior. The former involves Freud, and the movements stemming from his work, perhaps more than any other influence, but this stream has flowed through several channels — and in its course has influenced the sociologists and anthropologists in the group as well as the psychologists. Other influences have also been important in their effect on personality theory, particularly those documented in Gordon Allport's book on that subject. The study of animal behavior is, we believe, relatively catholic in its influence upon us.

Sociologically, we have been strongly influenced, especially through two of the group, by the work of the Europeans, Durkheim and Max Weber. Professor Stouffer, however, can be said to represent an almost wholly American influence, with the ideas of W. I. Thomas and Park especially prominent in his theoretical thinking. Finally, on the anthropological side, we also have a variety of sources: Boas, Kroeber, and Sapir stand out, but there are many others as well.

Another significant feature of the background of the group is that quite clearly the major trend of thinking of each member has been notably influenced by more than one "school" and more than one discipline. It might perhaps be said that the very fact that we do embody so many different influences has made it all the more urgent for us to attempt to synthesize our thinking. The process has not been altogether easy. Some of us have been closely associated over a considerable span of years. But when we tried to drive mutuality of understanding to deeper theoretical levels than was usual in our discourse, we frequently found unexpected and apparently serious differences — some of which, of course, were attributable to our having been educated in different academic disciplines, each with its sensitivities and blind spots. However, with patience and persistence, we have found it possible to make what, to us, is substantial progress toward agreement.

This fact, combined with the very diversity of the influences which, through their importance to us, have gone into this product, seems to us to bring out with peculiar vividness the fact that these many streams of thought are in the process of flowing together. We feel that the present effort belongs in the context of a major movement, whose significance to the future of social science far transcends the contributions of any one particular group. If we have helped to deepen the channel of the river and remove some obstacles to its flow, we are content.

Finally, those of us on the regular Harvard staff must acknowledge our special debt to our two visiting collaborators. They contributed not only their great knowledge, acute understanding, and fresh points of view, but through unfailing tact were able to serve as most effective catalytic agents. Their value to the project has been incalculable.

TALCOTT PARSONS

1

The General Theory of Action

1

Some Fundamental Categories of the Theory
of Action: A General Statement

1. INTRODUCTION

The present statement and the volume which it introduces are intended to contribute to the establishment of a general theory in the social sciences. Theory in the social sciences should have three major functions. First, it should aid in the codification of our existing concrete knowledge. It can do so by providing generalized hypotheses for the systematic reformulation of existing facts and insights, by extending the range of implication of particular hypotheses, and by unifying discrete observations under general concepts. Through codification, general theory in the social sciences will help to promote the process of cumulative growth of our knowledge. In making us more aware of the interconnections among items of existing knowledge which are now available in a scattered, fragmentary form, it will help us fix our attention on the points where further work must be done.

Second, general theory in the social sciences should be a guide to research. By codification it enables us to locate and define more precisely the boundaries of our knowledge and of our ignorance. Codification facilitates the selection of problems, although it is not, of course, the only useful technique for the selection of problems for fruitful research. Further than this, general theory should provide hypotheses to be applied and tested by the investigation of these problems. If research problems are formulated in terms of systematically derived theoretical hypotheses, the resulting propositions will in turn contribute toward both the validation and revision of the theory.

Third, general theory as a point of departure for specialized work in the social sciences will facilitate the control of the biases of observation and interpretation which are at present fostered by the departmentalization of education and research in the social sciences.

This statement does not itself purport to be the general theory which will adequately fulfill these three functions. It is rather a formulation of certain fundamental categories which will have to enter into the formulation of this general theory, which for many years has been developing through the convergence of anthropological studies of culture, the theory of learning, the psychoanalytic theory of personality, economic theory,[1] and the study of modern social structure.

2. THE FRAME OF REFERENCE OF THE THEORY OF ACTION

The present discussion will begin with an exposition of the fundamental concepts from which it is intended to develop a unified conceptual scheme for theory and research in the social sciences. In accordance with already widespread usage, we shall call these concepts the *frame of reference of the theory of action*. In order to make the rest of the exposition comprehensible, we shall define a considerable number of the concepts [2] and state their more general bearing on our problem.

ORIENTATION AND SITUATION

In the theory of action the point of reference of all terms is the action of an individual actor or of a collectivity of actors. Of course, all individual actors are, in one aspect, physiological organisms; collectivities of actors are made up of individual actors, who are similarly physiological organisms. The interest of the theory of action, however, is directed not to the physiological processes internal to the organism but rather to the organization of the actor's orientations to a situation. When the terms refer to a collectivity as the acting unit, it is understood that it does not refer to all of the actions of the individuals who are its members, but only to the actions which they perform in their capacity as members. Whether the acting unit is an individual or a collectivity, we shall speak of the actor's *orientation of action* when we describe the action. The concept *motivation* in a strict sense applies only to individual actors. The motivational components of the action of collectivities are organized systems of the motivation of the relevant individual actors. Action has an orientation when it is guided by the meaning which the actor attaches to it in its relationship to his goals and interests.

Each orientation of action in turn involves a set [3] of *objects of orientation*. These are objects which are relevant in the situation because they afford alternative possibilities and impose limitations on the modes of gratifying the

---

[1] See note at end of chapter.

[2] The authors are fully aware of the difficulty of standardizing terminology in the present state of social science. The difficulty is great particularly in view of the heterogeneity of the sources from which the terms here used have been drawn and the new emphasis we have often given them. We are not all equally satisfied with every term, and we do not regard ourselves as bound to use exactly this terminology each in his own work. We have merely endeavored to be as clear as possible, to avoid violent neologisms, and to use terms which would be as nearly acceptable to all members of the group as possible.

[3] The word *set* is used to designate a plurality of entities determinately limited in number and range of variation but not necessarily conceived as interdependent so as to constitute a system.

needs and achieving the goals of the actor or actors.[4] A situation provides two major classes of objects to which the actor who is the point of reference may be oriented. These are either (1) nonsocial, that is, physical objects or accumulated cultural resources, or (2) social objects, that is, individual actors and collectivities. Social objects include the subject's own personality as well as the personalities of other individuals. Where collectivities are objects, sectors of the action systems of a plurality of individual actors form a system which is an object for the actor or actors who are our point of reference. A specific combination of selections relative to such objects, made from among the possibilities of selection which were available in a specific situation, constitutes an orientation of action for a particular actor. The organized plurality of such orientations of action constitutes a system of action.[5]

The orientation of action to objects entails selection, and possibly choice. Selection is made possible by *cognitive* discriminations, the location and characterization of the objects, which are simultaneously or successively experienced as having positive or negative value to the actor, in terms of their relevance to satisfaction of drives [6] and their organization in motivation. This tendency to react positively or negatively to objects we shall call the *cathectic mode of orientation.* Cathexis, the attachment to objects which are gratifying and rejection of those which are noxious, lies at the root of the selective nature of action.[7] Furthermore, since selection must be made among alternative objects and gratifications at a single point of time or through time, there must be some evaluative criteria. The tendency of the organism toward integration requires the assessment and comparison of immediate cognized objects and cathectic interests in terms of their remoter consequences for the larger unit of evaluation. *Evaluation* rests on standards which may be either cognitive standards of truthfulness, appreciative standards of appropriateness, or moral standards of rightness. Both the motivational orientations and the value-orientations are modes of distinguishing, testing, sorting, and selecting. They are, in short, the categories for the description,

---

[4] The establishment of a definite relationship with objects (e.g., their possession or modification) or the creation of objects may be among the goals sought by actors. Objects once created may in turn become objects of orientation in ensuing actions.

[5] The word *system* is used in the sense that determinate relations of interdependence exist within the complex of empirical phenomena. The antithesis of the concept of system is random variability. However, no implication of rigidity is intended.

[6] By *drive* we mean the *organic energy* component of motivation with whatever elements of organization and directionality may be given with the *genetic constitution* of the organism.

[7] Human beings do much which is inhibiting or destructive of their interests in its consequences; hence the naïve hedonism which maintains that the gratification of a wish explains every overt act is clearly untenable. However, to deny that even self-destructive acts are motivated equally fails to make sense. The postulate that the course of behavior, at least at certain points where alternatives were open, has had motivational significance to the actor, that in some sense he "wanted" to do it, is essential to any logical theory of behavior.

on the most elementary level, of the orientation of action, which is a constellation of selections from alternatives.

It is essential to point out that a description of a system of action must refer not only to the particular constellation of orientations and sets of objects actually selected, but also to the alternative sets from which the selections might have been made but were not. In other words, we are concerned not only with how an actor actually views a situation, but also with how he might view it. This inclusiveness is required for the purposes of a dynamic theory of action which would attempt to explain why one alternative rather than another was selected.

The range of the alternatives of action orientation is determinate; it is inherent in the relation of the actor to the situation and derives ultimately from certain general properties of the organism and the nature of objects in their relation to such organisms. This determinate range of the alternatives which are available for selection marks the limits within which variability is possible.

DESCRIPTIVE AND DYNAMIC ANALYSIS

The complete analysis of a system of action would comprise description both of the state of the system at the given moment and of the changes in the system through time, involving changes in the relations of the constituent variables. This dynamic analysis would treat the *processes* of action and is the proper goal of conceptualization and theory construction. But we feel that it is uneconomical to describe changes in systems of variables before the variables themselves have been isolated and described; therefore, we have chosen to begin by studying particular combinations of variables and to move toward a description of how these combinations change only when a firm foundation for such analysis has been laid. Hence, it should be understood that when we describe the orientations of action in a given system, we are describing the state of the system at a given moment. The variables to which we refer in the analysis of given orientations are also those referred to in the analysis of the processes which maintain one system of orientation rather than another; these same variables are also dealt with in the analysis of the processes in which, through change in the values of the variables, one orientation changes into another. There is, thus, no difference between the variables involved in description of the state of a system and analysis of its processes. The difference lies in how the same variables are used.

PERSONALITY, SOCIAL SYSTEM, AND CULTURE

The frame of reference of the theory of action applies in principle to any segment of the total round of action or to any process of action of any complex organism. The elaboration of behavior to which this conceptual scheme is especially appropriate, however, occurs above all in human action.

In the formation of systems made up of human actions or the components of human action, this elaboration occurs in three configurations. First, the orientation of action of *any one* given actor and its attendant motivational processes becomes a differentiated and integrated system. This system will be called the *personality*, and we will define it as the organized system of the orientation and motivation of action of one individual *actor*.[8] Secondly, the action of a plurality of actors in a common situation is a process of inter-action, the properties of which are to a definite but limited extent independent of any prior common culture. This interaction also becomes differentiated and integrated and as such forms a social system. The social system is, to be sure, made up of the relationships of individuals, but it is a system which is organized around the problems inherent in or arising from social interaction of a plurality of individual actors rather than around the problems which arise in connection with the integration of the actions of an individual actor, who is also a physiological organism. Personality and social system are very intimately interrelated, but they are neither identical with one another nor explicable by one another; the social system is not a plurality of personalities. Finally, systems of culture have their own forms and problems of integration which are not reducible to those of either personality or social systems or both together. The cultural tradition in its significance both as an *object* of orientation and as an *element* in the orientation of action must be articulated both conceptually and empirically with personalities and social systems. Apart from embodiment in the orientation systems of concrete actors, culture, though existing as a body of artifacts and as systems of symbols, is not in itself organized as a system of action. Therefore, culture as a system is on a different plane from personalities and social systems.[9]

Concrete systems of action — that is, personalities and social systems — have psychological, social, and cultural aspects. For one thing, the state of the system must be characterized in terms of certain of the motivational properties of the individual actors. The description of a system of action must employ the categories of motivational orientation: cognition, cathexis, and evaluation. Likewise, the description of an action system must deal with the properties of the system of interaction of two or more individuals or collective actors — this is the social aspect — and it must note the conditions which interaction imposes on the participating actors. It must also take into account the cultural tradition as an object of orientation as well as culture patterns as internalized patterns of cognitive expectations and of cathectic-evaluative selection among possible orientations that are of crucial significance in the personality system and in the social system.

[8] The physiological aspect of the human organism is relevant to action theory only as it impinges on the orientation system. However, phantasies and imaginative productions, though they may not refer directly to any realistic situational objects, are unequivocally part of the orientation of personality as a system of action.

[9] Mr. Sheldon dissents from this view. His grounds are stated in Chapter II.

Cultural elements as constituents of systems of action may be classified in two ways. First, they may be differentiated according to the predominance of types of interests corresponding to the predominance of each of the modes of motivational orientation. Second, culture patterns as objects of the situation may be distinguished from culture patterns as internalized components of the orientation system of the actor. These two classifications cut across each other.

In the first method of classification it is convenient to distinguish the following three major classes of culture patterns. (1) Systems of ideas or beliefs. Although cathexis and evaluation are always present as orientational components, these cultural systems are characterized by a primacy of cognitive interests. (2) Systems of expressive symbols; for instance, art forms and styles. These systems are characterized by a primacy of cathectic interests. (3) Systems of value-orientations. Here the primary interest is in the evaluation of alternatives from the viewpoint of their consequences or implications for a system of action or one of its subsystems.

With respect to the second classification, it is quite clear that culture patterns are frequently objects of orientation in the same sense as other types of objects.[10] The actor knows their properties (for example, he understands an idea); he "responds" to them (that is, he is attracted or repelled by them); and he evaluates them. Under certain circumstances, however, the manner of his involvement with a cultural pattern as an object is altered, and what was once an object becomes a constitutive part of the actor. When, for example, he cannot violate a moral rule without intense feelings of guilt, the rule is functioning as a constitutive part of his system of orientation; it is part of his personality. Where this occurs a culture pattern has been internalized.

Before we continue with an elaboration of each of the above three major types of system into which the components of action become organized and differentiated — personality, cultural systems, and social systems — it is essential to review briefly certain other categories of action in general, particularly those that have been developed in behavior psychology.

3. Some Fundamentals of Behavior Psychology

NEEDS AND THE ORGANIZATION OF BEHAVIOR

Certain trends in psychological theory have placed the primary sources of the organization of behavior into the constitution of the organism. They

---

[10] A special position is occupied by physical artifacts which are the products of action. Like the objects of the natural environment they do not *interact* with the actor. They are situational objects which cannot be internalized into the orientation system of the actor. They might serve as instrumental objects in action systems or they might have "meaning" conferred on them by value-orientation systems, in the same way that meaning is conferred on objects of the natural environment.

have done this through some version of the "instinct" theory. This tendency has continually been challenged by demonstrations of the range of plasticity of the organism and the corresponding importance of "learning" — a challenge which has been greatly accentuated by the cultural relativity disclosed through the work of social anthropology and sociology.

The present analysis will observe a rule of parsimony with regard to assumptions about the constitutional organization of the tendencies of behavior. There is certainly a system of viscerogenic needs which are grounded in the interchange of the organism as a physiological system with its environment. Some of them are highly specific: the need for food is relatively specific; the needs for sleep and for breathing are much more so. The object which is constitutionally most appropriate for the cathexis of a viscerogenic need is, however, seldom absolutely specific. But, on the other hand, the range of variability open to action and cultural definition always has some limits. Among these needs which come to be of primary importance for action, however, the degree of specificity usually tends to be slight, particularly in the mode as distinct from the fact of gratification. In general, there is a wide range of variability of the objects and modes of gratification of any constitutionally given need. In addition to the viscerogenic needs there seem to be certain needs for "social relationships." These might be constitutionally given or they might, by being indirectly necessary for the gratification of viscerogenic needs, be derivative in their origin and come subsequently to acquire autonomy.

We assume then a set of needs which, although initially organized through physiological processes, do not possess the properties that permit these physiological processes to be exclusively determinative in the organization of action. In other words, the direction and modes in which these needs can determine action is modifiable by influence emanating from the situation of action. Moreover, the needs themselves can be modified, or at least their effect on action is modifiable, by the process of becoming embedded into need-dispositions.

However, even though the set of viscerogenic needs has initially a physiological organization, it possesses one persistent property which plays a central role as the set of needs evolves into the system of need-dispositions. It is incipiently organized with respect to a positive-negative discrimination; that is, it discriminates between need-gratifying and need-blocking or need-depriving aspects [11] of the situational object system. This discrimination is

---

[11] *Deprivation* is to be understood here as subsuming: (1) the withdrawal of gratifying objects already possessed by the actor; (2) the obstruction of access to gratifying objects which the actor does not possess and for which he is striving; (3) the enforced relationship with objects which are not gratifying, e.g., physical or psychological suffering of positive pain or injury (this category includes both actively encountering and passively receiving pain, etc.); (4) the threat of any of the foregoing. Responses by the actors to each of these types of deprivation might vary considerably.

the point of departure of a complex process of further differentiation into need-dispositions [12] which might possess varying degrees of specificity. In addition to the specific viscerogenic needs and the wider discrimination between gratification and deprivation, the human organism has a constitutional capacity to react to objects, especially other human beings, without the specific content or form of the reaction being in any way physiologically given. This reactive capacity or potentiality may be likened to the capacity to learn language, which is certainly not constitutionally specific to any particular language, and if the individual is not exposed to speech of other human beings, may not be activated at all. The human organism has a "sensitivity" to other objects, a potentiality of cathecting them as objects in various ways, depending on the context of orientation and situation.

This sensitivity extends to nonsocial objects but it is especially significant where *inter*action is involved. Moreover, this sensitivity is, like the discriminatory tendency to which we have already referred, inherently responsive to experience in interactive relationships. On the one hand, gratifying experience with an object engenders a positive attachment-seeking and -forming tendency; on the other, deprivation from an object predisposes the actor to a reaction of flight, escape, or aggression, a tendency to avoid or injure the object in order to control or forestall the deprivational effect of its action.

COGNITIVE AND CATHECTIC ORIENTATION IN THE ORGANIZATION OF ACTION

Impelled by its drives and needs, the acting organism is oriented to social and nonsocial objects in two essential, simultaneous, and inseparable modes. First, it "cathects" particular objects or classes of objects through attributing to them significance for direct gratification or deprivation of impulse-needs.[13] It may become attached to an object as a source of gratification [14] or

[12] The term *need-disposition* has been chosen to emphasize that in action the unit of motivation faces two ways. On the one hand, it is involved in the equilibrium of the actor as a personality (and organism), and on the other, it is a disposition to act in relation to one or more objects. Both references are essential. It is to be distinguished from *need* by its higher degree of organization and by its inclusion of motivational and evaluative elements which are not given by viscerogenic needs.

[13] A distinction between *affect* and *cathexis* is desirable for present purposes. *Affect* refers to a state of the organism — a state of euphoria or dysphoria or qualitative variants thereof. *Cathexis* refers to a state of the organism — a state of euphoria or dysphoria — in relationship to some object. Thus the term *cathexis* is broader in its reference than the term *affect*; it is *affect plus object*. It is *object-oriented affect*. It involves attaching affective significance to an object; although it involves attachment to one or more properties of the object, as used here it does not itself refer to a property of the object, but to a *relation* between actor and object. Furthermore, there is no connotation either of activity or passivity in the actor's relation to the object implied in the concept.

[14] The content of the gratifications need not be specified here. Gratifications may of course include those experiences or states which are normally viewed as pleasures, such as love, physical comfort; they may also under certain conditions include certain experiences ordinarily conceived as deprivational, such as pain, horror, disgust, but which because of the organization of a given personality system may have gratifying consequences.

repelled by it as a source of deprivation. Second, it cognizes the object field, discriminating any particular object from others and otherwise assessing its properties. Only when the actor knows the relations of objects to one another and to his own needs can his behavior become organized with reference to cathectic-cognitive discriminations.

The essential phenomena in motivational orientation are thus cognitive and cathectic discriminations among objects. When these discriminations become organized in a stable way, they form a system of orientation. The actor *selects* or is *committed* to culturally imposed selections among accessible objects with respect to their potentialities for gratification; he also selects from among the modes of their possible significance to him. The most primitive forms of this selectivity are perhaps acceptance — for instance, incorporation of food, remaining in a comfortable place, etc. — and rejection — spitting out, withdrawal from, or avoidance.

Cathectic-cognitive orientation toward the object world, in any system of behavior extending through time, always entails *expectations* concerning gratifications or deprivations receivable or attainable from certain objects and classes of objects. Action involves not merely discrimination and selection between immediately present objects, and the directly ensuing striving, acceptance, or rejection, but it involves also an orientation to *future* events with respect to their significance for gratification or deprivation. A discrimination between immediately available and future gratifications and the assessment of their relative value is an essential aspect of action.

EXPECTATIONS AND EVALUATIONS

Where there are alternative opportunities for gratification in a present situation and alternatives distributed among present and expected situations, the actor must have some means of deciding which of the alternatives or combinations of alternatives he should follow. The process of deciding among alternatives, of assessing them in the light of their ramified consequences, is called *evaluation*. Evaluation is the more complex process of selection built upon the discriminations which make up the cognitive-cathectic orientation.

There is a variety of possible ways in which action can be organized with respect to expected events. One of the most important categories of reaction to expectations is that of activity-passivity. On the one hand, the actor may *actively* seek out objects and manipulate them in the interest of his goals,[15] or he may explore the situation seeking previously unrecognized opportunities. Alternatively, he may passively *await* the impact of expected situations

---

[15] The cognitive-cathectic and evaluative orientations are connected by the "effort" of the actor. In accordance with a value standard and/or an expectation, the actor through effort manipulates his own resources, including his own body, voice, etc., in order to facilitate the direct or indirect approximation to a certain cathected goal — object or state.

and renounce interest in positive but still unattained goals. (There are various possible combinations of active and passive elements, such as the positive effort to escape from a situation expected to be threatening or enlisting the aid of others to cope with a threat.)

Learning [16] becomes relevant at this point in the development of the frame of reference of the theory of action. Learning is not merely the acquisition of "information" (that is, specific items of cognitive orientation) about the properties of the object world; it is also the acquisition of new "patterns of orientation." That is, it involves acquiring new ways of seeing, wanting, and evaluating; these are predispositions to approach or avoid, to seek actively in certain types of situation or to "lie low" and wait, to keep away from noxious objects or to control them.

Of fundamental importance in learning is the degree and incidence of generalization [17] which is introduced into the actor's orientations to his object world. Generalizations are modes of defining the actor's orientations to particular objects of which he has not yet had experience. This entails the categorization of the particular, concrete objects of his situation into general classes. In the acquisition of systems of cultural symbols, generalization is perhaps the most important of the learning mechanisms. As frames of reference, as the content of communication, and as the foci of common orientations, cultural patterns must possess content with a degree of generality which transcends the particularity of all concrete situations and experiences. Generalization through a cognitive process has consequences for the cathectic aspect of orientation. For example, through generalization it is possible to cathect categories of objects as well as particular objects.

Generalization as a cognitive mechanism orders the object world and thereby defines the structure of alternatives open to the orientation of action. The world in the actor's expectations comes to be composed of classes of objects, as well as particular objects, defined and differentiated by properties significant to the actor. Furthermore, the experiences of gratification or deprivation from particular objects may be generalized to other objects which are, in the actor's definition of the situation, classified with the original objects.

---

[16] Learning is the acquisition of changed modes of orientation to the object world, including in the latter the actor's personality, ideas, culture, social objects, etc.

[17] It is recognized that the term "generalization" has two principal current meanings: (1) the discrimination of the objects in what had previously been a single undifferentiated category to constitute two or more classes still possessing certain common features, and (2) the discernment of common properties in a group of events previously discriminated as different. The common element of the two meanings is the organization of the object world into categories. If it is important to distinguish the two meanings, the applicable meaning will be made clear.

CONSTITUTIONAL AND LEARNED COMPONENTS OF
GENERALIZED NEED-DISPOSITIONS

Anxiety is one type of generalized expectation of deprivation from a class of objects to which the actor is also simultaneously attached. There is a constitutional basis for the reaction to danger which is usually called fear. We speak of anxiety when this reaction to danger is generalized and organized as a need-disposition to anticipate a large class of deprivations. Anxiety exists where the actor "cries before he is hurt"; whether the anticipated deprivation is attributed to his inadequacy, to others, or to "circumstances" is a further distinction which we need not consider here. An anxiety, which might have originated in the fear of a specific class of objects, might become so highly generalized as to permeate virtually the whole system of orientation of a personality. Corresponding to anxiety and fear is the obverse generalized expectation of gratification in what is commonly referred to as optimism or a sense of security.

Some psychologists have tended to treat "aggressiveness" as a set of impulses constitutionally given in the organism.[18] It seems probable that a disposition to "strike back" if attacked or under certain types of intense strain is at least latent in normal human organisms. This disposition will be activated under certain conditions and if it is not overlaid by conflicting motives. However, such an innate disposition does not in any simple way determine responses to an experience or expectation of deprivation. Such responses, when organized as part of the actor's orientation, and if they include a disposition to injure or destroy the object felt to be the source of the deprivation, may be called *aggressiveness*. Aggressiveness, powerful and fundamental as it is, may take many forms; by itself it is one among a set of alternative responses to threats of deprivation. The other responses include withdrawal and avoidance or simply waiting passively for deprivations to occur. Furthermore, aggressiveness as a need-disposition may well be associated with actions which overtly are not aggressive. Which of these alternatives is chosen seems to depend on the prevalence of integrative predispositions[19] in the actor's personality system, which may suppress the expression of aggressive impulses in favor of alternative actions, such as a general tendency to "mastery" over situations as against a tendency to "passivity." Aggressiveness, then, is here treated as the manifestation in the organized orientation of action of the need-disposition to remove, injure, or destroy an object; the constitutional capacity for anger is a part of the organized need-disposition of aggressiveness.

---

[18] The capacity to experience anger may be different from the disposition to strike back if attacked. Both, of course, may be learned; but they seem to have some innate foundation.

[19] Including internalized cultural norms and the influence of the particular situation.

CONFLICT, EVALUATION, AND MOTIVATIONAL BALANCE

The individual actor possesses a large set of need-dispositions, some of which are active at the same time that others are quiescent. The gratification and quiescence of one need-disposition may be the signal for the activation of another and vice versa. Two or more need-dispositions are often concurrently activated, pressing the actor toward the performance of conflicting actions which are incompatible in the sense that gratifying one of the need-dispositions entails the deprivation of others. The actor seeking to achieve gratification and avoid deprivation is seldom, within a short time, capable of extirpating or extinguishing a well-established need-disposition even though its overt gratification may entail serious consequences for him. Through the process of evaluation, which operates unconsciously as well as deliberately, he will very often strike some sort of compromise among his conflicting need-dispositions, both simultaneously and over a period of time. Since deprivation is to be avoided or minimized, and since the situation makes some deprivation unavoidable, the compromise represents in some sense the best available in the circumstances, given both the exigencies of the situation and the actor's own personality structure. He will often perform actions which, taken alone, are self-deprivational but which, when seen in the wider constellation of his need-disposition system, represent the most gratifying total balance of action possibilities which could be performed under the circumstances.

So far, little has been said of the internal differentiation of the actor's object world except that it is differentiated along the axis of potentialities for gratification or deprivation. But even on this elementary level it has been possible to show the roles in action of the fundamental categories of orientation and their derivatives, of cognition and need, of evaluative and instrumental orientation, of discrimination and choice, of learning and generalization. When all of these elements are organized into a relatively coherent system of action, then a stable balance between the interest in increasing gratification and in the minimization of deprivation is made possible. This organization would consist of a relatively stable, interrelated set of discriminations or choices which has as a necessary counterpart a relatively stable set of expectations.

INTERACTION AND THE COMPLEMENTARITY OF EXPECTATIONS

Before entering into further discussion of the organization of systems of action, it is necessary to discuss one of the differentiations in the structure of the object world which is very crucial in relation to the actor's gratification interests. Only the potentiality of gratification or deprivation from objects is more crucial. We refer here to the distinction between objects which interact [20] with the acting subject and those objects which do not. These

---

[20] This is a technical usage of the term *interaction*. It implies a relationship both parties to which are actors in the technical sense. It is thus distinguished from the sense in which *interaction* is synonymous with *interdependence*.

interacting objects are themselves actors or egos [21] with their own systems of action. They will be referred to as *social objects* or *alters*. A potential food-object, at least as it approaches the state of edibility, is not an alter, because it does not respond to ego's expectations and because it has no expectations of ego's action; another person, a mother or a friend, would be an alter to ego. The treatment of another actor, an alter, as an interacting object has very great consequences for the development and organization of the system of action.

When we analyze the interaction of ego and alter, we shift from the analysis of the orientation of a single given actor to the consideration of two or more interacting actors as a system. In this case, the expectations of ego are oriented both to the range of alternatives for alter's actions (i.e., the alternatives open to alter in the situation) and to alter's selection, which is intentionally contingent on what ego himself does, within the range of alternatives. The obverse is true for alter. Ego does not expect the behavior of a nonsocial object to be influenced by expectations regarding his own behavior, although, of course, ego's behavior is influenced by his expectations concerning the behavior of the nonsocial object. It is the fact that expectations operate on *both* sides of the relation between a given actor and the object of his orientation which distinguishes social interaction from orientation to nonsocial objects.

This fundamental phenomenon may be called the *complementarity of expectations*, not in the sense that the expectations of the two actors with regard to each other's action are identical, but in the sense that the action of each is oriented to the expectations of the other. Hence the system of interaction may be analyzed in terms of the extent of *conformity* of ego's action with alter's expectations and vice versa. We have seen that an actor's system of action is oriented to the polarity of gratification and deprivation. Social interaction introduces a further complication in that the motivational significance is no longer attributed only to the properties of the immediate object alone, but also to alter's expectations with regard to ego. The contingent reactions of alter to ego's action may be called *sanctions*. Their efficacy derives precisely from the gratificational significance to ego of alter's positive reactions and the deprivational significance of his negative reactions. The significance of these secondary gratifications and deprivations to ego rests on two bases: (1) Any need-disposition can be directly or indirectly gratified or deprived through the consequences of alter's reactions to ego's actions. (2) Personalities certainly develop need-dispositions directly for certain types of response from actors who are significant objects to them, whatever the

---

[21] This usage of the term *ego* is different from that current in psychology. Here it refers only to an actor taken as a point of reference in his relation to another actor referred to as *alter*. The term as here used is parallel to anthropological usage in the description of kinship systems.

constitutional basis of this fact. In other words, they develop social-relational needs.

Thus, sanctions have two kinds of significance to ego. First, alter's intentional and overt action, which can change ego's objective situation, may have direct significance to ego by increasing his opportunities for gratification or limiting them, insofar as alter controls important aspects of ego's situation of action. But ego through generalization also becomes sensitive to alter's attitudes toward him and his action, so that even where alter has no specific intentions in the situation, it will still matter to ego whether alter approves or disapproves of his action — whether he shows love, hostility, or some other attitude toward him.

Thus consideration of the place of complementarity of expectations in the processes of human interaction has implications for certain categories which are central in the analysis of the origins and functions of cultural patterns. There is a *double contingency* inherent in interaction. On the one hand, ego's gratifications are contingent on his selection among available alternatives. But in turn, alter's reaction will be contingent on ego's selection and will result from a complementary selection on alter's part. Because of this double contingency, communication, which is the precondition of cultural patterns, could not exist without both generalization from the particularity of the specific situations (which are never identical for ego and alter) and *stability* of meaning which can only be assured by "conventions" observed by both parties.

Furthermore, the double contingency implies the normative orientation of action, since alter's reaction of punishment or reward is superadded to alter's "intrinsic" or direct behavioral reaction to ego's original selection. If punishment or reward by alter is repeatedly manifested under certain conditions, this reaction acquires for ego the meaning of an appropriate consequence of ego's conformity with or deviation from the norms of a *shared symbolic system*. A shared symbolic system is a system of "ways of orienting," plus those "external symbols" which control these ways of orienting, the system being so geared into the action systems of both ego and alter that the external symbols bring forth the same or a complementary pattern of orientation in both of them. Such a system, with its mutuality of normative orientation, is logically the most elementary form of culture. In this elementary social relationship, as well as in a large-scale social system, culture provides the standards (value-orientations) which are applied in evaluative processes. Without culture neither human personalities nor human social systems would be possible.

4. INTERACTION AND THE DEVELOPMENT OF PERSONALITY

The *inter*active element in the system of action, when joined with the fundamental variables of the organization of behavior discussed above, ac-

counts for the enormously complicated differentiation and organization of
the social and personality systems. In interaction we find the basic process
which, in its various elaborations and adaptations, provides the seed of what
on the human level we call personality and the social system. Interaction
makes possible the development of culture on the human level and gives culture its significance in the determination of action.

SOCIALIZATION

Before we begin our analysis of the personality system, we shall examine
briefly the significance of interaction in the socialization process. We have
referred above to the social-relational needs [22] of the infant. The importance
of these needs centers on the infant's state of initial dependency. As a result
of this dependency, the social-relational context in which viscerogenic needs
are gratified or deprived becomes perhaps just as important as the intrinsic
gratification or deprivation of the viscerogenic needs themselves. The child's
overwhelming sensitivity to the reactions of the significant adult objects, particularly to the reactions of the mother, opens the door to new possibilities of
frustration and even trauma. The child develops needs for appropriate attitudes on the part of these adults. It is on the basis of these new needs that the
human attains levels of organization beyond those open to animals.

The learning of the behavior patterns characteristic of the adult culture
requires new kinds of generalization, including symbols which abstract from
particular situations and which refer to classes of objects by means of language. In order to learn such generalizations, particularized attachments
which are essential in the earliest stages must be superseded. This substitution takes place through a mechanism like the following: the child forms a
social attachment which transcends any particular viscerogenic gratification
which the object confers. This attachment makes it possible for the child to
accept the necessary deprivations which are involved in renouncing earlier
types of gratification and to acquire the new attachment in that although con-
tinuance of the old gratifications is made more difficult still favorable
reactions from the significant social object are received. The newly learned
generalization is acceptable if the child feels that the adult wants it to do
the things in question and that it is loved.

Although the problem is still obscure, there is approximate agreement that
the development of identification [23] with adult objects is an essential mechanism of the socialization process. For present purposes the most significant

---

[22] When subsequently we use the term *relational needs* it should be understood to refer
to what we are here calling *social-relational needs.*

[23] It is well known that use of this term is by no means consistent. It seems essential
to distinguish (1) the internalization of the values but not the role of the model from
(2) internalization of his specific role. Though there are still other meanings of the
term, these two seem to be the most important for present purposes. In both cases, what
is taken over is a value pattern and not an action.

characteristic of identification in this sense is the child's acceptance of the adult's values in the relevant contexts; in other words, what the adult wants for the child, the child comes to want for itself. The extent to which this necessarily involves the child's formation of an ideal image of itself as similar to the adult in all respects (for example, with respect to sex, even though the adult is of the opposite sex) remains an open question.

The value-orientations and other components of the culture, as well as the specific accumulated objects which make up the cultural tradition in the form of skills, knowledge, and the like, are transmitted to the on-coming generation. Through the process of socialization, however, expectation systems become organized into patterns of selection in which the effective criterion is the differential significance of the various alternatives for the gratification-deprivation balance of the actor. To say then that a system of action has a degree of stability as a system is to say that there is a certain stability and consistency in its choice patterns. Such stability and consistency are prerequisites of the development of the higher levels of cultural behavior.

Because the child is dependent on the adult, the latter's reaction patterns become crucially important factors in the organization of the child's choice patterns. The child becomes oriented to the wishes which embody for him the values of the adult, and his viscerogenic needs become culturally organized needs, which are shaped so that their gratification is sought in directions compatible with his integration into this system of interaction.

PERSONALITY AS A SYSTEM

The child's development of a "personality" (or an "ego structure") is to be viewed as the establishment of a relatively specific, definite, and consistent system of need-dispositions operating as selective reactions to the alternatives which are presented to him by his object situation or which he organizes for himself by seeking out new object situations and formulating new goals. What will be needed, therefore, for the coherent description and analysis of human personality *as a system* will be the categories and hypotheses bearing on four main sets of variables.

1. Fundamentals of behavior psychology of the sort discussed above: motivation, the gratification-deprivation balance, primary viscerogenic and possibly social-relational needs, cognition and learning, as well as the basic mechanisms of cognitive and cathectic-evaluative learning and adjustment. The latter involves the examination of such learning mechanisms as differentiation and generalization, where cognitive interests have primacy, and reinforcement, extinction, inhibition, substitution, identification, and imitation, where cathectic or evaluative interests have primacy.

2. The allocative processes,[24] by which the strivings toward gratification

[24] By *allocation* we mean the distribution of significant components *within* a system in such a way as to be compatible with the functioning of the system in a given state. The term is borrowed from economics.

are distributed among the different available objects and occasions and gratification opportunities are distributed among the different need-dispositions. These processes keep conflict and anxiety within the limits necessary for the working of the personality system; the failure of their smooth operation calls the special mechanisms of defense and adjustment into play.

3. The mechanisms, classifiable as those of defense and adjustment,[25] by which the different components of need-dispositions are integrated internally as a system and directed toward objects.

4. The integration of the various need-dispositions into an "on-going" personality capable of some degree of self-control and purposeful action. The character of the on-going personality cannot be understood without reference to the relatively independent subintegrations within the personality structure and the adjustive mechanisms which relate them to each other.

The constitutional foundations of the need-disposition structure of personality continue to function throughout life. But because of the plasticity of the human organism they directly determine the behavior of the human adult far less than in many other species. Through learning and interactive experience they become integrated with the symbolic structures of the cultural tradition to form an interdependent system of acquired need-dispositions, many of the latter being closely fused into specific object attachments and systems of role-expectations. In comparison with its physiological base, the structure of human personality is highly autonomous and socialized. In addition, the personality usually has a high degree of autonomy vis-à-vis the social situation at any particular moment, in the sense that the variations in the social situation do not bring about completely corresponding variations in the personality systems.

PERSONALITY AND SOCIAL ROLE

One particular crucial aspect of the articulation of personality with the social system should be mentioned briefly. Once an organized system of interaction between ego and alter becomes stabilized, they build up reciprocal expectations of each other's action and attitudes which are the nucleus of what may be called *role-expectations*. Alter expects ego to behave in given situational conditions in certain relatively specific ways, or at least within relatively specific limits. Alter's reaction will then, contingent on the fulfillment or nonfulfillment of his expectations, be different; with fulfillment leading to rewards and/or favorable attitudes, and nonfulfillment leading to the reverse. Alter's reaction is in turn meaningfully interpreted (not necessarily correctly — distortion is of course possible and frequent) by ego and this

---

[25] By *mechanisms of defense* we mean the motivational processes by which conflicts internal to the need-disposition system of a personality are resolved or the severity of their consequences mitigated. *Mechanisms of adjustment*, on the other hand, are the processes by which *strains* on the actor's relations to objects are coped with. Complete resolution may occur through normal learning, but short of this special mechanisms operate.

interpretation plays a part in shaping the next stage in the process of his action toward alter (all this, of course, takes place in reverse too). The pattern of expectations of many alters, often generalized to include all of those in the status of ego, constitutes in a social system the institutionalized [26] definition of ego's roles in specified interactive situations.

Ego's system of need-dispositions may or may not predispose him to conform with these expectations. There are, of course, many complex possibilities of variation between dispositions to complete conformity and to drastic alienation — that is, predispositions to avoid conformity, to withdraw, or to rebel. There are also many complex possibilities of accommodation between dispositions not to conform, in varying modes and degrees, and interests in avoiding the sanctions which nonconformity might incur.

Moreover, alienative and conformist responses to institutional role-expectations do not exhaust the possibilities. Some actors possess, to a high degree, the potentialities of elaborating their own goals and standards, accepting the content of institutional role-expectations but simultaneously modifying and adding something new to them. These are the creative personalities whose conformity or alienation is not motivated mainly by a need-disposition to accept or reject the given institutional role-expectations, but rather by the need to discover, elaborate, and conform with their own ego-ideal.

The group of problems centering around conformity, alienation, and creativity are among the most crucial in the whole theory of action because of their relevance to problems of social stability and change. It is essential, in order to make progress in this area, to have conceptualized both the personality and social system adequately so that the points of empirical articulation where integration and unintegratedness are in balance can be analyzed.[27]

5. Cultural Aspects of Action Systems

INTERNALIZED ORIENTATIONS AND CULTURAL OBJECTS

We have already stated that the organization of the basic alternatives of selective orientation is fundamental to any system of action. Without this organization, the stable system of expectations which are essential to any sys-

---

[26] By *institutionalization* we mean the integration of the expectations of the actors in a relevant interactive system of roles with a shared normative pattern of values. The integration is such that each is predisposed to reward the conformity of the others with the value pattern and conversely to disapprove and punish deviance. Institutionalization is a matter of degree, not of absolute presence or absence.

[27] Although many schemes will allow the *ad hoc* analyses of some of the points of articulation, the scheme presented here seems to have the advantage of proceeding systematically from the elements of orientation. This permits the formulation of concepts which reveal the points of conceptual correspondence among the different types of systems — and this in turn offers a basis for a more comprehensive and more rigorous analysis of the points of empirical articulation.

tem of action could not exist. Not only does the child receive the major organization of his own selective orientations from adults through the socialization process, but consensus with respect to the same fundamental selections among alternatives is vital to a stable social system. In all societies the stabler and more effective patterns of culture are those which are shared in common — though in varying interpretations with varying degrees of conformity, idiosyncrasy, creativity, and persistence — by the members of societies and by groups of societies. The pattern of "commitment" to a particular set of such selections among the potentially open alternatives represents the point of empirical articulation of systems of actions.

Once the analysis of the organization of systems of action is pursued to the levels of elaboration which are necessary for the analysis of the structure of personalities, it also becomes necessary to examine the direct articulation with the patterns of cultural orientation, which have come to be one of the principal objects of anthropological study. The same basic set of categories of the selective alternatives which is relevant for the analysis of personality structures will also be involved in the macroscopic differentiation and classification of the cultural orientations or traditions of social systems.

THE ORGANIZATION OF CULTURE PATTERNS IN SYSTEMS

A cultural system is a highly complex constellation of elements. We may refer here to the two parallel classifications of the actor's modes of motivational orientation as cognitive, cathectic, and evaluative, and of the basic cultural orientations as systems of ideas or beliefs, systems of expressive symbols, and systems of value-orientation (as set forth above). Each type of culture pattern might then be regarded as a solution of a type of orientation problem — systems of ideas are solutions of cognitive problems, systems of expressive symbols are solutions of problems of how "appropriately" to express feelings, and systems of value-orientations are solutions of problems of evaluation, particularly but not exclusively in social interaction.

Value-orientation patterns are of particularly decisive significance in the organization of systems of action since one class of them defines the patterns of reciprocal rights and obligations which become constitutive of role-expectations and sanctions. (Other classes of value-orientation define the *standards* of cognitive and appreciative judgments.)

Cultural patterns tend to become organized into systems. The peculiar feature of this systematization is a type of integration which we may call *consistency of pattern.* Whether it be the logical consistency of belief system, the stylistic harmony of an art form, or the rational compatibility of a body of moral rules, the internal coherence of a body of cultural patterns is always a crucial problem for the student of culture.

The determination of the extent of the consistency of pattern and deviations from it in a given culture presents serious difficulties to the analyst. The overt or explicit culture almost always appears fragmentary at first, and its parts seem disconnected. Only under special conditions — for example, in highly sophisticated systems of ideas or legal systems — is explicit systematization carried out by the creators and bearers of the culture themselves. In order therefore to determine the existence of systematic coherence where there has not been explicit systematization, it is necessary for the student of culture to uncover the implicit culture and to detect whatever common premises may underlie apparently diverse and unconnected items of orientation. Very close approximations to complete consistency in the patterns of culture are practically never to be found in large complex social systems. The nature and sources of the mal-integration of cultural patterns are as important to the theory of action as the integration itself.

THE INTERNALIZATION OF CULTURE PATTERNS

It has already been made clear that, whatever its systematic form, a cultural pattern may be involved in action either as an object of the actor's situation or it may be internalized to become part of the structure of his personality. All types of cultural patterns may be internalized, but particular importance is to be attributed to the internalization of value-orientations, some of which become part of the superego structure of the personality and, with corresponding frequency, of institutionalized role-expectations.[23]

Cultural patterns when internalized become constitutive elements of personalities and of social systems. *All concrete systems of action, at the same time, have a system of culture and are a set of personalities* (or sectors of them) *and a social system or subsystem.* Yet all three are conceptually independent organizations of the elements of action.

Because of this empirical interrelatedness, there is a dynamic theory of culture which corresponds to that of the dynamic theory of personality and social systems. It is concerned with the conditions under which certain types of systems of culture can exist in certain types of personalities or societies. It analyzes the processes of cultural innovation and change in terms of their motivational determinants, as these operate in the mechanisms of the social system and in the mechanisms of personality. It is concerned with the imperfections in the integration of cultural patterns and accounts for them in terms of the empirical interdependence of culture orientations with the strains and processes of the social and personality systems.

[23] This fact of the internalization of values was independently and from different points of view discovered by Freud in his theory of the superego and by Durkheim in his theory of the institutionalization of moral norms. The fact that the two men, working from different premises, arrived at the same conclusion is one of the landmarks of development of modern social science.

6. THE SOCIAL SYSTEM

When, in the above discussion of action, we reached the point at which interaction of an actor with other persons or social objects became crucial, we disclosed the nucleus of the development of social systems. Personality as a system has a fundamental and stable point of reference, the acting organism. It is organized around the one organism and its life processes. But ego and alter in interaction with each other also constitute a system. This is a system of a new order, which, however intimately dependent on them, does not simply consist of the personalities of the two members.

ROLE AS THE UNIT OF SOCIAL SYSTEMS: SOCIAL SYSTEM AND PERSONALITIES

In the present terms a social system is a system of the interaction of a plurality of persons analyzed within the frame of reference of the theory of action. It is, of course, composed of relationships of individual actors and only of such relationships. The relationships themselves are constellations of the actions of the parties to the relationship oriented toward one another. For most analytical purposes, the most significant unit of social structures is not the person but the role. The role is that organized sector of an actor's orientation which constitutes and defines his participation in an interactive process. It involves a set of complementary expectations concerning his own actions and those of others with whom he interacts. Both the actor and those with whom he interacts possess these expectations. Roles are institutionalized when they are fully congruous with the prevailing culture patterns and are organized around expectations of conformity with morally sanctioned patterns of value-orientation shared by the members of the collectivity in which the role functions.

The abstraction of an actor's role from the total system of his personality makes it possible to analyze the articulation of personality with the organization of social systems. The structure of a social system and the functional imperatives for its operation and survival or orderly change as a system are moreover different from those of personality.[29] The problems of personality and social structure can be properly treated only if these differences are recognized. Only then can the points of articulation and mutual interdependence be studied.

When we recognize that roles rather than personalities are the units of social structure, we can perceive the necessity of an element of "looseness" in the relation between personality structure and the performance of a role. Role situations are situations with potentially all the possible significances to

[29] A further distinction between social and personality systems lies in the fact that a social system is not tied to any one *particular* aggregate of organisms. Furthermore, there is no reason to believe that when, having undergone a change of personnel, the social system remains the same, the new actors who have replaced those which were lost are necessarily identical in all the details of their personality with their predecessors.

an actor that situations can have. Their significance and the resultant effect on the motivation of behavior will be different with different personalities. But, in the organization of the latter's reactions where the stability of the sector of the social system in question is maintained, there are certain "control mechanisms" which serve to keep the potential dispersion of the actor's reactions within limits narrower than would be produced by the combination of the total situation and the actor's personality without this specificity of role expectations.

An important feature of a large proportion of social roles is that the actions which make them up are not minutely prescribed and that a certain range of variability is regarded as legitimate. Sanctions are not invoked against deviance within certain limits. This range of freedom makes it possible for actors with different personalities to fulfill within considerable limits the expectations associated with roughly the same roles without undue strain. It should also be noted that role-expectations and sanctions do exert "pressures" on individual actors which may well generate types of strain which have important repercussions in various parts of the personality. These will be manifested in types of action which in turn have a variety of social consequences and often result in either the development of further mechanisms of social control or the generation of pressures toward change, or in both. In this manner, personality and role structure constitute closely interdependent systems.

ROLE TYPES AND THE DIFFERENTIATION AND INTEGRATION OF SOCIAL SYSTEMS

The structural roles of the social system, like the structure of need-dispositions of the personality system, must be oriented to value alternatives. Selections are of course always actions of individuals, but these selections cannot be inter-individually random in a social system. Indeed, one of the most important functional imperatives of the maintenance of social systems is that the value-orientations of the different actors in the same social system must be integrated in some measure in a *common* system. All on-going social systems do actually show a tendency toward a general system of common cultural orientations. The sharing of value-orientations is especially crucial, although consensus with respect to systems of ideas and expressive symbols are also very important determinants of stability in the social system.

The range of variation and the shape of the distribution of the types of roles in a social system is neither parallel to nor fully congruous with the range of variation and the distribution of the personality types of the actors filling those roles. The actual operation of this structure of roles as an ongoing system is, of course, possible in the last analysis only because the component personalities are motivated to act in the requisite ways and sufficient gratification is provided to enough individuals within the immediate system of roles itself or in the more embracing system of roles. There are functional imperatives limiting the degree of incompatibility of the possible kinds of roles in the same action system; these imperatives are ultimately related to the conditions of maintenance of a total on-going social system of the type in which the more constitutive of these roles are found. A social system, like a personality, must be coherently organized and not merely a random assortment of its components.

As in the case of personality, the functional problem of social systems may be summarized as the problems of allocation and integration. There is always a differentiation of functions within any action system. There must accordingly be an allocation of such functions to different classes of roles; the roles must be articulated for the performance of collaborative and complementary tasks. The life span of the individual being limited, there must be a continual process of replacement of personnel within the system of roles if the system is to endure. Furthermore, both the facilities necessary to perform functions and the rewards which are important to the motivation of individual actors are inherently scarce. Hence their allocation cannot be left to an unregulated competitive process without great frustration and conflict ensuing. The regulation of all these allocative processes and the performance of the functions which keep the system or the subsystem going in a sufficiently integrated manner is impossible without a system of definitions of roles and sanctions for conformity or deviation. With the development of a considerable complexity of differentiation there emerge roles and subsystems of roles with specifically integrative functions in the social system.

This determination of functions and allocation and integration of roles, personnel, facilities, and rewards in a social system implies a process of selection in accordance with standards of evaluation applied to characteristics of the objects (individual and collective). This does not mean that anyone ever deliberately works out the "plan" of most social systems. But as in the other types of action systems it is not possible for the choices of the actors to fall at random and still form a coherently organized and functioning social system. The structure of the social system in this respect may be regarded as the cumulative and balanced resultant of many selections of many individuals, stabilized and reinforced by the institutionalization of value patterns, which legitimize commitment to certain directions of selection and mobilize sanctions in the support of the resultant orientations.

The patterns of commitment which, in their function as institutional role-expectations, are incorporated into the structure of social systems are, in at least one fundamental aspect of their content (that is, in the commitments which define rights and obligations) identical with the cultural value-orientation discussed above. The latter, in the form of the general moral consensus regarding rights and obligations, constitutes therefore one fundamental component of the structure of the social system. The structural differences between different social systems will often be found to reside in differences in the content and range of this consensus.

Although the moral consensus of the pattern of value-orientation provides the standards and sets the limits which regulate the allocations, there must also be special institutional mechanisms through which the allocative decisions are made and implemented. The institutional roles to which power and prestige are attached play a preponderant part in this process. The reason for this lies in the fact that power and prestige possess a highly general significance for the distribution of other facilities and rewards. The distribution of power and prestige and the institutional mechanisms which regulate that distribution are therefore especially influential in the working of a social system.

The general requirement for integration, therefore, demands that the control of allocative and integrative processes be associated with the same, or with closely interacting, roles; and that the mechanisms regulating the distribution of power and prestige apportion sufficient power and prestige to these allocative and integrative roles. And finally, it is essential that the occupants of these roles perform their allocative and integrative functions with a view to conforming with the value consensus of the society. These allocative and integrative roles (whether they be roles filled by individuals or by subcollectivities) may be considered to be important integrative mechanisms of the society. Their absence or defectiveness causes conflicts and frustrations.

It must be recognized that no social system is ever completely integrated just as none is ever completely disintegrated. From the sectors of unintegratedness — where expectations cannot be fulfilled in institutional roles or where need-dispositions are frustrated by institutionalized expectations or where the strain is not absorbed in safety-valve mechanisms — from these sectors some of the most important sources of change and growth are to be found.

Any system of interactive relationships of a plurality of individual actors is a *social system*. A *society* [30] is the type of social system which contains within itself all the essential prerequisites for its maintenance as a self-subsistent system. Among the more essential of these prerequisites are (1) organization around the foci of territorial location and kinship, (2) a system for determining functions and allocating facilities and rewards, and (3) integrative structures controlling these allocations and regulating conflicts and competitive processes.

With the institutionalization of culture patterns, especially value-orientation patterns, in the social structure, the threefold reciprocal integration of personality, social system, and culture comes full circle.[31] Such value pat-

[30] Partial social systems, so long as their relation to the society of which they are parts is made clear, are certainly legitimate objects of empirical investigation.

[31] Although — as must almost inevitably be the case with each individual signer — there are some things I should prefer to see said somewhat differently, there is only one point on which I remain slightly uncomfortable. This is the relation of social structure,

terns, institutionalized in the social structure, through the operation of role mechanisms, and in combination with other elements, organize the behavior of adult members of society. Through the socialization process, they are in turn constitutive in establishment of the personality structure of the new adult from the plasticity of early childhood. The process of socialization, it is clear from the above, is dependent upon social interaction. Adults in their orientation to the child are certainly acting in roles, very largely institutionalized, and almost from the beginning the child himself develops expectations which rapidly become role-expectations. Then within the framework of the personality structures thus formed, adults act both to maintain and to modify the social system and the value patterns in which and by which they live, and to modify or keep within the pattern the personality structures of their living descendants.

The reader should bear in mind that what we have presented in the foregoing pages is a highly general and abstract scheme. We are fully aware that *by itself* it cannot do justice to the immense richness and particularity of the human scene. But it can help us to analyze that scene and organize our knowledge of it.

The general outlines of the nature of action systems sketched here, the interrelations of the various components and the interdependence of the system levels of organization of those components, seems to be quite clearly implied in much contemporary theory and research. But the empirical complexity is immense, and the unexplored areas are, in the light of present knowledge, Stygian in their darkness. To us, progress toward unraveling that complexity and illuminating some of the obscurity depends, along with empirical investigation, on more precise and explicit conceptualization of the components of action and of the ways in which they are interrelated.

Talcott Parsons	Henry A. Murray, Jr.
Edward A. Shils	Robert R. Sears
Gordon W. Allport	Richard C. Sheldon
Clyde Kluckhohn	Samuel A. Stouffer

Edward C. Tolman

---

social system, role, and culture. Many anthropologists (and certainly the undersigned) will agree today that there is an element in the social (i.e., interactive) process which is not culturally patterned, which is in some sense autonomous from culture. Nevertheless, one whose training, experiences, and prejudices are anthropological tends to feel that the present statement does not give full weight to the extent to which roles are culturally defined, social structure is part of the cultural map, the social system is built upon girders supplied by explicit and implicit culture. On the other hand, whatever my reservations, I welcome the publication of the statement in its present form because I am convinced that in the present stage of social science it is highly useful to behave experimentally with reference to conceptual schemes — Clyde Kluckhohn.

The general preoccupations and terminology of the foregoing statement are those current in the disciplines of psychology, sociology, and social anthropology. It is reasonable to ask about the relevance of the theoretical interests of the well-established social science disciplines of economics and political science.

Economics is today, in a theoretical sense, probably the most highly elaborated, sophisticated, and refined of the disciplines dealing with action. It was by far the earliest to conceive of the relevant phenomena in terms of a system of interdependent variables and thus to interpret particular phenomena in the light of their interrelations with others in a system. It has also achieved a high level of technical refinement of its concepts and analytical methods.

Most certainly economic theory is a part of the theory of action in the present technical sense. It has not, however, been explicitly dealt with above because most of its problems arise only at points of elaboration and differentiation in the development of social systems beyond those to which we have carried our analysis.

It is true that there is an "economic" aspect of *all* empirical action systems — that aspect which we have designated as the "allocative," by borrowing a term from economics. But this concept of economics is so general as to preclude its being used as the basis of a technical theoretical development. This latter occurs only with the emergence of specially differentiated types of orientation of action within a correspondingly differentiated social system. Only with the development of money, of markets, and of the price mechanism or other differentiated mechanisms of allocation of resources do the phenomena of special technical interest to the economist appear on a substantial scale.

Economic theory is the conceptual scheme for analyzing such phenomena as production — as oriented to a set of market conditions or allocative policies — exchange, and determination of particular prices and of price levels. As such its technical basis rests on the fundamentals of action theory as here set forth — particularly instrumental orientation as an action type and the conditions of mutuality of such orientation. Its empirical relevance, on the other hand, rests on certain types of development of social systems. Just as the economic variant of instrumental orientation must be placed relative to other types and the particular combinations of action components they involve, so must the empirical processes of special interest to the economist be placed in terms of their relations to those other aspects of the total social system which are not susceptible of analysis in terms of economic theory.

Economic theory, then, is the theory of a particular set of processes or of a subsystem within a class of highly differentiated social systems. This subsystem is of very great strategic significance in these societies. Economic theory has its conceptual foundations in the categories of action theory here set forth, but only becomes a distinctive subtheory of the general theory on a considerably more elaborate level of differentiation than that reached here.

The case of political science is somewhat different. Its historical focus has been much more on a class of concrete phenomena, those of government, than on a disctinctive conceptual scheme. What has traditionally been called political theory has contained more of philosophical and ethical explication of the problems of government than of empirical analysis of its processes and determinants. In the sense of a distinctive *empirical conceptual scheme,* political theory has clearly not been in the same category with economic theory.

Since government constitutes one of the most strategically important processes and foci of differentiated structures within social systems, its study is clearly a legitimate basis for the specialization of a discipline within the social sciences. But, like economics, its special relevance does not emerge until degrees of differentiation on both theoretical and empirical levels beyond those reached in the present general statement have appeared.

It appears, furthermore, that the processes and structures of government necessarily have highly diffuse functions in social systems. It seems likely, therefore, that if the empirical focus of political science is to remain on the phenomena of government, it will not as a discipline be able to attain a sharpness of theoretical focus comparable to that of economics. It is more likely to draw from a much wider range of the components of the general theory of action and to find its distinctiveness in the way it combines these components in relation to its special empirical interests, rather than in the technical elaboration of a narrow and sharply focused segment of the theory of action, as is the case with economics.

2

RICHARD C. SHELDON

Some Observations on Theory

in Social Science[1]

Social science deals with one sector of the activity of human beings. Basically, activity can be considered to be any expenditure of energy of any part of the organism. It includes the biochemical processes which go on in the body. But social science does not deal with biochemical processes as such; they are in the domain of physiology. Social science is concerned with activity as related in some manner to things outside the organism itself — activity in terms of *principles of relationship* — and its basic task is to discover such principles and develop them into a coherent body of science.

By "things outside the organism itself" I do not necessarily mean material entities with independent existence. Such things as beliefs and images of the self and its capacities of course do not exist independently except insofar as they may be written down on paper; but it is true that they are developed in the course of contact with independent entities, usually other people. A relatively small number of things such as bodily pains may have no apparent external connections, and parts of the body are not outside the organism, but they can be behaved toward as though they were separate entities. In general, "things outside the organism itself" includes those things which can be behaved toward and which may exist in the past, present, or future, in material or nonmaterial form. Their designation is an integral part of the principles expressing the relationship between them and the organism which manifests activity; hence we need be concerned with their existence or location only as a part of the theoretical structure which we erect.

Since social science does not deal with activity in all its forms, abstraction is necessary. The sector of activity which is abstracted for study can be called by any convenient term. *Behavior* is one possible term, but it generally connotes observable bodily movements and does not include thoughts, and it often

[1] I am grateful for discussions and criticisms to Professor Clyde Kluckhohn and Edward C. Tolman and to Drs. Florence Kluckhohn, Gardner Lindzey, and Ivan D. London. I have incorporated many of their suggestions in this article, but the final form of the article is my own development, and the responsibility for any possible misuses of their suggestions is of course mine.

refers to individual styles of movements which may or may not be relevant to the study at hand. A more neutral term and one which has gained some currency in social-scientific thought is *action,* the term which has been adopted for this book. Action is activity which is related in some manner, by principles of relationship (or one may prefer the term *interrelationship*), to things outside the organism. It is the basic unit with which social science deals.

This basic unit may be broken down into certain components. *Environment* refers to all those things "outside" the organism to which action may be related. *Situation* refers to the organism and the environment in theoretical relationship but without action of the organism having taken place. Both terms, *environment* and *situation,* involve abstraction, but of different types. In describing environment one must abstract because one cannot describe everything. In describing situation one abstracts because the principles of relationship which are involved select features of the environment and of the organism for study, and the abstraction is done in terms of the theory which designates the principles of relationship. The features of the environment which are abstracted in the study of situations are *objects*; the abstraction from the organism is the *actor.* Although the situation consists of both actors and objects, it is convenient to speak of actors and situations as though the two were to some extent independent concepts: one speaks of actors in situations. If more precision is necessary for certain purposes, one can use the term *object situation* as differentiated from the *total situation,* which includes both objects and actors. It is *actors* in *situations* who *act* (manifest *action*); *organisms* in *environments* have *activity.* In other words, that which impinges upon our senses and which our measuring instruments record is the activities of organisms in environments; what we deal with on the scientific level are the actions of actors in situations, which are abstractions in terms of principles of relationship.

The crucial problem of social science is to develop these principles — to develop, in other words, the principles of action. The major portion of this book represents an attempt toward a solution of this problem. The principles of action, the operational ways in which they are connected to sense data, and the logical modes of their relationship to one another form the *theoretical structure of social science.* Because of the importance of the problem, it is useful to discuss at some length some of the characteristics of such a theoretical structure.

Possibly the most fundamental statement which can be made about the general principles that make up a body of science is that these principles are the free creations of the human intellect, as Poincaré has shown: [2] they do not necessarily reflect something inherently "given" in the phenomena observed, nor do they come from the inherent makeup of the human mind.

[2] Henri Poincaré, "Science and Hypothesis," *The Foundations of Science* (New York: The Science Press, 1929).

Therefore they are not imposed by the material dealt with. They are useful in a practical sense, however, only insofar as they can be identified in some manner with sense data, so that they can be used to predict occurrences which can be observed. Thus, although there is an infinite range of possibilities open in forming principles, experiment can indicate which are most useful for present purposes. To take a simple example, it is well recognized now that Euclidean geometry is based on a set of postulates which are not self-evident truths but are a set of conventions regarding the use of such terms as *line* and *point*. Because operations can be found to connect these terms with sense data, and because Euclidean geometry in connection with these operations produces predictable results for a certain range of phenomena, Euclidean geometry is useful. But assumptions of postulates other than Euclidean ones produce geometries which are consistent and do not lead to contradictions, and for certain purposes these non-Euclidean geometries have proved to be more useful than Euclidean geometry. One cannot, however, say which geometry is true, for the geometries are products of the intellect and are not imposed by nature. Likewise statements involved in such general principles as the law of inertia are not descriptions of pure facts which can be observed as such; they are conventions regarding the use of certain terms — definitions of expressions such as *uniform motion along a straight line*. We cannot be sure whether we are observing uniform motion or a straight line in any absolute terms, terms imposed by the data themselves. Instead we develop operations which if they produce certain results are said to indicate that uniform motion along a straight line has taken place. By doing this we have made an operational definition of a general principle. The principle itself is the free creation of the human intellect; the operations are necessary to connect it with sense data. Only after it has been so connected can we subject it to experimental test to see whether or not it is useful.

It can be seen from the above that for a system of propositions to have scientific meaning it must involve at least two sets of definitions. One set is a series of conventions about how to use certain terms; the other is a series of conventions about how to attach these terms to observable events. If the second set is not present, propositions involving only the first set of definitions are not susceptible to observational test and might be factually meaningless although they may be logically perfect. This does not mean that propositions involving only the first set of definitions — the free creations of the human intellect — should not be developed. Operational uses of such sets of propositions may be discovered later, as the history of non-Euclidean geometry shows. But in order for such propositions to become useful, they should be stated in terms which can be subjected to operational test when the time comes. Let us consider a common proposition of social science: "Human beings act as if they seek goals," or briefly, "Human beings have goals." This proposition has a certain observational base: we observe that organisms engage in activity and then cease activity; we say that they have achieved a goal. Such observation may be called an operational definition of a goal; the idea *goal* itself is a theoretical construction. But if we let the matter rest at this, the proposition, "Human beings have goals," does not have scientific meaning because the operations used to connect it with observable events are the same operations used to establish the convention about how the term *goal* is to be used. The proposition is analogous to one such as "Bodies move when force is applied." It is a principle which relates the organism to the environment, but it is not useful because it is not stated in terms subject to empirical test. It is merely a statement that *goal* is one of the concepts that will be used in whatever discussion follows.

In order, therefore, that a proposition be empirically testable it must be stated in such a way that the concepts involved may be attached to empirical data by operations other than those which merely restate the proposition. Usually this is done by expressing a relationship between two or more concepts, each of which can be defined by independent operations. Then what is tested is whether this relationship is stated correctly or not. The concepts and postulates of a theoretical system are by their nature untestable, but if from them logical conclusions are drawn and stated in terms of a relationship, it can be shown whether this stated relationship is correct or wrong, provided the relationship is stated precisely enough. The logical system which enables conclusions to be drawn and stated in terms of relationships is the third ingredient of a scientific theoretical structure; the first ingredient is the concepts and postulates, the free creations of the mind, and the second is the operational ways in which these concepts are attached to sense data. Because it is the relationships and not the other ingredients that are tested, this third ingredient is of enormous importance. This is why mathematics is such a powerful tool, because in mathematics one has at hand a magnificently developed system for drawing logical conclusions and because relationships can be stated with great precision by the use of that simple symbol, the equals sign. I do not propose here to enter the controversy as to whether the social sciences should be mathematized or can be mathematized. My purpose is to point out the necessity for very careful examination of the processes by which logical conclusions are drawn in the social sciences and of the terms in which relationships are stated, for it is only with these processes and terms that we can test the usefulness of our concepts.

In the social sciences relationships are usually stated in terms of the language of the person who describes them. The implications of this should be carefully examined. Let us take a purely hypothetical example. Suppose that in a given society it is observed that infants are brought up to their mothers' breasts but have to spend some time seeking the nipple before they get nourishment. It is also observed that there is a high amount of creative intellectual effort among the adults of this community: they seek new ideas. One might relate the one set of these seeking actions to the other. I have no doubt over-drawn this example to get the point across, but the point is this: there is an implicit assumption here that whenever the term *seeking*, as commonly un-derstood, can be applied to two sets of data, these data are equatable. Modern linguistics has shown that the implicit categories embedded in language are such that one should subject such a procedure to careful analysis before plac-ing too much reliance in it.[3] The use of language in this manner is often felt to be justified because there is a common feeling that "the social sciences have not advanced far enough yet to use more exact methods of the natural sciences." The result is that investigators often go on developing more and more observational categories without worrying much about how these cate-gories can be related to one another.

But if a consistent body of social scientific theory is to be developed, one must give considerable thought to the relationship of categories. One of our most prominent theorists of science, Philipp Frank, has this to say about the nature of theory:

The traditional presentation of physical theories frequently consists of a system of statements in which descriptions of observations are mixed with mathematical considerations in such a way that sometimes one cannot dis-tinguish clearly which is which. It is Poincaré's great merit to have stressed that one part of every physical theory is a set of arbitrary axioms and logical conclusions drawn from these axioms. These axioms are relations between signs, which may be words or algebraic symbols; the important point is that the conclusions that we draw from these axioms are not dependent upon the meanings of these symbols. Hence this part of a theory is purely conventional in the sense of Poincaré. It does not say anything about observable facts, but only leads to hypothetical statements of the following type: "If the axioms of this system are true, then the following propositions are also true," or still more exactly speaking: "If there is a group of relations between these sym-bols, there are also some other relations between the same symbols." This state of affairs is often described by saying that the system of principles and conclusions describes not a content but a structure.[4]

If the system of principles and conclusions that make up a scientific theory describe not a content but a structure, then an adequate theory for the social sciences must take into cognizance the means whereby by structural relation-ships are established. A multiplication of observational categories which are related more or less intuitively by the structure of the language of the observer is not sufficient for really rigorous theory; it produces what one may call metaphorical theory.

It is important to remember that the relationship between the symbols in the theory is contained in the theory itself and not in nature. Gravity, for

[3] See, for example, B. L. Whorf, *Four Articles on Metalinguistics* (Washington: Depart-ment of State, Foreign Service Institute), 1949.

[4] Philipp Frank, *Modern Science and Its Philosophy* (Cambridge: Harvard Uni-versity Press, 1949), p. 12.

example, is a relationship between symbols in Newtonian mechanics, not in nature, and it disappears in relativity mechanics. The conclusions we draw from it are not dependent upon the meanings of the symbols. Lack of the realization of this fundamental fact of the construction of theory can lead to difficulties. Such difficulties are at the bottom of the dissatisfaction that many social scientists feel with the functional approach in social science, which assumes that every action has the function of promoting the maintainance of a system, either a multipersonal, sociocultural system or a stable personality. "Function" is a principle relating action to object, but it is dependent upon the meaning of the symbols related; the relationship is assumed to be in nature. We can say that eating is functional because it promotes maintenance of the life of the actor, but it serves no end to say that A is functional because it promotes B. Such a statement has no meaning apart from specific meanings of A and B, which means that it contains nothing that enables us to draw logical conclusions about other relationships, and hence the axioms of the theory are not testable. The relationships are assumed to be in nature, and the theory has content but not structure. All one can do with such a theory is to fill in the content, and the end result can be statements such as, "Suicide is functional because it promotes peace of mind." [5]

Let us consider an example from social science in which there is a structure apart from the meanings of the symbols. One of the things anthropologists are concerned with is the degree of behavioral fit to ideal patterns. Given a tribe with a certain culture, the anthropologist can determine what per cent of the tribe's members do a certain thing which is ideally prescribed; then if the anthropologist is confronted by another settlement or tribe with an identical culture, he can predict what per cent of its members will do the same thing. Stated very briefly, the reasoning process involved is something like this:

1. Given A, B, C (usually actions or products of action), we say that X (a cultural pattern) is present.

2. Having determined X in a situation P (a tribe), we observe that such and such a percentage of R's (actors) do S (an action or group of actions). (S is usually connected in some way with A, B, or C, but for the purposes of this example, the connection is irrelevant.)

3. We then set up the hypothesis that given X, such and such a percentage of R's do S.

4. In situation Q (another tribe), we observe A, B, and C.

5. Therefore X is present and we predict that in situation Q such and such a percentage of R's will do S.

---

[5] The above discussion has been confined to the narrow functional concept that all actions must be functional. However, if it is considered that some actions may be dis-functional, or functional in one context but disfunctional in another, the basic point of the discussion nevertheless remains unchanged.

6. This prediction is then subjected to experimental test.

Such a line of reasoning is structural; it arrives at the expression of a relationship which by its nature can be shown to be true or false, and operations can be designed to connect the categories used with sense data. But although neutral symbols without meaning can be used to show the reasoning process — that is, although the relationships can be *stated* independently of the meaning of the symbols used — and although the categories used can be called operational, let us not say that the meaning of the symbols is irrelevant or that the formulation is operational to the extent of being merely a sum of defined operations. Any set of propositions such as the above is rooted in a great deal of observation and intuitional hunch that derives directly from the content of the things observed. Such a simple distinction as that between situation P and situation Q is made because situations P and Q originally had meaning, and the distinction is far from purely operational: although operations can be devised to distinguish the two situations, the fact that the distinction is made or is thought to be possible involves a reasoning process that comes before the operations and is quite distinct from them. Thus, although the system of principles and conclusions that makes up a theory indeed describes not a content but a structure, the devising of the theory involves far more than mere formal manipulations of symbols with meanings which are purely "operational": it involves immersing oneself first in the facts as known and then getting some good intuitions.

I emphasize this point because I have noticed that it is often thought that the facts follow the theory, on the grounds that all observation is in terms of a conceptual scheme. While it is true that all observation is in terms of a conceptual scheme and that a fact is a sense datum in terms of a conceptual scheme,[6] this does not mean that one must have a fully worked out theory in order to do any observation at all. The history of science indicates that the most fruitful theories have been those developed to explain known facts: the motions of the planets were fully known before Newton provided laws from which to derive these motions. From the original theories are then deduced additional facts to be discovered in nature, but the starting point has been the setting up of principles from which already known facts could be derived, and these known facts have usually been quite limited in range. Theories which encompass many facts start from a few. An example of this sort of thing is given in the reasoning process outlined above: the culture pattern X. Why, it may be asked, does one need this culture pattern? Why not merely say, given A, B, and C, such and such a percentage of R's do S? Such a statement would be analogous to one such as: given day, night follows. The culture pattern relates S to A, B, and C and tells us why S should be expected. For the purposes of the reasoning process, I said that the relation-

[6] See Talcott Parsons, *The Structure of Social Action* (New York: McGraw-Hill, 1937), p. 41.

ship of S to A, B, and C, was irrelevant, but it was irrelevant only because of the intent of the example. For the purposes of building a theory of action, it is very relevant, for then the same principles evolved to relate A, B, and C also extend to S; and the more S's that can be subsumed under one or a few principles, the more adequate the theory is. The aim of the theory is generality. But the theory begins with the relating of A, B, and C — known facts — and then is gradually extended to other facts.

How has the development of general theories — theories which fit a wide range of facts — proceeded? I am speaking here of those theories which produce statements that can be shown empirically to be true or false, not of theories which are general systems of knowledge. Usually they have begun by fitting a small range of facts, and as they were extended to fit more facts, they have been changed and have become more and more complicated and cumbersome. There may also have been a number of disparate theories which fitted the same or similar facts. Finally a fundamental revision of the theory has been made which has restored simplicity, and then the process has begun all over again. Such at least has been the course of development in physics. I do not by any means maintain that the same kinds of theories which are used in physics must be used in the social sciences, but the spectacular successes of the theories in physics at least suggest that the procedure followed in devising these theories might be fruitful for the social sciences. If something like this procedure is not followed, the theories of social science are in danger of being too far removed from the observational facts of activity; and while such theories may be useful as means of organizing thoughts, it is difficult to produce from them statements the affirmation and denial of which imply a difference capable of empirical test, which is the only way the theory may be given practical meaning. In general, the most fruitful all-embracing theories are developed from relatively small beginnings, and although they are free creations of the human intellect, they are rooted in observational fact (some of the theories of mathematics are exceptions, but these theories were developed as logical systems and not as models for events of physical existence).

Let us sum up the argument to this point. The crucial problem of the social sciences is to develop the principles of action into a theoretical structure or structures. Such structures, like all theories, consist of certain categories and axioms which are free creations of the human intellect; in the case of social science these are abstractions from organisms and environments and the relational principles which deal with these abstractions. By means of various operations the free creations can be attached to sense data. The structural aspect of the theory is produced by means of some system of logical derivations whereby there are stated relationships other than those originally stated in the categories and axioms. These derived relationships are the statements that are put to empirical test, and such derivations must be made if the theory is to have factual meaning. The categories and axioms are devised through familiarity with the data and with the help of intuition, and through refinement of already existing theories. Their starting point is the setting up of principles from which we can derive already known facts of rather limited range, and the use of the principles is then extended to encompass new facts, which may be discovered through logical derivation from the theory or may become known through other sources.

The setting up of a theory or theories of action, or indeed the setting up of any scientific theory, involves the assumption that action is *ordered*, that there is a certain regularity which permits of systematic study. Strictly speaking, the statement that there is order in action means this: that there can be set up a set of principles of such a nature that a very large number of actions can be derived from the principles. In other words, we do not need a different set of principles to explain each individual action, and hence action, or at least large segments of it, can be predicted. In speaking of individual actions, we must recognize the possibility that there may be large numbers of individual actions that are not predictable, just as in physics single subatomic events are not predictable, but that in the aggregate many such actions average out or converge,[7] which makes the application of general principles possible. It must be remembered that the order is in the principles and that different kinds of order will emerge with the use of different kinds of principles; as long as this is remembered, it is acceptable to say, for simplicity's sake, that action is ordered. On a simple level, we know that much action is ordered — we know when neckties will be worn, that the language which is comprehensible today will be comprehensible tomorrow, and so forth. On a more complex level, certain aspects of the ordered features of action have crystallized into foci of study.

One such focus has been the actor *qua* actor, or the actor as distinguished from other actors in similar situations. Actors exhibit certain regularities of action over a period of time and also exhibit what might appear to be certain inconsistencies. Insofar as principles can be set up from which these inconsistencies can be derived, the inconsistencies are ordered as much as the regularities. In social science it has become common to impute to the actor certain drives, needs, habits, traits, attitudes, beliefs, cognitions, etc., by which, in the proper admixture, to account for his actions. The study of these concepts, their content, their mechanisms, their interrelations in the actor, and their positions in the situation constitutes the discipline of psychology. The relatively ordered system of resultant actions in one actor is called his *personality*. One of the main foci of interest in psychology is the degree and manner of such ordering. (Remember that action is an abstract concept, that the ac-

[7] See Ivan D. London, "Some Consequences for History and Psychology of Langmuir's Concept of Convergence and Divergence of Phenomena," *Psych. Review*, LIII (May 1946), 170–188.

tivities from which it is abstracted are not just simple bodily movements, and that it always implies a relationship. This is not a Watsonian behaviorism or an oversimplified stimulus-response psychology, although both of these types of psychology would fit in.)

A second focus of the study of order in action has been around groups of actors. There is order in groups of actors — i.e., there are ordered systems of different personalities — of such a nature that it does not become apparent in the study of single individuals and which develops in various lines as more and more actors become encompassed in a study. This is the field of sociology and social or cultural anthropology. It is futile to try to draw a fine line of distinction between the disciplines of sociology and anthropology, but it may be said that in their common field the principles of order fall into two relatively distinct although interrelated types. The first type of principles derive from the fact that in a given situation there are a certain number of interacting actors with certain characteristics. The simplest example of this sort of thing is probably the peck order of chickens. The second type of principles of order are those that deal with learned, historically transmitted types or patterns of action which do not derive directly from the actors themselves or from the situations as such. These patterns are part of the body of *culture*, which also includes the products of action. Of course, culture ultimately derives from actors in situations, but it is transmitted beyond the original actors and situations, and at a given moment only relatively few of its components will be new. Leaving out psychological considerations for the moment, in any given situation action is partly determined by situational exigencies — that is, it can be treated by principles of order of the first type — but most of the action is determined to a greater or lesser degree by transmitted culture.

To say that action is determined by culture is, of course, merely a convenient way of speaking. Culture is a theoretical model, and the abstractions and principles from which it is made up are free creations of the mind. Some of these abstractions and principles deal with matters that are close to the minds of the individual culture bearers, who can tell you, for example, that certain actions are prescribed at certain occasions. This aspect of culture is usually called *explicit culture* or some similar term. Other aspects of culture, the *implicit culture*, are so generalized that in many cases the culture bearers are unable to formulate them — these are the "ways of life," tacit premises about how things are. All aspects of culture, however, are abstractions from activity, and the abstractions are put together by ordering principles. These principles refer chiefly to patterned action, the patterns of which are transmissible, and hence one can deal with culture itself alone, without having to refer in each instance to the actions of specific actors in specific situations. As the structure of cultural theory becomes more highly developed, one is able to treat more and more adequately the makeup of the patterns and the interrelations of patterns among themselves. It is at present possible, for example, to make statements about the probability of the coexistence of certain types of kinship terminology and residence and about the developmental direction that such complexes can take.[8] Similar theoretical formulations are needed on the level of implicit culture. But whatever the nature of the formulation, we must remember that culture is a set of such formulations, a theoretical model, a system of categories and principles set up in such a fashion as to give order to action; or, more loosely speaking, we may say that culture is a system, or structure, of ordered action.

When dealing with groups of actors, a somewhat different, although related, approach puts more emphasis on particular actors in particular situations. Situations are grouped, according to regularities of action in them, into *institutions*; an institution is thus a concept which states that many separate situations have features in common, in terms of principles of abstraction or order, and in which, in the same terms, actors exhibit the same or closely similar actions. These similar actions are said to be *institutionalized* if the actors expect them to occur and there are cultural sanctions opposing nonconformity with expectations. In the formal description of institutions the position of the actor is described by saying that he occupies a *status*. When he acts in this status he is said to be acting out a *role*. Thus institutions are in another sense systems of roles. Institutions, or systems of roles, are grouped into larger systems called *social systems*. There are other meanings of social system in current usage, but the above is the one adopted in the theory which forms the major portion of this book.

We turn now to a brief examination of this theory from the point of view of the considerations contained in the preceding paragraphs. The theory, which is presented in Part II, "Values, Motives, and Systems of Action," is an attempt to provide a general basis on which subordinate theories of personality, culture, and social system can be worked out, all using the same or similar categories and concepts, thus providing opportunity for cross-disciplinary fertilization and coöperation and, in the end, for a more or less unified body of social scientific theory. In the theory of Part II the concepts personality and social system are used much as they have been presented in the preceding paragraphs, but the concept of culture is given a somewhat different meaning from what has been stated above. Most action which the anthropologist would call cultural is put in the social system (and to some extent into personality) as institutionalized norms, role behaviors, and so forth. For the category of culture proper is left only systems of ideas and beliefs, systems of expressional symbols (for example, art forms), and systems of value-orientations. And in the working out of the theory by far the major attention is paid to value-orientations, because much of the theory is concerned with the selection by actors of objects and gratifications in terms

[8] G. P. Murdock, *Social Structure* (New York: Macmillan, 1949).

of normative prescriptions, in which "should" and "ought" statements —
values — play a large role. This procedure produces a dichotomy in the use
of the concept of culture. That part of what, in ordinary anthropological usage,
is generally called culture which is put into the social system and into personality is considered to be an element in the orientation of action; the part of
culture that remains as a system in itself is considered to be an object of
orientation.

What are the implications of this procedure? The implications are stated
above in the General Statement: "Apart from embodiment in the orientation
systems of concrete actors, culture though existing as a body of artifacts and
as systems of symbols is not in itself organized as a system of action. Therefore culture as a system is on a different plane from personalities and social
systems." Culture as a system is thus considered to be a body of artifacts and
symbols, not a set of theoretical principles for ordering action as such.
Action is considered to be confined to specific actors in specific situations. It would be foolish to worry about whether a certain item of action should be put into a category labeled "culture" or "social structure,"
but one may legitimately inquire whether something may not be lost by
confining the application of theoretical principles to specific actors in specific
situations, particularly when one is dealing with implicit culture. In the past
there has been demonstrated the utility of dealing with basic action configurations in terms that are not specifically situational; in fact, aspects of action
patterns in specific situations can only be derived from the more general
configurations. Such a category as Benedict's "Dionysian," for example, is
not action in a specific situation, nor is it a system of ideas, expressional symbols, or values considered as objects toward which action can be oriented,
although it colors all of these things. It is an ordering principle, a free creation of the intellect. It is a principle which orders action just as the principles
involved in the conceptions of personality and social system order action.

Culture, personality, and social system — all three — are theoretical
models, systems of free concepts and principles. All are abstractions from
activity and relate activity to things outside the organism. If this fact is accepted, one can by definition restrict culture to objects and put the ordering
principles of culture all in personality and social system if one wants to;
but one does this by definition and not because of the inherent nature of
action or of the concepts personality, social system, and culture. In its opposition of "action" systems (personality and social systems) to culture,
which "is not organized as a system of action," the proposal for a theory of
action contained in Part II of this book seems to be making a classification
along the lines of what is conceived to be the inherent nature of the concepts.
And by doing so it rules out some of the demonstrated benefits of the use of
the concept of culture and also rules out future developments of this concept along lines which have been shown to have been fruitful. Of course, if

such a ruling out is done from purely logical considerations, one should not
object to it for *a priori* reasons but must await empirical demonstrations that
it constitutes an advance in our conceptual treatment of action. Such a demonstration is always possible, and in any event a demonstration of usefulness is
the final criterion no matter how the theory is arrived at. But if the ruling
out is done from what appears to be a misconstrual of the theory at hand, and
if it appears that the ruling out restricts the usefulness of conceptual advances
already made, then a reëxamination of the theory is in order.

As the title of this book indicates, the theory of action which will be
presented in the following pages does not purport to be a final, fully worked
out theory. In large measure it is a statement of the categories, or variables,
which are to make up a complete general theory for the social sciences. In the
General Statement which introduces the book it is stated that "the present
statement . . . is a formulation of certain fundamental categories which will
have to enter into the formulation of this general theory." These categories
are designed so as to codify and provide a common language for existing
knowledge in all branches of social science and to facilitate common effort
in increasing knowledge. Such categories are needed and are highly useful.
But I believe that one should make with considerable caution statements that
such and such a set of categories *have* to be used. Considering the nature of
theory in general, one can never be sure that one's categories are the best possible for handling the data at hand; and as I have pointed out, the experience
of science has shown that a set of data does not impose theoretical categories
which have to be used. This is a matter of fundamental importance and is not
hairsplitting. Mechanistic physics got into a cul-de-sac in the later nineteenth
century by assuming that observations had to be presented in terms of what
Frank has called "a certain preferred analogy" [9] — the laws of Newtonian
mechanics — and it was not until it had been shown that there was nothing
in nature which imposed such a theoretical framework that physics was able
to progress into fields which had hitherto been thought to be inaccessible. In
social science it should always be recognized that no matter how fruitful a
theory or approach has been, it may be possible to make a great advance by
completely revising the categories of that theory. A fruitful approach should
be followed through as thoroughly as possible, but it should not be taken as
gospel.

The basic assumption of Professor Parsons and Shils's proposal for a
theory of action (see Part II) is that the actor strives to achieve goals. In his
goal-seeking the actor is oriented to objects, and the orientation is assumed
to be in three modes: cognitive, cathectic, and evaluative. These modes are
the basic principles which relate actors to objects and are thus the basic
principles by which activity is conceptualized as action. Objects of orientation

[9] Philipp Frank, *Einstein, His Life and Times* (New York: Knopf, 1947), p. 47.

are assumed to be relevant in the situation because they afford alternative possibilities and impose limitations on the ways of gratifying the needs and achieving the goals of the actor. Orientation of action toward these objects hence entails selection. Actors, objects, and modes of orientation (principles relating actors to objects) being the basic conceptual material of personality, culture, and social systems, it should be possible to provide a unified basis for the development of these latter three categories in terms of the basic conceptual material. A very complicated classification and cross-classification of modes, objects, and alternative possibilities of selection among them is developed which crosscuts and intermingles with the concepts of personality, culture, and social system and allows the categorization of a tremendous number of kinds of action. The theory is indeed an all-embracing one, and the potentialities for developing a unified social science theory are high, provided one can give factual meaning to the categories in terms of operations and provided one can derive from these categories relationships subject to empirical test.

It is on these two "provideds" that the theory will stand or fall, and for the present we must await their full testing. The theory of action as it now stands does not purport, as I have said, to be developed to the state of being a complete general theory for the social sciences. It is a system of categories, which belong — speaking in terms of abstract theory — to the type of concepts which have been called here free creations of the intellect (this does not mean, of course, that the categories have been created out of thin air; they are based on years of empirical work by social scientists). The other two major ingredients of a general theory are not specifically contained in the theory of action as presented in Part II: the operations whereby the categories are to be connected to sense data, and the principles independent of the original assumptions whereby relationships subject to empirical test can be derived. The theory of action in its present form is propounded to be used for "describing the state of the system at a given moment" (see General Statement) rather than for "dynamic" analysis — describing changes in the system through time. But a description of the system at a given moment here means classifying action according to the categories of the theory, and such a classification remains in the realm of the untestable assumptions of the theory. Testable relationships can be derived from categories regardless of whether the system is considered to be changing or not, and it is the derivation of these relationships which is the immediate problem; dynamism refers merely to a certain type of derived relationships. The theory of action is not used in this general derivational manner in its present state of development. It can be used to say, "Given the present state of the system, certain variables must be present in certain situations," but such a statement is a definition of what the state of the system is assumed to be and of what the variables are, not an independent derivational statement. If it is recognized that such a statement is not imposed by the nature of the data treated but is a freely created theoretical supposition, then the way is cleared for developing the necessary theoretical and operational procedures for deriving from it relational statements susceptible to empirical test. When this is done, we shall have a complete theory.

In the body of social science as it now exists there is much to aid in the development of this complete theory. In particular, there are many operations already developed to connect hypothesis with sense data. If these operations can be coördinated with a set of general categories such as are contained in the present theory of action, much will be gained in generalizing the present departmentalized categories of social science. It is not the purpose of this chapter to outline specific ways in which this should be done. The history of science indicates that such a procedure should be closely coördinated with experiment and applied first to the explanation of relatively restricted areas of already known facts, and each step in the procedure could in itself be the subject of a complete article. My purpose here has been merely to indicate the kind of statements and assumptions which the experience of science has shown to be nontestable and what it has shown to be testable, and how inherently nontestable but necessary assumptions are utilized in developing fruitful theories. If the various components of a theory are recognized for what they are, one can stay out of blind alleys and one can most efficiently direct his energies toward developing ways for predicting action, which is the final goal. The theory of action presented in Part II is not complete as it stands, nor is it supposed to be complete, but if its development produces results, it provides promise, because of its wide range, of being an important step toward that goal.

2

Values, Motives, and Systems of Action

TALCOTT PARSONS

EDWARD A. SHILS

With the assistance of
JAMES OLDS

Introduction

This section is, in a sense, a continuation of the enterprise started in the General Statement of Part I. That statement sets forth a conceptual scheme concerning the nature of action. It holds that the elements of action can be organized into three different interdependent and interpenetrating, but not mutually reducible, kinds of systems. These three kinds of systems — personalities, social systems, and cultural systems — are all important in social theory.

The conceptual scheme set forth in the General Statement is the framework we share with our collaborators. It underlies our work and it will be taken for granted here. Our aim in the present section is to develop, from these starting points, a more technical and more highly differentiated conceptual scheme.

The body of Part II falls into four chapters. The first chapter defines more completely than has been done heretofore certain elements of the orientation of action and certain elements of the structure of the situation. These elements of orientation and structure are important in all three kinds of systems. In the same chapter, a further analysis of the interrelations of these elements is carried out. Specifically, the scheme of five "pattern variables" of value-orientation will be developed as a tool for analysis of such interrelations. The pattern-variable scheme presents a systematization of one of the crucial points of articulation of the three kinds of systems.

The second chapter is concerned with the way the action of the individual is organized into a personality system. The chapter attempts to organize certain motivational variables with those of the theory of action so as to form the two into one coherent system. Particularly, it points up relationships that obtain between motivational and value-orientation variables. And, it tries to show the relationship of the latter to the defensive and adjustive mechanisms by which the individual personality system copes with the exigencies of its situation.

The third chapter is concerned with culture. It takes up the systematic analysis of value patterns themselves and their organization into systems. It places them in the context of larger culture systems and analyzes their articulation with social systems and personalities. Sources of imperfect integration of certain value systems are also discussed; these are such as expose the systems to processes of change.

The fourth chapter takes up the social system, analyzing its bases of organization and its functional problems. It shows how value-orientation patterns enter into the institutionalization of roles and of the allocative and integrative structures of the social system and how the motivation of individual actors is channeled into role behavior. There is also consideration of the problem of the bases of structural variability and change of social systems. The final chapter briefly summarizes the main analysis and suggests certain lines of promising work for further development.

The most important thread of continuity running through Part II is the "pattern variable" scheme. It might be well to familiarize the reader with this scheme here at the outset so that he will be prepared for some of the complex material that will precede its technical introduction into the text of this work. The following paragraph, therefore, will show the reader something of what is to come.

The pattern-variable scheme defines a set of five dichotomies. Any course of action by any actor involves (according to theory) a pattern of choices with respect to these five sets of alternatives.[1] Ignoring technical terminology, we may define the five dichotomies as follows. The first is that between accepting an opportunity for gratification without regard for its consequences, on the one hand, and evaluating it with regard to its consequences, on the other. The second is that between considering an act solely with respect to its personal significance, on the one hand, and considering it with respect to its significance for a collectivity or a moral code, on the other. The third is that between evaluating the object of an action in terms of its relations to a generalized frame of reference, on the one hand, and evaluating it in terms of its relations to the actor and his own specific relations to objects, on the other. The fourth is that between seeing the social object with respect to which an action is oriented as a composite of performances (actions), on the one hand, and seeing it as a composite of ascribed qualities, on the other. The fifth is that between conceding to the social object with respect to which action is oriented an undefined set of rights (to be delimited only by feasibility in the light of other demands), on the one hand, and conceding to that social object only a clearly specified set of rights on the other.

The pattern-variable scheme to be presented below will attempt to formulate the way each and every social action, long- or short-term, proposed or concrete, prescribed or carried out, can be analyzed into five choices (conscious or unconscious, implicit or explicit) formulated by these five dichotomies.

We should perhaps give a brief résumé of the problems which gave rise to this method of analysis. Certain elements of this scheme were developed some years ago in an attempt by one of the authors to systematize the analysis of

---

[1] Actions may be long-term or short-term; they may be planned or concrete; they may be prescribed or carried out. A long-term action may be comprised by a sequence of shorter-term actions. A planned action may or may not eventuate in a concrete action; similarly, a prescribed course of action may or may not be carried out. Nevertheless, any specifiable course of action, short- or long-term, proposed or concrete, prescribed or carried out, is by theory analyzable into a pattern of choices with respect to these five dichotomies.

social role-patterns.[2] This attempt in turn grew out of dissatisfaction with then current dichotomous classifications of types of social relationships, of which Toennies' *Gemeinschaft* and *Gesellschaft* was the most prominent. Though applied to the analysis of professional roles and elsewhere, the pattern-variable scheme remained incomplete and its grounding in general theory obscure. This line of thought converged with ideas derived by the other author largely from critical consideration of Max Weber's four types of action and the difficulties in Weber's scheme.[3]

The problems posed by these concepts have proved to open up one of the main paths to the higher level of systematic integration of theory presented here. It appeared above all that these variables were not peculiar to social structure but were grounded in the general structure of action — they were hence involved in personalities as well as in social systems. It further appeared that they were patterns of value-orientation and as such were part of culture. This insight contributed greatly to the understanding of culture and of the ways in which it became integrated in personalities and social systems. The pattern variables have proved to form, indeed, a peculiarly strategic focus of the whole theory of action.

Several questions may arise about whether the substance of this monograph constitutes a "system" in the theoretical sense.[4] In one sense every carefully defined and logically integrated conceptual scheme constitutes a "system," and in this sense scientific theory of any kind consists of systems. Beyond this, however, there are three questions relevant to the "systematic" nature of a theoretical work. The first has to do with the generality and complexity of the scheme. The second is concerned with the degree to which it may claim "closure"; here the problem is whether the implications of its assertions in some parts are systematically supported or contradicted by assertions in other parts. The third is concerned with the level of systematization; that is, with how far the theory is advanced toward the ultimate goals of science.

Let us propose, in advance, some answers to these questions about the systematic nature of our work. Since we carry deductive procedures further than is common in the social sciences (excluding, perhaps, economic theory), we may justly be called system-builders on the first count. In default of formal, logical, or mathematical tests of completeness or closure, however, we are unable to judge how far the present scheme approaches such a standard; it seems almost certain that it is relatively incomplete in this sense. We do feel

[2] Cf. Talcott Parsons, *Essays in Sociological Theory*, esp. chap. viii.

[3] E. A. Shils, "Some Remarks on the Theory of Social and Economic Organization," *Economica*, 1948.

[4] Here the notion of a "theoretical system" should be kept separate from the notion of an "empirical system." The latter notion will be defined and discussed at the end of Chapter I. In the present section we are concerned with whether or not our conceptual scheme constitutes a theoretical system. Thus we are asking about the coherence and utility of our scheme. The other question (about an empirical system) has to do with criteria for coherence and harmony to be applied to some specific body of subject matter.

that we have carried the implications of our assumptions somewhat further than others have carried theirs; yet we do not feel that the fruitful implications of our assumptions have been even nearly exhausted. We believe that there is much more to be done.

So far as the "level" of systematization is concerned, it seems useful to distinguish four different levels of systematization of conceptual schemes, in order of their "primitiveness" relative to the final goals of scientific endeavor: (1) *ad hoc* classificatory systems, (2) categorial systems, (3) theoretical systems, and (4) empirical-theoretical systems.

The first type involves the use of more or less arbitrary classes for the sake of making summary statements about the subject matter. No attempt is made to fit the classes to the subject matter in such a way that the relations among the classes will be patterned upon the relations among the items of the subject matter summarized by these classes. The classes are quite independent of one another and any relations which may be discovered must come from *ad hoc* researches. Such common-sense classifications as that of "fish, flesh, or fowl" are illustrative of this type of classificatory system.

The second, the categorial type, involves a system of classes which is formed to fit the subject matter, so that there are intrinsic relations among the classes, and these are in accord with the relations among the items of the subject matter. Thus, in these systems, the principles of classification,[5] themselves, include statements of certain relationships among classes. The elements are so defined as to constitute an interdependent system. And the system has sufficient complexity and articulation to duplicate, in some sense, the interdependence of the empirical systems which are the subject matter. A categorial system, thus, is constituted by the definition of a set of interrelated elements, their interrelatedness being intrinsic to their definition. Thus in classical mechanics such concepts as space, time, particle, mass, motion, location, velocity, acceleration and their logical interrelations constitute a categorial system. A categorial system in this sense is always logically prior to the laws which state further relations between its elements. The laws state generalized relationships of interdependence between variables in the system. The laws presuppose the definitions of the variables, and they presuppose those relations which are logically implied by the definitions and by the kind of system in question. Insofar as specific laws can be formulated and verified, a categorial system evolves into a theoretical system. Thus a categorial system whose laws relating elements have been formulated is a theoretical system. But it is quite possible to have a categorial system or many parts of one before we have more than a rudimentary knowledge of laws.

In the field of action, our knowledge of laws is both vague and fragmentary. We know, for instance, that there is a positive relationship between reward and learning, but we cannot say in any specific situation how reward

---

[5] The principles of classification *are* the definitions of the elements of the system.

or its absence will interact with other variables; we do not know, that is, what effect will be produced by a concrete interaction of many variables even when reward is one of the ingredients of the situation. We do know, of course, that certain variables are highly significant, and we know certain things about the direction of their influence and how they combine with other variables. Knowing that a variable is significant, having a definite conception of it and its logical distinctions from other variables and other aspects of the empirical system is categorial knowledge; and that is where most of our theoretical knowledge of action stands today.

We have already said that a theoretical system is a categorial system whose laws relating elements have been formulated. The classical mechanics is the commonest example of what we mean here by a theoretical system. By logical manipulation of this system it is possible to make detailed predictions about the consequences of specific changes in the values of specific variables; this is because the general laws of the system are known. It should be noted, however, that the classical mechanics does not tell us how empirical systems will actually behave; it tells us rather how they might behave if an ideal set of scientific or "standard" conditions were to exist. Insofar as an empirical system can be subjected to such standard conditions in a laboratory, or insofar as it exists in some "pure" medium, so far is the theoretical system an adequate tool for the prediction of the changes which actually occur in the empirical system. Thus, in certain empirical fields, such as the astronomy of the solar system, the theoretical system of classical mechanics is, to a close approximation, empirically adequate. But in other fields, such as ballistics, or practical mechanics, the classical system by itself gives only much rougher approximations. This is because of the intervention of such variables as airresistance and friction. The latter variables, insofar as they have no place in the system itself, bring about "error" in prediction, that is, error in the fit between the theoretical and the empirical systems.

This gives us the basis for our definition of empirical-theoretical systems. We speak of an empirical-theoretical system whenever a sufficient number of relevant variables can be brought together in a single (theoretical) system of interdependence adequate for a high level of precision in predicting changes in empirical systems outside special experimental conditions. This is the long-term goal of scientific endeavor.

It has often been said that in our field we have a "structural-functional" theory. This refers to the fact that we have achieved in our field the stage where the categorial requirements are relatively well met; the knowledge of laws has not yet reached far enough to justify calling ours a theoretical system in the sense of the classical mechanics. The progress of knowledge will, however, move it steadily in that direction.

The present monograph is a straightforward exposition of a conceptual scheme. We deliberately decided to forego documentation by references to the relevant literature. This would have been a heavy task, would have greatly increased the already considerable bulk of the monograph, and would have substantially delayed publication. We would like this monograph to be received as an essay in theory construction as such, not as a work of scholarship in the traditional sense.

It is always difficult to acknowledge adequately indebtedness for others' contributions to such a work. In the deepest sense our debt is to the work of the great founders of modern social science theory, among whom we may single out Durkheim, Freud, and Max Weber; but in addition to these many other psychologists and anthropologists have influenced us greatly. More directly, our collaborators in the present project have stimulated us profoundly through many discussions, formal and informal; by their criticisms; and, of course, by their writings. Among them Professor Tolman and Mr. Sheldon, with whom we shared the privilege of release from normal academic obligations, stand out. Members of the Harvard Department of Social Relations also played a very important part. The debts to our Harvard colleagues are relatively immediate because of the discussions in which we have jointly participated. These acknowledgements should not obscure the great indebtedness we feel to many colleagues and writers outside Harvard.

The final draft of this manuscript was turned over to Mr. James Olds for careful editing in the interest of clarity and readability. Mr. Olds's services were on a level far above that normally expected of an editor. He has contributed substantially to the content of the monograph at a number of important points as well as to the improvement of the presentation. We are most happy to acknowledge his contribution and to have him associated with us in the authorship of the monograph.

Finally, because of their close relationship to this work, we should mention two publications. *The Social System,* by Talcott Parsons, will be published in 1951 by the Free Press of Glencoe, Illinois. This book could be regarded as a second volume to the present monograph; it takes essentially the subject matter of Chapter IV and elaborates it into a full volume. The general foundations in the theory of action on which it builds are those developed in the General Statement of Part I and the present monograph. *The Primary Group in the Social Structure* by Edward A. Shils, will also be published by the Free Press. In a somewhat more special field, it analyzes the interrelations of personality systems, primary groups, and larger social systems, using much of the conceptual scheme presented here in Part II.

T. P.

E. A. S.

1

Categories of the Orientation and

Organization of Action

ACTION AND ITS ORIENTATION

The theory of action [1] is a conceptual scheme for the analysis of the behavior of living organisms. It conceives of this behavior as oriented to the attainment of ends in situations, by means of the normatively regulated expenditure of energy. There are four points to be noted in this conceptualization of behavior: (1) Behavior is oriented to the attainment of ends or goals or other anticipated states of affairs. (2) It takes place in situations. (3) It is normatively regulated. (4) It involves expenditure of energy or effort or "motivation" (which may be more or less organized independently of its involvement in action). Thus, for example, *a man driving his automobile to a lake to go fishing* might be the behavior to be analyzed. In this case, (1) *to be fishing* is the "end" toward which our man's behavior is oriented; (2) his situation is the road and the car and the place where he is; (3) his energy expenditures are normatively regulated — for example, this driving behavior is an *intelligent* [2] means of getting to the lake; (4) but he does spend energy to get there; he holds the wheel, presses the accelerator, pays attention, and adapts his action to changing road and traffic conditions. When behavior can be and is so analyzed, it is called "action." This means that any behavior of a living organism might be called action; but to be so called, it must be analyzed in terms of the anticipated states of affairs toward which it is directed, the situation in which it occurs, the normative regulation (e.g., the intelligence) of the behavior, and the expenditure of energy or "motivation" involved. Behavior which is reducible to these terms, then, is action.

---

[1] The present exposition of the theory of action represents in one major respect a revision and extension of the position stated in Parsons, *The Structure of Social Action* (pp. 43–51, 732–733), particularly in the light of psychoanalytic theory, of developments in behavior psychology, and of developments in the anthropological analysis of culture. It has become possible to incorporate these elements effectively, largely because of the conception of a system of action in both the social and psychological spheres and their integration with systems of cultural patterns has been considerably extended and refined in the intervening years.

[2] Norms of intelligence are one set among several possible sets of norms that function in the regulation of energy expenditure.

Each action is the action of an actor, and it takes place in a situation consisting of objects. The objects may be other actors or physical or cultural objects. Each actor has a system of relations-to-objects; this is called his "system of orientations." The objects may be goal objects, resources, means, conditions, obstacles, or symbols. They may become cathected (wanted or not wanted), and they may have different significances attached to them (that is, they may mean different things to different people). Objects, by the significances and cathexes attached to them, become organized into the actor's system of orientations.

The actor's system of orientations is constituted by a great number of specific orientations. Each of these "orientations of action" is a "conception" (explicit or implicit, conscious or unconscious) which the actor has of the situation in terms of what he wants (his ends), what he sees (how the situation looks to him), and how he intends to get from the objects he sees the things he wants (his explicit or implicit, normatively regulated "plan" of action).

Next, let us speak briefly about the sources of energy or motivation. These presumably lie ultimately in the energy potential of the physiological organisms. However, the manner in which the energy is expended is a problem which requires the explicit analysis of the orientation of action, that is, analysis of the normatively regulated relations of the actor to the situation. For, it is the system of orientations which establishes the modes in which this energy becomes attached and distributed among specific goals and objects; it is the system of orientations which regulates its flow and which integrates its many channels of expression into a system.

We have introduced the terms *action* and *actor*. We have said something about the goals of action, the situation of action, the orientation of action, and the motivation of action. Let us now say something about the *organization* of action into systems.

Actions are not empirically discrete but occur in constellations which we call systems. We are concerned with three systems, three modes of organization of the elements of action; these elements are organized as social systems, as personalities, and as cultural systems. Though all three modes are conceptually abstracted from concrete social behavior, the empirial referents of the three abstractions are not on the same plane. Social systems and personalities are conceived as modes of organization of *motivated* action (social systems are systems of motivated action organized about the relations of actors to each other; personalities are systems of motivated action organized about the living organism). Cultural systems, on the other hand, are systems of symbolic patterns (these patterns are created or manifested by individual actors and are transmitted among social systems by diffusion and among personalities by learning).

A *social system* is a system of action which has the following characteristics: (1) It involves a process of interaction between two or more actors; the interaction process as such is a focus of the observer's attention. (2) The situation toward which the actors are oriented includes other actors. These other actors (alters) are objects of cathexis. Alter's actions are taken cognitively into account as data. Alter's various orientations may be either *goals* to be pursued or *means* for the accomplishment of goals. Alter's orientations may thus be objects for evaluative judgment. (3) There is (in a social system) interdependent and, in part, concerted action in which the concert is a function of collective goal orientation or common values, [3] and of a consensus of normative and cognitive expectations.

A *personality system* is a system of action which has the following characteristics: (1) It is the system comprising the interconnections of the actions of an individual actor. (2) The actor's actions are organized by a structure of need-dispositions. (3) Just as the actions of a plurality of actors cannot be randomly assorted but must have a determinate organization of compatibility or integration, so the actions of the single actor have a determinate organization of compatibility or integration with one another. Just as the goals or norms which an actor in a social system will pursue or accept will be affected and limited by those pursued or accepted by the other actors, so the goals or norms involved in a single action of one actor will be affected and limited by one another and by other goals and norms of the same actor.

A *cultural system* is a system which has the following characteristics: (1) The system is constituted neither by the organization of interactions nor by the organization of the actions of a single actor (as such), but rather by the organization of the values, norms, and symbols which guide the choices made by actors and which limit the types of interaction which may occur among actors. (2) Thus a cultural system is not an empirical system in the same sense as a personality or social system, because it represents a special kind of abstraction of elements from these systems. These elements, however, may exist separately as physical symbols and be transmitted from one empirical action system to another. (3) In a cultural system the patterns of regulatory norms (and the other cultural elements which guide choices of concrete actors) cannot be made up of random or unrelated elements. If, that is, a system of culture is to be manifest in the organization of an empirical action system it must have a certain degree of consistency. (4) Thus a cultural system is a pattern of culture whose different parts are interrelated to form value systems, belief systems, and systems of expressive symbols.

Social systems, personality systems, and cultural systems are critical subject matter for the theory of action. In the first two cases, the systems themselves are conceived to be actors whose action is conceived as oriented to

---

[3] A person is said to have "common values" with another when either (1) he wants the group in which he and the other belong to achieve a certain group goal which the other also wants, or (2) he intrinsically values conformity with the requirements laid down by the other.

goals and the gratification of need-dispositions, as occurring in situations, using energy, and as being normatively regulated. Analysis of the third kind of system is essential to the theory of action because systems of value standards (criteria of selection) and other patterns of culture, when *institutionalized* in social systems and *internalized* in personality systems, guide the actor with respect to both the *orientation to ends* and the *normative regulation* of means and of expressive activities, whenever the need-dispositions of the actor allow choices in these matters.

COMPONENTS OF THE FRAME OF REFERENCE OF THE THEORY OF ACTION

1. *The frame of reference of the theory of action* involves actors, a situation of action, and the orientation of the actor to that situation.

a. One or more *actors* is involved. An actor is an empirical system of action. The actor is an individual or a collectivity which may be taken as a point of reference for the analysis of the modes of its orientation and of its processes of action in relation to objects. Action itself is a process of change of state in such empirical systems of action.

b. A *situation* of action is involved. It is that part of the external world which means something to the actor whose behavior is being analyzed. It is only part of the whole realm of objects that might be seen. Specifically, it is that part to which the actor is oriented and in which the actor acts. The situation thus consists of objects of orientation.

c. The *orientation of the actor to the situation* is involved. It is the set of cognitions, cathexes, plans, and relevant standards which relates the actor to the situation.

2. The *actor* is both a system of action and a point of reference. As a system of action the actor may be either an individual or a collectivity. As a point of reference the actor may be either an actor-subject (sometimes called simply *actor*) or a social object.

a. The *individual-collectivity* distinction is made on the basis of whether the actor in question is a personality system or a social system (a society or subsystem).

b. The *subject-object distinction* is made on the basis of whether the actor in question occupies a central position (as a point of reference) within a frame of reference or a peripheral position (as an object of orientation for an actor taken as the point of reference. When an actor is taken as the central point of reference, he is an actor-subject. (In an interaction situation, this actor is called *ego*.) When he is taken as an object of orientation for an actor-subject, he is a social object. (In an interaction situation, this actor is called *alter*.) Thus, the actor-subject (*the* actor) is an orienting subject; the social object is the actor who is oriented to. This distinction cross-cuts the individual-collectivity distinction. Thus an individual or a collectivity may be either actor-subject or social object in a given analysis.

3. The situation of action may be divided into a class of social objects (individuals and collectivities) and a class of nonsocial (physical and cultural) objects.

a. Social objects include actors as persons and as collectivities (i.e., systems of action composed of a plurality of individual actors in determinate relations to one another). The actor-subject may be oriented to himself as an object as well as to other social objects. A collectivity, when it is considered as a social object, is never constituted by all the action of the participating individual actors; it may, however, be constituted by anything from a specified segment of their actions — for example, their actions in a specific system of roles — to a very inclusive grouping of their actions — for example, all of their many roles in a society. Social objects, whether individuals or collectivities, may be subjected to two further types of classification which cross-cut each other: they may be divided on the basis of whether they are significant to the actor-subject as "quality" or "performance" complexes; and they may be divided on the basis of the "scope of their significance" to the actor-subject.

i. The *quality-performance* distinction: In the first place, social objects may be significant to the actor-subject as *complexes of qualities*. When the actor-subject sees another actor solely in terms of what that actor *is* and irrespective of what that actor *does,* then we say that actor-object is significant to the subject as a complex of qualities. In other words, whenever the actor-subject considers another actor only in terms of that actor's *attributes,* and whenever the actor-subject is not, in the specific context, concerned with how the actor will perform, then the actor being oriented to is a *complex of qualities.* The qualities are those attributes of the other actor which are for the nonce divorced from any immediate connection with the actor's performances. The significant question about the object is what it *is* at the relevant time and in the relevant context, regardless of actual or expected activities. For our purposes, qualities in this sense shall include *memberships* in collectivities and *possessions,* whenever the possession of an acknowledged claim to property is considered as one of the actor's attributes.

In the second place, social objects may be significant to the actor-subject as *complexes of performances.* When the actor-subject sees another actor solely in terms of what that actor *does* and irrespective of what that actor *is,* then we say that the actor-object is significant to ego as a complex of performances. In other words, whenever the actor-subject considers another actor only in terms of that actor's capacity to accomplish things (what that actor has done in the past, what he is doing, what he may be expected to do) then the other actor is a complex of performances.

ii. The *scope of significance* distinction: In the first place, social objects may have such a broad and undefined significance for the actor-subject that he feels obliged to grant them any demand they make of him, so long as the granting of the demand does not force him to fail in other obligations higher on a priority scale of values. In this case we may say the object has for the actor-subject a broad scope of significance. Its significance is *diffuse*.

In the second place, social objects may have such a narrow and clearly defined significance for the actor-subject that the actor-subject does not feel obliged to grant them anything that is not clearly called for in the definition of the relationship which obtains between them. In this case we say the scope of significance of the object for the actor-subject is *specific*.

b. Nonsocial objects are any objects which are not actors. Nonsocial objects may be classified on the basis of whether they are physical objects or cultural objects.

i. *Physical objects* are those objects which are located in space and time; which do not "interact" with the actor-subject, as other actors do; and which constitute only objects, not subjects, of cognitive, cathectic, and evaluative orientation. Thus they can constitute instrumentally significant means, conditions, goal objects, obstacles or significant symbols.

ii. *Cultural objects* are elements of the cultural tradition or heritage (for example, laws, ideas, recipes) when these are taken as *objects* of orientation. These too may be objects of cognitive, cathectic, and evaluative orientation in the sense that one may understand the meaning of a law, want a law, decide what to do about a law. Also, these may serve as normative rules, as instrumentally significant means, and as conditions or obstacles of action, or as systems of significant symbols.

These cultural objects are the laws, ideas, and so forth, as the actor-subject sees these things existing outside of himself. The same laws and ideas may eventually become internalized elements of culture for the actor-subject; *as such* they will not be cultural objects but components of the actor-subject's system of action. Cultural objects as norms may be divided into classes (cognitive, appreciative, and moral) exactly parallel to the three classes into which the value standards of the motivational orientation of the actor will be divided in the next section of this outline. Since these three classes will be defined at that point, we need not define them here.

4. The *orientation of the actor to the situation* may be broken down into a set of analytic elements. These elements are not separate within the orientation process; they might be conceived as different aspects or different ingredients of that process. They may be divided into two analytically independent categories: a category of elements of *motivational orientation* (appearances, wants, plans), and a category of elements of *value*-orientation (cognitive standards, aesthetic standards, moral standards).

a. Motivational orientation refers to those aspects of the actor's orientation to his situation which are related to actual or potential gratification or deprivation of the actor's need-dispositions. We will speak of three *modes* of motivational orientation.

i. The *cognitive* mode involves the various processes by which an actor *sees* an object in relation to his system of need-dispositions. Thus it would include the "location" of an object in the actor's total object-world, the determination of its properties and actual and potential functions, its differentiations from other objects, and its relations to certain general classes.[4]

ii. The *cathectic* [5] mode involves the various processes by which an actor invests an object with affective significance. Thus it would include the positive or negative cathexes implanted upon objects by their gratificational or deprivational significance with respect to the actor's need-dispositions or drives.

iii. The *evaluative mode* involves the various processes by which an actor allocates his energy among the various actions with respect to various cathected objects in an attempt to optimize gratification. Thus it would include the processes by which an actor organizes his cognitive and cathectic orientations into intelligent plans. These processes make use of cognitive norms (bits of knowledge) in order to distribute attention and action with respect to various objects and their possible modalities, with respect to various occasions for gratification, and with respect to the demands of different need-dispositions. Evaluation is functionally necessary for the resolution of conflicts among interests and among cognitive interpretations which are not resolved automatically; and which thus necessitate *choice,* or at least specific selective mechanisms.

b. Value-orientation [6] refers to those aspects of the actor's orientation which commit him to the observance of certain norms, standards, criteria of selection, whenever he is in a contingent situation which allows (and requires) him to make a choice. Whenever an actor is forced to choose among various means objects, whenever he is forced to choose among various goal objects, whenever he is forced to choose which need-disposition he will gratify, or how much he will gratify a need-disposition — whenever he is forced to make any choice whatever — his *value-orientations* may commit him to certain norms that will guide him in his choices. The value-orientations which commit a man to the observance of certain rules in making selections from available alternatives are not random but tend to form a system of value-orientations which commit the individual to some organized set of rules (so that the rules themselves do not contradict one another). On a cultural level we view the or-

---

[4] Tolman's concept "cognitive mapping" well describes this mode. The extent to which this involves instrumental orientation will be taken up below, pp. 75–76.

[5] It is through the cathexis of objects that energy or motivation, in the technical sense, enters the system of the *orientation of action.* The propositions about drive in the General Statement are here taken for granted. Their implications for action will be further elaborated in Chapter II.

[6] Standards of value-orientation are of course not the whole of a system of cultural orientation. This has been made clear in the General Statement. They are however *strategically* the most important parts of culture for the organization of systems of action. Their relation to the other parts will be more fully analyzed in Chapter III, below.

ganized set of rules or standards as such, abstracted, so to speak, from the actor who is committed to them by his own value-orientations and in whom they exist as need-dispositions to observe these rules. Thus a culture includes a set of *standards*. An individual's value-orientation is his commitment to these standards. In either case our analysis of these standards of value-orientation commitment may be the same.

We shall speak of three modes of value-orientation, which parallel the modes of motivational orientation.

i. The *cognitive* mode of value-orientation involves the various commitments to standards by which the validity of cognitive judgments is established. These standards include those concerning the relevance of data and those concerning the importance of various problems. They also include those categories (often implicit in the structure of a language) by which observations and problems are, often unconsciously, assessed as valid.

ii. The *appreciative* mode of value-orientation involves the various commitments to standards by which the appropriateness or consistency of the cathexis of an object or class of objects is assessed. These standards sometimes lay down a pattern for a particular kind of gratification; for example, standards of taste in music. The criterion in formulating such appreciative standards is not what consequences the pursuit of these patterns will have upon a system of action (a person or a collectivity). Rather, these standards purport to give us rules for judging whether or not a given object, sequence, or pattern will have immediate gratificatory significance.

iii. The *moral* mode of value-orientation involves the various commitments to standards by which certain consequences of particular actions and types of action may be assessed with respect to their effects upon systems of action. These standards define the actor's responsibility for these consequences. Specifically, they guide the actor's choices with a view to how the consequences of these choices will affect (a) the integration of his own personality system and (b) the integration of the social systems in which he is a participant.

Fig. 1 is an attempt to summarize this outline. It shows that the frame of reference of the theory of action includes subjects and objects. Only actors are subjects; objects include actors and nonsocial objects. The box in the center shows how social systems and personalities interpenetrate one another whether they are subjects or objects: a role is the segment of a personality's actions (or orientations) which goes into the constitution of any particular group (the concept will be discussed in detail later). At the bottom of the diagram is a section that indicates how cultural systems are abstracted from the action frame of reference. (All figures referred to in Part II are grouped, in sequence, following page 245.)

COMMENTARY ON THE FRAME OF REFERENCE

The frame of reference of the theory of action is a set of categories for the analysis of the relations of one or more actors to and in a situation. It is not directly concerned with the internal constitution or physiological processes of the organisms which are in one respect the units of the concrete system of action; its essential concern is with the structure and processes involved in the actor's *relations* to his situation, which includes *other actors* (alters) as persons and as members of collectivities. There is an inherent relativity in this frame of reference. The determination of which is actor and which is object in a situation will depend on the point of reference required by the problems under consideration. In the course of an analysis this point of reference may shift from one actor to another and it is always important to make such a shift explicit. It is also fundamental that a *collectivity* may be chosen as a point of reference, in which case the relevant segments of the action of its members do not belong to the situation, but to the collectivity as actor.[7] By the same token the actor himself, as either an organism or personality or as both, may be treated as an *object* of his own orientation. It is very important to understand that the distinction between actor and situation is *not* that between *concrete* entities distinguished in common-sense terms. It is an *analytical* distinction, the concrete referents of which will shift according to the analytical uses to which it is put.

The frame of reference of the theory of action differs in two ways from the biological frame of reference which has, explicitly and implicitly, in-

---

[7] The collectivity as an action system, whether it be subject or object in a given analysis, is not the simple sum of the actions of the individual actors involved. It is rather composed of the segments of their action; specifically, those segments of their action which are oriented to and in this collectivity. To the individual actors the collectivity is an object of orientation, that is, a social object (thus an alter), and the actions of the collectivity may themselves be more specific objects of orientation for the individual actor. But when the collectivity is taken as the actor-subject, the actions of these individuals (the members of the collectivity) insofar as they are oriented to the collectivity, are the *actions of the collectivity*. Thus, when the collectivity is the actor, then the collectivity-oriented actions of its members are not objects of orientation for the collectivity; they are the actions of the collectivity. A collectivity may be viewed as an actor in either of the following senses: (1) as a social system in relation to a situation outside itself. In the most important case, the collective actor is a subsystem of the larger social system interacting as a unit with other subsystems and/or individual actors (which are taken as objects of *its* situation). Viewed internally the collective actor must be interpreted as a concert of actions and reactions of individual actors, and the conceptual scheme for its analysis will thus be that used for the analysis of *social systems*. The conceptual scheme used in the analysis of personality systems is hence inappropriate for the description of a collective actor, especially in the imputation of motivation. The *mechanisms* which explain the action of the collective actor are those of the social system, *not* of the personality. (2) A collectivity may be viewed as an actor when it is the point of reference for the orientation of an individual actor in a *representative role*. In this usage, a member of a collectivity acts on behalf of his collectivity, his role as representative being accepted by fellow members and by those who are the situational context of the collective actor. (Collectivities as systems of action may of course be treated as objects by the actors in a situation.)

fluenced much current thought about behavior. In the first place, the theory of action is not concerned with the internal physiological processes of the organism. It is concerned instead with the organization of the actor's processes of interaction with objects in a situation; in this sense it is *relational*. The course of a stream may be said in the same sense to be a *relational* matter; it is no property of water to flow in one direction rather than another, nor is it the contour of the land alone which determines the direction of the flow. The stream's course is determined by a relationship between the properties of the water and the contour of the land; however, the map-maker can chart the flow of a stream by means of *relational* concepts without recourse to any but a few of the intrinsic properties of land or water. The map-maker is not interested in the principles of moisture-absorption, condensation, and gravitation, which, in a sense, account for the direction of the stream's flow; he is satisfied merely to plot the structure of the channel which actually guides the water's flow. The structure of the river system, thus, is not the structure of the water, but it is a structure — in this case, of the water's relationships to the earth's undulations. Similarly, the structure of action is *not* the structure of the organism. It is the structure of the organism's relationships to the objects in the organism's situation.

One of the apparent paradoxes of the theory of action stems from this lack of concern for internal structure. The paradox is that with all its emphasis on structure, the theory of action describes an actor who sometimes does not seem to have any internal structure at all. This paradox arises only on one level of conceptualization; [8] that level in which the actor is treated as the unit of interaction within a larger system of action. On the level dealing with the dynamic analysis of social interaction, however, the actor does indeed have very much of a structure. When we go beyond the description of an orientation and seek to *explain* what has occurred, the actor is not only a *point* of reference, but also definitely a system of action which we call personality. Even at this level, however, the internal, physiological process of the organism, although highly relevant to the concrete phenomena of action, is

[8] When the individual actor is seen as the interacting unit within a larger scale structure (for example, within a social system, or within the total action frame of reference which comprehends both actors and objects) the actor does not seem to have a structure. This is similar to the notion that any molecule of water in the stream is simply an unstructured unit of flow to the man charting the river. But this is true only on one level of conceptualization: both the molecule and the actor may be analyzed as systems in themselves if one seeks explanation on a deeper level. When we treat the actor as a unit in the system of interaction with the object world, our abstraction ignores the internal structure and processes of that unit and considers *only* its relations with the situation. Nevertheless, any particular act of this unit may in fact be a very complex resultant of internal personality factors. When these internal complications are an object of study the personality is not treated merely as an actor but as a system of action. It will be recalled that there is just as much *interaction* between elements within the personality as a system as there is between persons in the social system.

only relevant insofar as it affects the system of orientations. The physiological process will enter the picture as the source of the viscerogenic drive or energy of action and in various ways as part of the object system, as a system of qualities and of capacities for performance. We emphasize, however, that only the empirical *consequences* of this aspect of the organism, formulated in terms of their *relevance* to the system of action, interest us here.

In the second place, the frame of reference of the theory of action differs from common biologically oriented approaches in the categories used to analyze the interaction of organism and environment. The most obvious difference is the *explicit* concern of our theory with *selection* among alternative possibilities and hence with the evaluative process and ultimately with value standards. Thus, our primary concern in analyzing systems of action with respect to their aims is this: to what consequences has this actor been committed by his selections or choices? [9] This contrasts with the primary concern of biological theorists, who, in a motivational analysis, would ask a parallel but quite different question: what does this person have to do in order to survive? In the system of action the question is what does this actor strive for, not what does he *have* to strive for in order to survive as an organism. Further, we ask: on what bases does the actor make his selections? Implicit is the notion that survival is *not* the sole ground of these selections; on the contrary, we hold that internalized cultural values are the main grounds of such selective orientations.

The role of choice may be implicit in much biological analysis of behavior, but in the frame of reference of the theory of action it becomes explicit and central.[10]

The *empirical* significance of selective or value standards as determinants of concrete action may be considered problematical and should not be prejudged. But the theory of action analyzes action in such a way as to leave the door open for attributing a major significance to these standards (and their patterning). The older type of biological frame of reference did not leave this door open and thus prejudged the question.

The theory of action formulates the components of the action frame of

[9] The terms *selection* and *choice* are used more or less interchangeably in this context. Where alternatives exist which cannot all be realized, a selection must result. The mechanisms by which this occurs are not at issue at this stage of the analysis. The present problem is, then, analysis of the structure of the system of alternatives, not the determinants of selection between them.

[10] The notion of selection or choice in the present discussion is closely connected with the notion of expectations and normative orientations in the General Statement of Part I. These concepts all underline and define the voluntaristic or purposive aspects of systems of action as conceived by the present analytical scheme. Without this purposive aspect, most of the elements of the orientation of action under consideration here — and above all the patterns of value-orientation — would become analytically superfluous epiphenomena.

reference in terms of their direct relevance to *choice orientation*.[11] The situation is treated as a constellation of objects among which selections must be made.[12] Action itself is the resolution of an unending series of problems of selection which confront actors.

It is against the background of these observations that the subjective viewpoint of our frame of reference should be considered. We do *not* postulate a substantive entity, a mind which is somehow dissociated from the organism and the object world. The organization of observational data in terms of the theory of action is quite possible and fruitful in modified behavioristic terms, and such formulation avoids many of the difficult questions of introspection or empathy.[13] In Tolman's psychology, it is postulated that the rat is oriented to the goal of hunger gratification and that he cognizes the situation in which he pursues that goal. Tolman's concepts of orientation and cognition are ways of generalizing the facts of observation about the rat's behavior. The concept of expectation is also essential to this mode of organizing data. By broadening this notion to include the "complementarity of expectations" involved in the action of an ego and the *reaction* of an alter, we have all the essential components of the analysis of action defined in Tolman's manner without raising further difficulties. What the actor thinks or feels can be treated as a system of *intervening variables*. The actor and his cognitive, cathectic, and evaluative processes are neither more nor less real than the "particle" of classical mechanics and its composition.

CLASSIFICATION OF OBJECTS

The foregoing discussion constitutes a commentary on items one and two of our outline. We have tried to give the reader a general familiarity with the significant features of the action frame of reference, and in the course of the discussion we have sought to clarify the relation of the actor-subject to the frame of reference. We shall proceed now to a discussion of the objects of the situation, item three of our outline. Specifically, we shall discuss the classification of objects in terms of the *object modalities*. A *modality* is a property of an object; it is one of the aspects of an object in terms of which the object may be significant to an actor. Some (if not most) objects have several modalities in terms of which they may have meaning to an actor. A given actor may "choose" to see the object only in terms of one, or a specific set, of these modalities. The relevant action of the actor will be a function of the modalities he chooses.

[11] The terms *choice orientation, selective orientation,* and so forth, refer to the actor's acts of choosing. That is, they refer to the subjective processes involved while the actor is making a choice.

[12] Actually choices are not made so much with respect to the objects themselves as among possible relations to these objects.

[13] This procedure does not necessarily commit one to any specific position on the more ultimate epistemological problem of the nature of our knowledge of other minds.

The most fundamental distinction bearing on the object system is that between the *social* and the *nonsocial* modalities of objects. By *social* in this context, we mean interactive. A social object is an actor or system of action, whose reactions and attitudes are significant to the actor who is the point of reference. The social object, the alter, is seen by ego to have expectations which are complementary to ego's own. The distinction between those objects which do and those objects which do not have expectations complementary to ego's is fundamental to the theory of action. It should, however, be clear that the same *concrete* object may be social or nonsocial in different contexts. Thus, on the one hand, a human being may be treated *only* as a physical object and no account taken of his possible reactions to ego's action, and, on the other, an animal may be a social object.

Within the category of social objects a further discrimination has been made between complexes of qualities and complexes of performances. In one sense, of course, all action is performance and all social objects are "performers"; yet it is possible to orient objects either (1) in terms of characteristics they possess regardless of their performances, or (2) in terms of characteristics they possess by virtue of their performances.

A social object is a complex of qualities when the actor, in the orientation of action to the objects, overlooks actual or possible performances and *focuses* on "attributes" [14] as such. These attributes may in the further developments of interaction be related to performances in many ways, but in the immediate situation, it is the attribute which is the basis of discrimination. Thus, to take a very obvious example, for the normal heterosexual person, the sex of an object rather than its "capacity for giving erotic gratification" may be the *first* criterion of object-choice. Only within the category of those possessing the quality of *belonging to the opposite sex* from ego do performance criteria become relevant.[15]

A social object is a complex of performances when the actor, in the orientation of action to the object, *focuses* on its processes of action and *their outcomes* rather than its qualities or attributes. The significant focus is not a *given state.* It may be remarked that orientation to performance has become so central in Western society that there has been a tendency to assimilate all social objects to this modality. A comparative perspective will dissolve this illusion.

Certainly the most obvious reason for emphasis on the distinction is the very great importance in the organization of social relations of ascriptive

[14] Confusion is very easy here because logically *anything* predicated of an object may be considered an attribute. Here we have a special definition of the term in mind. An attribute of a social object is some quality or descriptive term which would characterize the object irrespective of any action that object might perform.

[15] Of course the two aspects are so fully integrated in the actual system of our cultural orientations that it never occurs to most of us to make such a distinction, and in daily life, there is no reason why it should be done.

qualifications for status. But the distinction will be seen to permeate systems of action very generally. It should be emphasized here that this distinction, like the distinction between social and nonsocial objects, refers to aspects of objects, not to discrete concrete entities. The same object may, in different contexts of the same system of action, be significant for its qualities or for its performances.[16]

In addition to the quality-performance distinction, a scope-of-significance distinction can also be applied to social objects. An object's scope of significance is not really a modality of the object; it is rather a special relationship which obtains between the actor and the object. Thus a social object, whatever the content of an actor's concern for it, may be significant to him in terms of one, several, or numerous of its aspects. The range or scope over which the object is significant to the actor cannot be deduced from, and is thus analytically independent of, the modalities of the object. It is likewise analytically independent of motivational orientations and value-orientations, and it might thus be regarded as an additional category of orientation.

The category of nonsocial objects comprises both physical and cultural objects. They have in common the fact that they do not, in the technical sense, *interact* with actors. They do not and cannot constitute alters to an ego; they do not have *attitudes* or *expectations* concerning ego. Both may, however, be immediately cathected as objects; they may constitute conditions or means of instrumental action, and as symbols they may become endowed with meaning.

Although physical and cultural objects have these features in common, there is a crucial set of differences which centers on the fact that cultural objects can be internalized and thereby transmitted from one actor to another, while only *possession* of claims to physical objects can be transmitted. This difference rests on the fact that the cultural object is a pattern which is reproducible in the action of another person while it leaves the original actor unaffected. Only in a figurative sense does an actor *have* patterns of value-orientation. In a strict sense he *is*, among other things, a system of such patterns. Of course, another actor, an alter, cannot be internalized either. Only his cultural patterns — for instance, his values — can be "taken over" by orientation or identification.[17]

The distinction between cultural patterns as objects, on the one hand, and as components of the actor's system of orientation, on the other, must be held separate from the classification of *types* of culture patterns themselves — that is, from the classification in terms of belief systems, systems of expressive symbols, and systems of value-orientations. The first distinction is not a differentiation among the parts of a cultural system; it distinguishes

---

[16] The term *performance* has been chosen to avoid confusion with the general meaning of the term *action*. Orientation to an object in terms of its qualities is action.

[17] See Chapter II, pp. 116, 130.

modes of the relationship of cultural patterns to action, regardless of the type of the pattern. In principle *every* kind of cultural object is capable of internalization. It is this "transferability" from the status of object to the internalized status and vice versa which is the most distinctive property of culture and which is *the fundamental reason why culture cannot be identified with the concrete systems of action.*

The Freudian hypothesis concerning the formation of the superego has made the internalization of patterns of value-orientation widely known. It is also strategically the most important case for us. But the internalization of instrumental and expressive patterns such as skills and tastes is also of the highest importance in the analysis of action.

Before leaving the problem of objects, we should speak briefly about the problem of the "phenomenological" approach to the object world which we use. We are interested in the object world not as an abstract scientific entity but as something which significantly affects the action of an actor. Thus we are only interested in those aspects of that world which do affect, which are relevant to, ego's action. But, to become relevant to ego's action, all classes of objects must be known or cognized in some way or other. Thus our tendency is to pattern our abstraction of the object world after ego's cognition of that world. There is always a distinction between the actually and the potentially known. Only the hypothetical mind of God is omniscient. An observer may, however, know many things about another actor's situation and his personality which the other actor himself does not know. The observer might thus well know much more than ego about those properties of the objects in ego's situation which affect ego's behavior indirectly.

We should therefore recognize the implicit if not always explicit distinction between the situation as known to or knowable by an observer and as known to the actor in question. Of course, ego's knowledge may be increased by processes of investigation; and through the search for knowledge, as well as by other processes arising from the properties of the object situation, new objects not previously part of the situation of action may enter. The most usual condition is for relatively few of the knowable properties of the object situation to be known to the actor. He will seldom know the systemic interconnections of the objects of his situation which the scientific observer might know and would have to know in order to account for their behavior.

Let us turn now now from item three of our outline, the situation, to item four, the orientation of the actor to that situation, and discuss the categories for analysis of the actor's system of relations to the object world.

ORIENTATION TO THE SITUATION

What can we say about the actor's orientation to a situation? At the outset we must mention two general features which characterize and perhaps define all such orientations, but which are of such a general nature that they are not treated as separate modes of orientation. These are (1) the choice aspect and (2) the expectancy aspect of the orientation. The first implies that every orientation is explicitly or implicitly an orientation to alternatives; the orientation involves a scanning of several possible courses of action and a choice from them. The second implies that every orientation is an "expectancy" in the sense that it is an orientation to the future state of the situation as well as to the present. We mention these two points at the outset as they pervade the following discussion of the modes or orientation.

Besides the aspects mentioned above, the salient features of an actor's orientation are these: (1) There is orientation to discriminated and related objects; various things are seen or expected, and they are seen or expected in relational contexts. (2) There is orientation to goals; various things are wanted. (3) There is orientation to the gratification-deprivation significance of the various courses of action suggested by the situation, and there is comparison of the gratification-deprivation balance presented by each of the alternative courses. (4) There is orientation to standards of acceptability which (a) narrow the range of cognitions, sorting "veridical" from "nonveridical" object-orientation; (b) narrow the range of objects wanted, sorting "appropriate" from "inappropriate" goal objects; and (c) narrow the number of alternatives, sorting "moral" from "immoral" courses of action.

Points one, two, and three make up the three modes of the motivational orientation in our classificatory scheme. Point four is the value-orientation. We will discuss first the three modes of motivational orientation and then the three modes of value-orientation.

The first two modes of motivational orientation, the cognitive and cathectic modes, are the minimal components of any act of orientation. Similarly they are the minimal components of any act of selection or choice (this is redundant in the sense that any orientation involves an explicit or implicit choice, but it serves to emphasize another aspect of the problem). One cannot "orient" without discriminating objects, one cannot discriminate an object without its arousing some interest either by virtue of its intrinsic gratificatory significance, or by virtue of its relationships to other objects. Similarly, one cannot make a choice without "cognizing" the alternatives; and also one cannot select except on the basis of the cathectic interest aroused by the alternatives. The discrimination of objects is the cognitive mode of motivational orientation. The having of interest in an object is the cathectic mode of motivational orientation. The "expectancy" aspect of the orientation enters into both modes; both modes, that is, have a future reference: the cognitive discrimination of an object includes a cognitive prediction regarding a future state of the situation; the cathectic interest in an object includes a readiness to receive gratification and avoid deprivation.

Let us dwell for a moment on the notion, implicit in the paragraph above, that cognition and cathexis are simultaneously given and only analytically separable. In the first place, there can be no *orientation* to the cathectic or gratificatory significance of objects without discrimination, without location of the relevant object or objects in relation to others, without discrimination between objects which produce gratification and those which are noxious. Thus the cognitive mapping of the situation, or relevant parts of it, is one essential aspect of any actor's orientation to it. Nor can there be cognition without an associated cathexis. Each object of cognition is cathected in some degree either by virtue of its intrinsic gratificatory significance or by virtue of its relationships to other objects of intrinsic gratificatory significance. The limiting case is the object of "pure knowledge," and even this is cathected in the limited sense implied by the existence of a cognitive interest in it. Furthermore, the standards of cognitive judgment must certainly be objects of cathexis and the act of cognition might also be cathected.

Of these two modes of orientation, the cathectic mode is most specifically *relational* in the sense that we have already said the orientation itself is relational. That is, a cathexis relates an actor and an object. Specifically it refers on the one side to a motivation — that is, a drive, need, wish, impulse, or need-disposition — and on the other side to an object. It is only when the motivation is attached to a determinate object or objects through the cathectic mode of motivational orientation that an organized system of behavior [18] exists.

We have just said that a cathexis relates a motive to an object, and in the section of the General Statement on behavior psychology, quite a bit is said about the motivation that makes up one side of this picture. Hitherto, however, we have said nothing about the kinds of objects that become cathected — that is, the kinds of objects which gratify need-dispositions — and it is not possible to do more than indicate them briefly here. Except for the objects which gratify specific organically engendered need-dispositions, the most pervasive cathected object is a positive affective response or attitude on the part of alter and the corresponding positive affective attitude on the part of ego toward alter or toward himself as object (e.g., love, approval, esteem). The sensitivity to which we alluded in the General Statement is primarily a sensitivity to these positive affective attitudes. This sensitivity enters as an ingredient into many need-dispositions with complex institutional objects, such as the need-dispositions for achievement, charity, and so forth. The sensitivity is learned through a series of processes in which generalization, substitution, and identification play preëminent parts.

---

[18] The degree to which this organized system of behavior is an active pursuit of gratification or merely a state of passive receptive gratification may of course vary. In either case we have action in the sense that the active pursuit or passive reception is selected from alternatives by the actor. Both activity and passivity share elements of "expectancy." Activity involves the expectation of gratification in consequence of performance. Both are directed toward future developments in the situation in both cognitive and cathectic modes.

When an object is sufficiently gratifying to the need-dispositions or set of need-dispositions which are directed toward it over time, we may speak of an object-attachment. The actor will recurrently seek out the object when the need-disposition is reactivated or he will seek to maintain (or possess) at all times a given relation to it. This possession of objects, or maintenance of relationships to them, serves to stabilize the availability of objects and thus to stabilize the orientation system of the individual actor (that is, he knows where to find things; his little world is not a chaos). Finally, it should be remembered that through the mechanisms of generalization, *categories* of objects may be themselves objects of attachment.

The third of the three basic modes of motivational orientation is evaluation. The evaluative mode is essentially the organizational or integrative aspect of a given actor's system of action and hence it is directly relevant to the act of choice. It operates wherever a selection problem is presented to the actor, where he wants or could want two or more gratifications, both of which cannot be attained — where, in other words, there is actually or potentially a situation in which one "wants to eat one's cake and have it too." [19] That this situation exists on the level of animal behavior is amply attested by Tolman's work. It becomes particularly significant on the human level with the involvement of culture and cultural standards in the act of choice.

Several things are to be said about this evaluative mode. The first is that it cannot be understood properly except as an aspect of the cognitive-cathectic orientation process; the evaluative mode tends to be inextricably related to the cognitive mode whenever cognition is at all complex. The second is that it is our organizational concept which parallels the system of instincts in biological analysis of behavior. The third is that it is to be sharply distinguished from the value standards of the value-orientation. The fourth is, on the other hand, that it designates the point in the system of motivation at which these value or cultural standards of the value-orientation become effective in guiding behavior.

Let us return to our first point, the relation between the evaluative and cognitive modes. The evaluative process in some sense transforms the function of the cognitive mode of motivational orientation. Abstracted from the evaluative mode, cognition is simply in the service of specific motivations

---

[19] The emphasis on choice, choice alternatives, patterns of choice, etc., which is central to this scheme of analyses, should not be interpreted to mean that the actor always deliberately and consciously contemplates alternatives and then chooses among them in the light of a value standard. The decision regarding which of the realistic alternatives he should choose is often made for him through his acceptance of a certain value-orientation. (In a figurative sense, it might be said that the value-orientations which are part of the cultural value system by being institutionalized come to make the choice rather than the actor.) From one point of view, the function of the institutionalization of value standards is to narrow the range of effective choice to manageable proportions.

or need-dispositions, being instrumental to their gratification. In conjunction with the evaluative process, cognition begins to serve not only the specific motives one at a time, but the functional harmony of the whole. The actor learns to take account of the *consequences* of immediate gratification; in the absence of evaluation, he only takes account of how to arrive at that gratification. Thus, whenever cognition is involved in the solution of any sort of conflict problem, it is inextricably related to the evaluative mode.

Second, let us point out what we mean by saying that evaluation is our organizing principle. In any complex system, some mediating mechanism is required to accomplish the discipline of the parts with a view to the organization of the whole. Biologically oriented theorists have been wont to postulate "instincts" or "systems of instincts" as the mechanisms which mediate this discipline. Instincts were innate organizers, or innate systems of discipline. In our theory, instincts thus defined account for little of the over-all organization. That is, we believe that such innate organization as may exist leaves a wide area of freedom; there is a certain plasticity in the relation of the organism to the situation. Having given up instinct as the over-all organizing principle, we require some compensative element of organization. For us, that element is the evaluative mode of motivational orientation. It regulates selection among alternatives when several courses of action are open to the actor (owing to the plasticity of his relationship to the situation).

Third, let us distinguish clearly between the evaluative mode of motivational orientation and the value standards of value-orientation. The evaluative mode involves the cognitive act of balancing out the gratification-deprivation significances of various alternative courses of action with a view to maximizing gratification in the long run. The value standards are various recipes or rules (usually passed from person to person and from generation to generation) which may be observed by the actor in the course of this balancing-out procedure. They are rules which may help the actor to make his choice either by narrowing the range of acceptable alternatives, or by helping the actor foresee the long-run consequences of the various alternatives.

Fourth, we say that the evaluative mode designates the point in the system of motivation at which these value or cultural standards of the value-orientation become effective. The way is *cleared* for the orientation of value standards to have a decisive effect upon behavior whenever there is a significant degree of behavioral plasticity of the organism, that is, whenever the motivational orientation allows two or more alternative courses of behavior. But it is precisely at this point that the evaluative mode becomes relevant. The evaluative mode itself concerns the weighing of alternatives and the act of choosing. When this evaluation is made with an eye to any standards for guiding choice, then the evaluative mode has brought in some aspect of the value-orientation. It should be remembered that the *act of choosing* is essentially the aspect of orientation implied by the term *evaluative mode*; the *standards on which choices are based* are the aspects of the orientation implied by the term *value-orientations*.

At this point, we shall proceed to a discussion of the value-orientation as such, and its various modes.[20] We have already said that the way is cleared for value standards to be effective whenever the plasticity of the organism leaves a realm of freedom in the relation between the situation and the organism and we said that value standards are involved in the *evaluative mode* of the motivational orientation as rules and recipes for guiding selections. We have said too that the value standards themselves constitute what we call the value-orientation and we have mentioned in passing that these standards guide selection (*a*) by narrowing the range of alternatives open and (*b*) by amplifying the consequences of the various alternatives. In much the same vein, we have said these are standards of acceptability and that they (i) narrow the range of cognitions, (ii) narrow the range of objects wanted, and (iii) narrow the number of alternatives.

We have also pointed out that cultural values are effective in two main ways. On the one hand, through interaction, they become built into the structure of personality through the learning process; on the other hand, they are objects in the situation which become particularly significant through their involvement in the sanction system which is associated with roles in the social structure. It is only *through* these channels that value standards enter the motivational process and play a part in the determination of action.[21] By the same token a cathexis must be involved before action is affected. If not the standard itself in an abstract sense, then at least the objects which are chosen in accord with it, must be cathected for value standards to influence behavior.

Value standards are classified on the basis of their relationship to the three modes of motivational orientation. Action is organized by cognitive, cathectic, and evaluative modes of motivational orientation. There are regulatory standards applicable to all three aspects of orientation; thus there are cognitive, appreciative, and moral standards. Classification of standards along these lines offers great convenience for the analysis of action. In the following paragraphs we take up the three categories or modes of value-orientation formulated by this method of classification.

[20] Let us emphasize that we are not turning our attention from one kind of orientation to another kind. The three elementary modes of motivational orientation do not define any type of concrete act even when they are all taken together. The motivational orientation is inherently involved in every act, but so also are the modes of value-orientation, and the objects of the situation. It is only when the three sets of components — objects, motivational orientations, and value-orientations — combine that we even begin to be able to discuss concrete actions and types of actions.

[21] It may again be noted that value-orientation standards are only *part* of culture. We do not mean, moreover, to imply that a person's values are entirely "internalized culture" or mere adherence to rules and laws. The person makes creative modifications as he internalizes culture; but the novel aspect is not the cultural aspect.

Every concrete action involving a cognitive component (by definition, this is true of every action) entails the operation, usually only below the level of deliberation, of standards of cognitive validity. The standards of cognitive validity enter into the construction of expectations (predictions), the testing of observations. The category of cognitive value-orientation is present in all cultural value systems, although there may be variations in the content of the standard with regard to different types of knowledge; for example, the standards of validity of empirical knowledge might vary from those applied in the demonstration of religious beliefs.[22] It is desirable to distinguish between the standards of cognitive validity and the *organization* of cognitive content and perception;[23] cognitive content comes more properly under the cognitive mode of motivational orientation.

The appreciative mode of value-orientation corresponds to the cathectic mode of motivational orientation. It is particularly important here to bear in mind that we are discussing *standards*, not motivational content. The standards applied in the evaluation of the alternatives involved in cathectic choices[24] are at issue here. As in all evaluation, there is a disciplinary aspect of appreciative standards. The choice always involves at least an implicit sacrifice, in that an actor cannot have *all* of what are in one sense potential gratifications, and choosing one involves a "cost" in that it excludes alternatives. The payment of this cost is the disciplinary element.[25]

The use of the term *appreciative* diverges from common usage. In its literal sense, *aesthetic* as connoting desirability would be preferable, but it has come to be used so largely with regard to the fine arts, and so forth, that it is too narrow for our purposes. The term *expressive* has been suggested. If the choices governed by these standards were simply choices with respect to which need-disposition should be expressed, this term would suffice; but choices between objects, modalities, and occasions also come under this head. Thus a broader term is needed. The term *expressive* will be reserved for the *type* of action in which cathectic interests and appreciative standards have primacy.

The category of *moral* value standards extends and makes more explicit the common meaning of the term *moral*. Moral value standards are the most comprehensive integrative standards for assessing and regulating the *entire system of action under consideration*, whether it be a personality or a society

---

[22] But whatever the range of criteria of validity which may be represented as clustering about a mode, no fundamental epistemological question is raised here concerning the validity of the criteria of empirical truth.

[23] The organization of cognitive content might involve the selection of foci of attention, or the organization of knowledge.

[24] Cathectic choices may be among objects, object modalities, need-dispositions, or occasions.

[25] Freud's conception of the "economic" aspect of libido theory, which is the allocation of gratifications within a feasible system, is the psychoanalytic equivalent of the disciplinary element.

or a subsystem of either. They are the "court of last appeal" in any large-scale integrative problem within the system.

Any specific system of morals is adapted to the specific integrative problems confronted by the action system which it, in one sense, controls. Morals, in this sense, are relative. It is the relativity of moral standards to the social system which may be an unfamiliar element in the present definition of moral standards. We live in a culture where the standards are mainly "universalistic," and we therefore tend to think of a moral standard as transcending the particular system of action of the society in which it is exercised. The student of society is concerned with the comparative analysis of different systems of action. He needs a category of value integration which is relative to the system of action in question. The category of moral value standards [26] serves such a purpose for us. The significant criterion for definition of the moral concept is concern for the broader consequences for a system of action.[27]

The concluding paragraphs of this discussion will be concerned with various *kinds* of orientations or actions. It has been stressed throughout our discussion of the *modes* of orientation that these various modes are not different kinds of orientation but simply different aspects that might be abstracted from any orientation. Now we are going to be concerned explicitly with the problem of different kinds or types of action.

It is certanly fair at times to speak of an intellectual activity, an expressive activity, and a responsible or moral activity. Since these are types of concrete action, all of them entail all modes of motivational orientation and some value standards. How, then, are the various kinds of action differentiated? Two problems of emphasis are involved.

In the first place, motivation attaches to activity as well as to objects; that is, certain activities are cathected in their own right as means or goal objects; even cer.ain modes of activity may be cathected. When we speak of a cognitive interest, a cathectic interest, or an evaluative interest, we refer to the fact that these modes of the action process are, to some small or large degree, cathected in their own right.

In the second place, when there is orientation to standards, and these standards are guiding choices, then. if several kinds of standards are oriented at once, there is always the possibility of a conflict. When there is a conflict among standards, there is a problem of primacy. One standard or set of standards must be emphasized, given primacy; it must dominate, the other must give way. In any specific action, primacy may be given to cognitive, appreciative, or moral standards.

---

[26] The moral value standards might be universalistic, that is, concerned with the consequences for a class of phenomena wherever found; or they might be particularistic, that is, concerned with the consequences for a collectivity of which the actor is a member.

[27] It may be noted that this is in accord with the usage of Sumner, Durkheim, and the French anthropologists.

In order to make a basic classification of *types of action*, we will conjoin the problems of interest (in the modes of motivational orientation) and of primacy (among the modes of value-orientation). Thus the three basic types are: (*a*) *intellectual activity*, where cognitive interests prevail and cognitive value standards have primacy (i.e., investigation or the "search for knowledge"); (*b*) *expressive action*, where cathectic interests and appreciative standards have primacy (i.e., the search for direct gratification); and (*c*) *responsible* or *moral action*, where evaluative interests and moral standards have primacy (i.e., the attempt to integrate actions in the interest of a larger system of action).

A special position is occupied by another derivative but very prominent type: *instrumental action*. Here, the goal of action is in the *future*. Cathectic interests and appreciative standards have primacy with respect to the goal, yet cognitive standards [28] have primacy with respect to the process of its attainment.[29] The primacy of cognitive considerations therefore bifurcates into the purely cognitive type, here called "intellectual activity" or investigation, and the instrumental type in the interest of a cathected goal.

Before leaving our discussion of the frame of reference, we should give some brief treatment to the allocative and integrative foci for the organization of empirical systems. When we begin to treat this problem, we find we must first differentiate the distinctive types of action systems from each other. Then we must give the two types separate treatment. The point is that when action occurs (when something is wanted or chosen and thus brings forth action) it is simultaneously embraced in two types of action systems: personality systems and social systems.

As we said in the General Statement, these two systems are distinguished by the differences in the foci around which they are organized. The personality of the individual is organized around the biological unity of the organism. This is its integrative focus. The allocative mechanisms within the system are the need-disposition (and other motivational) systems which serve to relate orientations to one another. The social system is organized around the unity of the interacting group. This is the integrative focus. The allocative mechanisms within this system are the roles which serve to relate various orientations to one another.

The system of interaction among individuals, however, cannot be organized in the same way as the system of action of the individual actor; they each face different functional problems. Personality and social systems, thus, are constituted by the same actions and they are in continuous causal interdependence, but as systems they are not reducible to one another.

---

[28] Where an orientation is only to immediate gratification, only cathectic-appreciative (and possibly moral) interests and standards apply.

[29] Evaluation is, of course, also involved; it places both the particular goal and the processes of attaining it within the larger system of action.

Neither systems of value-orientation nor systems of culture as a whole are action systems in the same sense as are personalities and social systems. This is because neither motivation nor action is directly attributable to them. They may conjoin with motivation to evoke action in social systems or personalities, but they themselves cannot act, nor are they motivated. It seems desirable to treat them, however, because of the great importance of the particular ways in which they are involved in action systems.

With the transition to the analysis of systems of action — personalities and social systems — the descriptive structural analysis with which we are particularly concerned here begins to shade into dynamic analysis. Dynamic problems emerge as soon as we begin to deal with the functional problems of allocation and integration. Our knowledge of the fundamentals of motivation, as it will be analyzed in the next chapter, is of course crucial for the analysis of dynamic processes. Much empirical insight into dynamic problems on *ad hoc* levels has already been achieved. But without further analysis of the structure of action, we could not have the coördinates which would raise empirical insight to a higher level of systematic generality.

Dilemmas of Orientation and the Pattern Variables

Those who have followed our exposition thus far have acquired a familiarity with the definitions of the basic elements of the theory of action. There are further important conceptual entities and classificatory systems to be defined, but these, in a sense, derive from the basic terms that have already been defined. The point is that the further entities can be defined largely in terms of the entities and relationships already defined, with the introduction of a minimum of additional material.

The next section of the present chapter will be devoted to the highly important, derived, classificatory system, the pattern-variable scheme. If one were to look back over the sections of this chapter devoted to the objects of the situation and to the orientation of the actor to the situation (items three and four in our outline), he would see that an actor in a situation is confronted by a series of major dilemmas of orientation, a series of choices that the actor must make before the situation has a determinate meaning for him. The objects of the situation do not interact with the cognizing and cathecting organism in such a fashion as to determine automatically the meaning of the situation. Rather, the actor must make a series of choices before the situation will have a determinate meaning. Specifically, we maintain, the actor must make five specific dichotomous choices before any situation will have a determinate meaning. The five dichotomies which formulate these choice alternatives are called the *pattern variables* because any specific orientation (and consequently any action) is characterized by a pattern of the five choices.

Three of the pattern variables derive from the absence of any biologically given hierarchy of primacies among the various modes of orientation. In the first place, the actor must choose whether to accept gratification from the immediately cognized and cathected object or to evaluate such gratification in terms of its consequences for other aspects of the action system. (That is, one must decide whether or not the evaluative mode is to be operative at all in a situation.) [30] In the second place, if the actor decides to evaluate, he must choose whether or not to give primacy to the moral standards of the social system or subsystem. In the third place, whether or not he decides to grant primacy to such moral standards, he must choose whether cognitive or appreciative standards are to be dominant, the one set with relation to the other. If cognitive standards are dominant over appreciative standards, the actor will tend to locate objects in terms of their relation to some generalized frame of reference; if appreciative standards are dominant over cognitive, the actor will tend to locate objects in terms of their relation to himself, or to his motives.

The other pattern variables emerge from indeterminacies intrinsic to the object situation: social objects as relevant to a given choice situation are either quality complexes or performance complexes, depending on how the actor chooses to see them; social objects are either functionally diffuse (so that the actor grants them every feasible demand) or functionally specific (so that the actor grants them only specifically defined demands), depending on how the actor chooses to see them or how he is culturally expected to see them.

It will be noted now that the three pattern variables which derive from the problems of primacy among the modes of orientation are the first three of the pattern variables as these were listed in our introduction; the two pattern variables which derive from the indeterminacies in the object situation are the last two in that list.

At the risk of being repititious, let us restate our definition: a *pattern variable* is a dichotomy, one side of which must be chosen by an actor before the meaning of a situation is determinate for him, and thus before he can act with respect to that situation. We maintain that there are only five *basic* pattern variables (i.e., pattern variables deriving directly from the frame of reference of the theory of action) and that, in the sense that they are *all* of the pattern variables which so derive, they constitute a system. Let us list them and give them names and numbers so that we can more easily refer to them in the future. They are:

1. Affectivity–Affective neutrality.
2. Self-orientation–Collectivity-orientation.
3. Universalism–Particularism.
4. Ascription–Achievement.
5. Specificity–Diffuseness.

[30] In a limited sense the evaluative mode is operative, even when no thought is given to the consequences of immediate gratification; this in the sense that aesthetic (apprecia-

The first concerns the problem of whether or not evaluation is to take place in a given situation. The second concerns the primacy of moral standards in an evaluative procedure. The third concerns the relative primacy of cognitive and cathectic standards. The fourth concerns the seeing of objects as quality or performance complexes. The fifth concerns the scope of significance of the object.

These pattern variables enter the action frame of reference at four different levels. In the first place, they enter at the concrete level as five discrete choices (explicit or implicit) which every actor makes before he can act. In the second place, they enter on the personality level as habits of choice; the person has a set of habits of choosing, ordinarily or relative to certain types of situations, one horn or the other of each of these dilemmas. Since this set of habits is usually a bit of internalized culture, we will list it as a component of the actor's value-orientation standards. In the third place, the pattern variables enter on the collectivity level as aspects of role definition: the definitions of rights and duties of the members of a collectivity which specify the actions of incumbents of roles, and which often specify that the performer shall exhibit a habit of choosing one side or the other of each of these dilemmas. In the fourth place, the variables enter on the cultural level as aspects of value standards; this is because most value standards are rules or recipes for concrete action and thus specify, among other things, that the actor abiding by the standard shall exhibit a habit of choosing one horn or the other of each of the dilemmas.

From the foregoing paragraph, it should be obvious that, except for their integration in concrete acts as discrete choices, the pattern variables are most important as characteristics of value standards (whether these be the value standards of a personality, or the value standards defining the roles of a society, or just value standards in the abstract). In the sense that each concrete act is made up on the basis of a patterning of the choices formulated by the scheme, the pattern variables are not necessarily attributes of value standards, because any specific concrete choice may be a rather discrete and accidental thing. But as soon as a certain consistency of choosing can be inferred from a series of concrete acts, then we can begin to make statements about the value standards involved and the formulation of these standards in terms of the variables of the pattern-variable scheme.

What is the bearing of the pattern variables on our analysis of systems of action and cultural orientation? Basically, the pattern variables are the categories for the description of value-orientations which of course are in various forms integral to all three systems. A given value-orientation or some particular aspect of it may be interpreted as imposing a preference or giving

---

tive) standards may be invoked to determine the "appropriateness" of the form of gratification chosen. Only in this limited sense, however, does evaluation enter the immediate gratification picture.

a primacy to one alternative over the other *in a particular type of situation*. The pattern variables therefore delineate the alternative preferences, predispositions, or expectations; in all these forms the common element is the direction of selection in defined situations. In the personality system, the pattern variables describe essentially the predispositions or expectations as evaluatively defined in terms of what will below be called ego-organization [31] and superego-organization. In the case of the social system they are the crucial components in the definition of role-expectations. Culturally, they define patterns of value-orientation.

The pattern variables apply to the *normative* or ideal aspect of the structure of systems of action; they apply to one part of its culture. They are equally useful in the empirical description of the degree of conformity with or divergence of concrete action from the patterns of expectation or aspiration. When they are used to characterize differences of empirical structure of personalities or social systems, they contain an elliptical element. This element appears in such statements as, "The American occupational system is universalistic and achievement-oriented and specific." The more adequate, though still sketchy, statement would be: "Compared to other possible ways of organizing the division of labor, the predominant norms which are institutionalized in the American society and which embody the predominant value-orientation of the culture give rise to expectations that occupational roles will be treated by their incumbents and those who are associated with them universalistically and specifically and with regard to proficiency of performance."

These categories could equally be employed to describe actual behavior as well as normative expectations and are of sufficient exactitude for first approximations in comparative analysis. For more detailed work, however, much more precise analysis of the degrees and incidence of deviance, with special reference to the magnitude, location, and forms of the tendencies to particularism, to ascriptiveness, and to diffuseness would have to be carried out.

We will now proceed to define the five pattern variables and the problems of alternative selection to which they apply. They are inherently patterns of cultural value-orientation, but they become integrated both in personalities and in social systems. Hence the general definitions will in each case be followed by definitions specific to each of the three types of systems. These definitions will be followed by an analysis of the places of the variables in the frame of reference of the theory of action, the reasons why this list seems to be logically complete on its own level of generality, and certain problems of their systematic interrelations and use in structural analysis.

---

[31] The term *ego* is here used in the sense current in the theory of personality, not as a point of reference.

THE DEFINITIONS OF PATTERN VARIABLES

1. *The dilemma of gratification of impulse versus discipline.* When confronted with situations in which particular impulses press for gratification, an actor faces the problem of whether the impulses should be released or restrained. He can solve the problem by giving primacy, at the relevant selection points, to evaluative considerations, at the cost of interests in the possibility of immediate gratification; or by giving primacy to such interests in immediate gratification, irrespective of evaluative considerations.

a. Cultural aspect. (1) *Affectivity*: the normative pattern which grants the permission for an actor, in a given type of situation, to take advantage of a given opportunity for immediate gratification without regard to evaluative considerations. (2) *Affective neutrality*: the normative pattern which prescribes for actors in a given type of situation renunciation of certain types of immediate gratification for which opportunity exists, in the interest of evaluative considerations regardless of the content of the latter.

b. Personality aspect. (1) *Affectivity*: a need-disposition on the part of the actor to permit himself, in a certain situation, to take advantage of an opportunity for a given type of immediate gratification and not to renounce this gratification for evaluative reasons. (2) *Affective neutrality*: a need-disposition on the part of the actor in a certain situation to be guided by evaluative considerations which prohibit his taking advantage of the given opportunity for immediate gratification; in this situation the gratification in question is to be renounced, regardless of the grounds adduced for the renunciation.

c. Social system aspect. (1) *Affectivity*: the role-expectation [32] that the incumbent of the role may freely express certain affective reactions to objects in the situation and need not attempt to control them in the interest of discipline. (2) *Affective neutrality*: the role-expectation that the incumbent of the role in question should restrain any impulses to certain affective expressions and subordinate them to considerations of discipline. In both cases the affect may be positive or negative, and the discipline (or permissiveness) may apply only to certain qualitative types of affective expression (e.g., sexual).

2. *The dilemma of private versus collective interests,* or the distribution between private permissiveness and collective obligation. The high frequency of situations in which there is a disharmony of interests creates the problem of choosing between action for private goals or on behalf of collective goals. This dilemma may be resolved by the actor either by giving primacy to interests, goals, and values shared with the other members of a given collective

---

[32] A role-expectation is, in an institutionally integrated social system (or part of it), an expectation *both* on the part of ego and of the alters with whom he interacts. The same sentiments are shared by both. In a less than perfectly integrated social system, the concept is still useful for describing the expectations of each of the actors, even though they diverge.

unit of which he is a member or by giving primacy to his personal or private interests without considering their bearing on collective interests.

  a. Cultural aspect. (1) *Self-orientation*: the normative pattern which prescribes a range of permission for an actor, in a given type of situation, to take advantage of a given opportunity for pursuing a private interest, regardless of the content of the interest or its direct bearing on the interests of other actors. (2) *Collectivity-orientation*: a normative pattern which prescribes the area within which an actor, in a given type of situation, is obliged to take directly into account a given selection of values which he shares with the other members of the collectivity in question. It defines his *responsibility* to this collectivity.

  b. Personality aspect. (1) *Self-orientation*: a need-disposition on the part of the actor to permit himself to pursue a given goal or interest of his own — regardless whether from his standpoint it is only cognitive-cathectic or involves evaluative considerations — but without regard to its bearing one way or another on the interests of a collectivity of which he is a member. (2) *Collectivity-orientation*: a need-disposition on the part of the actor to be guided by the obligation to take directly into account, in the given situation, values which he shares with the other members of the collectivity in question; therefore the actor must accept responsibility for attempting to realize those values in his action. This includes the expectation by ego that in the particular choice in question he will subordinate his private interests, whether cognitive-cathectic or evaluative, and that he will be motivated in superego terms.

  c. Social system aspect. (1) *Self-orientation*: the role-expectation by the relevant actors that it is *permissible* for the incumbent of the role in question to give priority in the given situation to his own private interests, whatever their motivational content or quality, independently of their bearing on the interests or values of a given collectivity of which he is a member, or the interests of other actors. (2) *Collectivity-orientation*: the role-expectation by the relevant actors that the actor is *obliged*, as an incumbent of the role in question, to take directly into account the values and interests of the collectivity of which, in this role, he is a member. When there is a potential conflict with his private interests, he is expected in the particular choice to give priority to the collective interest. This also applies to his action in representative roles on behalf of the collectivity.

  3. *The dilemma of transcendence versus immanence.* In confronting any situation, the actor faces the dilemma whether to treat the objects in the situation in accordance with a general norm covering *all* objects in that class or whether to treat them in accordance with their standing in some particular relationship to him or his collectivity, independently of the objects' subsumibility under a general norm. This dilemma can be resolved by giving primacy to norms or value standards which are maximally generalized and which have a basis of validity transcending *any* specific system of relation-

ships in which ego is involved, or by giving primacy to value standards which allot priority to standards *integral* to the *particular* relationship system in which the actor is involved with the object.

a. Cultural aspect. (1) *Universalism*: the normative pattern which obliges an actor in a given situation to be oriented toward objects in the light of general standards rather than in the light of the objects' possession of properties (qualities or performances, classificatory or relational) which have a particular relation to the actor's own properties (traits or statuses). (2) *Particularism*: the normative pattern which obliges an actor in a given type of situation to give priority to criteria of the object's particular relations to the actor's own properties (qualities or performances, classificatory or relational) over generalized attributes, capacities, or performance standards.

b. Personality aspect. (1) *Universalism*: a need-disposition on the part of the actor in a given situation to respond toward objects in conformity with a general standard rather than in the light of their possession of properties (qualities or performances, classificatory or relational) which have a particular relation to the actor's own. (2) *Particularism*: a need-disposition on the part of the actor to be guided by criteria of choice particular to his own and the object's position in an object-relationship system rather than by criteria defined in generalized terms.

c. Social system aspect. (1) *Universalism*: the role-expectation that, in qualifications for memberships and decisions for differential treatment, priority will be given to standards defined in completely generalized terms, independent of the particular relationship of the actor's own statuses (qualities or performances, classificatory or relational) to those of the object. (2) *Particularism*: the role-expectation that, in qualifications for memberships and decisions for differential treatment, priority will be given to standards which assert the primacy of the values attached to objects by their particular relations to the actor's properties (qualities or performances, classificatory or relational) as over against their general universally applicable class properties.

4. *The dilemma of object modalities.* When confronting an object in a situation, the actor faces the dilemma of deciding how to treat it. Is he to treat it in the light of what it is in itself or in the light of what it does or what might flow from its *actions*? This dilemma can be resolved by giving primacy, at the relevant selection points, to the "qualities" aspect of *social objects* as a focus of orientation, or by giving primacy to the objects' performances and their outcomes.

a. Cultural aspect. (1) *Ascription*: the normative pattern which prescribes that an actor in a given type of situation should, in his selections for differential treatment of social objects, give priority to certain attributes that they possess (including collectivity memberships and possessions) over any specific performances (past, present, or prospective) of the objects. (2) *Achievement*:

the normative pattern which prescribes that an actor in a given type of situation should, in his selection and differential treatment of social objects, give priority to their specific performances (past, present, or prospective) over their given attributes (including memberships and possessions), insofar as the latter are not significant as direct conditions of the relevant performances.

b. Personality aspect. (1) *Ascription*: the need-disposition on the part of the actor, at a given selection point, to respond to specific given attributes of the social object, rather than to their past, present, or prospective performances. (2) *Achievement*: a need-disposition on the part of the actor to respond, at a given selection point, to specific performances (past present, or prospective) of a social object, rather than to its attributes which are not directly involved in the relevant performances as "capacities," "skills," and so forth.

c. Social system aspect. (1) *Ascription*: the role-expectation that the role incumbent, in orienting himself to social objects in the relevant choice situation, will accord priority to the objects' given attributes (whether universalistically or particularistically defined) over their actual or potential performances. (2) *Achievement*: the role-expectation that the role incumbent, in orienting to social objects in the relevant choice situation, will give priority to the objects' actual or expected performances, and to their attributes only as directly relevant to these performances, over attributes which are essentially independent of the specific performances in question.

5. *The dilemma of the scope of significance of the object.* In confronting an object, an actor must choose among the various possible ranges in which he will respond to the object. The dilemma consists in whether he should respond to many aspects of the object or to a restricted range of them — how broadly is he to allow himself to be involved with the object? The dilemma may be resolved by accepting no inherent or prior limitation of the scope of the actor's "concern" with the object, either as an object of interest or of obligations, or by according only a limited and specific type of significance to the object in his system of orientation.

a. Cultural aspect. (1) *Diffuseness*: the normative pattern which prescribes that in a given situation the orientation of an actor to an object should contain no prior specification of the actor's interest in or concern with or for the object, but that the scope should vary with the exigencies of the situation as they arise. (2) *Specificity*: the normative pattern which prescribes that in a given type of situation an actor should confine his concern with a given type of object to a specific sphere and not permit other empirically possible concerns to enter.

b. Personality aspect. (1) *Diffuseness*: the need-disposition to respond to an object in any way which the nature of the actor and the nature of the object and its actual relation to ego require, actual significances varying as occasions arise. (2) *Specificity*: the need-disposition of the actor to respond to a given object in a manner limited to a specific mode or context of significance of a social object, including obligation to it, which is compatible with exclusion of other potential modes of significance of the object.

c. Social system aspect. (1) *Diffuseness*: the role-expectation that the role incumbent, at the relevant choice point, will accept any potential significance of a social object, including obligation to it, which is compatible with his other interests and obligations, and that he will give priority to this expectation over any disposition to confine the role-orientation to a specific range of significance of the object. (2) *Specificity*: the role-expectation that the role incumbent, at the relevant choice point, will be oriented to a social object only within a specific range of its relevance as a cathectic object or as an instrumental means or condition and that he will give priority to this expectation over any disposition to include potential aspects of significance of the object not specifically defined in the expectation pattern.

Of the five pattern variables defined above, the first three are determined by primacies among the interests inherently differentiated within the system of value-orientation itself and in the definition of the limits of its applicability; the other two are determined by the application of value-orientations to the alternatives which are inherent in the structure of the object system, and in the actor's relation to it. The derivation of the pattern variables from the basic categories of the action scheme is presented in diagrammatic form in Fig. 2. (Figures follow page 245.)

The first of the pattern variables, affectivity versus affective neutrality, represents the problem of whether any evaluative considerations at all should have priority. It is thus the marginal choice between complete *permissiveness*, without reference to value standards of any kind, and *discipline* in the interests of any one of the various kinds of value standards.

This dilemma is inherent in any system of action. There can in principle be no such dilemma involving cognitive and cathectic modes of orientation, since both modes are inherently operative in any action whatever. But as soon as *consequences* for the functioning of a system come into the picture, a problem of evaluation arises and it becomes necessary to impose some discipline in order to restrict damaging consequences and facilitate favorable ones. This is, therefore, in a sense, the most elementary dilemma of systems of action.

The second pattern variable essentially reproduces the same basic dilemma in a somewhat different perspective and with an additional complication deriving from a difference of level. In the pattern variable of affectivity–affective neutrality there is no reference to the beneficiary on whose behalf discipline is exercised. This problem becomes preëminent in the pattern variable of self-orientation versus collectivity-orientation. The same basic distinction between permissiveness and discipline is repeated, but permissiveness is no longer solely for immediate gratification in the psychological sense; it now includes action in terms of "ego-organization," with all the discipline associated with that. The occurrence of this problem in the personality system is dealt with in a very similar way in Freud's later writings about ego and superego organization.[33]

When the actor accepts discipline, the problem of the standards and the objects in behalf of which discipline is to be exercised requires solution. Collectivity-orientation is the resolution of one of these problems through the primacy of the moral value standards, either over other types of value standards or over nonevaluative modes of orientation. In this connection it is important to refer to the earlier definition of moral values (pp. 60, 73–74). What is at issue here is *not* the concrete *content* of the relevant moral standards but — whatever this may be — their primacy over other nonmoral standards. Moral standards were specifically defined as those which refer to consequences for the system of relation in question, whether it be the society as a whole, a subcollectivity, or even a deviant "subculture." Sometimes moral standards are, as is usual in our culture, universalistically defined, in which case they do in fact transcend the particular relational system. But this is a matter of the concrete content of moral values, not of the definition of what moral values themselves are.

Cognitive and appreciative values may be more or less fully integrated with moral values in the total value system. The area in which they are allowed primacy of a permissive or deviant nature may vary in scope. These problems must be reserved for the discussion of the patterns of value-orientation. Here we are merely concerned with defining the variable elements which go into them.

Even when the actor has selected the moral value standards as his guiding star, he still must make a decision about how he is to judge the object. Is he to respond to it in the light of cognitive or appreciative standards? Is he to judge objects by the class categories which he can apply to all of them, or is he to judge them by what they mean to him in their particular relationship to him? Cognitive standards are by their very nature universalistic. They are assessments of events, the demonstration of the existence of which does not depend for validity on any *particular* actor's need-dispositions, value patterns, or role-expectations. The criteria of whether a proposition is true or false are not bound to a particular time or place or object-relationship.[34] If a proposition is true, it is, for the conditions (explicit or implicit) to which it applies,

[33] The distinction between *id* and *ego* in Freud's later theory is essentially the same as our distinction between affectivity and discipline. Indeed the first two pattern variables form the major axis of Freud's conception of the organization of personality or what psychoanalysts sometimes call the structural point of view.

[34] Ideas, to the contrary, are, to be sure, current, especially among proponents of the "sociology of knowledge," but they rest on epistemological confusions, failing to distinguish between the qualifications and adaptations in the *content* of knowledge which are indeed relative to and necessitated by the "perspective" of the actor, and the *criteria of validity*, which are not.

true. It is not true for one person and false for somebody else. Its *significance*
for or *relevance* to action may, of course, vary in different relational contexts,
but not its validity. A value standard, then, in which cognitive propositions
have primacy — and which may be put into the form, "this is valid for me as
a standard guiding my action because such-and-such a proposition is cognitively true" — is universalistic, and its applicability transcends any particular
relational context.

On the other hand, insofar as purely appreciative criteria are given primacy in the determination of a standard, the values concerned have their
validity *in their relationship to the actor* who is judging. The ultimate basis
of validity of the appreciative standard comes to be that the actor (or actors)
admires or enjoys the object, which is thought or felt to be in a suitable or
appropriate relationship with him; "suitability" or "appropriateness" means
here harmony with a pattern which may have already been internalized. Thus
the standard itself is *particularistic*; that is, it is *immanent* in the particular
relationship complex or system of action of which it is a part. There is a
possible source of confusion here, similar to that involved in the concept of
moral standards. In a culture where universalistic values are prominent,
many *concrete* appreciative values are also universalistically defined. This
is not the result of the primacy of appreciative criteria in their definition; it
happens rather because the *particular* appreciative standards are part of a
general system of value-orientation in which cognitive standards have primacy,
and the cognitive standards therefore shape appreciative values as well as
others.[35]

These first three pattern variables exhaust the possibilities of relative
primacies within the system of modes of orientation. The fourth and fifth
pattern variables derive from choices that must be made with respect to the
modalities and scope of significance of the object system. The distinction between the modalities of qualities and performances as foci for action orientation [36] has already been discussed and does not need to be elaborated upon
here, except to note that it presents an authentic selection alternative involved
in all systems of interaction.

[35] Here as elsewhere a clear distinction must be made between the analytical and the
concrete. In a concrete standard contained in judgments in the appreciative field, it is
possible for cognitive, appreciative, or moral criteria to have primacy. This is true also
of the concrete standards governing cognitive or moral judgments. But the present concern is not with this concrete level. It is with the classification of types of *criteria* of
value judgments and the consequences of differences of relative primacies among such
types of criteria.

[36] This distinction, in its obverse form, is related to that frequently made in psychological analysis in the distinction between *activity* and *passivity*. Achievement criteria require activity, as a qualification of the actor not the object, while ascriptive criteria do
not. See below, Chapter II. This distinction has become known in Anglo-American anthropological and sociological literature through Linton's *The Study of Man*, in which it is
applied to the analysis of social structure.

The fifth pattern variable presents the alternative modes of delimiting the actor's relationship to a social object. It also is distinctly a *relational* category, specifying neither a general characteristic of the actor nor an intrinsic property of the object, but rather one aspect of the way a given actor is related to a specific object. A social object either has "defined" rights with respect to ego, or it has the rights of "residual legatee." Let us be more explicit. In the first place, if a social object is related to ego at all, then it has some "rights," in the sense that it has some significance. Ego, that is, is granting alter some rights as soon as alter becomes a social object for him. This happens because alter's action has consequences within ego's orientation of action and thus functions among the determinants of ego's action.[37] The rights of a social object with respect to ego are either defined (so that ego and alter know the limits of ego's obligations) or they are undefined (so that ego must render to alter such of his efforts as are left over when all of his other obligations are met). The social object, that is, either has specific (segmental) significance for ego (in which case obligations are clearly defined); or it has diffuse significance (in which case obligations are only limited by other obligations).

The segmental significance of an object may, in a concrete orientation, coincide with the primacy of one mode of motivational orientation, such as the cognitive-cathectic. But analytically these ranges of variation are independent of one another.

The most feasible empirical criterion of the difference between the two alternatives is the "burden of proof." If a question arises concerning the determination of the range of responsibility, in the case of specificity, the burden of proof rests on the side that claims a certain responsibility to exist (to be included in the contract, so to speak). A possible right of alter which is not included in the mutual expectations which defines the relation between ego and alter is *prima facie* to be excluded as irrelevant, unless specific argument for its inclusion can be adduced. In the case of diffuseness, the burden of proof is on the opposite side, on the side that claims a responsibility does not exist. Any possible right of alter is *prima facie* to be regarded as valid, even though neither ego nor alter has heretofore given the right in question any thought, unless ego can adduce specific other and more important obligations which make it impossible for him to grant alter this right.

Thus, even if an object's significance is defined in diffuse terms, the range of obligation is not unlimited, because the allocation of orientation interests among objects is a basic functional imperative of all action systems. Therefore, the range of diffuseness can never be unlimited, because this would lead directly to encroachment on the interests in, and obligations to, other objects. In the case of diffuseness, it is always the potential conflict with the relations

---

[37] To grant an object "rights" in the last analysis is nothing else than to allow it to affect one's action. Alter's rights over ego, that is, refer to those things which ego "has to do" because of alter's relations to ego's motives and ego's system of values.

to other objects which limits the orientation to the first object; whereas it is the set of expectations concerning the particular object which brings about the limitation in the case of specificity. When, therefore, a question of evaluation arises, the justification for rejecting a claim, in the case of specificity, is simply the denial of an obligation (e.g., "it wasn't in the contract"). In the case of diffuseness, the rejection of a claim can be justified only by the invocation of other obligations which are ranked higher on some scale of priority.

As with the other pattern variables, the dilemma presented in the specificity-diffuseness pattern variable is inherent in any orientation of one actor to another. Almost invariably an explicit choice has to be made. If the contact between two people is fleeting and casual, the significance of one for the other may be highly specific without any explicit choice occurring. But if the relationship continues, the problem of its scope becomes explicit. The possibility of diffuse attachments will then become more pressing and a decision will have to be made.

THE INTERRELATIONS OF THE PATTERN VARIABLES

We hold that the five pattern variables constitute a *system* covering all the fundamental alternatives which can arise directly out of the frame of reference for the theory of action. It should be remembered that the five pattern variables formulate five fundamental choices which must be made by an actor when he is confronted with a situation before that situation can have definitive (unambiguous) meaning for him. We have said that objects do not automatically determine the actors "orientation of action"; rather, a number of choices must be made before the meaning of the objects becomes definite. Now, we maintain that when the situation is social (when one actor is orienting to another), there are but five choices which are completely general (that is, which must always be made) and which derive directly from the action frame of reference; these choices must always be made to give the situation specific defined meaning. Other choices are often necessary to determine the meaning of a situation, but these may be considered accidents of content, rather than genuine alternatives intrinsic to the structure of *all* action. To be a pattern variable, a set of alternatives must derive directly from the problems of dominance among the modes of orientation, or from the problems arising from the ambiguities of the object world which require choice on the part of ego for their resolution. In order to show that our five pattern variables constitute a system, we must show that they exhaust these problems. Let us take up first the problems of dominance among modes of orientation, and second, problems arising from the ambiguities of relation to the object world.

There are only three completely general problems of dominance arising directly from the modes of orientation. Since the cognitive and cathectic modes of motivational orientation are so inseparable as to abnegate any problem of primacy, we do not find any conflict between them. Thus, the first pattern variable is between them acting alone, on the one hand, and an evaluative orientation, on the other. The problem is: Will evaluation enter into the determination of this course of action? A decision must always be made (explicitly or implicitly, consciously or unconsciously).

The other two pattern variables arising from primacy problems with respect to orientation modes are not on the same level as the first in terms of generality within the concrete act, because if affectivity is selected in the concrete situation instead of affective neutrality, the problems presented by pattern variables two and three never arise. (If an actor does not evaluate, he does not have to decide which standards will get primacy within the evaluative process.) However, in discussing the orientation *habits* which make up a value, a role-expectancy, or a need-disposition, we can see that the second two pattern variables have just as much generality as the first. Although an actor may be regarded in affective terms in some concrete situations, and even though ego may have the habit of affectivity with respect to alter, this still does not mean that the "affectivity attitude" will apply to alter all of the time. (The habit implies that in perhaps a majority of the situations an attitude of affectivity will apply, but no relationship between human beings can remain always on the affectivity level — this, perhaps, is what we mean by saying "we are not beasts".) When on rare or frequent occasions the affectively neutral attitude is assumed, when evaluation of the relationship evokes value standards, the problems formulated in pattern variables two and three immediately become relevant, and choices must be made.

Thus, one must choose, if one evaluates, whether or not to give primacy to collectivity-integrating moral standards. If moral standards are invoked at all, they will have primacy owing to their status as the "final court of appeal" on any problem of integration. Cognitive and appreciative standards, on the contrary, are always invoked in any evaluative problem; thus, the problem of their relative primacy with respect to one another always arises, whether or not moral standards are invoked. Hence, the problem of the relative primacy of appreciative and cognitive standards must always be resolved. If cognitive standards are to dominate appreciative ones, then the objects will be judged primarily in terms of their relationship to some generalized frame of reference; if appreciative standards are to dominate cognitive ones, then objects will be judged primarily in terms of ego as the center of the frame of reference. Thus, these three problems of choice and only these three, derive directly from problems of dominance among the modes of orientation.

Similarly, there are only two completely general ambiguities with respect to social objects as these are defined in our frame of reference. These are (1) the quality-performance ambiguity and (2) the diffuseness-specificity ambiguity. In every social situation, anywhere, ego either implicitly or explicitly has to resolve these two ambiguities by choosing one side or the other of both dichotomies before the social object can have determinate meaning for him. Thus, we complete our case for the exhaustiveness of our list of pattern variables.

Certain other pairs of concepts, representative and autonomous roles for instance, are derivatives from pattern variables. The pair in this example are derivatives of the second pattern variable — self versus collectivity-orientation — on a more concrete level. Let us show how this derivation is made. First, a distinction must be made, in dealing with a collectivity, between the internal relations of its members, and their relations outside of the collectivity. In analyzing their relations outside of the collectivity, the bearing of their membership on the external relations must be taken into account. Now, a representative role is characterized as follows: in external relations a member is oriented primarily to the role-expectations which govern his conduct as a member of the collectivity; this primacy of collectivity-orientation over self-orientation defines the representative role. Correspondingly, an autonomous role is one in which the actor is free (oriented independently) of his roles as a member of the collectivity in external relations; the primacy of self-orientation defines the autonomous role.

Similarly, rational as opposed to traditional action has been suggested as a pattern variable. This seems to be a complex derivative from the pattern variables. It has a special relation to the universalism-particularism dichotomy, because cognitive standards are inherently rational. But the reference in the rational-traditional dichotomy is not to the generality of the frame of reference (as it is in universalism) but to the stability of patterns over time. Thus the rational-traditional dichotomy is a way of formulating alternative ways of adapting primary (pattern variable) value-orientation patterns over a period of time in an empirical action system.

In another sense, the rational-traditional dichotomy may be seen as a way of characterizing any long-run sequence of pattern-variable choices. In choosing the various sides of the pattern-variable dichotomies, a person may choose in a rational or traditional fashion. That is, he may shift his choices in accord with the pragmatic exigencies of the situation (in which case the choices would be considered rational), or he may select in accord with his life-long idea of the way his group, or his family, has always made selections in a given matter (in which case his whole set of pattern-variable choices would be considered traditional). Thus, the rational-traditional variable is in some sense a characteristic of the content of a person's patterned choices over a period of time. The more consistent a person's selections, independent of varying situations, the more traditional we say he is; the more his choices vary with the situations, the more rational we say he is. This distinction, however, is certainly not on the same level as the pattern variables; it is not a choice which must be made in addition to other pattern-variable choices before the situation has determinate meaning. Rather it is a characteristic of the pattern-variable choices themselves; or if it is a choice alternative at all, it stands on a level antecedent to the pattern variables, being perhaps a choice which ego will make in deciding what will be the basis for his pattern-variable choices.[38]

There are three assumptions in our contention that the five pattern-variable dilemmas are an exhaustive set. These assumptions are: (1) acceptance of the basic frame of reference as we have defined it; (2) acceptance of the level of generality on which we are proceeding, which is the *first* level of derivation from the basic frame of reference; (3) acceptance of our method of derivation through the establishment of primacies among types of interest and the resolution of ambiguities intrinsic to the world of social objects.

Finally, it should be emphasized that the variables as we have stated them are dichotomies and not continua. In a series of concrete actions, a person may be partly "affective" and partly "neutral." But this series would be composed of dichotomous choices; no specific choice can be half affective, half neutral. The same is true of the other pattern variables. One who has carefully read the definitions and discussions will see that each concept sets up a polarity, a true dilemma.

CLASSIFICATION OF NEED-DISPOSITIONS AND ROLE-EXPECTATIONS

The pattern variables are tools for the classification of need-dispositions and role-expectations, which, as has been pointed out, represent allocative foci for both personality and social systems. Before we go into the classification of these units, it might be wise to recapitulate briefly the way the allocative and integrative foci fit into the frame of reference of the theory of action. We have said that action systems, as either actors or social objects, may be personalities or collectivities, both of which are abstracted from the same concrete action. The different principles of abstraction used in locating the two systems derive directly from the notion that personalities and collectivities have different kinds of allocative and integrative foci. The integrative foci are, in some sense, the principles of abstraction used in locating or delimiting the system: thus, the individual organism is the integrative focus of a personality system and the interacting social group is the integrative focus of a social system. The integrative foci are therefore used for abstracting social systems themselves from the total realm of possible subject matter.

The allocative foci, on the other hand, are the primary units used for analyzing the action system into elements or parts. The allocative foci of personality systems are need-dispositions. The personality system is in a sense

---

[38] Other pairs of concepts, such as dominance-submission and autonomy-heteronomy should similarly be regarded as being on a different level of complexity. Some of these will be considered in more detail in later chapters.

composed of a variety of need-dispositions; each of these assures that some need of the personality system will be met. The referent of a need-disposition is, in a sense, a set of concrete orientations. That is, a need-disposition is an inferred entity; it is inferred on the basis of a certain consistency of choosing and cathecting in a wide variety of orientations. Thus, when we speak of a need-disposition, we will sometimes seem to be talking about a real entity, causally controlling a wide variety of orientations and rendering them consistent; other times we will seem to be talking about the consistent set of orientations (abstracted on the basis of the postulated entity) themselves. Logicians have shown that it is usually fair to use interchangeably the inferred entity postulated on the basis of a set of data and the whole set of data itself. The postulated entity is, in some sense, a shorthand for the set of data from which it is inferred.

The allocative foci of social systems are roles or role-expectations. The social system is in a sense composed of a variety of roles or role-expectations; each of these assures that some need of the social system will be met. The referent of a role, like that of a need-disposition, is a set of concrete orientations; the role or role-expectation is an inferred entity in exactly the same fashion as is the need-disposition. Each orientation, according to postulate, is a joint function of a role (which partly controls it), a need-disposition (which also partly controls it), and probably of other factors not mentioned here.[39] When orientations are grouped (or abstracted) according to the need-dispositions that control them, and according to the individual organisms who have these need-dispositions, we are dealing with personality systems. When orientations are grouped (or abstracted) according to the roles or roles-expectations that control them, and according to the interacting groups to which they belong, we are dealing with social systems.

Now, since none of the depth variables (allocative foci, etc.) are effective except as they influence the orientation of action (which is not necessarily either conscious or rational), and since all orientations tend to have not only the allocative foci of both social and personality systems as ingredients but also value standards (which, when internalized, are depth variables similar to need-dispositions and role-expectations), no need-disposition, nor any role-expectation, is effective except in conjunction with certain value-orientations with which it is systematically related (at least in the sense that both control the same orientation for the moment). Hence, in discussing personalities or social systems, using as the primary units of abstraction need-dispositions or role-expectations, we may regard the value-orientation components of the orientations so grouped to be the value-orientation components of the need-dispositions or role-expectations themselves. Thus we

---

[39] As will be seen in a moment, each orientation is in some sense a function of the value standards which partly control it. Furthermore, each orientation is certainly partly a function of the present object situation.

can classify the need-dispositions and role-expectations in terms of the value-orientations with which they tend to be linked.

In principle, therefore, *every* concrete need-disposition [40] of personality, or every role-expectation of social structure, involves a combination of values of the five pattern variables. The cross-classification of each of the five against each of the others, yielding a table of thirty-two cells, will, on the assumption that the list of pattern variables is exhaustive, produce a classification of the basic value patterns. Internalized in the personality system, these value patterns serve as a starting point for a classification of the possible types of need-dispositions; as institutionalized in the system of social action, they are a classification of components of role-expectation definitions.[41]

It should be clear that the classification of the value components of need-dispositions and of role-expectations in terms of the pattern variables is a *first step* toward the construction of a dynamic theory of systems of action. To advance toward empirical significance, these classifications will have to be related to the functional problems of on-going systems of action.[42]

As a last word before taking up the problem of classification itself, we should mention that of the logically possible combinations of the pattern variables, not all are likely to be of equal empirical significance. Careful analysis of their involvement in a wide variety of phenomena shows that they are all in fact independently variable in some contexts and that there is no tautology in the scheme. Nonetheless there are certainly tendencies for certain combinations to cluster together. The uneven distribution of combinations and the empirical difficulty, or even perhaps impossibility, of the

[40] A need-disposition as the term is used here always involves a set of dispositions toward objects. In abstraction from objects the concept becomes elliptical. Only for reasons of avoiding even greater terminological cumbersomeness is the more complex term "need-disposition toward objects" usually avoided. However, such a need-disposition and the *particular* objects of its gratification are independently variable. The mechanism of *substitution* links the need-disposition to various objects that are not its "proper" gratifiers.

[41] The classification of role-expectations and need-dispositions according to value patterns is only a part of the larger problem of classifying concrete need-dispositions and role-expectations. Other components of action must enter the picture before a classification relevant and adequate to the problem of the analysis of systems is attainable. For example, one set of factors entering into need-dispositions, the constitutionally determined components, has been quite explicitly and deliberately excluded from the present analysis. So far as these are essential to an adequate classification of the need-disposition elements of personality, the classification in terms of pattern variables obviously requires adjustment.

[42] This means above all that the motivational *processes* of action must be analyzed as processes in terms of the laws governing them, and as mechanisms in terms of the significance of their outcomes for the functioning of the systems of which they are parts. In due course the attempt to do this will be made. Also, it should be noted that the necessary constitutional factors which are treated as residual in this conceptual scheme will find their place among the functional necessities of systems.

realization of some combinations in systems of action will raise important dynamic problems.

To classify need-dispositions and role-expectations, we must begin by making the cross-classification tables mentioned above. In constructing such tables we find that certain of the pattern-variable dichotomies are of major importance with respect to need-dispositions (and hence personality systems). Similarly, certain pattern-variable dichotomies are of major importance with respect to role-expectations (and hence social systems). Furthermore, the pattern variables of major importance for classification of need-dispositions are not the same as those of major importance for classification of role-expectations. In fact, the two sets are more or less complementary; those of major importance for need-dispositions are the ones of minor importance for role-expectations, and vice versa.

The only one of the pattern variables equally applicable to both need-dispositions and role-expectations is the self-collectivity variable (number two). Of the other four, the first, affectivity-neutrality, and the fifth, specificity-dffuseness, are chiefly important with respect to need-dispositions. The third, universalism-particularism, and the fourth, ascription-achievement, are chiefly important with respect to role-expectations.

Figs. 3 and 4 present the formal classifications of types of need-disposition orientation and of role-expectation orientation, respectively. In each case, for the sake of simplicity, the pattern variable concerning the distribution between private and collective values and interests is omitted. This variable seems to occupy, as we shall see presently, a special place in the comprehensive integration of systems of action and is the only one which has a fully symmetrical relation to both diagrams. It is therefore possible to omit it here and introduce it when personality systems and social systems are discussed in more detail subsequently.

The characterizations of each of the types in the cells of the main diagrams and the illustrations in the supplementary ones indicate that each of the cells makes sense empirically. Concrete phenomena can be adduced as illustrations without distortion. The two figures do not have an identical arrangement. Figure 3 is divided into four major "blocks" by the cross-classification of the first and the fifth pattern variables while the further subdivision within each of the blocks is the product of cross-classification of the other two variables, universalism-particularism and ascription-achievement. In Fig. 4 the four main blocks are the result of the cross-classification of universalism-particularism and ascription-achievement, while the subdivisions within the major types are produced by cross-classifying affectivity-neutrality and specificity-diffuseness. The pattern variable, self- versus collectivity-orientation, is not involved in the symmetrical asymmetry of these fundamental classificatory tables and is omitted.

Let us discuss for a moment the reasons why the pair of pattern variables primary for personality is the obverse of the pair primary for social systems. Personality systems, as we have said, are primary constellations of need-dispositions. The primary problems regarding need-dispositions and the orientations they control are these: (1) On the orientation side of the orientation-object division, the primary question is whether or not the need-disposition allows evaluation. Metaphorically, we might ask whether the need-disposition interacts peacefully with the other need-dispositions in the system. If it allows evaluation, it interacts peacefully, if it disallows evaluation, it competes for all or no affective control of the organism. (2) On the object side, the question is whether the need-disposition which mediates attachment to any given object is segmental (being perhaps an uncomplex residue of the biological drive system, or some very segmental learned motivational system), or whether it is a complex integration of many drives and motives into one diffuse and complex need-disposition that can be aroused by many different situations and conditions. These two problems are primary because they concern the most basic aspects of the relations which obtain between need-dispositions; thus, the selections of the various need-dispositions on these questions are in a sense constitutive of the nature of the personality system in question.

Social systems, we have said, are primarily constellations of roles or role-expectations. The primary problems relative to role-expectations and the orientations they control are these: (1) On the orientation side, the question is whether or not the role's mutual relationships to other roles (or to the role-expectations which define the role) are based on cognitive or appreciative standards. (If this role is related to other roles on the basis of cognitive standards, then, its chief characteristics do not derive from its specific relations to other social objects; and its characteristics do not change so much depending on the alter with which it is interacting.) (2) On the object side, the question is whether this role (qua object) is related to other roles on the basis of the performance or the quality characteristics of its incumbents. These two problems are primary because they concern the most basic aspects of the relations which obtain between roles; thus, the selections of roles (or occupants of roles) on these questions are in a sense constitutive of the nature of the social system in question.

At this point, it would be wise to turn to Figs. 3, 3a, 4, and 4a (pp. 249–252). Fig .3 presents the major classification of need-dispositions; that is, according to the affectivity-neutrality variable and the specificity-diffuseness variable. Fig. 3a presents the further cross-classification of Fig. 3 by the two pattern variables of secondary importance for personalities, universalism-particularism and quality-performance. Fig. 4, similarly, presents the major classification of roles; that is, according to the universalism-particularism variable and the quality-performance variable. Fig. 4a presents the further cross-classification of Fig. 4 by the two pattern variables of secondary importance for social systems, affectivity-neutrality and specificity-diffuseness.

Fig. 5 illustrates the "symmetrical asymmetry" pointed out above. It shows that affectivity-neutrality and diffuseness-specificity apply most directly to problems of motivational orientation and thus to systems composed of motivational units and that universalism-particularism and ascription-achievement apply most directly to problems of value-orientation and thus to systems composed of units established by social values and norms (that is, systems of roles and role-expectations). Finally, it shows that the self-orientation — collectivity-orientation variable applies equally to problems of motivational and value-orientation, and thus equally to personality and social systems.

For those who already comprehend the diagrams, the following explanation is unnecessary. A new topic begins on page 98. Similarly, those who are interested in the outline but not the finer details of our theory may proceed to that page. For those who wish it, however, we give a brief discussion of these diagrams.

The four main types of need-dispositions (given in Fig. 3) are variants of the actor's attitudinal attachments to any object, further differentiated by the scope of the attachment to the object. Two of them (Cells I and III) represent the actor's needs for direct gratification through specific or diffuse attachments. In the former there are *specific* relations to objects (e.g., objects for the gratification of hunger or erotic needs). In the latter, the attachment is diffuse and involves a large portion of ego's action system in the relation to the object. The attachment to the object comprises both the reception of the attitudes of the object and the possession of the reciprocally corresponding attitudes toward the object. A lack of reciprocality in this responsiveness-receptiveness structure of a need-disposition (which mediates an attachment) is, however, extremely frequent empirically. Thus it presents a major problem in the dynamic analysis of personalities and social systems. It must be analyzed by the introduction of other variables in addition to those so far considered (see below, Chapter II).

The other two main types of need-disposition (Cells II and IV) are directed toward less immediate, less intensely positive affective gratification. The value standards figure more prominently in them. In the *specific* variant of this more disciplined need-disposition, the needed attachment is to a specific quality or performance. Again there is receptive-responsive reciprocality — the need-disposition is to approve of the qualities or performances of other persons and to be approved by others for one's own qualities or performances in conformity with some specific value standards (which have been internalized in the personality). In the diffuse variant the needed attachment is to a whole person; the need is to be esteemed by others on the basis of conformity to a set of standards applying to the whole person, and to esteem others on the basis of their conformity to similar standards. It should be stressed that the cathexis which is fundamental here covers both phases of the attachment, to loved and loving objects, to esteemed and esteeming objects, and so on.

In commenting on this simplified systematic classification of need-dispositions, we ought to point back and show whence it is derived; then point to examples and show that the different kinds of need-dispositions do exist; then, perhaps, show how these need-dispositions are generated within the personality. However, in such an essay as this we cannot spell out all steps completely. Suffice it to say that the categories are derived from our basic categories of action through the pattern variables. We have tried to make the steps of this derivation explicit. As for pointing to examples, we will not here go into all of the specific kinds of need-dispositions that fill our various categories, but we can point out that there are these needs to receive certain attitudes from others and to respond with certain attitudes to others. If it is asked how ego comes to be so concerned about the attitudes of approval, love, esteem, and so forth, which alter directs toward ego (and which ego directs toward alter) we must point to the cathectic *sensitivity* to the attitudes of others which is developed in the course of socialization. The child learns to need the love or approval or esteem of others and in the same sense he learns to need to love or approve or esteem others through identification. In somewhat different form, the same is true of the need for specific attachments to objects as immediate sources of gratification. There are perhaps physical components of all these need-dispositions, according to which they also might also be classified. And ultimately, of course, they are genetically derived from organic sources in the infant's dependency — his needs as a biological organism — but in their operation as parts of a system of need-dispositions they acquire a very far-reaching functional autonomy in the form of the personality system.

The fundamental reason why Fig. 4 is constructed from pattern variables omitted from Fig. 3 has already been given. We may expand it briefly. Personality systems are primarily systems of need-dispositions; the primary questions about need-dispositions (which always govern orientations of actors to objects), when we are concerned with a system of them, are: (1) Does the need-disposition in question integrate harmoniously with other need-dispositions in the system? (2) Is the need-disposition in question diffusely related with many other sectors of the system, or is it more or less segmental and cut off with respect to the other aspects of the system of which it is a part? Hence in the description of the fundamental need-dispositions, the primarily relevant pattern variables are (1) that derived from the problem whether or not evaluation is called for (whether the need-disposition has to be integrated with others) and (2) that derived from the problem of whether the object shall be endowed with diffuse or specific significance (whether the need-disposition which mediates the object attachment involves much or little of the action system of ego).

A social system is primarily a system of roles. The primary questions about roles (which govern mutual orientations of individuals within a social system) when we are concerned with a system of these roles, are: (1) Does the role in question integrate with other roles on the basis of universalistic or particularistic principles of organization? (2) Are the roles in question defined and thus related in terms of the quality or performance characteristics of their occupants? It should be remembered that the determination of how roles are related in this respect is largely a function of the value standards institutionalized in the social system. Consequently, the pattern variables most relevant to the description of the normative patterns governing roles (i.e., role-expectations) are achievement-ascription and universalism-particularism. The four main types of role-expectations are presented in the four cells of Fig. 4. Fig. 4a is constructed by further cross-classifying each main type of role-expectation. What are classified in Fig. 4 are only the primary value-orientation components of the role-expectations and most emphatically *not* the concrete roles themselves.

These two diagrams in a slightly different formulation also constitute classifications of constellations of the alternatives of choice which make up systems of value-orientations themselves. They are components of "patterns of culture." Again it should be emphasized that they are classifications of constellations of *components* of systems of value-orientation, not of *types* of such systems. Types of systems are formed from such constellations when they are related to the more concrete "problems" presented by the situation of action. These and related questions will be taken up in the analysis of systems of value-orientation in Chapter III.[43]

CLASSIFICATION OF COMPONENTS OF THE OBJECT SITUATION

Here we shall recapitulate briefly what has been said above about the structure of the object world and elaborate further on the classification of the components of that structure.[44] The structure of the object world in the most

[43] There is one implication of the above discussion which may be noted now for further analysis. The symmetrical asymmetry which has been discussed implies a difference between the systematic focus of a value-orientation system for personality, and the corresponding one for the social system (see Fig. 5). A system of personal values will be organized primarily around the actor's motivational problems, such as permission and restraint, and the scope of the significance of objects. The patterns of relationship between persons beyond these bases of interest will be conceptually secondary, although of course they will have to be integrated with the primary foci. A system of *social values*, on the other hand, will be organized more about the problems of choice between the types of normative patterns which govern the relations among individuals and the aspects of those individuals which are to be constitutive of their social statuses and roles. This asymmetry may be of considerable importance in defining the relations between the study of culture and personality, on the one hand, and culture and society, on the other. Fig. 5 presents in schematic form the relationship of the pattern variables of motivational orientation on the one hand, and role-expectation on the other. The second pattern variable, self- or collectivity-orientation, belongs equally to both and is central to neither.

[44] Every action system has, in one sense, three components: a pattern of value-orientation, a structural object world, and a set of allocative and integrative foci. Of these three sets of components, the value patterns and the object world are common, without essential differences, to personality and social systems and even to cultural systems. The

general terms takes form from the distinction between social and nonsocial objects, the further differentiation of the former into the categories of qualities and performances, and the further differentiation of the latter into the categories of physical and cultural objects. Nonsocial objects, it will be remembered, are distinguished by the fact that ego does not see them as having expectations about ego's behavior. Ego knows that social objects "expect" him to do certain things; he does not see nonsocial objects as having such expectations. Cultural objects, it will be remembered, are distinguished from physical objects in that the former are subject to "internalization," the latter are not.

Taking these distinctions as our starting point we will now further differentiate objects along lines which are of maximal significance in the orientation of action.

Social objects may be distiguished as individual actors and collectivities, which are systems of action involving a plurality of individual actors but which are treated as units. Among physical objects one subclass in particular has such importance for action that it must be singled out. This is the organism of the individual actor, whether it be ego's own body or that of alter. Within the class of individual social objects it is desirable to distinguish the personality of alter from that of ego himself as an object. Internalized cultural objects are no longer distinct objects but parts of the personalities of ego and alter and of the structure of collectivities.

Finally, we must divide objects in accordance with whether the properties on the basis of which actors are oriented toward them are attributes of a class (of qualities or performances) or whether they are possessed by virtue of a relationship. This distinction is not identical with the quality-performance distinction; in fact, it cuts across it. Nor is it derived from the distinction between universalism and particularism, though it is closely related to it. It is derived from the distinction between the actor as such and the system of action which involves status and role in relationships. The actor *in abstracto* is simply a set of properties by which he can be classified; in action he is involved in a system of relationships. Hence social objects can be distinguished by certain properties which they have independently of their relationships as well as by those which they have in their capacities of participants in a relationship which may be social, biological, or spatial.

Fig. 6 presents in schematic form the structure of the object world. Each of the "units" listed at the left may be integrated into action in several (or many) different ways. It is, of course, a different kind of object, depending on how it is integrated into action. The columns which make up the body

differences between personality, social, and cultural systems lie (1) in the different allocative and integrative foci, and (2) in the empirical organization and integration of these elements in the concrete control of action. Thus the components of the object situation, like the patterns of value orientation, can be analyzed once and for all, and the categories so developed should be applicable to all three kinds of systems.

of the chart show the various ways each of the units may be integrated as an object. (Fig. 6 is on page 254.)

The distinction of modalities applies chiefly to social objects and only these form interactive relationships; the first two columns therefore present this distinction for social objects. The nonsocial objects appear separately in the right-hand column, since the quality-performance distinction is inapplicable to them.[45] The latter are relevant to action as empirical and symbolic means, conditions, and obstacles of the gratification of need-disposition.

The classification of social objects within each of the modalities follows the distinctions employed in our analysis of actor and situation: the actor as an individual as an object, alter as an individual as an object, and a collectivity as an object.

We have already remarked that the actor is a special sort of methodological abstraction, a point of reference. The particular actor who is performing the particular action at a particular moment cannot be an object of an orientation which has a future reference. Only the empirical system of action which has duration and which is referable to that point of reference (i.e., the personality) can be an object. From the point of view of any given actor, ego, *his own* personality (i.e., his system of action or any part of it which is larger and more extensive in time than the action which he is performing at the moment) may be an object and is, as a specific, concrete object, differentiated from the personality of any other actor. The inclusion of the personality of ego, expressly *as an object* and not only as the actor, is fundamental to the theory of action. It is only through the employment of this device that many of the most crucial analytical operations of the theory of action, such as the use of the mechanism of identification and the corresponding concept of the "internalization" of cultural norms, become possible. Common sense, we may say, lays *all* the stress on the *difference* between ego and alter as two separate entities. The theory of action accepts this difference as fundamental and embodies it in *one* of its major classifications. But it also employs a classification according to which certain analytical distinctions, such as that between the object modalities, apply equally to ego and to alter because, both being objects precisely to ego, the categories which are significant for the orientation to objects apply to both of them. It then becomes possible to relate ego's own personality as an object to the rest of the object world in a way which would not be possible so long as a rigid qualitative distinction is maintained between the self as a concrete entity and all objects which are classified as belonging to the "outside" world. In essence we are *analytically* splitting the concrete self into two components, the self as actor and the self as object.

[45] There seems to be one exception to this rule. Organisms, as physical objects, seem amenable to the quality-performance distinction; thus the nonsocial column is placed at the bottom of the diagram.

These distinctions are indispensable for the analysis of the interaction of social objects and make possible the basic structural homology [46] between various personalities (on other than constitutional, biological bases) and between personalities and social systems, which is fundamental to our analysis of the interdependences between the two systems.

The second basic distinction within the category of social objects is that between the individual actor and the collectivity as action systems. It should be remembered that the individual actor (as a personality or a subsystem of it) is here defined as a system of action. A collective system of action, of which the actor may or may not be a member, can be an object of orientation just as an individual can. The collectivity in this case may be either a whole society (a self-subsistent social system) or a partial social system.

In a collectivity as a system of action no one actor or his personality is the point of reference, and indeed, strictly speaking, the individual personality as such is not a relevant point of reference at all when we speak of a social system from an analytical standpoint. (Empirically, of course, the personality system of the members will be very relevant to our understanding of the working of a collectivity as a social system.) When ego and alter are oriented toward one another, the question whether they are or are not members of the same collectivity will be important in their orientation; it will determine the relational qualities of alter and ego. They will not in these terms be orienting themselves toward collectivities as objects but toward alters as objects having relational or membership qualities. For this reason memberships are classified in Fig. 6 as the qualities of individuals as objects and not as the qualities of collectivities. Its membership composition (i.e., the number and kinds of members) *is*, on the other hand, a quality of the collectivity.

It is nonetheless important to bear in mind that collectivities as such, past, present, and future, may well be objects of orientation. The actions of individuals in membership, representative, or executive roles are oriented toward collectivities (other collectivities and their own) as *systems* of actions, and not merely toward individuals with membership qualities. The maintenance by an executive of a given system of relationships within a corporate body or collectivity, as well as the discontinuance or prohibition of certain corporate practices, is an orientation toward a collectivity. It is not just an orientation to a single alter as an object, but toward a system of relationships among a plurality of alters who form a system.

It is particularly important to realize that the collective object is usually a *partial* social system. The individual actor, on the other hand, is typically a member not of one but of many collectivities. He is a member of all the subsystems in which he has distinguishable roles. The concept of the collectiv-

[46] The term *homology* refers to certain formal identities. It will be discussed at the end of this chapter.

ity of which the actor is himself a member *as an object of orientation* by others is fundamental to the concept of role, which is crucial to the analysis of social systems. From this point of view, the actor's role in a particular collectivity is an organized subsystem of his total system of action. It is a normatively regulated orientation to a collectivity as an object, i.e., to an organized plurality of alters in terms of the reciprocal interlocking of ego's role-expectations concerning his own action, with his expectations of *their* interindividually organized or concerted contingent reactions to the various possibilities of his behavior.

Within the category of nonsocial objects as units, a further distinction appears which is not directly relevant to the classification of modalities: the distinction between organisms and other nonsocial objects.[47] In its conceptualization, the theory of action does not treat the *actor* as an organism — the common, though usually implicit, assumption that he is, is a basic biological fallacy in the analysis of behavior. The concrete *individual* who behaves is, however, also *in one aspect* always an organism. He must be distinguished from other objects since in his personality aspect he is "tied" to a particular organism. This is of course equally true both for ego and for alter. The qualities and the propensities for performance of the organism provide criteria which may become fundamentally important foci for action orientation, again both ego's own organism and alter's. For instance, the significance of ego's own sex for his personality structure, as in his "acceptance" of his sex role, is to be analyzed in terms of the role of this particular "trait" of his body *as an object* in his orientation, by virtue of which he "classifies himself" with fellow persons of the same sex as distinguished from those of opposite sex. The same holds, of course, for performance capacities or propensities, such as physical strength or agility.

It should be quite clear that we are here speaking of the organism or the body *as an object*. This excludes the organism as a source of motivation, or in its significance as the id.[48] The energy which the physiological organism supplies for action, according to the paradigm of the theory of action, is in-

---

[47] It will be noted in the diagram that this is a very particular class of nonsocial objects, as the quality-performance distinction does apply to it, whereas it does not apply to other nonsocial objects. This is because concretely the actor's personality and the organism are not separate.

[48] In relation to the action schema, the psychoanalytic conception of the id fails to differentiate between two things: (1) the organic energy which enters into action as motivation, and thus is prerequisite to personality; (2) certain aspects of dispositions which are organized within the personality in relation to the object world. The latter component in present terms is definitely part of, not prerequisite to, personality as a system of action. In recent psychoanalytic theory the tendency seems to have been to include most of the latter in the unconscious parts of the ego. The distinction between points 1 and 2 is vital in the theory of action. Whether and at exactly which point a line corresponding to that drawn by Freud between Id and Ego should be drawn *within* the personality as a system of action, rather than *between* it and the organic need-motivation system, is a question which may be deferred until Chapter II.

corporated into the *modes of motivational orientation. It does not go into but only toward the constellation of objects.* The distinctions among ego's body, ego as personality, and ego as actor underlies much that is specific to action theory. This is essential to avoid the confusions involved in much of the traditional biological way of looking at human action. But, however fundamental these distinctions, it is also equally fundamental clearly to distinguish the organism, whether of ego or of alter, as an object from other physical objects in the situation.

The rest of the nonsocial object system is classified into physical objects and cultural objects. However important the distinction between physical and cultural objects for many purposes, *relative* to social objects they have much in common: on the one hand, they constitute objects of immediate cognitive-cathectic significance; on the other, they are instrumentally significant means — that is, "resources" — conditions, and obstacles. In the present context, it is as *units* of the object system, as distinguished from other units, that the first lines of distinction are drawn. A house, an automobile, a tree, or a book are different objects of orientation in the sense that they are distinguishable — one house as a unit from another house, and a house from an automobile — but they are also all distinguishable from actors as units and from the bodies of actors. However within the class of nonsocial objects the distinction between cultural and physical objects remains as of very marked conceptual and empirical significance.

A particularly important class of such nonsocial units are, however, concretely both physical and cultural. Of those mentioned, only a tree is a purely "natural" object. But a house or an automobile is primarily significant as a *humanly shaped and adapted* physical object; whereas a book is primarily a cultural or symbolic object, which has a "physical embodiment." It is the "content" of the book, not the paper, ink, and covers, which primarily makes the book into an object of orientation.

Just as the motivation of ego is not an object of orientation, neither are his *internalized* culture patterns. We have already remarked that for analytical purposes internationalized value standards are treated as an independent category of the system of action, *not* as part of the object world.

We should also repeat here a point which has rather general bearing. The system of objects is known to the actor(s) in question. It is only when known (i.e., cognized) [49] that it is a set of objects of orientation. We must therefore distinguish the known situation from those features of the situation "as it really is" which may be known, or are intrinsically knowable, to an observer, but are not at the moment known to the actor(s). The interrelations between the actor's situation as he is oriented toward it and the situation as discerned by a contemporary or later observer raises some of the

[49] Cognition need not be explicit or conscious.

most important problems of empirical analysis. In principle, the same is true of new elements which may come into the situation and which may be predictable to an observer. Hence the distinction between what is known to the actor and what is not is always potentially important. For a standard by which to assess this, it is necessary to have an appraisal of the situation as it is known to or knowable by an observer.

The cognitive orientation of the actor may not only pass over an object completely so that the actor is ignorant of it, but it may also be distorted. It may involve errors of perception and interpretation. This is of first importance to the analysis of action, and again can only be assessed with reference to a conception of the situation "as it really is," which is the equivalent of its being known by an observer. The observer's knowledge need not and cannot be absolute; it is only necessary that it should be adequate to the problem in hand.

Another source of complexity and possible misunderstanding is the question of whether ego's orientation to an object must, in whole or in part, be conscious. The answer is quite clear; it is not necessary. The criterion is whether ego acts toward the object in a meaningful way so that it is reasonable to interpret his action as based on his orientation to what the object is, has been, or is expected to be. This means of course that a given "situation" will often be the object of several cognitions by the actor: he will perceive it in accordance with the current canons of valid perception, and he will also perceive it as possessing the properties imputed to it by his unconscious need-dispositions to attribute certain probably empirically invalid properties to objects that he has already perceived to possess certain other properties. For example, an action by a person in an authoritative role will be interpreted (i.e., perceived) unconsciously as also having certain properties of aggressiveness. The *unconscious* in the psychoanalytic sense can be analyzed in terms of the theory of action, and its actual formulation in present-day psychoanalytic theory is not very far removed from the terms of the theory of action. In other words, the line between conscious and unconscious has nothing to do with the limits of analysis in terms of the frame of reference of the theory of action, including, of course, cognitive orientation.

Neither of these two problems creates any difficulties for our classification of objects — although they add greatly to the complexities of empirical analysis. The "real" situation (of the observer) and the "cognized" situation (of the actor) can both be described in terms of our classification of objects. The consciously perceived situation of the mildly neurotic adult, and the distortedly perceived situation of his unconscious reinterpretation, are likewise subject to description in the same categories. Indeed, this possibility of describing discrepancies contributes to the formulation of many important problems in the study of personality and social systems.

In conclusion, it may again be pointed out that the scheme of the pattern variables as the variable components of value-orientations and the classification of the structural components of the object system are *common to all three* types of system in which action elements become organized: personalities, social systems, and systems of cultural orientation. It is this which gives unity to the theory being developed here. This conceptual unity and its consequent advantages for systematic empirical analysis will be indicated in the three chapters which follow, in which we will attempt to present a systematic account of each of the three types of system and certain of their conceptual and empirical interrelations. No effort will be made to demonstrate the empirical hypotheses derived here, since our aim will be to show only that they can be derived from this conceptual scheme. It should not be forgotten, however, that applicability to the study of the real behavior of human beings is the ultimate test of *any* theoretical scheme.

The Basic Structure of the Interactive Relationship

The interaction of ego and alter is the most elementary form of a social system. The features of this interaction are present in more complex form in all social systems.

In interaction ego and alter are each objects of orientation for the other. The basic differences from orientations to nonsocial objects are two. First, since the outcome of ego's action (e.g., success in the attainment of a goal) is contingent on alter's reaction to what ego does, ego becomes oriented not only to alter's probable *overt* behavior but also to what ego interprets to be alter's expectations relative to ego's behavior, since ego expects that alter's expectations will influence alter's behavior. Second, in an integrated system, this orientation to the expectations of the other is reciprocal or complementary.

Communication through a common system of symbols is the precondition of this reciprocity or complementarity of expectations. The alternatives which are open to alter must have some measure of stability in two respects: first, as realistic possibilities for alter, and second, in their meaning to ego. This stability presupposes generalization from the particularity of the given situations of ego and alter, both of which are continually changing and are never concretely identical over any two moments in time. When such generalization occurs, and actions, gestures, or symbols have more or less the *same* meaning for both ego and alter, we may speak of a common culture existing between them, through which their interaction is mediated.

Furthermore, this common culture, or symbol system, inevitably possesses in certain aspects a normative significance for the actors. Once it is in existence, observance of its conventions is a necessary condition for ego to be "understood" by alter, in the sense of allowing ego to elicit the type of reaction from alter which ego expects. This common set of cultural symbols becomes the medium in which is formed a constellation of the contingent actions of both parties, in such a way that there will simultaneously emerge a definition of a range of *appropriate* reactions on alter's part to each of a range of possible actions ego has taken and vice versa. It will then be a condition of the stabilization of such a system of complementary expectations, not only that ego and alter should *communicate*, but that they should *react appropriately* to each other's action.

A tendency toward consistent appropriateness of reaction is also a tendency toward conformity with a normative pattern. The culture is not only a set of symbols of communication but a *set of norms* for action.

The motivation of ego and alter become integrated with the normative patterns through interaction. The polarity of gratification and deprivation is crucial here. An appropriate reaction on alter's part is a gratifying one to ego. If ego conforms with the norm, this gratification is in one aspect a reward for his conformity with it; the converse holds for the case of deprivation and deviance. The reactions of alter toward ego's conformity with or deviance from the normative pattern thus become sanctions to ego. Ego's expectations vis-à-vis alter are expectations concerning the roles of ego and of alter; and sanctions reinforce ego's motivation to conform with these role-expectations. Thus the complementarity of expectations brings with it the reciprocal reinforcement of ego's and alter's motivation to conformity with the normative pattern which defines their expectations.

The interactive system also involves the process of generalization, not only in the common culture by which ego and alter communicate but in the interpretation of alter's discrete actions vis-à-vis ego as expressions of alter's *intentions* (that is, as indices of the cathectic-evaluative aspects of alter's motivational orientations toward ego). This "generalization" implies that ego and alter agree that certain actions of alter are indices of the *attitudes* which alter has acquired toward ego (and reciprocally, ego toward alter). Since these attitudes are, in the present paradigm, integrated with the common culture and the latter is internalized in ego's need-dispositions, ego is sensitive not only to alter's overt acts, but to his *attitudes*. He acquires a need not only to obtain specific *rewards* and avoid specific *punishments* but to enjoy the favorable attitudes and avoid the unfavorable ones of alter. Indeed, since he is integrated with the same norms, these are the same as his attitudes toward himself as an object. Thus violation of the norm causes him to feel shame toward alter, guilt toward himself.

It should be clear that as an ideal type this interaction paradigm implies *mutuality* of gratification in a certain sense, though not necessarily equal distribution of gratification. As we shall see in the next chapter, this is also the paradigm of the process of the learning of generalized orientations. Even where special mechanisms of adjustment such as dominance and submission or alienation from normative expectations enter in, the process still must be described and analyzed in relation to the categories of this paradigm. It is thus useful both for the analysis of systems of normative expectations and for that of the actual conformity or deviation regarding these expectations in concrete action.

In summary we may say that this is the basic paradigm for the structure of a solidary interactive relationship. It contains all the fundamental elements of the role structure of the social system and the attachment and security system of the personality. It involves culture in both its communicative and its value-orientation functions. It is the nodal point of the organization of all systems of action.

THE CONCEPT OF SYSTEM AND THE CLASSIFICATION OF TYPES OF SYSTEMS

With our discussion of interaction we have entered upon the analysis of systems. Before we discuss more fully personality and social systems, it is desirable to state explicitly the principal properties of empirical systems which are relevant for the present analysis. The most general and fundamental property of a system is the interdependence of parts or variables. Interdependence consists in the existence of determinate relationships among the parts or variables as contrasted with randomness of variability. In other words, interdependence is *order* in the relationship among the components which enter into a system. This order must have a tendency to self-maintenance, which is very generally expressed in the concept of equilibrium.[50] It need not, however, be a static self-maintenance or a stable equilibrium. It may be an ordered process of change — a process following a determinate pattern rather than random variability relative to the starting point. This is called a moving equilibrium and is well exemplified by growth. Furthermore, equilibrium, even when stable, by no means implies that process is not going on; process is continual even in stable systems, the stabilities residing in the interrelations involved in the process.

A particularly important feature of all systems is the inherent limitation on the compatibility of certain parts or events within the same system. This is indeed simply another way of saying that the relations within the system are determinate and that not just anything can happen. Thus, to take an example from the solar system, if the orbit of one of the planets, such as Jupiter, is given, it is no longer possible for the orbits of the other planets to be distributed at random relative to this given orbit. Certain limitations are imposed by the fact that the value of one of the variables is given. This limitation may in turn be looked at from either a negative or a positive point of view. On the one hand, again using the solar system as example, if one of the planets should simply disappear, the fact that no mass was present in that particular orbit would necessitate a change in the equilibrium of the system. It would make necessary a readjustment of the orbits of the other

---

[50] That is, if the system is to be permanent enough to be worth study, there must be a tendency to maintenance of order except under exceptional circumstances.

planets in order to bring the system into equilibrium. This may also be expressed in the statement that there is a change in the structure of the system. On the other hand, the same problem may be treated from the standpoint of what would happen in the case of the coexistence of "incompatible" elements or processes within the same system. Incompatibility is always relative to a *given* state of the system. If, for example, the orbits of two of the planets should move closer to each other than is compatible for the maintenance of the current state of the system, one of two things would have to happen. Either processes would be set up which would tend to restore the previous relation by the elimination of the incompatibility; or if the new relation were maintained, there would have to be adjustments in *other* parts of the system, bringing the system into a new state of equilibrium.

These properties are inherent in all systems. A special additional property, however, is of primary significance for the theory of action. This is the tendency to maintain equilibrium, in the most general sense stated above, within certain boundaries relative to an environment — boundaries which are not imposed from outside but which are self-maintained by the properties of the constituent variables as they operate within the system. The most familiar example is the living organism, which is a physicochemical system that is not assimilated to the physicochemical conditions of the environment, but maintains certain distinct properties in relation to the environment. For example, the maintenance of the constant body temperature of the mammal necessitates processes which mediate the interdependence between the internal and the external systems in respect to temperature; these processes maintain constancy over a wide range of variability in environmental temperatures.

The two fundamental types of processes necessary for the maintenance of a given state of equilibrium of a system we call, in the theory of action, *allocation* [51] and *integration*. By *allocation* we mean processes which maintain a distribution of the components or parts of the system which is compatible with the maintenance of a given state of equilibrium. By *integration*, we mean the processes by which relations to the environment are mediated in such a way that the distinctive internal properties and boundaries of the system as an entity are maintained in the face of variability in the external situation. It must be realized that self-maintenance of such a system is not only maintenance of boundaries but also maintenance of distinctive relationships of the parts of the system *within* the boundary. The system is in some sense a unity relative to its environment. Also, self-maintenance implies not only control of the environmental variations, but also control of tendencies to change — that is, to alteration of the distinctive state — coming from within the system.

[51] The term *allocation* is borrowed from the usage of economics, where it has the general meaning here defined. Specifically, economists speak of the allocation of resources in the economy.

The two types of empirical systems which will be analyzed in the subsequent chapters are personalities and social systems. These systems are, as will be repeatedly pointed out, *different* systems which are not reducible to each other. However, there are certain conceptual continuities or identities between them which derive from two sources. (1) They are both systems built out of the fundamental components of action as these have been discussed in the General Statement and in the present chapter. These components are differently organized to constitute systems in the two cases; nevertheless, they remain the same components. (2) They are both not only systems, but both are systems of the boundary-maintaining, self-maintenance type; therefore, they both have properties which are common to systems in general and the more special properties which are characteristic of this particular type of system. (3) A third basis of their intimate relation to each other is the fact that they *interpenetrate* in the sense that no personality system can exist without *participation* in a social system, by which we mean the integration of *part* of the actor's system of action as *part* of the social system. Conversely, there is no social system which is not from one point of view a mode of the integration of parts of the systems of action which constitute the personalities of the members. When we use the term *homology* to refer to certain formal identities between personalities and social systems which are to be understood in terms of the above considerations, it should be clear that we in no way intend to convey the impression that a personality is a microcosm of a social system, or that a social system is a kind of macrocosmic personality.

In spite of the formal similarities and the continuous empirical interdependencies and interpenetrations, both of which are of the greatest importance, personalities and social systems remain two distinct classes of systems.

2

Personality as a System of Action

The preceding chapter dealt with certain common features of systems of action. Besides their common properties as systems, systems of action have certain common substantive features. In *both* social systems and personalities, the actions which make up the systems are oriented to the same classes of objects and entail selections from and commitments to the same system of alternatives of value-orientation. Having stated the general properties of systems, we will show how these substantive components are organized to form personalities. We will accordingly turn to a further discussion of motivation as it was treated in the General Statement of Part I and develop some of the categories and hypotheses presented there in order to lay the groundwork for showing systematic relationships of (1) the patterns of value-orientation and (2) the organization of objects to (3) the components of motivation (which are the allocative foci of personality systems). This will require a certain amount of recapitulation of our earlier argument. At the end of the chapter we shall analyze certain aspects of the interrelation of this system with the social system in which the actor lives.

MOTIVATIONAL CONCEPTS

Since this chapter will be concerned largely with the relation between the motivation of action and the orientation of action, we shall start out by defining carefully the important terms, chiefly the term *motivation* itself. We must define also the other motivational terms *drive*, *drives*, and *need-dispositions*.

The term *motivation* has at least two accepted meanings; the use of the word without distinguishing these two meanings serves only to confuse the reader. When we speak of an animal or a human being as having "a lot of motivation," we refer to the amount of energy being released in the course of the animal's behavior. In this sense, motivation is the organically generated energy manifested in action. It is sometimes called *drive*. When, on the other hand, we say "the motivation of an organism," referring to the organism's "motives" or "drives," [1] we refer to a set of tendencies on the part of the organism to acquire certain goal objects (or really, certain relationships to goal objects).

Motivation (or motives) in this last sense may be conceived as denoting certain more or less innate systems of *orientations* involving cognition of and cathectic attachment to certain means and goal objects and certain more or less implicit and unconscious "plans" of action aimed at the acquisition of cathected relationships to goal objects. Motivation in the former sense (as energy) supplies the energy with which such plans of action are conceived and carried out.

When *motivation* refers to the tendency to acquire these relationships to goal objects, then it is (as the paragraph above implies) also a tendency to "orient" in a certain fashion (that is, to see certain things, to want certain things, and to do certain things). Thus its referent may be either the group of orientations which follow the pattern marked out by the "tendency," or a postulated entity which, by hypothesis, controls or brings about orientations of this kind.

From now on, we will use the term *drive* [2] to refer to the physiological energy that makes action possible. We will use the term *drives*, or such terms as *a drive* or *sex drive*, to refer to the *innate* tendencies to orient and act in such a fashion as to acquire cathected relationships to goal objects. The term *need-dispositions* will be used to refer to these same tendencies when they are not innate but acquired through the process of action itself. Need-dispositions may integrate one or several drives, together with certain acquired elements, into very complex tendencies of this nature. We will avoid *ad hoc* hypotheses about the amount of biologically determined structuring of drives which would beg the empirical and conceptual questions of the extent and ways in which structuring is a need-disposition problem. That is, we will not try to decide in advance how much the structuring of tendencies is innate and how much it is a function of the structure and situation of action.[3]

The term *motivation* itself will be reserved as a general term to refer to all the phenomena discussed above. Thus action may be said to be motivated by "drive," or by "drives," or by "need-dispositions," depending on what is meant by *motivation*, and depending on the stage of development of the personality involved, and the type of action being discussed. Some actions are perhaps jointly motivated by drives and need-dispositions, in an organism where some drives are organized into need-dispositions and others are not.

[1] For example, the organism's hunger-drive or sex-drive.

[2] This term is only singular (an animal's drive, an amount of drive, and so forth) when it refers to energy; when we speak of "a drive," the animal's "drives," the term refers to a tendency.

[3] A statement of the general problem of the relation of constitutional elements in behavior to action elements was made in the General Statement of Part I and need not be repeated here.

All actions are in one sense motivated by the physiological "drive" of the organism insofar as the ultimate energy of behavior comes from the organism as a physiological system. Nevertheless, the important question of how this energy expenditure will take place, what behavior will result, what will be accomplished, requires analysis of *drive* and *need-dispositions* in the categories of action, rather than an analysis of where the energy or drive comes from. Therefore, our chief concern with motivation in this chapter will be with the orientation and action tendencies which are denoted by the terms *drive* and *need-disposition*. Moreover, since we are most concerned with the analysis of the action of human beings (and usually human beings with some degree of maturity), we will usually be more concerned with need-dispositions than with drives.

For our purposes, the drives may be regarded as action tendencies in which the chief objects are the actor's own organism and those physical objects which are necessary to achieve some state of the organism. (We include under physical objects the physiological organisms of other persons.) We need not for the time being go in detail into the degree of specificity of the physical objects or the content of the states of the actor's own organism as an object which is required for activating the drive or bringing it to quiescence. All we need say is that there are varying degrees of specificity in the two classes of objects and that there is always some plasticity in the organization of the orientation toward the objects. *All* concrete drives and need-dispositions (in relation to objects) on the personality level — that is, above the most elementary organic level — have a structure which can be analyzed in the categories of the theory of action. They can be analyzed only in terms of orientation to an object world, which varies of course through time, and in terms of the organization of value-alternative selections and commitments into patterns of need-dispositions and value-orientations which make up the personality.

One significant difference between drives on the most elementary organic level [4] and drives and need-dispositions as these are formulated in terms of the theory of action is that the former are conceived as "automatic" regulatory devices. The animal orients to the object; the object orientation automatically engages a drive; the drive implants a cathexis on the oriented object; action and consummation automatically ensue. No selection or choice is involved. There is no orientation to anything beyond the present and immediately given aspect of the situation of action. We might say the system of orientation seems to have no time dimension. No orientation to the future may take place; thus the animal is *driven* by the situation of the moment, he cannot choose on the basis of the long-run integration of his action system.

[4] The notion of drives on the most elementary organic level may, of course, be simply a limiting case not existing in either animals or human beings; there may be no such things.

Whatever may be the case on purely organic levels, when drives and their modes of gratification become organized into and with symbolic systems on the cultural level, the system of orientation necessarily *acquires* a temporal dimension. The orientation of action is not directed merely to the situation at the moment but also to future states of the system and to the potentialities for future occurrence or change of the objects in the situation. The future therefore is cognitively differentiated and its probabilities evaluated above all as differing alternatives of action. Gratification then is not merely associated with responses to a current situation; it is *distributed in time* in connection with *expectations* concerning the future development of the situation. The conception of the orientation of action by selection from a set of alternatives thus includes future as well as present alternatives and attendant consequences. A need-disposition therefore has as one of its essential properties an orientation of expectancy relative to future possibilities.[5]

We proceed on the postulate that drives tend toward gratification through the cathexis of objects. The interruption of any established process of gratification is a disturbance of equilibrium. The possible sources of interruption are twofold: first, changes in the situation which make maintenance of an unchanged relation to the cathected object impossible; second, internal processes which motivate the actor to change his relations to objects. Thus our conception of the actor's drives is that they are organized in an equilibrated system of relationships to an object world and that this system, if disturbed, will set in motion forces tending either to restore a previous state of equilibrium or to make stable a new state. This conception will underlie all our analysis of learning processes and of the operation of the personality as an on-going system.

In action, therefore, drives do not ordinarily operate simply to gratify organic needs in a pure form. They are integrated into need-dispositions,[6] which are for us the most significant units of motivation of action. A need-disposition represents the organization of one or more drive elements, elaborated into an *orientation* tendency to a more differentiated object situation than is the case with elementary drives. The drive component of a need-disposition is *organized* with cognitive and evaluative elements. Cognitively, objects of the situation are more finely discriminated and more extensively generalized in need-dispositions than in the simpler cognitive organization of drives. At the same time the selection from value alternatives is not so "automatic" but entails relatively complex and stable orientations to selective standards.

The equilibrium of drive gratification thus operates within the context of

[5] Without the property of "future-orientedness" in need-dispositions it would be difficult to understand the nature of such phenomena as anxiety.
[6] See p. 10, n. 12, of the General Statement of Part I.

an equilibrium of need-dispositions and their systems. It is not a direct gratification of elementary drives.

A common formula describing the relations of drive to action is the "tension reduction" hypothesis. For our purposes this theory is inadequate for
three reasons. First, it fails to take explicit account of the organization of the
drive element into the system of need-dispositions. Second, "tension" tends
to be merely a name for an unknown; hence an explanation of action by tension reduction tends to be a tautology to the effect that tension is reduced
because it is the nature of tension to seek reduction. Third, explanation of
action by tension reduction tends to translate action into an oversimplified,
relatively undifferentiated rhythm of tension activation and quiescence, so
that specific differentiation in relation to elements of the situation and of
orientation of action are obscured.

However, whether formulated in terms of tension reduction or otherwise,
the careful study of the process of gratification of particular drives has made
important contributions to our understanding. It has produced a first approximation to an analysis of the motivation of behavior. Our concern here, however, is to consider the problems on more complex levels of organization of
motivation involved in human action.

To make this advance from the simplifying hypothesis of need reduction,
we must remember that a need-disposition does not operate in isolation in the
sense that it may become activated, impel action, culminate and come to rest
independently of a whole constellation of other need-dispositions, some of
which work in opposition to (or even as defenses against) the originally activated need-disposition.

This brings to a close our general discussion of motivational concepts. Our
next major step will be to show how need-dispositions (as the elements of the
personality system) are related to one another, to the personality system as
a whole, and to the world of objects, by means of certain processes which
mediate these relationships. Then we must show how these processes, when
classified in terms of the ways they serve to solve the various major problems
of personality systems, comprise the *mechanisms* of personality. Before we do
this, however, it seems wise to give some special discussion to the specific kind
of motivational variable with which we will be most concerned, that is, the
need-disposition.

NEED-DISPOSITIONS

Need-dispositions, we have said, are tendencies to orient and act with respect to objects in certain manners and to expect certain consequences [7] from

---

[7] The expectations of consequences is nothing more than the cognition of a certain
object as leading to a certain set of consequences and the cathexis of an object in the
light of its antecedent relationship to a more cathected set of consequences. In other words,
the expectation is nothing more than the cognition and cathexis of a means object qua
means to an end.

these actions. The conjoined word *need-disposition* itself has a double connotation; on the one hand, it refers to a tendency to fulfill some requirement of the organism, a tendency to accomplish some end state; on the other hand, it refers to a disposition to do something with an object designed to accomplish this end state. We have already said that its denotation is a group of orientations (or the postulated variable which controls that set of orientations), all following a pattern involving the discrimination of an object or a group of objects, the cathecting of an object or group of objects, and the tendency to behave in the fashion designed to get the cathected relationship with the object. In the last analysis, the identifying index of a need-disposition is a tendency on the part of the organism to "strive" for certain relationships with objects, or for certain relationships between objects. And the tendency to "strive" is nothing more than the tendency to cognize and cathect in certain ways and to act in a fashion guided by those cognitions and cathexes. The differences between a need-disposition and a drive, we have said, lies in the fact that it is not innate, that it is formed or learned in action, and in the fact that it is a tendency to orient and select with an eye to the future, as well as with an eye to immediate gratification.

Three different types of need-dispositions are chiefly important in the theory of action: (1) Need-dispositions vis-à-vis the attitudes of and relationships with social objects (these need-dispositions mediate person-to-person relationships); (2) need-dispositions vis-à-vis the observance of cultural standards (these need-dispositions are the internalized social values); and (3) role-expectations, which are on a somewhat different level from the other two.[8] Other types of need-dispositions enter as variables into personality systems, but none has nearly the importance of these as determinants of action, particularly when (as is always the case) the various aspects of the per-

---

[8] Here we are classifying need-dispositions in terms of their foci; that is, in terms of objects and relationships at which they direct the actor's attention and toward which they direct his strivings. Chiefly important for our system are *two* fundamental foci of need-dispositions — *social objects* and *value patterns*. Thus, the first two classes of need-dispositions are listed. Role-expectations, although they incorporate components of both of the first two, are not a special subclass of either but a special way of organizing them together. A role *always* involves both. It is defined by the *complementarity* of expectations (such that ego and alter must, in some sense, both have need-dispositions which require one set of actions and attitudes by ego and another set by alter; and ego must require of himself what alter requires of him; conversely, alter must require of himself what ego requires of him). The complementary expectations are both cognitive and cathectic in their relevance to both personalities. And the expectations (in order to have this complementary "fit" with one another) must be subject to (or governed by) common value patterns, as was pointed out in the General Statement. There can be need-dispositions to cathect objects or (object relationships) without this complementarity. And there can be value patterns which do not help mediate the complementarity of role-expectations. Nevertheless, a role-expectation itself may legitimately be called a need-disposition within the personality, but it tends to be a slightly different sort of abstraction (from the concrete orientation of the actor), since it gets some of its components from those elements which make up values and some from those elements which make up need-dispositions vis-à-vis social objects.

sonality system are also integrated into social systems and cultural systems. Note that these three types of need-disposition variables in the personality system correspond to the three types of system which we are considering: the first subsume pure personality-personality relations, the second subsume personality–cultural system relationships, the third subsume personality–social system relationships. Let us discuss briefly the way in which all of these three types of variables are in fact need-dispositions on the personality level and the way they are all classifiable in terms of the pattern variables, and thus the manifold ways the pattern variables may enter as characterizations of personality systems or of their subsystems.

In the first place, need-dispositions vis-à-vis social objects are exemplified by the need-dispositions for esteem, love, approval, and response, when these are directed toward specific human beings or classes of human beings, or toward collectivities of them. In their broadest sense, these need-dispositions include more than role-expectations. In a sense, they constitute the foundations for the internalization of role-expectations and values. They are dispositions to discriminate and group social objects in certain fashions, to cathect some social objects or groups of them (or, specifically, certain relationships with social objects), and thus to behave in certain ways vis-à-vis these classes of social objects.

Values or internalized value standards are, as we have repeated several times, need-dispositions. That is, they are, on the one hand, *needs* to realize certain functional prerequisities of the system. (Specifically, they aim at those end states which are not in conflict with and which are demanded by such cultural value standards as have been internalized and have come to define, in part, the system.) On the other hand, they are dispositions to handle objects in certain fashions in order to bring about the cathected relationships.

Role-expectations are "needs" to get "proper" responses and attitudes from alter and "dispositions" to give "proper" attitudes and responses to alter. In another sense, they are needs to cognize a set of cathected complementary relationships between ego and alter and dispositions to manipulate the self and the objects in order to bring about the set of cathected relationships. Note how the role expectation organizes a need-disposition vis-à-vis a social object with a value in terms of which the attitudes, and so forth, are judged "proper."

In the personality system, all of these variables, as we have said, are need-dispositions. Now, we add that all have value-standard components, and thus all three types of need dispositions are classifiable in terms of the pattern variables. Need-dispositions vis-à-vis social objects tend to have value-standard components, in the sense that (as was said in the last chapter) any relationship between ego and a social object tends in the long run to be controlled by value standards, and these long-run relationships are the ones mediated by need-dispositions. Role-expectancies are internalized values as integrated with object relationships, thus they obviously involve value standards. And finally the *value* need-dispositions are themselves the internalized cultural standards which are above all classifiable in terms of the pattern variables. Let us show how the pattern variables enter the picture at this level of the organization of personality. (We point out, however, before we start, that the pattern variables enter the personality picture at several other levels: they may be used to characterize the personality as a whole, or the *mechanisms* which integrate the variables which we are discussing here.) At this level they constitute a method for classifying need-dispositions, which are the basic variable of personality systems.

With respect to any particular need-disposition, the most elementary alternative is whether or not it is to be released in action in the particular situation. The alternative which we have called *affectivity* refers to the inability of the need-disposition to present any internal barrier to direct release or gratification. The opposite alternative is for the need-disposition to respect inhibition from immediate gratification when this is demanded for the good of the system. Where the need-disposition can be held in check — that is, where the mechanism of inhibition may operate — we shall speak of *affective neutrality*.

The second pair of alternatives refers to the scope of significance of the object. In the one case the orientation is defined by the specificity of that significance, in the other, by its diffuseness in the form of an attachment.

The third pair of alternatives defines the basis on which the relation between actor and object rests. In the one case the significance of the object rests on its membership in a general category, so that any object conforming with the relevant general criteria would be equally appropriate as an object for cathexis and evaluation in relation to this particular need-disposition or combination of them. This is the universalistic alternative. In the other case the significance of the object may rest on its standing in a particular relationship to ego. Regardless of its general attributes, no other object is appropriate unless the particular relationship to ego exists or can be established. This is the particularistic alternative.

Ego is an object to himself. As such all the other categories of object-orientation apply to him, but in particular he must categorize himself as an object in value-orientation terms. The most fundamental basis of categorization, since it defines the characteristics peculiar to social objects, is the distinction between an object as a complex of *given qualities* and an object as an *actor*, striving toward goals. In his self-image or ego-ideal (i.e., the set of need-dispositions which relate him to himself as a social object), the actor may emphasize either the given qualities of his personality, by which he *ascribes* himself to categories, or he may emphasize his *achievement*, past or potential. Similarly, the need-dispositions which relate him to social objects may emphasize *their* qualities or their achievements. Thus the fourth of these pairs of alternatives is *ascription-achievement*.

Finally, any specific gratification may be sought in isolation from any potential significance of the object other than that of its power to gratify the need-dispositions of ego. This alternative, since it disregards any significance of the object other than its capacity to gratify ego, we call self-orientation. On the other hand, the gratification may take place in the framework of an attachment to the particular object from which the gratification is being sought or to some other object which will be affected by the change in the relationship between ego and the former object. In this case, the object as an entity acquires significance to ego. Its "welfare" is therefore a value for ego independently of the specific gratifications he receives from it directly. Since by such an attachment, when the object is a social object, ego and alter constitute a collectivity, we call this *collectivity-orientation*.[9]

When we take the step from the consideration of the particular need-disposition to the description of a system of need-dispositions, we must examine the basis on which the different need-dispositions in the system are differentiated from each other. The starting point for this analysis is provided by the pattern variables in their relevance to the constituents of motivation. These five variables when cross-classified provide thirty-two possible types of orientations. These, however, as we have seen, are not all equally relevant to personality. The problems of which need-dispositions are to be gratified in a given situation and of whether the object has a specific or a diffuse significance are the primary problems because of their direct impingement on motivation. The variable of affectivity-neutrality comprehends the alternative possibilities of direct gratification and inhibition in relation to objects and occasions, while that of specificity-diffuseness refers to the breadth of the cathexis of the object.

How affectivity can characterize a need-disposition is immediately obvious. The case of neutrality is more complex. Affective neutrality in itself does not contain a gratification interest, the term referring simply to the fact of inhibition relative to certain immediate objects or occasions. But it does mean that the gratification interest is focused on a future goal, or on some other aspect of the object or situation or relation, to which the inhibition, including the attitude of alter applies. Neutrality therefore characterizes the state of a need-disposition system in which potential immediate gratifications may be renounced because of their incompatibility with other gratification interests of the system. A need-disposition system is *never* affectively neutral in its entirety but only vis-à-vis certain *specific* opportunities for gratification.

Accepting the predominance of these two pattern variables for personality, we can construct a classification of four major types of need-dispositions as presented in the four main sections of Fig. 3 in Chapter I. The concurrence of affectivity and specificity has been called the *specific gratification* need-

---

[9] The element of collectivity-orientation is the core of what Freud called the *superego*. Its source in the processes of identification will be evident from the above.

disposition. Such a need is gratified in specific object cathexis, or attachments, and not in diffuse attachments (e.g., foods, appreciation of specific qualities or acts). In relation to a social object it is the need for receptiveness and/or response in a specific context on the part of the object.

When affectivity occurs together with diffuseness, however, the specific gratification is no longer possible in isolation, since the other components of the object of diffuse attachment cannot be disregarded. Such an attachment entails the reorganization of specific gratification interests into a system focused on the object as a totality, and in the case of social objects, inherently connected with expectations of reciprocation. In such a case we may speak of a need for a diffuse attachment, or in current terminology, a need for love objects. The need to be loved is its reciprocal in relation to a social object; it is derived conceptually from the complementarity of expectations.

The combination of specificity and affective neutrality in orientation toward a social object represents one of the variants of the basic sensitivity toward positive response which, as we have already indicated, is the basic substantive need-disposition of the human being in relation to social objects. It involves the postponement of gratification pending the attainment of a goal or the occurrence of an anticipated situation. There may also be direct gratification through alter's and ego's own attitudes of approval. Such an orientation toward a person toward whom there is an attachment, and toward whose responsiveness one is sensitive, will be called approval. It is a response to a specific type of action or quality, and it is restrained or disciplined. The need for this kind of response from social objects to whom we are attached is to be called the need for approval.

It is, however, also possible for affective neutrality to be combined with a diffuse attachment as well. In this case the relation of the postponed or otherwise renounced gratification interests to each other and to the object is essentially the same as in the case of the need for love, with the difference that there is a less immediate affectual content. This we shall designate as the need for esteem. In the present conceptual form, this is complementary and covers both the need to grant esteem and the need to be esteemed. Here again we have the need for positive responsiveness, but in this particular case, the response is given to the attachment without reference to specific qualities or actions.

Within these four basic orientations there is the possibility of a further differentiation through subclassifying each orientation according to the values of the other three. There is space here for only a brief consideration of a few of these possibilities. For example, achievement-ascription differentiates the basic orientations on the dimension of whether a need-disposition is a tendency to orient to alter on the basis of his active strivings or given qualities.[10]

Universalism-particularism presents still another possible range of varia-

---

[10] If ego orients himself in terms of qualities, he is more apt to be passive.

tion. In this case, the object of the basic need-dispositions may be chosen by either of two criteria. On the one hand, the object may be chosen from a plurality of objects on the basis of its universalistically defined capacities or qualities independently of a particular relation to ego except that established by the selection. On the other hand, an alter who stands in a given particular relation to ego may, by virtue of the fact, be selected as the object of one of the basic need-dispositions. Thus, in the case of an object of attachment, the basis of cathexis may be the fact that the object stands in a given particular relation to ego (e.g., *his* mother or *his* friend). The basis of the attachment may be instead the possession by the object of universalistically defined qualities or performance capacities independently of any particular relationship (e.g., the possession of certain traits of beauty or character).

Finally, any one of the four major types may be subdivided according to whether the orientation is or is not in terms of obligation toward a collectivity-orientation. Thus in the need-disposition for approval (neutrality-specificity) the goal may be shared with alter which means that the actor seeks the approval not only for himself but also for the collectivity of which he is a member. However, ego's orientation may be independent of the bearing of his actions on alter's values or gratifications. In the need-disposition for love, normal reciprocity is collectivity-oriented since sensitivity to alter's needs and gratifications is an essential part of the relationship. This sensitivity, however, may be subordinated to an interest of ego which motivates him to disregard the bearing of his action on alter's need-disposition.

The need-disposition system of different personalities will contain different proportions of these basic types of need-dispositions and their differences in their distribution in a society. There will, however, be certain clusters where the range of variability is narrower than chance would produce because of the particular significance of certain types of need-dispositions in the relevant areas.

FUNCTIONAL PREREQUISITES OF THE PERSONALITY SYSTEM

In any system we may discuss the conditions of equilibrium which are in the last analysis the conditions of the system's being a system. Here, we shall discuss these problems as they affect the personality system. When viewed from the outside, the conditions which must be met in order that the system shall persist are the functional prerequisites of the system. When viewed from the inside (from the actor's point of view rather than the observer's), these are the functional foci of action organization. The over-all problem of personality systems thus may be viewed in two ways: (1) from the outside, or from the scientific observer's viewpoint, it is the problem of maintaining a bounded system; in other words, it is the personality's problem of continuing to be the kind of system it is. (2) From the inside, or from the actor's viewpoint, it is the problem of optimization of gratification. We have already discussed to some extent the external aspect of this problem, and we will take up in a moment its specific meaning for personality systems. Let us discuss briefly here, however, the way this problem looks from the actor's point of view.

To the actor, all problems may be generalized in terms of the aim to obtain *an optimum of gratification*. The term *optimum* has been deliberately chosen as an alternative to *maximum*. The latter is too involved in the traditional hedonistic fallacy which rests on the tautology that gratification is held to be both the result and the motive of every action, even that which appears to be deprivational in its immediate consequences. It ignores the consequences of the interrelations of need-dispositions in systems, which in cases of conflict often entail the inhibition and hence deprivation of many particular need-dispositions. In this sense self-deprivation is a common phenomenon. The term *optimum* avoids this difficulty by emphasizing that the level of gratification toward which the personality system tends is the optimum relative to the existing set of particular need-dispositions in the particular situation. Out of their conflicts within the system often come commitments to particular self-deprivations. The optimum of gratification is the best that can be obtained from the existing conditions, given the existing set of need-dispositions and the available set of objects. The personality may thus be conceived as a system with a persistent tendency toward the *optimum* level of gratification. This proposition involves no judgment about the absolute level of gratification or the specific gratifications sought or the trend of development of the personality toward higher or lower levels. It simply asserts that at any given time, and with a given set of need-dispositions, mechanisms will be in operation which will adjudicate among conflicting need-dispositions and will tend to reduce the state of dysphoria (the subjective experience of deprivation) to tolerable limits.

Our classification of the problems of personality systems is the same whether we are looking at the problems from the outside or from the inside. Nevertheless, the problems will be stated primarily in terms of the *ways they appear to the actor*. Therefore, they may be construed as the various modes in which the problem of optimization of gratification appears to him. The following classification is in terms of the kinds of problems to be solved. After this classification has been discussed, we will take up the way the problems break down again depending on the kinds of processes which solve them.

Problems can be classified first on the basis of where the actor sees the problem to lie, that is, in terms of the phenomenological place of the problem. On the one hand, problems may be seen to lie in the external [11] world: these are cognitive and cathectic problems involving perceived and cathected facts (or objects) which may be seen to conflict with need-dispositions (in the sense

---

[11] It should be noted that the term *external* when applied to the phenomenological place of a problem is quite different from the term *outside* which is used to distinguish the way the system looks to an observer.

that those need-dispositions implant negative cathexes upon the perceived facts). On the other hand, problems may be seen to lie within the personality system: these are evaluative problems involving the allocation of functions or time and effort to different need-dispositions, or the adjudication of conflicts between need-dispositions.

Problems can also be classified in terms of the kind of problem presented: (1) problems of allocation and (2) problems of integration. This classification crosscuts the external-internal distinction. Problems of allocation are primarily problems of seeing that the system gets done all of the things that need to be done. Thus, in the personality system, it breaks down into two kinds of problems: (*a*) allocating *functions* to the various units of the system or subsystems, (*b*) allocating time or action among the various units so that they may accomplish their functions. External allocation problems involve chiefly the allocation of cathexes (and thus attention) among different possible goal and means objects (so that all the demands of the situation will be met). Internal allocation problems involve chiefly the allocation of functions and time to the various need-dispositions so that all of the requirements of the system will be met.

Problems of integration are primarily problems of adjudicating conflicts between various elements of the system. External integration problems involve chiefly the problems posed when cognized facts conflict with one another or when these facts "conflict" with need-dispositions. A fact is in conflict with a need-disposition whenever it is negatively cathected (since all cathexes arise out of need-dispositions). These problems are all solved by actions which change the perception or cognition of the situation: these may be overt operations which change the situation, and thus change the perception of it, or they may be operations of reorganization of the perceived facts so they no longer conflict, or they may be merely operations which change the perceptions without either changing the situation (as the observer sees it) or getting a new organization of the facts. These are all primarily cognitive problems.[12] Internal integration problems involve chiefly the resolution of conflicts between need-dispositions.

From the foregoing it can be seen that the external-internal distinction when crosscut by the allocative-integrative distinction provides in some sense a parallel structure to the cognitive-cathectic evaluative analysis which runs through our whole work. This is because the cognitive and cathectic aspects of an orientation (or an orientation group, that is, a need-disposition) are those aspects which relate the actor to the external world. The actor cognizes and

---

[12] Role conflicts may be either internal or external integrative problems, depending on whether or not the roles in question have been internalized. If they are not internalized, the actor cognizes a fact (to wit, that he must do two incompatible things or incur sanctions), which fact is negatively cathected by the need-dispositions to avoid the sanction involved. If they are internalized, the actor wants to do two incompatible things at the same time and he has a conflict between need-dispositions.

cathects objects. Here, also, the cognitive is the integrative aspect; it relates objects to one another as all in one class, associated in time, associated in space (being context to one another), or associated as cause and effect. And the cathectic is the allocative aspect; it serves to distribute attention and interest among the objects.

The evaluative aspects of an orientation or system of orientations, on the other hand, are those aspects which relate one internal variable to other internal variables. The evaluative aspects handle both allocative and integrative problems at the internal level. That is, they relate variables in the system to one another (which is the integrative function) and they relate variables to the system as a whole (which is the allocative function).

We turn now to the kinds of processes or changes in the personality system which can function to solve the problems we have presented.

Learning Processes and Performance Processes

There are two kinds of systematic changes that occur within the personality system; these changes are always governed by the systematic requirements set forth above. First, there are changes determined by the structure of the personality system itself; these we may call the changes of normal performance, or the performance processes. These processes transmit changes from variable to variable without changing the structure of the system. They are like the processes whereby the energy of the automobile motor is transmitted to the wheels without changing the structure of the machine involved. Second, changes in the structure or pattern of the system itself are occurring all of the time along side of (and partly determined by) the performance processes of the system. These we may call the changes of learning, or the learning processes. It is as if the structure of the automobile's transmission system were being constantly changed while the engine is driving the car.

When the performance and learning processes of a system are interpreted (or categorized) in terms of the ways they solve the functional problems outlined in the previous section, they constitute the *mechanisms* of the personality system. The next sections will deal with these mechanisms as such and with their various classifications. There is, however, an important superordinate problem concerning mechanisms which depend entirely on the learning-performance distinction (when this is taken as relevant to the over-all problem of the system — the optimization of gratification). It is the controversial problem of the law of effect. Since all changes in personality systems are governed by the general prerequisite of maintaining the system (that is, of optimization of gratification), it is possible to interpret the effects of any of these processes in terms of the way it serves to solve or help solve this problem. This means that all processes are governed by what psychologists have termed the "law of effect." This says nothing more than has already been said; namely, that all processes can be interpreted in terms of what they do for the maintenance of the boundaries of the system (or, again, in terms of their contribution to the optimization of gratification).

The problem of the law of effect, however, breaks down into two problems based on the learning-versus-performance distinction. The "law of effect as a law of learning" is prominent in the psychology of the Yale school. The "law of effect as a law of performance" is prominent in the psychology of Tolman. The standard argument in psychology is whether the former is simply a derivative consequence of the latter (as is maintained by Tolman); or whether the latter is a derivative consequence of the former (as "law of effect" psychology maintains).[13] This question (even if the truth is all on one side, as may not be the case) need not concern us here; for in either case, we do have a "law of effect" in action and it crosscuts the distinction between learning changes and performance changes in systems of action. It is simply another way of saying that the system is a system in both its learning and performance processes.

There are still many controversial questions concerning the nature of the processes by which the outcome of action motivated by a given need-disposition serves to strengthen or weaken the disposition to repeat the action in future situations. There can, however, be no doubt that in a broad sense an orientation or action which has repeatedly led to more gratification than deprivation of drives and need-dispositions in a given type of situation is more likely to be repeated or strengthened than if the experience has been one of repeated deprivation. For our purposes this is the essential point about the law of effect. This point is particularly crucial to the theory of action because of its bearing on the significance of sanctions in interactive relations. It seems probable that many of the complications of the reinforcement problem relate to the interrelations of many need-dispositions in a system rather than to the conditions of strengthening or weakening a particular orientation tendency by virtue of its gratificatory significance to one need-disposition taken in abstraction from the operations of other need-dispositions. Our main reservations about some current learning theory are concerned with the implications of this hypothesis.

A particularly important case in point is the significance to ego of alter's attitudes as distinguished from alter's particular overt acts. The attitude of an alter is rarely a specific reward or punishment in the sense in which that term is used in learning theory. It usually constitutes an organized and generalized pattern under which many particular sanctions are subsumed. The generality of such an attitude as love or esteem renders it impossible for its relevance to

---

[13] Hull's statement would be that, since those actions which foster the maintenance of the system are *learned* at the expense of those which don't, performances which foster maintenance of the system tend to occur. Tolman would say that since the animal tends to do those things which he knows will foster the maintenance of the system, and since frequency of performance fosters learning, the animal therefore learns the things that foster the system better than those that don't.

be confined to a single need-disposition. Alter's attitude therefore affects a broad sector of ego's system of need-dispositions.

All of the processes we have discussed above can be categorized in terms of the way they serve to meet the problems of the system. When the processes of learning and performance are classified on the basis of the way they serve to meet the requirements of the system, they are termed mechanisms. That is, a process is a mechanism, insofar as it is viewed in terms of its relevance to the problems of the system.

Fig. 7 gives us a classification of the mechanisms of personality systems. We have three kinds of distinctions relevant to the classification of the mechanisms: (1) the distinction between the types of process that may be involved — thus mechanisms may be learning or performance mechanisms; (2) the distinction based on the phenomenological place of the problems involved — thus mechanisms may be relevant to external or internal problems; (3) the distinction based on the type of problem involved — thus mechanisms may be mechanisms of allocation or mechanisms of integration. It should be noted that each of these bases for classification cuts across the other two; thus there should be eight different types of mechanisms. We will take up below those portions of Fig. 7 (page 255) most relevant to the psychological problems of action.

The mechanisms of learning. Learning is perhaps best defined as the acquisition and extinction of orientation and action tendencies. Thus, for our purposes, the important learning mechanisms deal with acquisition or extinction or any other changes in habits of cognition, cathection, and evaluation (including changes in internalized value standards). We have already said that our term *mechanisms* of learning implies that there is a "law of effect" in the field of learning — that is, all mechanisms are in some sense functional with respect to the maintenance of the systems. Thus the learning mechanism must involve the acquisition of those tendencies which better maintain the system at the expense of those which are detrimental to the system.

The learning mechanisms may be analyzed into categories on the basis of whether they are chiefly cognitive, cathectic, or evaluative; or they may be classified as external, internal, allocative, integrative. The two methods of classification will in general accomplish the same thing, as external-integrative is almost equivalent to cathectic. Internal, integrative, and allocative is almost equivalent to evaluative. Actually, all learning occurs within the whole cognitive-cathectic-evaluative matrix; thus all of it involves some changes in all these aspects of motivational orientation. Similarly, all learning has ramifications for internal and external, allocative and integrative problems. The question of the primacy of one of the modes or categories has to do simply with which aspect of the orientation must undergo greatest change in order to solve the problem. The terms *cognitive, cathectic*,[14] *evaluative* define the aspects of orientation process which can be more or less independently varied. The terms *external, internal, integrative, allocative* define types of problems. The parallelism derives from the fact that the changes required to solve these different types of problems ordinarily take place mainly in the parallel aspect of the orientation. Thus external-integrative problems are always solved by a series of changes of orientation; *ordinarily* this series of changes (which will involve changes in all aspects of orientation) will involve most change in the cognitive aspect. We will discuss three different kinds of learning, (1) cognitive, (2) cathectic, and (3) evaluative: these will be different learning processes each of which involves changes in all aspects of orientation, but each of which involves most changes in that aspect after which it is named. And, owing to the considerations above, these three kinds of learning can be seen as also comprising (1) the external-integrative, (2) external-allocative, and (3) internal, integrative, and allocative mechanisms of learning.

First, let us take up the mechanisms of cognitive learning. We shall confine our consideration here to two, discrimination and generalization. The first concerns the cognition of differences between different objects and different attributes of the same objects in terms of the significance of these differences for the actor. Generalization is the process by which different objects and groups of them are classed together with respect to those properties which they have in common and which are significant to the orientation of action. These are both aspects of the "cognitive mapping" of the situation.

The cognitive mechanisms enter into all systems of action oriented toward objects because knowledge or cognitive orientation is inseparably associated with cathexis and evaluation, and the latter cannot occur without it. As we go on to discuss the other mechanisms of the personality system, we will see that generalization is a necessary condition for substitution and for many of the mechanisms of defense. It is a prerequisite for the emancipation from particular object attachments, as well as of any extensive capacity for instrumental manipulation of the situation.

Because of both the continual changes in the situation and the equally continual process of reorganization of the actor's own personality (need-disposition) system, nothing like a stable system of orientations would be possible without some capacity for flexibility in the transfer of orientations from one object to another. Thus, the learning process by which different objects are rendered functionally equivalent is essential to the establishment of systematic stability and equilibrium.

Similarly, because of the very different consequences which may ensue upon very slightly different situations, the personality system becomes sensitized to the very slight differences between objects which are indices of im-

---

[14] In learning, cognitive and cathectic are more independently variable than in performance. This is because an actor may retain his principles of grouping but learn to give the objects involved different cathexes (or their value as means or goals changes).

portant and big differences in consequences. Thus the learning process by which similar objects become discriminated on the basis of their radically different consequences is very important to the adjustment of the personality system to its environment.

Next, we take up the mechanisms of cathectic learning. Here we are faced with the problem of the choice of concrete objects (or classes of objects). A given need-disposition or combination of them has the alternative at any given time of remaining attached to the same objects or transferring cathexis to new objects. The process of transfer is called *substitution*. Substitution is the process of replacing one particular object of a given need-disposition by another, which may be in the same class or another class but which in terms of gratification of the need-disposition is to some degree the equivalent of the relinquished object. Particularly, of course, in the developmental process, object attachments which may be essential at one stage must be given up if a higher stage of personality organization is to be attained. Substitution is the mechanism by which this giving up and transfer to another object takes place. As in the case of other mechanisms, the concept substitution refers to the outcome in the working of the system of a class of processes. Even though certain regularities in such outcomes are known, much about the processes is obscure and can only be understood after much further research. In very general terms, however, we may say that there usually must be some combination of barriers to access or retention of the old object (which may be inhibitions or situational barriers) and, as well, positive incentives to cathect the new object. (All of which is to say that there is a law of effect operating here as there is everywhere in the mechanisms.)

Now let us turn to the mechanisms of evaluative learning. The expression of a need-disposition is not dependent on its own strength alone but also on its compatibility with other need-dispositions in the same system. Learning theory hitherto has rightly tended to treat the unimpeded carrying out of a motivational pattern as unproblematical. Where it has been impeded as a result of conflict with other need-dispositions, the term *inhibition* has been employed. The basic problem here is, of course, that of choice of need-dispositions to be satisfied. *Inhibition* refers to a very generalized aspect of this highly complex set of choice phenomena. The chief features of the concept are two: first, the checking of the impulse to release a need-disposition into action; second, the fact that the source of the inhibition is internal to the personality. The enormous significance of this mechanism comes directly from the nature of personality as a system which maintains distinctive patterns and boundaries. Incompatible motivational tendencies are inherently operative; unless the system had modes of protection against the potentially disruptive consequences of the conflicts involved, it could not function as a system.

This concludes our classification of the mechanisms of learning insofar as that classification is based upon the phenomenological place of problems, the type of problems, and the kind of learning processes chiefly responsible for solution of the problems. It should be noted, however, that the cognitive learning processes, generalization and discrimination, which taken together constitute the learning how to perceive and how to construct an integrated cognitive map of the situation, are the normal *learning* processes used in the solution of external-integrative problems. (Thus, whether the problem be one of conflict between two facts, between a fact and a need-disposition, or between two different role-expectations, if the problem is solved as an external problem,[15] and if it is solved by learning, its solution consists in learning new ways to perceive and thus new ways to manipulate the situation.) It should be noted too that the cathectic learning process, substitution, is the normal learning process used in the solution of external-allocative problems. (Thus, whenever there is a problem of how to distribute attention between different objects or events in the external world, if the problem is solved by learning, it constitutes the learning of a new cathexis, that is, the substitution of a new object of interest for an old.) Finally, it should be noted that the evaluative learning process (the learning of inhibition) is the normal learning process used in the solution of internal, allocative, and integrative problems, insofar as the problems require that one or several need-dispositions be held in check while others are being allowed gratification. (Thus, whenever there is a problem of conflict between two need-dispositions or a conflict over which need-dispositions should get most time and effort for the good of the organism, if the problem is solved by learning, its solution constitutes the learning of an order of inhibition whereby various need-dispositions may be inhibited by others.)

At this point we are going to take up a different method for classification of learning processes, which again cuts across all the classifications made above. We shall classify the learning processes on the basis of the kind of relationship which obtains between the learning actor and the environmental objects while the learning is going on. When classified on this basis, learning turns out to be "invention," "imitation," or "identification." The learning of cognitive, cathectic, and evaluative patterns can, any of them, be either invention, imitation, or identification. A need-disposition, as we have seen, is organized in terms of patterns of orientation. A personality confronts the problem of acquiring these patterns for itself by creating new ones, or by acquiring them from some existing pattern which serves as a model. In the former case we have invention. In the latter case, we have either imitation or identification (which are both ways that patterns may be acquired from social objects).

---

[15] Such problems can become internal problems, as we have said elsewhere, when the fact which conflicts with a need-disposition (which is negatively cathected in terms of that need disposition) arouses that need-disposition into active conflict with other need-dispositions active at the same time. When this happens, the problem is internal, and if it is solved by a learning process, the process is an evaluative learning process.

In the case of invention, the actor has no specific "learning-relevant" relationship with another social object during learning. That is, he has no model for either imitation or identification. He has run into a problem which requires a new pattern (because the old pattern has got the system into some sort of problem), so he simply tries different patterns until one of them solves the problem. Invention may be either trial-and-error learning, in which the actor tries new patterns at random until one of them works; or it may be "insight" learning in which the actor constructs a new pattern systematically on the basis of several old ones.

The two major mechanisms for the learning of patterns from social objects are *imitation*, which assumes only that alter provides a model for the specific pattern learned without being an object of a generalized cathectic attachment; and *identification*, which implies that alter is the object of such an attachment and therefore serves as a model not only with respect to a specific pattern in a specific context of learning but also as model in a generalized sense. Alter becomes, that is, a model for general orientations, not merely for specific patterns.

With imitation and identification we come to the distinctive part played by social objects in learning. Knowledge and other patterns *may* be acquired through independent discovery by the actor himself. But more frequently knowledge is taken over from other actors.[16] (This is the type of learning that forms the basis of the cultural accumulation of knowledge — and of other cultural orientations as well.) The acquisition of patterns in such a fashion (like all learning), is instrumental to fulfilling certain requirements of the personality system (or of the need-dispositions which are subsystems). Thus, we may say that all such learning must be motivated in the sense that it must result from some need-disposition tendency of the personality (or from some tendency generated by a problem of the system as a whole).

It is possible and common for ego to be motivated to acquire a specific pattern from alter without any attachment to alter extending beyond this particular process of acquisition. Alter thus is significant only as an object from which the pattern is acquired. It is the pattern not the attitudes of alter as a person which is the object of cathexis. Alter is only its bearer. This is the meaning of the term *imitation*. Imitation is very prominent in the acquisition of various specific elements of culture, such as specific knowledge, technical skills, and so forth. It is much less important in the acquisition of more general patterns of orientation, such as standards of taste, fundamental philosophical or ethical outlooks, and above all, patterns of value-orientation.

---

[16] The relation of ego to the alter from whom he learns a cultural pattern need not involve direct personal contact. He may for example read a book which alter has written. This mediation by independent physical embodiments of culture adds only a further elaboration of the same fundamental elements which enter into learning through direct personal contact and need not be analyzed here.

By *identification,* on the other hand, we mean the acquisition of *generalized* patterns of orientation motivated by an attachment to a social object. An attachment, as we noted in the last chapter, develops at the point where not only alter's specific acts are significant to ego as sanctions but where by generalization ego has become sensitive to alter's attitudes toward him as a person, to his responsiveness when it takes the form of granting or withholding his approval, love, or esteem. In this case the object is not the cultural *possessions* of alter — what he *has* — but alter himself as a person — what he *is*. The cultural patterns acquired by ego are in fact, as we have seen, part of alter's personality. They are patterns that alter has internalized. It is, however, the characteristic feature of cultural patterns as objects that, being systems of symbols, they are transmissible. Ego cannot himself become alter, nor can any part of alter's personality so become part of ego's personality that it is lost to alter — in the way, for example, in which a particular article of clothing once worn by alter cannot, if worn by ego, simultaneously be worn by alter. An orientation *pattern,* however, can be adopted without necessitating a change in alter's personality.

When alter is cathected *as a person,* as distinguished from specific attributes, possessions, or actions, we speak of an *attachment.* (Alter as a person is a complex constellation of attributes, possessions, and actions, significant in a multiplicity of aspects which focus on the significance of his attitudes.) An attachment thus exists when alter possesses a general significance as an object for ego, when not merely his specific acts, qualities, and possessions are significant to ego. This generalized significance for ego focuses on ego's concern with alter's attitudes toward him, and it underlies the development of a need-disposition to attain and maintain certain types of such attitudes. For example, instead of the specific gratification of a hunger need being the focus of the significance of the mother, her provision of food becomes generalized into an appropriate expression of her love or approval. Once the retention of such a favorable attitude has become important for ego, it is possible for other actors to impose frustrations of particular needs and to have them accepted as long as they can gratify the need to retain the favorable attitude.

Because of the element of generality in attachments, the patterns of value-orientation taken over through identification are necessarily *generalized* patterns of orientation. They are not *specific* skills or perceptions or appreciative judgments. The patterns of cultural value-orientation, because of their generality, are acquired for the most part through identification. Specific skills, appreciative judgments, and cognitive propositions, however, are often acquired *by imitation* within the framework of an identification. The imitative process may be greatly facilitated by its coincidence with identification.[17]

[17] It should be borne in mind that because our knowledge of the mechanisms consists of empirical generalizations, no definitive list can be drawn up. The number of such mechanisms into which it is convenient to divide the empirical problems involved is a conse-

The patterns acquired through identification are general patterns of orientation which vary as a function of variations in the character of the underlying attachments. These variations we shall analyze in terms of the two basic pattern variables for motivational orientation: specificity-diffuseness and affectivity-neutrality. The four combinations of the values of these two variables define the major types of attitude on alter's part, the security of which can become the primary focus of ego's attachment to alter.

This concludes our discussion of the mechanisms of learning. The mechanisms of allocation and integration will be discussed below. This discussion may have relevance to some of the mechanisms of learning, when these are taken in their broader context as mechanisms of allocation and integration (including learning and performance processes) rather than merely as learning mechanisms. Nevertheless, since learning has been covered here, the ensuing discussion will tend to emphasize the performance mechanisms of allocation and integration.

The mechanisms of allocation. The structure of personality is the result of a cumulative process of commitments between the alternatives of orientation and their consequences for defense or resolution within the system, and *adjustment* to the situation. Each possible alternative selection point confronts the actor with a situation in which he cannot perform two conflicting actions simultaneously. There are inherent limitations on what is possible, arising from the nature of alternatives and the consequences attending commitment to them. The choice of one of a pair of alternatives not only excludes the other alternative but it also affects the direction of choice in other categories as well.

The result of these limitations is the necessity for an *allocative distribution* among the possibilities which are logically open. By allocation we mean the processes by which the action of a system is distributed among its different parts in such a way that the conditions necessary for the maintenance of the system, or an orderly pattern of change, are met. Allocative distribution in the personality system may be analyzed into two constituent distributions, the importance of each of which is inherent in the structure of the action system. The first is external allocation — the distribution of object-selections or event-selections relative to any *particular* need-disposition. (The distribution of time and effort to different need-dispositions is primarily an internal problem; thus the choice of one event or occasion over another may be an internal rather than an external allocative problem, unless both events are cathected by

---

quence of the structure of the system and the functional "problems" of the system. But it is also a function of the state of theoretical knowledge at the time. An advance in the latter may well make it necessary to make a distinction which had not previously been current, or make it possible to consolidate two mechanisms which it had previously been necessary to treat separately. As an illustration of the former change, the mechanism of identification seems to have entered the picture as a result of Freud's discoveries of the ways in which the significant object-relations of childhood lay at the foundation of an individual's unconscious "self-image." Before Freud the empirically crucial problem covered by the concept of identification was not in the field of psychological attention.

the same need-disposition and are mutually exclusive for some nontemporal reason. The distribution of cathexis in terms of place and context is simply a subhead of distribution among objects; since objects, in the last analysis, are constituted by their place or context.) The second is internal allocation — the distribution of gratification opportunities among *different* need-dispositions.

We will take up internal allocation first, because it constitutes the more important of the two allocative mechanisms for personality systems. Need-dispositions relative to the object world become organized into a differentiated structure. A variety of specific need-dispositions (for gratifications, for love from particular types of objects, for approval for particular qualities or per-formances, etc.) develop from the original drives and energy of the organism in interaction with the situation. It is inherent to motivational phenomena that there is a drive for more gratification than is realistically possible, on any level or in any type of personality organization. Likewise it is inherent to the world of objects that not all potentially desirable opportunities can be realized within a human life span. Therefore, any personality must involve an organi-zation that allocates opportunities for gratification, that systematizes preced-ence relative to the limited possibilities. The possibilities of gratification, simultaneously or sequentially, of all need-dispositions are severely limited by the structure of the object system and by the intra-systemic incompatibility of the consequences of gratifying them all. The gratification of one need-disposition beyond a certain point is only possible at the cost of other need-dispositions which are important in the same personality.[18]

Next, we turn to external allocation. Each particular need-disposition generally involves a more or less definite set of cathexes to particular objects or classes of objects. Hence the allocation of objects is very closely associated with the allocation of gratifications. Nevertheless, it is desirable to distinguish the allocation of object choices relative to a need-disposition as another of the functional problems of a personality system. Certain types of commitments to one object preclude assignment of the same significance to another object. For example, if there is to be a plurality of objects of sexual attachment, certain features of an exclusive attachment to one object become impossible. Even though a need-disposition for a certain *type* of object relationship has been granted precedence, the allocation of the relevant cathexes between ap-propriate particular objects is still a problem which requires solution if the system is to operate.[19]

The allocative aspect [20] of the organization of the total need-disposition system (i.e., of the personality system) is in a sense the "negative" aspect of

[18] Therefore, the allocation of opportunities for gratification between different need-dispositions is as fundamental to personalities as the allocation of wealth-getting or power-getting opportunities between persons, or classes of persons, is to social systems.
[19] The fact that ego is in competition with other actors for objects, especially the response of social objects, is of course fundamental to this aspect of the allocative problem.
[20] It is this allocative aspect which Freud called the "economic."

its selectivity. It designates the structure arising in consequence of the necessity of being committed to only one of each of a number of pairs of intrinsically desirable alternatives and thus rejecting, or relegating to a lesser place, the other alternative of the pair. The second major aspect of the systemic structure is the integration (into a system) of the various elements which have been allocated. The allocative and integrative aspects of the personality system are complementary. The allocative commitments distribute time and attention among various need-dispositions, objects, and so forth. This distribution is regulated by the over-all requirements of the personality system; once the distribution of functions has been made, each of the need-dispositions constitutes a subsystem with its own systemic requirements. This introduces the possibility of conflict; integrative mechanisms prevent or alleviate conflict. We next turn our attention to them.

The mechanisms of integration. As we have said, integration is a function peculiar to the class of systems which maintain distinctive internal properties within boundaries. In such a system certain processes become differentiated as mechanisms which solve actual conflicts and prevent threatened conflicts by integrating the internal variables with one another and by integrating the whole system with the situation outside of it. In relation to personality, therefore, integrative mechanisms have two main classes of functions. The first is the integration of the subsystems created by the allocation of functions into one over-all system. This involves the forestalling of potential conflicts and minimizing their disruptive consequences for the system when they arise. This class of functions is handled by what we have called the *internal integrative mechanisms.* They are also sometimes called the mechanisms of *defense.* The second class of functions is the adjustment of the system as a whole to threatened (or actual) conflicts between it and the external environment. This class of functions is handled by what we have called the *external integrative mechanisms.* They are also sometimes called the mechanisms of *adjustment.*

We will discuss first the *mechanisms of defense.* These, as we have said, handle conflicts between different need-dispositions. Though many features of conflict between need-dispositions are specific to the particular need-dispositions concerned and the particular situation, there are certainly general properties of conflict and the response to it which we can analyze here.

Before we can give a complete discussion of these general properties of conflict and the responses to it, however, we must introduce the problem of fear. Although fear is in fact out of place here, as it is one of the chief problems of *external* integration, we must nevertheless discuss it briefly because it is the genetic antecedent of several important problems of internal integration. (It will be discussed further when we take up the external-integrative mechanisms.) Fear is the cognition and cathexis of a negatively cathected fact in the external world. Since all cognition-cathexes have a temporal dimension (that is, they are expectancies) we can say that fear is the cognition of an expected deprivation. The negatively cathected object (that is, the expected deprivation) is placed phenomenologically in the external world. Thus fear is an important antecedent to the mechanisms of external integration; it may be seen as a superordinate situational antecedent for a whole set of mechanisms of adjustment. For our present purposes, we must show the relationships of fear to pain and anxiety, both of which are relevant to mechanisms of internal integration. Anxiety is internalized fear. That is, when a fear of deprivation has been experienced often, the organism develops a need-disposition to avoid the objects involved and to avoid the situations in which the fear arises. The arousal of these internalized fears constitutes anxiety.

Pain is the actual deprivation of need-dispositions (fear is only an expectancy of that deprivation; anxiety is a specific need-disposition aimed at avoiding even the fear of deprivation). Both anxiety and pain are problems of internal integration.[21] An aroused anxiety need-disposition conflicts with other need-dispositions; it constitutes an internal threat to the system. Similarly, any deprived need-disposition conflicts with the requirements for the functioning of the system and constitutes an internal threat to the system. Finally, any internal conflict, whether generated by a specific anxiety, a specific deprivation, or simply a recurrent conflict between need-dispositions, generates its own "anxiety" need-disposition which constitutes, now, a need to avoid the conflict. In this last sense anxiety may be interpreted as a warning signal within the system for the personality to mobilize its resources in order to meet any threatened conflict and minimize disruptive consequences. It is a universal correlate and condition of activation of the mechanisms of defense.

Complete resolution of a threatened conflict would necessitate modification of either one or both of the relevant need-dispositions so that in relation to the exigencies of the situation no deprivation would be imposed. *Resolution* in this sense is continually going on in normal personalities and should authentically be called the first mechanism of defense. It may well be that cognitive generalization plays a particularly important part in the process. A variety of other processes may be involved in resolution. The strength of one or both of the need-dispositions may be altered so one gives way. Their structure may be changed to eliminate the particular strains. Objects or occasions may be reallocated.

The resolution is always accomplished by giving primacy to one or the other (or to some superordinate value) of the conflicting need-dispositions. Thus normal resolution may be seen as always involving choice, which, as we have shown, is based on values and the pattern variables. Therefore, evaluation itself might be seen as the normal mechanism of defense.

Frequently, however, the strength and rigidity of either or both sides are too great for much or full resolution to take place. Then special mechanisms

---

[21] Pain may also be a problem of external integration, as will be seen.

of defense are resorted to. Before we continue, we must introduce a digression to explain the nature of our list of these special mechanisms. The reader will remember that we held the distinction between external and internal integrative problems to be roughly parallel to the distinction between the cognitive and evaluative aspects of orientation. This parallelism, we said, was due to the fact that external integrative problems were usually solved by changes in the cognitive aspect of orientation and internal integrative problems by changes in the evaluative aspects of orientation. This parallelism held up fairly well in discussion of the learning mechanisms. Also, in our discussion of the allocative mechanisms, the external allocative mechanisms involved chiefly changes in evaluative procedures. Finally, the normal performance aspect of the internal integrative mechanisms (that is, the resolution of conflicts between need-dispositions by application of standards of primacy relations based on pattern-variable choices) were evaluative, as they should be according to our parallelism. As we will see later, the normal external integrative mechanisms will involve chiefly cognitive changes, as they should according to the parallelism. The abnormal or rigid internal mechanisms, however, apparently are not open to interpretation in these parallelistic terms. This seems to be owing to the fact that the problems of conflict, which are actually internal conflicts between need-dispositions and are thus internal problems, are often not recognized by the actor as internal problems at all. On the contrary, they are often localized by him in the external world, and thus solved as though they were external problems of integration. We are forced to make a choice: we see that phenomenologically they seem to be problems of adjustment for the subject involved; yet we know that there is behavior which indicates a real (although perhaps subconscious) subjective awareness that these are internal problems.

Thus we list all of the mechanisms aimed at the resolution of internal problems as mechanisms of defense, even though we know that the actor-subject is not always aware that these are mechanisms for the resolution of internal problems. It will be remembered that external integrative problems are resolved primarily by cognitive changes; this will be seen to hold true when we take up the mechanisms of adjustment. It was said that internal integrative problems are solved largely by evaluative changes; it will be seen in the following paragraphs that many if not most internal integrative problems are so distorted as to constitute seemingly external integrative problems for the actor. Therefore, most of the mechanisms which solve them will involve primarily changes in the cognitive sphere.

Here we will simply list and define briefly each of the special mechanisms of defense.

First is *rationalization*. This involves a distorted perception by the actor of the relation which obtains between his need-dispositions and the goal of an action. The goal is "seen" to be relevant to (and cathected by) one set of need-dispositions (need-dispositions of which the person is proud — often his values). Actually the goal is cathected by another set of need-dispositions, which are not even seen to be operative in this situation. Usually the need-dispositions which are kept out of the picture would come into conflict with some value need-dispositions of the actor if they were allowed in the picture. Thus a conflict is averted by the technique of rationalization. Although this mechanism is primarily a method for handling problems generated by internal conflicts, the problem often appears to the actor as one of adjustment. Ego is threatened by the negatively cathected perception of himself (if he sees himself as possessing a characteristic which he does not like, he will be constantly uncomfortable in the presence of the perceived trait, which, by definition, constitutes a deprivation). Therefore, ego chooses to distort the facts so that he may perceive himself as a cathected object. The problem can be perceived as an external problem by ego, because of the fact that ego as actor can perceive himself as an object. Rationalization occasionally arises as a purely *adjustive* mechanism (i.e., dealing with really external problems) when it is used as a method of distorting a negatively cathected fact that really arises out of the external world (as when one justifies something which he wants to believe with sophistic arguments).

Second is *isolation*. This is the refusal to cognize and cathect an object in terms of one need-disposition, A, while it is being cognized and cathected in terms of another conflicting need-disposition, B. Thus an overt conflict between A and B is avoided. This involves a distorted perception of the object which will obscure its relevance to A.

Third is *displacement*. This is the removal of the positive cathexis implanted by need-disposition A from an object which is negatively cathected by need-disposition B; and the attachment of that positive cathexis to a new object which is not negatively cathected. This is nothing more than substitution, which has already been discussed, under conditions of conflict and for the purpose of resolving conflict.

Fourth is *fixation*. This is the obverse of displacement. It is the compulsive retention of a cathexis on the least threatening object in order to avoid some conflict that would be engendered by the substitution that would normally occur in the development of the personality.

Fifth is *repression*. Repression involves the destroying of internal systematic interconnections between some threatening need-disposition and the rest of the system; this is accompanied by radical repression of the offending need-disposition. The threatening need-disposition is cut off from normal internal interdependence with the rest of the personality system and at the same time it is denied direct gratification.

Sixth is *reaction formation*. This is a special case of repression. When the threat is originally engendered by a conflict between two need-dispositions, the more threatening of the two is repressed, and the one with which it conflicted is reinforced.

Seventh is *projection*. This is a combination of repression, reaction formation, and rationalization, in a special fashion. Ego represses a threatening motive and reinforces the motive which did not allow tolerance for the repressed motive, just as in the case of reaction formation. Then ego refuses to see himself as possessing the repressed motive, and he explains the anxiety generated by the repression by seeing alter as possessing the motive which he cannot tolerate. Thus, the "reaction" need-disposition (the one that does not allow tolerance) can negatively cathect alter instead of implanting a negative cathexis on ego himself, which would involve continual deprivation and pain.

These are the principal classical mechanisms of defense.[22] In each case normal learning mechanisms are operative with the addition of special features imposed by the situation of conflict, in consequence of which modifications of both intensity and direction occur. If full resolution of conflicts fails, the other mechanisms of defense reduce conscious anxiety and otherwise minimize the disruptive potentialities of conflict. But at the same time, this is possible only at the cost of impairment of potential activities, which will be severe according to the degree of failure of full resolution. The overt manifestations of these impairments of function are the symptoms of psychopathological disorders.

The consequences of the mechanisms of defense, which are operative to some degree in every personality, are the introduction of a set of modifications of the need-dispositions.

The *mechanisms of adjustment* solve external integrative problems. Here we are confronted with problems of two types: there may be conflicts between facts, or there may be conflicts between facts and need-dispositions. In the first case (which is less important for the whole personality system) we have a conflict between two possible ways of perceiving (i.e. cognizing) the external world; and since the actions of the actor are determined by his orientations, these conflicting facts bring about impulses to conflicting actions.

The latter case, which is of prime importance for personality systems, involves what we called the conflict between a fact and a need-disposition. How, one may ask, can a fact conflict with a need-disposition? For our purposes, a fact is nothing more than the cognition of an object or an event. It has simply the status of any phenomenological object. An object can be said to conflict with a need-disposition whenever it is negatively cathected. Any need-disposition which implants negative cathexes on anything (and it seems that all need-dispositions negatively cathect some deprivational objects) constitutes a tendency to withdraw from or to abolish the deprivational phenomenological object. In the case of a negatively cathected fact, the tendency of the need-disposition is to change those facts which conflict with it. Facts can

---

[22] Sublimation is not a special mechanism of defense in this sense but a special case of the normal learning mechanism of substitution. It may, of course, play a highly important part in resolution of conflicts.

be changed by means of actions that change the actual relations between objects and thus change the perception of those relations (the perceptions being the facts) ; or facts can be changed by merely distorting the perceptions of the relations between objects without really altering the relations at all. In either case the problem is solved by constructing a new set of perceptions in which the "facts" cognized are no longer in conflict with the need-dispositions; that is, by bringing about a situation where the negatively cathected facts are not cognized. Insofar as there is a personality problem here, it is chiefly a problem of altering the cognitive aspect of the orientation.

Every personality problem, of course, involves need-dispositions, and thus it involves cognitions and cathexes and (usually) evaluations too. The question in classifying the problems, however, is this: which aspects of the orientation (and the system too, since every change in the orientation is at least a superficial change in the system) is chiefly important in the changes which must be made to solve the problem.

Usually conflicts between need-dispositions and facts are of a rather superficial nature, in that the fact is not an actual deprivation of the need-disposition but rather simply a threat of deprivation — something instrumental to deprivation which, if allowed to continue, might result in actual deprivation. Such problems can be solved by changing the facts before the negatively-cathected threat of deprivation brings about the deprivation itself. If the threatened deprivation is not counteracted, actual deprivation may ensue, bringing about actual pain. In this case the deprived need-disposition comes into conflict with other need-dispositions and with the system as a whole by blocking normal process. At this point, the problem is no longer external but internal, and the mechanisms of defense come into operation to defend the system against the perseveration of the injured need-disposition (better amputate the diseased element than give up the whole system).

It can be seen that the entire discussion above may be interpreted as a discussion of fear. Whenever a perceived fact constitutes the threat of deprivation of one of the need-dispositions, then we have what we called fear. Thus, we can say that the mechanisms of adjustment are ways of doing away with fears, or with actual deprivations, by changing the relationships which are seen to obtain between the personality and the world of objects (chiefly, for our purposes, social objects). Also, referring back to the beginning of this section, we may say they are ways of solving conflicts between facts themselves.

Let us discuss briefly the method for adjudicating conflicts between two factual propositions, before we go on to discuss the methods for solving conflicts between facts and need-dispositions. The normal method for adjudicating conflicts between dissonant cognitive elements within one orientation is "reality testing." This has to do with allowing the law of effect to operate, insofar as it applies to the acceptance or rejection of cognitions in both learning and performance. It is the external equivalent of the internal tendency toward optimum gratification in the sense that it represents an adjudication of the various possibilities of cognition. It is the descriptive term for the process of selecting objects of attention, focusing on some and avoiding others as possibilities for gratification and dangers of deprivation. Like other functions this cognitive system is oriented to the future as well as the present. What it does is to adjudicate conflicts between different possible cognitions by looking into the future to see which actually serves to guide action in a fashion which is most gratifying and least deprivational in the long run.

Reality-testing is functionally crucial to the personality system as a link between the system and the situation. It imposes limits on the variability of action. It allows the actor to group objects in terms of their expected outcomes, and thus to stabilize, in some sense, the outcomes he gets from interaction with objects.

When we come to problems of conflict between facts and need-dispositions, a learning process similar to reality-testing provides the normal method for their resolution. The actor must learn to perceive new relationships which will guide action in such a fashion as to avoid the deprivation. This is the problem of inventing and learning new patterns of perception. For example, when ego is in some immediate danger, he must find some relationship — usually causal — between some event he knows how to produce by his own action and the event that he wants, that is, the averting of the calamity. He does this by reality-testing his invented patterns until one of them succeeds in avoiding the deprivation.

The normal techniques of adjustment are parallel to the normal mechanisms of defense (which involve simple evaluative choices based upon the pattern variables). As was true in that case, so it is true here that there are certain cases where rigidity prevents normal resolution of conflicts and thus gives rise to special mechanisms of adjustment. The cases where rigidity prevents normal external integration arise chiefly when the actor suffers real or threatened deprivation of cathected relationships with social objects. Four major types of problems are possible here. At this point the pattern variables enter the picture in a new way. They define certain typical problems of adjustment to which the personality is exposed in its relations to the social objects of the situation. These problems derive from the conditions required for the fulfillment of the four main types of need-dispositions arrived at in the table which cross-classified affectivity-neutrality with specificity-diffuseness. Each of these kinds of need-disposition presents the personality with a special kind of problem of adjustment. We will discuss these main types of need-dispositions only in terms of their relevance in mediating attachments to social objects.

First is the need-disposition that results from the combination of specificity and affectivity. This constitutes the case where the actor is striving for immediate specific gratification vis-à-vis an object. If there is no internal barrier to gratification, the primary factor on which gratification depends is the availability of the appropriate specific objects. A problem is occasioned by absence, or threatened deprivation, of the specific objects. Anxiety focuses on this possibility.[23] The need-disposition may, of course, cope with such a threat actively or passively.

Second is the need-disposition that derives from the combination of diffuseness and affectivity. This constitutes the case where the actor strives for love or affection. Here the problem is that of maintaining the security of the attachment, including the dependability of alter's attitude of diffuse love or affection.

Third is the need-disposition that derives from the combination of neutrality with specificity. This constitutes the case where the actor strives for approval by alter. Here again the problem is that of the availability of the appropriate object, which this time is the attitude of approval of alter. These attitudes may be actively sought, or they may be passively "hoped for."

Fourth is the need-disposition that derives from the combination of neutrality with diffuseness. This constitutes the case where the actor strives for esteem by alter. Here the problem is that of possible loss of esteem by alteration of ego's relationship to the object. It is not ego's immediate gratification opportunities which are threatened; rather, the danger is that ego will not fulfill his obligations to alter, these obligations being the conditions of future gratifications. Alter's attitudes, again, are of paramount significance. This time it is not a question of alter's approval of specific acts or qualities but of his esteem for ego as a person.

In all of these problems, the threat on which anxiety is focused is the possible disturbance of ego's cathected relationship to alter as an object. To resolve these problems, to cope with these threats, there are two fundamentally opposite directions in which ego's need-dispositions can be modified. Ego may intensify his motivation to retain and consolidate the relationship or he may accept the possibility of its relinquishment. The intensification of the need to retain the attachment to alter as an object results in *dependency*. If, on the other hand, the path of relinquishment is taken, we may speak of *compulsive independence*, which may concretely involve a reaction formation to dependency needs. When selections have been made from these alternatives, the question whether the search for security by retention or relinquishment is to be sought by active or passive devices still remains.

With this introductory discussion complete, we may now proceed to classify the special mechanisms of adjustment, which are all applicable to the four major types of problems of adjustment to social objects.

When ego chooses to cope with the threat by striving to retain the relationship with alter, we may speak of *dominance* as the active alternative and

[23] It is lack of receptiveness and/or responsiveness on which anxiety focuses.

submission as the passive alternative. Dominance thus means mitigation of the danger of loss or deprivation engendered by ego's attempting actively to control the object on which he is dependent or with whose expectation he must conform. Submission, on the other hand, seeks to forestall unfavorable reactions of alter by ego's ingratiating himself with alter and fulfilling his wishes. This presumably must be correlated with the renunciation of one set of ego's conflicting needs, a renunciation which may be possible only through the operation of the mechanisms of defense. Indeed, from one point of view the mechanisms of adjustment as ways of coping with threats or relations to objects must always have their counterparts in mechanisms of defense as ways of coping with threats arising within ego's own personality. This complementary relationship is inherent in the kind of significance and importance which object attachments have for the whole personality. It follows from this that the most strategic need-dispositions are those which mediate the reciprocal attachments.

Turning to the case of willingness to relinquish the attachment to alter, we again find the corresponding possibilities. *Aggressiveness* is the active alternative and *withdrawal* the passive. Aggressiveness is basically the need-disposition to get rid of a noxious object — to take active steps to render the object's noxious activities impossible. This may or may not entail what is ordinarily considered injury to or destruction of the object; it may be limited to the prevention of certain activities. The case where injury to the object is positively cathected is a further complication of aggressiveness; it may be called *sadism*. Withdrawal scarcely needs comment. It is renunciation of the object, accompanied either by inhibition of the need-disposition (which may require repression) or substitution of a new object (which may involve displacement). The logical relations of these four primary mechanisms of adjustment are shown in Fig. 8 (page 256).

As in the case of sadism, dynamic relations between the mechanisms of defense and of adjustment may be established from which many of the clinically familiar patterns of motivation may be derived. For example, masochism may be treated as involving the combination of submission as a primary pattern of adjustment with strong elements of guilt-feeling and hence a need-disposition to accept suffering. This combination may in turn favor a positive cathexis (e.g., in erotic terms) of certain states of suffering at the hands of an object of attachment. Or, to take another example, compulsive independence taking the passive form of withdrawal from love attachments may be combined with expression of a dependency need in the affectively neutral form of a compulsive need for approval.

The outcome of such motivational combinations may be a selective orientation as between the different types of attachment as formulated in terms of the basic pattern-variable combinations of Fig. 3. Thus a need to secure specific approval through dominance will pose quite different problems of execution from those entailed in a need to ensure an attitude of diffuse love on alter's part. To carry out all these possibilities would involve us in far too much classificatory detail for present purposes.

Before leaving these questions it is important to emphasize again that there are processes of *resolution* in this area as there were in the sphere of internal integration. The actor's relation to his world of objects is, in fact, continually changing, and adjustments to these changes must continually be made. So far as this adjustment is carried out without manifestation of strain or conflict, it is to be regarded *as a process of learning* and the normal mechanisms of learning will operate. There will be not only in the developmental period but throughout life a continual succession of new reinforcements and extinctions, inhibitions, substitutions, imitations, and identifications. The *special* mechanisms of adjustment come into operation only when the normal learning mechanisms fail to operate without strain, when the resolution is incomplete or absent.

The process of internal integration and situational adjustment are, as noted, interdependent with each other. A new adjustment problem which cannot be resolved by normal learning processes creates a strain that reacts not merely on one or two need-dispositions but has repercussions in the system of need-dispositions. If in turn these repercussions, which will always create some conflicts, cannot be adequately resolved, mechanisms of defense will come into operation. Conversely, the operation of a defense mechanism arising out of an internal conflict will create in the need-dispositions concerned needs either to intensify some of their cathexes or to withdraw them. Unless these needs can be fully inhibited, the result will be the intensification or creation of a problem of adjustment, which in turn may activate or intensify a mechanism of defense. Thus the processes of resolution, of defense, and of adjustment are all mutually interdependent.

Anxiety, as we have seen, is the danger signal given by anticipations of danger to the equilibrium of the personality from within. There are other dimensions of a diffuse feeling of dysphoria. One type of special significance to our study is that manifested in relation to ego's own violation (actual or anticipated as possible) of value standards which he has internalized. Here the relation to the internal integration of personality, on the one hand, and to situational objects, on the other, is significant. Such a dysphoric feeling directed toward ego's own internalized standards, in such a way that he himself is the judge, may be called *guilt*. If, on the other hand, the orientation is toward alter's reaction, according to what are interpreted to be his standards of approval or esteem, it may be called *shame*. If finally it is concerned *only* with *overt* consequences which will be injurious to ego, it is *fear*.

In the preceding section we have been discussing certain complex need-dispositions engendered by the problem of maintaining the level of gratification in the face of threats from within the personality and outside it. We have said nothing about the possibility of these need-dispositions becoming dominant features in the integration of the personality system. It is to this that we wish to give our attention at this point.

The personality system is an organized set of primary and complex need-dispositions which are related to one another in a hierarchical way. Certain of the need-dispositions are generalized and fused with more specific need-dispositions. Thus, such need-dispositions as aggressiveness, dominance, submissiveness, and so on, might find release simultaneously with more specific need-dispositions; for example need-dispositions for love, achievement, erotic gratification. This simultaneous gratification of several need-dispositions gives unity to the personality system. It provides what Murray has called the "unity thema"; but it does more than provide a unified pattern of orientation. It is also an allocative and integrative factor.

Integration, however, is not a homogeneous phenomenon. We may speak of total integration and subintegration. Subintegrations are groupings of need-dispositions around certain objects or classes of objects or around object or occasion modalities.[24] Particular sets of need-dispositions will be activated and gratified by certain objects; that is, they will press for release and will be released without disruptive conflict with their "co-operative" need-dispositions in connection with certain objects. Insofar as several need-dispositions (whatever their level of complexity) are simultaneously gratified in a stable recurrent manner about particular objects, object classes, or modalities, we shall speak of subintegrations (regardless of whether the simultaneous gratification is accompanied by resolution or by some mechanism of defense or adjustment).

These partial integrations within the personality structure are built up in the course of particular sequences of experience (experiences of action and interaction in a situation). They acquire a kind of relative independence in their functioning, a "functional autonomy." The situation which provokes one of the constituent need-dispositions of the integration system also provokes the others. Each subsystem, so far as it has become an integrated system, becomes a unitary need-disposition, itself, with its appropriate gratifications, more complex in structure and with wider systemic connections and ramifications than more elementary need-dispositions (e.g., for love, esteem, etc.). Through their repercussions in the personality system these subsystems may either indirectly or directly produce real conflicts with other subintegrations.

---

[24] A compulsive fixation on time-allocation is a familiar phenomenon. Special significance of particular places, such as a home, is also an example.

A subintegration such as a need-disposition for passively received love might come into conflict with some other need-disposition, primary or complex, or with another subintegration such as the compulsive need for independence from authority. Thus conflict might be dealt with by allocative resolution, as by the selection of love objects and sources which neither exercise nor symbolize authority; or it might be dealt with by some defense mechanism such as repression or reaction formation. With the mastery of conflicts between subintegrations of need-dispositions, we return to the phenomenon of the total integration of the personality system.

Again the hierarchical organization of need-dispositions plays a central part. One generalized complex need-disposition is especially significant here: namely, that built around the self-collectivity orientation alternative.

There are two primary aspects of this integration about collectively shared values. In the first place the values of the collectivity themselves define areas of control and areas of permissiveness. That is, there are areas in which ego is expected to be guided by considerations constitutive of his membership in the collectivity, and other areas of permissiveness, within which he is free to act and choose independently of obligations of membership. This distinction will exist with respect to every institutionalized role definition and normally will become incorporated into personality structure in the form of a generalized need-disposition, usually called a "sense of obligation." It will be a need-disposition to conform with institutional expectations. Insofar as ego's personality structure is integrated with and by such collective value-expectations which impose obligations upon him, we will speak of "superego-integration." When, in addition to the integration with collective values the area of permission to pursue his own interests and/or values irrespective of (*not* in conflict with) role-obligations in collectivities is included, we will speak of "ego-integration."

This distinction between modes of personality integration relative to collectivity membership obligations should be clearly distinguished from another set which is also important in the analysis of such obligations: "conformative" and "alienative" need-dispositions. The latter, exceedingly crucial distinction concerns in the first instance the articulation of the personality system with the role structure of the social system; it stresses the involvement of role structure (in one crucial respect) in the structure of personality. The value patterns institutionalized in the role-expectations of ego's roles may become an integrated part of his own personality structure, in which case he will have a need-disposition to conform with the expectations of the role in question. On the other hand, this integration may be absent, and he may have one of a number of possible types of need-disposition to avoid, or to rebel against, conformity with such expectations. A need-disposition to conformity or alienation acquires a special compulsive force when in addition to or in place of the general need-disposition there develops a specific anxiety about the attitudes of the object.

It should be clear from the whole foregoing analysis that a personality does not have in a simple sense *one* homogeneous "superego," but precisely because he is involved in a multiplicity of roles in as many collectivities, he has several superego-integrations in his personality. Very frequently the most important internal as well as external conflicts are not between obligations imposed by a general collective value system and "self-interest" but between the obligations of different roles, that is, between the constituent, more or less specific, need-dispositions in the superego. The actor is put in the position of having to sacrifice one or the other or some part of each. This is an authentically internal personality conflict, and not merely a conflict over the possible "external" consequences of sanctions; as such it is extremely important.

A certain trend of thought tends to treat personality simply as a cluster of what in the present terms would be called superego-integrations. The importance of this aspect of personality is indeed great, but it alone is not adequate and would introduce serious biases unless related to other aspects. Not only does there seem to be much evidence for the importance of areas of sheer gratificatory autonomy without reference to any role obligation, but also it is within the area of autonomy vis-à-vis defined role obligations that individual "creativity" [25] and personal morality occur. This autonomous area of individual action may occur within a zone of permissiveness provided by the institutional structure of the society; it might also exist in zones which are institutionally regulated, but in accordance with standards which are contrary to the predominant institutional expectations.

Another basic element in the comprehensive integration of the personality system is a "personal value system." This problem will be taken up in the following chapter. At this point it should be emphasized that the integration of a personality as a concrete empirical action system can never be a simple "reflection" or "realization" of a value system. It must involve the adjustment of such a value system to the exigencies of the object situation and to the exigencies of organic needs. There is, therefore, a presumption that the integration of the value system into action will be less than perfect. There will be necessary elements of compromise, evasion, and more or less open conflict. This is particularly true because of the "historical" character of both personal and social value systems. The personal value system is built up in the course of a career, the different components of which, especially in a complex society, may not articulate very well with each other. In general it can be said that the nonintegration of the personal value system is "veiled" by the mechanisms of defense. This means that the actor is usually only

---

[25] If individual "creativity" is required by a set of role-expectations, then, of course, it does not occur in the area of autonomy. Thus the scientist is expected to create theory.

partially aware of the structure and importance of many of his conflicting elements — unless, of course, he has been very thoroughly psychoanalyzed, and even then much will remain obscure.

But although the integration of personality in terms of the value system is always less than perfect — and is, in fact, usually considerably so — it does not follow that the degrees or modes of integration are unimportant. They are of primary significance.

For example, the characterization of *total* personalities, in terms of what Murray calls their "unity thema," clearly presupposes an analysis of the degree and nature of the integration of the personal value system. But because of its applicability to both personality and social system levels, it has seemed best to treat the general problem of the structure of value systems separately in the following chapter. It is clear that the results of this treatment should be incorporated into the analysis of personality as a system and are not to be thought of separately as relevant only to problems of "culture." Similarly, in the formulation of an over-all characterization of a personality, the manner and degree of its integration in the social structure presents a critical problem. The following discussion presents a first approximation to the solution of this problem.

The Articulation of Personality and Social Systems

In the analysis of the empirical interdependence of personality and social systems, the best point of departure would be an examination of the points of contact between the two types of system. This procedure has been rendered much more feasible from a theoretical standpoint by virtue of our derivation of all major concepts from a few basic categories of the theory of action. The use of the same set of basic categories for the description of discrete actions and for the description of systems allows us to study not the identities of the two types of system but the points of their integration and mal-integration which is the central empirical problem of this field of social science.

In Fig. 9 we have schematically summarized the component elements of the two systems with a view to showing the areas in each system which correspond to the other. In what follows we shall present some brief considerations on these points of empirical articulation or correspondence between the concrete structures in the two systems.

In the left-hand column Fig. 9 presents a minimum list of structural elements of a social system, all of which must be present in any empirical case. These are first the two primary classes of unit elements of the social system: (1) the ways in which actors are categorized as objects of orientation, that is, by qualities (age, sex, territorial location, collectivity memberships) and performance capacities, and (2) the ways in which the roles in which they act are defined, the types of pattern and their distribution. The two together

define the role structure of the system; the first defines the actors' characteristics on the basis of which they are assigned to roles, and the second defines those roles (in terms of who shall occupy them and of the requirements
the occupants must meet) and the relations of roles to one another within
the system. Next, every social system must have an organized allocation of
orientations vis-à-vis the two fundamental types of interests in objects, the
instrumental and the expressive. This includes the distribution of transfer-
rable objects of interest, facilities and rewards, and therefore it includes the
structure of the systems of power and of prestige. Finally, every social system has structures of primarily integrative (or in the social sense, moral)
significance — on both the cultural and the institutional levels. In the latter
case the most important phenomenon is the presence of roles which carry
special institutionalized responsibility and with it both authority and prestige greater than those of most actors in the system.

We may now begin to examine the implications of the existence of these
fundamentals of the social system for the personality organization of its component actors. In the first place, it is quite clear that there must be a fundamental correspondence between the actor's own self-categorization or "self-
image" and the place he occupies in the category system of the society of
which he is a part. Many aspects of this categorization, such as sex, age,
ethnic adherence, seem too obvious to consider explicitly. But even where
there is such an obvious biological point of reference as in the case of sex,
it is clear that self-categorization must be learned in the course of the socialization process, and the process is often very complex, and to some degree
the individual must learn to "see himself as others see him" (that is, to accept
the socially given definition of his status). Even in the case of sex, certainly
among children, fantasies of belonging to the opposite sex are very common,
and there is reason to believe that on deeper levels these fantasies may reflect
a serious difficulty in accepting the membership in the sex group to which
the individual has been biologically ascribed. Such pathological phenomena
indicate that categorization even by sex is not simply given with the anatomi-
cal structure of the organism but has to be built into the personality. Failure
for it to work out fully is very probably an important component in at least
some types of homosexuality. What is true of sex is much more obviously so
in such a case as ethnic membership. For a person of light skin color to
categorize himself as a Negro is obviously something which must be learned.
It should be remembered that the criterion of social ascription to the Negro
group is not physical characteristics as such, but parentage. *Any* child of a
Negro is in social terms a Negro, even if his physical characteristics are such
that he would have no difficulty in "passing."

Another important type of such categorization concerns performance
capacities and character traits. What the individual believes about himself —
with respect to his intelligence, his abilities to do various things, whether

he is honest or attractive and so forth — becomes constitutive of his personality itself. This is, of course, not merely a matter of cognitive belief alone
but of internalization as part of the need-disposition system.

Of course, in this as in so many other respects, the correspondence
between the personality structure and the social system is not exact. But the
elements of looseness and the frequency of discrepancies between self-image
and actual social role should not obscure the fundamental importance of a
broad correspondence.

In the second place, as we have so often pointed out, the social system
places every individual in a series of roles where he is expected to conform
with certain expectations of behavior. The need-disposition structure which
controls one's responses to the expectations defining one's various roles is
therefore one of the most fundamental aspects of any personality, for the
simple reason that social objects constitute the most important part of the
situation in which he acts. Therefore, in the performance as well as the quality modality of his involvement in the social system, the individual personality inevitably must be shaped around the definition of role-expectations.
There are, of course, the two primary aspects of this. Within the range permitted by biological plasticity, there is the possibility that, through the socialization process, the constitution of the need-disposition system itself will
be organized in terms of the motivation to fulfill role-expectations. Perhaps
the most important single instance of this is the internalization of value-orientation patterns through the processes of identification.

The second aspect is that, however the need-disposition system may come
to have been constituted, at every point in the life processes the individual
is confronted with the actions and attitudes of others as part of his situation
of action. Because he is a social being participating in processes of social
interaction, he can never escape being oriented to the reactions of others, to
their attitudes and the contingencies of their overt behavior. In this connection, then, the meaning of these role-expectations as expressed in the attitudes
and actions of his interaction partners is always a fundamental point of reference for his own motivations. Role-expectations are so fundamental to the
social system that all human social motivation closely involves the problem
of conformity with them. Hence one of the most important dimensions of any
need-disposition system of a personality must be what we have called the
conformity-alienation dimension. There may, of course, be widely varying
degrees to which a need-disposition for either conformity or alienation is
generalized in the personality, but whether it applies only to a narrow sector of the role-system or is highly generalized, it is always present.

The next two major aspects of the social system constitute in a sense a
further specification of the implications of these first two fundamental ones.
Each, however, has certain special features of its own which may be com-
mented upon briefly. As an essential part of every social system there is, as

has been noted, an allocation of (mutually oriented) instrumental activities to the various roles and a corresponding allocation of sanctions and rewards. As we shall see in discussing the social system later, there is a variety of possible ways in which these activities can be organized relative to other components of the social system. But whatever this organization may be, it has to have its counterpart in the motivational organization of the individual personalities involved.

This becomes particularly evident in two more or less antithetical contexts. First, it is clear that the more complex and sophisticated types of instrumental activity require high levels of self-discipline on the part of the individual. The person who is unduly responsive to every passing opportunity for immediate gratification is incapable of the sustained effort and implementation of planning which is necessary — the capacity for sustained work is essential. A wide development of the instrumental aspects of a social system therefore presupposes the development of personalities capable of the requisite levels of disciplined application — as well as other capacities, of course, such as that for handling abstract generalizations. Not least among these capacities is that for a certain *flexibility* of orientation. The personality which is too highly dependent on highly detailed "ritualistic" routines of life is not ordinarily capable of the higher levels of instrumental achievement.

At the same time, a stable system of action requires other elements than instrumental disciplines, and this leads us to the second aspect. A stable system requires above all the internalization of value-orientations to a degree which will sufficiently integrate the goals of the person with the goals of the collectivity. In the economy of instrumental orientations one of the principal points at which this problem arises is with respect to the control of "self-interest." In popular terms we are likely to say that in addition to instrumental capacities people must have certain levels of "moral integrity" and of "responsibility" to be satisfactory members of a society. The prerequisites for such qualities in the structure of personality are somewhat different from the prerequisites of instrumental efficiency or adaptiveness.

Each social system at the same time has an "economy" of rewards and of the expressive orientations and interests connected with them. In motivationally significant terms this comes down to the question of what are the most important immediate and ultimate gratifications, and how they are organized and distributed within the social system. It is here that perhaps the most important single inference from the paradigm of interaction needs to be drawn. Human society, we may say, is only possible at all because, within the limits of plasticity and sensitivity, sufficient basic human gratifications come to be bound up with conformity with role-expectations and with eliciting the favorable attitudes of others. Both the immediate presocial gratification needs and the individualistic type of instrumental reciprocity provide too brittle and unstable a basis for social order. The phenomena of attachment and of identification are altogether fundamental here.

There seem to be two primary dimensions to this significance. First, through the diffuseness of what has been called the love type of attachment, the mutuality of dependency is extended to the social object as a whole, which precludes his being "used" as a facility for specific immediate gratifications without regard to the totality of the attachment relationship. Second, the mechanism of identification in the context of role-orientation provides a motivation for the acceptance of still further disciplines by leading to the development of the needs for approval and esteem; that is, for favorable attitudes relatively independent of the provision of other immediate gratifications. This need to be approved and esteemed is sometimes a source of social strains, but it is a fundamental motivational basis for the acceptance of socially necessary disciplines. There is a sense in which, paradoxical as it may seem, the core of the reward systems of societies is to be found in the relevance of this element of the motivation of individuals. What people want most is to be responded to, loved, approved, and esteemed. If, subject, of course, to an adequate level of physiological need-gratification, these needs can be adequately gratified, the most important single condition of stability of a social system will have been met. Hence the study in personality of the conditions both of building up and of gratifying the need-dispositions in this area is crucial for the study of social systems. Conversely, the understanding of the social situation, both in the course of socialization and in adult interaction, is crucial to this phase of personality study.

It will be made clear in Chapter IV that institutionalization itself must be regarded as the fundamental integrative mechanism of social systems. It is through the internalization of common patterns of value-orientation that a system of social interaction can be stabilized. Put in personality terms this means that there is an element of superego organization correlative with every role-orientation pattern of the individual in question. In every case the internalization of a superego element means motivation to accept the priority of collective over personal interests, within the appropriate limits and on the appropriate occasions.

Certain aspects of this larger class of superego elements, however, are particularly significant in the articulation of personality with the social system. Of these two may be singled out. First is the organization of attitudes toward authority, which is of crucial significance, since, however great its variability, authority is always a functionally essential element of social systems. The significance of this dimension in personality development, with its close connections with the structure of the parent-child relationship, is well known, of course. Perhaps because we live in a society with an anti-authoritarian orientation, a converse problem has, however, received less attention: the problem of motivation to the acceptance of responsibility. This, like the problem of authority, of course, is closely involved with the general conformity-alienation problem. But there seems to be much evidence in our society of the great importance of deviance in the direction of withdrawal from responsibilities; the use of illness in this connection is a familiar example. This problem, in its significance to the social system, poses extremely important questions of the articulation of social systems with personality.

Up to this point we have been treating the points of articulation between personality and social systems in a manner which assumed, on the whole, a far-reaching integration of the personality into the social system. It was for the sake of convenience and emphasis in exposition that this integration was portrayed first. The articulation which we have presented does not depend, however, for its validity on any particular degree of empirical "closeness of fit" between personality and social system.

The validity of the conceptual scheme which we used in analyzing the articulation of highly integrated personality and social systems is thus not affected by cases in which the integration is far from perfect. In fact, the imperfections of integration can be described only by careful observance of the same conceptual scheme which analyzes the positive integration. To illustrate the equal relevance of the conceptual scheme to situations of mal-integration, we may enumerate some of the possibilities.

First, with respect to categorization: alienation of the actor from his collectivity will exist where the various categories of qualities and performance-relevant qualities are differently assessed; that is, where the expectations of the actor concerning himself do not correspond to the expectations which others have formed concerning him. The actor, identifying himself, for instance, with respect to certain categories of qualities or performance capacities on which he places a high evaluation, will have expectations regarding the obligations of others to him which will not be acknowledged by those whose image of him diverges from his own — unlike the situation where the general value-orientation of the actor and his fellows are similar. In such situations, the non-integration of the actor's personality with the social system with respect to categorization may become associated with ambivalences in the actor's own categorization of himself. When this happens, the unifying regulation of need-dispositions by a harmonious allocative scheme gives way to contradictory allocative standards and consequent instabilities of behavior and internal conflict, as well as conflict between the actor and the members of his collectivities.

Second, with respect to role systems and role orientations: an individual whose capacity for diffuse object-attachment is impaired so that he is, for example, unable to make object-attachments of certain types (e.g., with persons of the opposite sex) will very likely become isolated. He will be unable to conform with expectations in a way which will enable him to fulfill certain roles in certain types of solidary relationships (e.g., marriage). He will perhaps find his way into some subsystem populated by the types of persons with whom he can establish attachments but his performance in roles in relation to other members of the society will be impaired. Similarly, fear of diffuse attachments to members of his own sex may hamper his collaboration in some specific roles where there is a "danger" of the emergence of diffuse "homosexual" attachments.

Third, with respect to the allocation of instrumental functions of the roles in which a person performs: in most cases, individuals perform role functions in the division of labor which do not, as such, completely and directly gratify any specific need-disposition or any set of the need-dispositions of their personality system. It is the nature of instrumental action that it should be this way. Conformity with the role-expectations is possible, however, either through a generalized need-disposition to conformity or through instrumental orientations. The latter, while making possible conformity with role-expectations, do involve (as we have just said) the renunciation of certain gratifications and therewith the generation of strains in the personality system. In the extreme case, which is relatively infrequent because of prior allocative processes, the primary or derivative need-dispositions are so pressing that no adaptation is possible and the expectations (of alters) concerning the actor's behavior in a particular role in the division of labor are completely frustrated.

The disjunction between role-expectations (of alters) and need-dispositions (of ego) may in some instances be a product of an alienative adjustive mechanism, a derivative need-disposition to avoid conformity. The disjunction might in its turn, by virtue of the negative sanctions which it incurs, produce anxieties which have to be coped with by defensive mechanisms and which modify the functioning of both the personality and the social system. Another possibility is that the role expectations may be so general that they allow persons with diverse sets of need-dispositions to perform the role in accordance with their spontaneous tendencies. The gap between prestige allocation and need-dispositions for approval and esteem can likewise be viewed with respect to its effects on the social system and on the personality system. Under certain conditions, the gap might activate certain learning mechanisms, for example, inhibition of the approval and esteem need-dispositions or the substitution of other social objects; in either case the gap might reduce motivation for conformity with role-expectations and weaken the aspiration to approximate certain role models. Within the personality system, the irritated state of certain ungratified, rigid need-dispositions might cause a reorganization of the personality as an adaptation or defense against this deprivation.

Finally, with respect to the mechanisms of social control and the internalization of shared values, we have already indicated that the superego need not consist only of the more generally shared values. Insofar as this is true, the integration of the personality into the social system will be less than complete. Where this divergence among the superego contents of the members of the society becomes relatively widespread, it might result also in the modification of the position of the superego in the personality system. In some instances the integrative-controlling function of the superego is weakened through the withdrawal of the reinforcement which is provided by the perception of numerous other individuals whose action seems to show conformity with the same internalized value-orientations. As a reaction to this threat, in some personalities, the superego functions more repressively and this strengthens its position within the personality system.

It is clear that the development of the need-disposition system is a function of the interaction of the actor with the situation throughout life. The types of mal-integration discussed above are therefore markedly influenced and irritated by the actor's exposure to conflicting expectations from different significant objects or inconsistencies in the expectations which are directly toward him by significant social objects concerning the same type of situation at various times. But the way in which these strains are coped with and their consequences for the personality cannot be deduced from the behavior of the objects alone. They must be referred to his personality as a functioning system.

Thus the problems of the pathology of personality must be understood in terms of a complex balance between the internal conflicts and strains of the personality as a system and the difficulties of adjustment to the situation, the latter in turn having repercussions on the personality. It is both a "psychological" and a "sociological" problem.

From the foregoing it has become clear that the contact surface of the personality and social systems lies between need-dispositions of ego and role-expectations of various alters. We shall therefore undertake a somewhat more elaborate examination of this crucial zone of action theory.

NEED-DISPOSITIONS AND ROLE-EXPECTATIONS

The starting point is the *interaction* of persons or, to put it in other words, of ego with a system of social objects. From the beginning of the actor's life, the significant social objects in his situation act in roles, of which presumably the major elements are institutionalized. In consequence of his dependence on these social objects, the actor as an infant builds up a set of roles of his own response to his treatment by adults. Only by doing so is he able to survive.

This process takes the form of his establishment of expectations regarding the social objects in his situation — in the first instance, his mother — and of the formation of attachments to them. The social object is not, however, an inert source of gratification, but *reacts* toward him, so that there enters a *conditional* element into the fulfillment of expectations. Alter has expectations of ego and vice versa; this is what we have already called a "complementarity of expectations." At the very beginning the infant is perhaps almost an environmental object to the adult. But this aspect changes quickly, a reciprocity of responsiveness builds up, the infant's smile calls forth responses, and organization along the axis of gratification and renunciation becomes more differentiated. As all this happens, he begins to *play a role* in the social system; that is, he acts in accordance with expectations, just as the adult does.

The essential element in the role is the complementarity of expectations. The outcome of ego's action, in terms of its significance to him, is *contingent* on *alter's* reaction to what he does. This reaction in turn is not random but is organized relative to alter's expectation concerning what is "proper" behavior on ego's part. The reaction, then, is organized about the problem of whether, and to what degree, ego "conforms" with alter's expectations of what he should do. At the very beginning the expectations may be purely predictive, but very soon they acquire a normative content. (This normative aspect has indeed been included in the concept of expectation from the start.)

Ego, then, is oriented, not only to alter as an object in the immediate environment, but to alter's contingent behavior. His orientation follows the paradigm "If I do this, he will probably do (or feel) such and such; if, on the other hand, I do that, he will feel (and act) differently." These reaction patterns of alter, which are contingent on what ego does, we have called *sanctions*. Role-expectations, on the other hand, are the definitions by *both* ego and alter of what behavior is proper for each in the relationship and in the situation in question. *Both* role-expectations and sanctions are essential to the total concept of a "role" in the concrete sense of a segment of the action of the individual. Sanctions are the "appropriate" behavioral consequences of alter's role-expectations in response to the actual behavior of ego.

Both role-expectations and sanctions may be institutionalized to a greater or lesser degree. They are institutionalized when they are integrated with or "express" value-orientations *common* to the members of the collectivity to which both ego and alter belong, which in the limiting case may consist only of ego and alter. (Of course, for the newly born infant, role-expectations cannot be institutionalized.) But so far as he "internalizes" the evaluations of the social objects around him, his own expectations may become institutionalized, at least within his family circle. Only as this happens, as he develops a "superego," can he be said to be "integrated" in the collectivity in the sense of sharing its values.

Sanctions, being responses interpreted as gratifications or deprivations, are organized about a positive-negative axis. Ego's fulfillment of alter's expectations generally brings forth in some form positive sanctions; for example, the "granting" of gratifications such as love and approval and the performance of actions which gratify ego. Failure to fulfill expectations, on the other hand, generally brings forth negative sanctions; for example, the withholding of gratification, love, or approval, and "doing things" which are dis-advantageous or unwelcome to ego, such as imposing further deprivations or "punishments."

It is in the *polarity* of sanctions and their *contingency* that their special relevance to the learning process is to be found. By virtue of their efficacy in relation to the learning mechanisms, ego is forced into the path of conform-ity with alter's expectations. Thus is established the relationship with social objects that becomes so directly constitutive of personality structure. Early childhood is selected for illustration only because of the dramatic character of the influence of this interaction system on a highly fluid and unorganized personality. In principle, however, the same basic processes go on throughout life. It is through the mechanisms of the system of sanctions operating on the learning, adjustive, and defensive mechanisms of the individual that a social system is able to operate and especially to control the action of its component individuals.

INDIVIDUALITY

Because of the paramount significance to any personality of its system of relations to other persons, the institutionalized organization of roles (in rela-tion to significant social objects and through them to cultural and physical objects) is central to the organization of personality itself. The pattern of expectations governing one's system of relations to other persons comes to be internalized into the structure of one's personality. But this system of inter-nalized roles is not the only constituent of personality, for a variety of rea-sons, which may be briefly reviewed. In the first place, those concrete role-expectations which become internalized are themselves only partly the ones which are institutionalized. That is, not *only* the institutionalized role-expecta-tion patterns become incorporated into the personality but also other elements, which are important in particular interactive relationships. In relation to the social structure in question, these may be deviant elements or merely varia-tions within the limits of permissiveness. In either case, the institutionalized definitions of role-expectation will account for only part of the interaction.

Second, even to the extent that the component role-expectations in a given institution might be classed together as uniform, the sets of such expectations will probably vary for the different actors who participate in the institution. The degree to which this is true will vary for different types and parts of the social structure, but generally, and especially in our type of society, there will be considerable variations. Although there is some measure of uniformity, for example, in the mother-child relationship regardless of the sex of the child, there is also a difference of expectation on the mother's part regarding her male and her female children. The matter is further complicated by differ-ences of sex in relation to birth order — a boy who follows two girls will necessarily be treated differently from a first-born son. In school and in play groups too the treatment will vary according to the individual characteristics of the actor so that variations in expectations will offset uniformities. Hence there is, in the combinations of the role-expectation elements which affect different personalities, a basis for *differentiation* between personalities which have been exposed to the "same" experiences as other persons in the "same" category.

Third, it must be recalled that the organization of a personality occurs in a *particular* organism. This has two aspects. On the one hand, ego's own organism as an *object* has features which differentiate it, and therefore him, from others who may be in similar status-positions in the social structure. Ego, in this sense, may be tall or short, fat or thin, black-haired or blonde, strong or weak. All this creates an influential source of differentiation. There might, furthermore, be variations of energy and of the strength of organic needs and capacities, such as hunger-needs, erotic needs, and motor-activity capacities.

The upshot of these considerations is that, though in a fundamental sense personality is a function of the institutionally organized role-expectations of the social system in which ego is involved, in an equally fundamental sense, it cannot be even approximately fully determined by this aspect of its structure. In confrontation with a given pattern of role-expectations in any given situation, there is therefore every reason to believe that there will be a dispersed distribution of personality types which are faced with approximately the same specific role-expectations.

These observations imply that there can be no neatly schematic relation between the *role-expectations* (of ego and alter) and the *specific* organization of behavior and sanctions. The same reactive sanction behavior cannot be guaranteed to have a completely standardized impact on the personality of any ego. In the learning process relative to role behavior there are many possibilities of divergent development from essentially similar starting points, the divergences being a cumulative function of the aspects of the personality in question *other than* the specific role-expectation confronting the actor in the particular situation.

Deviance

Just as sanctions are contingent upon the fulfillment or nonfulfillment of alter's expectations, so the significance of the sanctions to ego will also vary in accordance with whether he is motivated by a predominantly conformative or alienative set of need-dispositions. Internalization of patterns of value is crucial in the integration of an actor in a role system. Insofar as internalization occurs without exceptionally great unmastered conflict, ego will develop need-dispositions to conform with expectations; [26] while faulty internalization

[26] It does not follow that this necessarily makes him a "conformist" in the popular sense of the term. Many of the values which are institutionalized in role systems enjoin

(internalization attended by ineffective defense mechanisms or incomplete resolution of conflicts) may produce alienative need-dispositions, which are derivative need-dispositions to refuse to fulfill expectations. According to the structure of his personality in other respects, ego, if alienatively disposed, will tend (1) toward withdrawal, or (2) to evade the fulfillment of expectations, or (3) to rebel by openly refusing to conform. The alternative which he selects will be dependent on the activity-passivity need-dispositions of his personality.

An alienative need-disposition in this sense does not by itself necessarily produce deviant behavior. Normally the operation of the sanction system will lead ego to have an interest in the avoidance of the negative sanctions which would be attached to overtly deviant behavior. He may thus control his deviant tendencies and conform overtly, but the alienative need-dispositions may still be highly important in his personality structure, and the failure to gratify them might engender strains. There is an almost endless range of possibilities of compromise.

Alienative need-dispositions may become unconscious through repression. This often takes place through defense mechanisms (such as reaction formation, displacement or projection of the associated aggressiveness) which serve to reduce the anxiety engendered by (1) the infringements on the superego and (2) the prospective thwarting of authority.

Furthermore, ego is an object to himself. And, although the ultimate sources of the role-expectations which become internalized in the personality must be sought in relations to external objects, once expectations are internalized their aspect as internal objects of orientation may become of crucial importance. Guilt and shame are indeed negative sanctions applied to ego by himself, as punishment for his failure to live up to his own and others' expectations respectively.

The balance within ego's personality between conformative and alienative need-dispositions is perhaps the primary source *in personality* of the dynamic problems and processes of the social system. There are, of course, sources of deviation from alter's role-expectations other than ego's alienative predisposition; for example, ego's exposure to conflicting role-expectations from one or more alters, or an instrumental orientation which leads ego to deviate from the immediate expectation because the expected result is more highly valued than alter's positive response. But alienative tendencies are ordinarily operative in deviant orientations when they occur on any considerable scale.

The absence of a simple correspondence between the structure of any given personality and the role-expectation structure of the roles he occupies

---

independence and initiative, as is true of many in our own society. The person who refuses to stand on his own feet or take initiative, because he is anxious about others' reactions, is not "conforming" to the role-expectation, though in another sense he may be conforming to what he *thinks* others want him to do.

means that conformity and deviance in overt action (any overt action, for that matter) can be understood neither as an "acting out" of ego's own need-dispositions alone nor as determined solely by the expectations of immediate and remote alters with their various powers to impose sanctions. The sanction system [27] interposes a set of intermediate determining factors into the operation of the various need-disposition constellations. Thus, there are *mechanisms* of social control other than the internalization of value-orientations as parts of the personality system.

Nonetheless, a stable social system does depend upon the stable recurrence of the mechanisms which render more probable those patterns of action essential to the make-up of the social system. The "same" patterns may have widely different functions in different personalities; the social problem is to get the patterns whatever their functional significance to the person. One example will suffice. A disposition in the direction of "economically rational behavior," (that is, methodical organization of resources and work habits, prudence, careful consideration of the future, an orientation toward specific rewards) may have quite different functional significances for different personality structures. In a large-scale industrialized social system, economically rational behavior has a very important, relatively definite, and uniform function. The effectiveness with which such a system operates will depend to a high degree on the presence of such complex need-dispositions on the part of a sufficiently large proportion of the population. It does not matter whether there are important differences among types of personality possessing this need-disposition as long as it exists. Moreover, it does not even matter greatly whether the dominant subintegrations of need-dispositions are not directly gratified by economically rational behavior as long as the personality systems allow them to carry out the action without more than a certain amount of strain, and as long as there are noneconomic institutions capable of absorbing and tolerating the repercussions of the strain. Furthermore, the sanction system provides a secondary "line of defense" for the social system, in that it is possible to secure conformity even though the need-disposition is relatively weak or even within limits, definitely alienative. What does matter is that there should be sufficient personalities capable of producing "economically rational behavior" either directly in response to the pressure of their own subintegrates of need-dispositions or the anticipated rewards or punishments.

---

[27] This includes both the impact of actual sanctions on ego and the influence of their anticipation on his behavior.

3

Systems of Value - Orientation

Patterns of value-orientation have been singled out as the most crucial cultural elements in the organization of systems of action. It has, however, been made clear at a number of points above that value-orientation is only part of what has been defined as culture. Before entering into a more detailed consideration of the nature of value systems and their articulation with the other elements of action, it will be useful to attempt a somewhat more complete delineation of culture than has yet been set forth.

The Place of Value-Orientation Patterns in the Organization of Culture

Culture has been distinguished from the other elements of action by the fact that it is intrinsically transmissible from one action system to another — from personality to personality by learning and from social system to social system by diffusion. This is because culture is constituted by "ways of orienting and acting," these ways being "embodied in" meaningful symbols. Concrete orientations and concrete interactions are events in time and space. Within the personality these orientations and interactions are grouped according to the need-dispositions denoting tendencies which the concrete orientations and interactions exhibit. Within the society they are grouped according to roles and role-expectancies denoting requirements which the concrete orientations and interactions both stipulate and fulfill. Both *need-dispositions* and *role-expectancies* are, in another sense, postulated entities, internal to personalities, and internal to social systems, controlling the orientations which constitute their concrete referents. As such, they cannot either of them be separated from the concrete actions systems which have and exhibit them. A need-disposition in this sense is an entity internal to a personality system which controls a system of concrete orientations and actions aimed at securing for the personality certain relationships with objects. A system of role-expectations is a system of need-dispositions in various personalities which controls a system of concrete mutual orientations and interactions aimed by each actor at gaining certain relationships with other social objects, and functioning for the collectivity in which it is institutionalized to bring about integrated interaction. In either case, the postulated entity is internal to and inseparable from the system of action which it helps to regulate. Cultural objects are similar to need-dispositions and role-expectations in two senses: (1) since they are ways of orienting and acting, their concrete referent consists in a set of orientations and interactions, a set which follows a certain pattern. (2) In another sense cultural objects are postulated entities controlling the orientations which constitute their concrete referents. However, unlike need-dispositions and role-expectations, the *symbols* which are the postulated controlling entities in this case are not internal to the systems whose orientations they control. Symbols control systems of orientations, just as do need-dispositions and role-expectations, but they exist not as postulated internal factors but as objects of orientation (seen as existing in the external world along side of the other objects oriented by a system of action).

Because of the internal character of need-dispositions and role-expectations, they cannot exist, except insofar as they represent actual internal (structural) factors in some concrete action system. This holds both for elemental need-dispositions and role-expectations and for complex patterned need-dispositions and role-expectations (these being complex structures of the simpler ones). Elemental symbols are similarly tied to concrete systems of action, in the sense that no external embodiment is a symbol unless it is capable of controlling certain concrete orientations in some action systems. (This means that each elemental symbol must have its counterpart in terms of a need-disposition on the part of an actor to orient to this object as a symbol, and thus to orient in a certain way wherever this symbol is given.) On the other hand, a complex "manner of orienting" (which can be termed either a complex cultural object or a complex symbol, the two terms meaning the same thing) can be preserved in an external symbol structure even though, for a time, it may have no counterpart in any concrete system of action. That is, symbols, being objectifiable in writing and in graphic and plastic representation, can be separated from the action systems in which they originally occurred and yet preserve intact the "way of orienting" which they represent; for, when they do happen to be oriented by an actor (to whom each element is meaningful) they will arouse in him the original complex manner of orientation.

By the same token, a complex external symbol structure (each element of which has a counterpart in terms of need-dispositions on the parts of the several actors who participate in a collectivity) can bring about roughly the *same* type of orientation in any or all of the actors who happen to orient to it. And since the concrete referent of the symbol is not the external object but rather the "way of orienting" which it controls, we may say that complex symbols are transmissible from actor to actor (i.e., from action system to action system). That is, by becoming a symbol, a way of orienting can be transmitted from one actor to another. This is because the physical embodiment of the symbol is a first or second order [1] derivative from the orientation of the actor who produces the symbol, and it controls (because it is a symbol) roughly the same orientations in the other actors who orient to it. Thus symbols differ from need-dispositions and role expectations in that they are separable from the action systems in which they arise, and in that they are transmissible from one action system to another.[2] Both of these differences derive from the fact that they have external "objective" embodiments, rather than internal "unobservable" embodiments. On the other hand, insofar as they are "ways or patterns of orienting and acting" and insofar as their concrete referent is a set of orientations (which follow a pattern, or better, of which the pattern is an ingredient), they have exactly the same status as role-expectancies and need-dispositions.

To show what symbolization does for action systems, we may point out that symbols or cultural objects involve "interpersonalizing" the kind of "abstraction" or "generalization" which characterizes all stable systems of orientation (which, by the same token, characterizes the organization of concrete orientations into the subsystems, here called need-dispositions). This calls for some digression to show how the word "generalization" (which was originally introduced in the General Statement in the section on behavior psychology) can be rendered equivalent to the term "abstraction" and used in this context. Action is said to be generalized when the *same* form of action (according to a set of criteria formulated either by ego or by an observer) is given in different situations or in different states of the same situation or by different persons, as we will show shortly. This is what is meant by the term when it is used in behavior psychology. In terms of the theory of action, this occurs whenever a need-disposition is constructed. For every need-disposition groups situations on the basis of selected criteria (thus constituting for the actor a generalized object) and causes them all to be oriented to in the same fashion (or as one object). Thus every need-disposition, when it is formed, constitutes a generalization of orientation, and by the same token "creates" an object (the object being created in terms of the criteria whereby the generalized orientation is rendered relevant). But here, it may be noted, we have the process called *abstraction*, which is nothing more than the creation of objects from the field of experience by grouping situations according to

---

[1] We say a first or second order derivative because action itself is the first order derivative from the orientation; that is, it is caused by the orientation. Sometimes the action itself is the symbol. Other times the symbol derives from (is caused by) the action.

[2] It can be noted here that role-expectations, insofar as they have a status at all different from complex need-dispositions (for social-object relationships), have that status by virtue of the fact that they are complex (internalized) need-dispositions which have symbolic counterparts, and which thus can be the same for both ego and alter. Thus role-expectations are a specific interpersonal class of need-dispositions controlling complementary expectations because they are symbols as well as need-dispositions.

selected criteria. Every need-disposition within a personality system is therefore a generalized orientation (or an abstraction, in one manner of speaking)
which allows the actor to orient different concrete events as all of one class,
and thus brings about roughly similar action with respect to all these events.
Within a personality, therefore, the term *generalization* refers to "orienting in
the same way" at several different times (and places). Or at least, such simi-
larity of orientations is generalization when it occurs by virtue of some systematic internal controlling factor and not by chance.

We have already suggested that a "way of orienting" may be exemplified
not only at different times within the same personality system, but also within
different personality systems, and this may be a systematic and not a random
occurrence if the various persons within whom the way of orienting occurs
are controlled by the same complex symbol system.[3] Thus, we say, symbolization allows "interpersonalized" generalization. It is this very capacity for
"interpersonal-generalization" which is the essence of culture. And, in turn,
this capacity is the prerequisite of its crucially important role in systems of
action; for it implies the transmissibility of ways of orienting from person to
person, and hence a dimension of development which is known only rudi-
mentarily among nonhuman species of the biological universe. In other words,
communication, culture, and systems of human action are inherently linked
together.

THE CLASSIFICATION OF THE ELEMENTS OF CULTURE

The various elements of culture have different types of significance. The
criteria of classification for these elements are to be sought in the categories
of the fundamental paradigm of action. Every concrete act, as we have seen,
involves cognitive, cathectic, and evaluative components organized together.
These categories provide the major points of reference for analyzing the
differentiations of the symbol systems (just as they do for need-dispositions).
Hence the content of clture may be classified in accordance with the primacies [4] of the three fundamental components of the orientation of action.

The classification of symbol systems based on these primacies runs as
follows. Symbol systems in which the cognitive function has primacy may be
called "beliefs" or ideas.[5] Symbol systems in which the cathectic function has

---

[3] This may of course involve broadening the criteria of "sameness" so that the various
orientations of different actors to one system of symbols may all be classified as following
one "manner of orientation."

[4] We have said that symbols are ways of orienting controlled by external physical
objects. Now, just as a single orientation may be primarily cathectic, evaluative, or
cognitive (as in the case where a person is "merely considering a fact" which has very
little motivational importance), so also may a *way* of orienting (a cultural object) be
characterized by the primacy of such modes.

[5] Beliefs, since they are primarily cognitive, always relate the individual to his environment. Thus they are all existential (even mathematics and logic provide concepts and rules
for assertion of existential propositions). On the other hand, existential beliefs may be

primacy may be called "expressive" symbols. As compared with cognitive symbols the primary reference of the orientations involved in cathectic symbols is more inward toward the affective state which accompanies the orientation than outward toward the properties of the object oriented to.[6] The object is significant as the occasion of the affective state in question and cognition of its properties is subordinated in this context. Symbol systems in which the evaluative function has primacy may be called "normative ideas" or "regulatory symbols." They are the standards of value-orientation or the value-orientation modes about which we have said so much. In a moment, we will see that these evaluative standards themselves can be subclassified into cognitive, appreciative, and moral standards. First, we must clarify briefly the distinction between the classification of symbols into cognitive symbols, expressive symbols, and value standards; and the classification of the standards themselves into cognitive, appreciative and moral standards.

We have already said that symbols are ways of orienting which are embodied in or controlled by the external symbolic objects. It is roughly true, now, to state the following equivalencies: (1) Systems of cognitive symbols (beliefs) are ways of cognizing, these ways being controlled by the external symbolic objects. (2) Systems of expressive symbols are ways of cathecting (similarly controlled by symbolic objects). (3) Systems of value-orientation standards are ways of evaluating (also controlled by symbolic objects); that is, ways of solving conflicts between various units. Thus they can be ways for solving conflicts between various beliefs, between various cathexes (or wants), and between various evaluative mechanisms.

It is immediately apparent, therefore, that the third type of symbols (the evaluative ones), which have been called the value-orientation standards, *can* be subclassified again on the basis of the cognitive-cathectic-evaluative distinction. Thus, the evaluative symbols which outline ways of solving cognitive problems are cognitive standards; those which outline ways of solving cathectic problems are appreciative standards; and those which outline ways of handling purely evaluative problems are moral standards.

The three types of systems of value standards, it must be noted, are all systems of evaluative *symbols*. And thus they are to be distinguished from systems of cognitive symbols and of expressive symbols. For example, a single belief may be a part of a system of cognitive symbols, but it is not necessarily part of a system of cognitive standards. A criterion of truth, on the other hand, on the basis of which the belief may be judged true or false, is a *cognitive standard* (and thus an evaluative symbol).

---

empirical or nonempirical, depending on whether or not they are amenable to the verification procedures of modern science.

   [6] Systems of expressive symbols will often be fused with elaborate systems of ideas, so that as a result aesthetic experience and criticism will often have a very profound outward tendency. The ultimate criterion remains, however, the actor's sense of fitness, appropriateness, or beauty.

It seems to us that these standards, which we have variously called patterns of *value-orientation, normative ideas,* and *evaluative symbols,* are symbols of a somewhat different type from the cognitive and expressive symbols. This is perhaps because they are ways the actor has of orienting to (and acting with respect to) his own orientations, rather than ways of orienting to objects outside alone.

Let us discuss for a moment the complex (and still poorly understood) differences between the standards and the other classes of symbols. In the first place, they all seem to represent in some fashion a synthesis of cognitive and cathectic elements. Objects *cognized* are *evaluated* in terms of whether or not they will help the actor get what he *wants.* Thus, in this sense, a cognition cannot be evaluated except insofar as its long-run cathectic consequences are taken into account. Similarly, a cathexis cannot be evaluated except insofar as the object cathected is cognized in its patterned relationships to other cathected objects.

In other words, when a particular cathectic component is *evaluated,* its implications must first be developed. It must be synthesized into a wider cognitive structure, and then the balance of cathectic attachment to the whole set or system of implications may be discovered. This is cathectic evaluation. Similarly, when a particular cognized object or fact is to be evaluated, its cathectic implications must be developed. One must, in a certain sense, find out whether a *fact* may be *cathected* as a truly instrumental means to some ulterior goal, before one can evaluate it as true or false.

In both of these cases of evaluation, therefore, the actor has a commitment to orient himself in terms of *a balance* of consequences and implications rather than being free to orient himself to the particular cultural symbol on its immediate and intrinsic merits. Thus his orientation to a particular complex of symbols must conform with the imperatives of the larger system of normative orientation of which it is a part. Otherwise, the normative system becomes disorganized.

It is, indeed, in the evaluative synthesis of cognitive and cathectic modes of orientation that the major lines of the patterns of value-orientation of a system of action emerge. This source of patterns of value-orientation helps to explain their particularly strategic significance in action. But it also helps to explain their relative lack of functional independence. The cognitive reference connects the orientation with the object world, particularly with respect to the anticipation of consequences, which flow from actual commitments to action and which might flow from hypothetical courses, which, because of these anticipated consequences, may indeed be rejected as alternatives in the situation of choice. The cognitive orientation provides one of the bases of the range of freedom which we have called choice, and of which one of the most important aspects is the choice among alternatives in time. There is also the cathectic dimension, which has its meaning in terms of gratification-deprivation. Alternatives are selected with respect to their different consequences for the actor on this level. Value-orientations become organized into systems of generalized, normative patterns which require consistency of cognitive-cathectic and consequently evaluative orientation from one particular situation to another.

Value-orientations elaborated into cultural patterns possess (in their categorial organizations) the potentiality of becoming the common values of the members of a collectivity. Concretely, value-orientations are overwhelmingly involved in processes of social interaction. For this reason consistency of normative orientation cannot be confined to one actor in his action in different situations and at different times; there must also be integration on an interindividual level. Rules, that is, must be generalized in a manner to apply to all actors in the relevant situations in the interaction system. This is an elementary prerequisite of social order. On a psychological level, systems of symbols may have cognitive or cathectic primacy in their relation to particular actions of individuals. Where they are constitutive of the role-expectation systems of a social system, however, they *must* necessarily involve an evaluative primacy, since roles must be organized relative to alternatives of time and situation. It does not follow that systems of cognitive symbols and of expressive symbols do not have functional significance. But there is a sense in which ideas and expressive symbols branch off from the trunk of the ramifying tree of action lower down than do the modes of value-orientation themselves.

Ideas, evaluative standards, and expressive symbols, respectively, can become the primary foci of orientation of certain types of *concrete action.* Action where cognitive beliefs have primacy in relation to the attainment of a given goal may be called *instrumental action.* Action where expressive symbols have primacy will be called *expressive action.* Where evaluative standards have primacy (and where there is usually a concern for the gratification of other actors) the action will be called *moral action.* Instrumental actions are subsidiary in the sense that the desirability of the goal is given by patterns of value-orientation, as is the assessment of cost which is felt to be worth while to pay for its realization (i.e., the sacrifice of potential, alternative goals). But *given* the goal and the assessment of the permissible sacrifice, the problem of action is instrumental, and is to be solved in accordance with given standards of efficiency. It becomes a question of what the situation *is*, and this is answerable in cognitive terms. Thus the cultural element in instrumental action consists solely of beliefs, or ideas. *Skills* constitute the integration of these ideas with the motivational and physiological capacities of individual actors. The ideas which enter into the skill have been internalized.

The category of instrumental actions is a very broad one indeed. It includes the cultural aspects not only of the skills ordinarily used in a utilitarian context but at least a large component of those employed in the expressive field, as in ritual and art. It also applies in such basic general activities as the use of language, which is, of course, not exhausted by it. The essential criterion is subordination of action in a particular situation to a *given* goal.

Expressive orientations of action are concerned not with goals beyond the immediate action context but with organized gratifications in relation to cathected objects. The element of normative ordering to which this gratification process is subjected in a culture is the manifestation of appreciative standards of value-orientation. These appreciative standards have the same function of furthering the generalized consistency of behavior in this field as cognitive standards perform in the instrumental field. The normative regulation of religious ritual or of artistic style are familiar examples.

The focus of moral value standards is, as we have asserted previously, on the integration of a larger system of action. Moral standards set the limits of the permissible costs of an expressive gratification or an instrumental achievement — by referring to the consequences of such action for the other parts of the system and for the system as a whole.

The basic components of the structure of culture may be classified as follows. (This analysis is based on the modes of orientation as these were given in Chapter I.)

(1) *Types of Cultural Symbol Systems.*[7] (*a*) Systems of ideas (cognitive primacy). (*b*) Systems of expressive symbols (cathectic primacy). (*c*) Systems of standards of value-orientation (evaluative primacy).

(2) *Types of Standards of Value-Orientation.* (*a*) Cognitive. (*b*) Appreciative. (*c*) Moral. .

(3) *Types of Orientation of Action.* (*a*) Instrumental: here, expressive and moral problems are treated by the actor as solved, and the primary focus of attention is on cognitive problems which must be solved by reference to cognitive standards. Thus the problem is one of discovering the most efficient means vis-à-vis a *given* goal, subject to *given* moral rules. (*b*) Expressive: here, cognitive and moral problems are treated as solved (the actor knows what the situation is, and he knows which actions are "good" in this situation), and the primary focus of attention is on cathectic problems which must be solved by reference to appreciative standards. Thus the problem is one of discovering whether or not it is appropriate for the actor to want or "like" a given cognized object, after it has already been determined that there is no moral reason why the object should be either liked or disliked. (*c*) Moral: here, cognitive and cathectic problems are treated as solved (the actor knows what he sees, and he knows what he wants), and the primary focus of attention is on evaluative problems which must be solved by reference to moral standards. Thus the problem is one of discovering whether or nor it is *right* (in the light of the norms expressing the values of the system of action as a

_____

[7] A good deal of confusion in the analysis of culture has arisen from failure to distinguish these three major aspects of culture.

whole) for an actor to adopt a certain course of action whose outcome is both known and wanted.

This is an *analytical* classification. In concrete cultural phenomena, many combinations and nuances are possible. The fact that by no means every empirical case can be put neatly into one and only one category of an analytical classification will not be a valid objection to the classification itself.

From the point of view of comparative cultural analysis, which is our primary interest here, an especially great significance rests with the category of cognitive orientation or, more specifically, existential beliefs. This is because systems of beliefs constitute in the nature of the case a generalizing, systematizing, organizing component of systems of action.

COGNITIVE SYMBOLS

Existential ideas are an integral part of the *system* of culture which in turn is an integral part of action systems. They are therefore in principle interdependent with all the other elements of action. A concrete system of ideas, therefore, is a *resultant* of this interdependence. Even science is not simply a reflection of reality,[8] but is a selective system of cognitive orientations to reality — to parts or aspects of the situation of action.

The cognitive element has special significance for the integration and consistency of a cultural system as well as for the adaptation of action to the exigencies of the situation. This is perhaps particularly true of the non-empirical aspects (those aspects not testable by modern, scientific methods of verification) of the system of existential ideas. As compared with empirical ideas, the nonempirical ones are less controlled by the process of verification. Choices among the cognitive possibilities are therefore less subject to control by the immediate consequence of action in the situation. They enjoy therefore a greater range of freedom. The question, "Is it a fact?" cannot so readily be given a definite answer. The larger measure of freedom permits more flexible adaptation and therefore a more harmonious relationship with other elements in the cultural system.

There are many reasons why noncognitive interests are often particularly pressing in many spheres in which empirical cognitive orientations cannot operate. In the areas which Max Weber called the "problems of meaning," [9] cognitive answers are required which cannot be conclusively demonstrated by empirical means. Thus, why rewards and deprivations should be so unevenly distributed among men, and what the relation of this distribution to their "deserts" may be, are not questions satisfactorily answerable in scientific terms. Whatever the ultimate state of knowledge may turn out to be, at any

[8] It is worth noting here that "facts" are not "realities" but *statements* about reality. They may be "true" and yet highly selective in relation to any conception of the "total reality."

[9] The word "meaning" here has a somewhat teleological import. It refers to the desire on the part of human beings to know why things ought to be one way or another.

given stage of the advancement of knowledge, there is always a range of cognitive problems which are vital to human beings but which cannot be authoritatively answered by science. Hence, because of their great importance in reconciling normative expectations and actual responses (rewards and allocations) *common* orientation through nonempirical ideas has great significance for the social system.

Various possibilities of disequilibrium arise from the fact that these nonempirical ideas are not always common to all the members of a collectivity (as they need to be in order to maintain stability). It is, in fact, more difficult to get common acceptance in this area owing to the relatively greater indeterminacy of the answers to nonempirical cognitive problems. However, these possibilities of disequilibrium are reduced by the intervention of noncognitive mechanisms in the "enforcement" of uniformity and stability in beliefs. These mechanisms are of two major types, "traditionalism" and authoritative or administrative enforcement. At the same time the functional necessity of resort to such mechanisms of control creates strains since in a system of cognitive values it is inherent that the ultimate criteria of truth should be cognitive, not traditional or authoritarian.

Systems of beliefs, or cognitive orientations relate the actor to his situation. Hence the classification of the elements of the situation, of the different types of object, should provide a set of invariant points of reference for the classification of the most important ranges of variation of systems of ideas. The classification set forth in Fig. 6 (page 254) may be used for this purpose. We have recurrently emphasized that the most important distinction is that between social and nonsocial objects. Here, however, the distinction between physical and cultural objects within the category of the nonsocial objects is also highly important. Hence the invariant points of reference of the cognitive orientations may be classified in four categories as follows: (1) *Persons* constitute one invariant point of reference. Although it is essential, in the analysis of action, to discriminate between ego as actor and alter as actor, in the analysis of systems of belief this distinction may be disregarded. A unified cultural tradition will not maintain fundamentally different sets of beliefs about the ways in which human beings act and hence they will not need to distinguish between ego and alter. They must accordingly be classed together in the cognitive orientation system as persons or human beings. Otherwise, without these common beliefs about human action, complementarity of orientation would not be possible. This sector of the cognitive orientation system of a culture may be called its *conception of human nature.* (2) The *collectivity* as an object is another invariant point of reference, whether or not ego is one of its members. The collectivity figures as an object of central importance in political and economic ideologies; for example, "capitalism" or "socialism." (3) From this we must distinguish cognitive orientations toward physical objects (including organisms) and their connections in systems and subsystems. In the Western world we ordinarily call this *nature*. (4) Finally the cultural tradition itself, the tradition of the society in question and of others of which knowledge is current,[10] will be the object of cultural orientations.

The question of the ranges of variation of cognitive orientations with respect to each of these classes of situational objects is complex and cannot be systematically explored here. Only a few suggestions may be made. First, the primacy of cognitive interests in relation to systems of belief means that the grounds of validity of beliefs are always a crucially important problem. Hence the "epistemology" which is always implicit, if not explicit, in a cultural tradition constitutes a highly significant set of problems with respect to which variant beliefs may be held. Second, the problem of the "meaning" of the phenomena in each of these categories, as they are cognized in the culture in question, will always be crucial. We refer here to the conceptions of their bearing on human interests and goals, and specifically the interests and goals of the actors in the society which incorporates the culture. The problem of meaning, as can be seen, is inevitably and intricately bound up with the gratification-deprivation balance. Hence it contains a judgment of objects on the basis of their relative favorableness or unfavorableness to what are conceived as the worth-while human goals and interests. Nature, for instance, may be thought of as compliant or resistant in its relation to human goals.

Finally, there must be an over-all integration of a culture's system of ideas or beliefs which may be more or less explicitly worked out in cognitive terms. This will include, so far as it is explicit, a set of beliefs about man's relation to time and the ordering of his actions in time and to the nonempirical grounds of the world in general. This is essentially the cosmology of the culture, its way of looking at the universe and life, which is the primary cognitive foundation of the "ethos" of the culture. It is not possible to go further at present. But the next step would be to attempt to approach the problem of working out a typology of cognitive orientation systems.

EXPRESSIVE SYMBOLS

Systems of expressive symbols also may be differentiated according to the classes of objects in relation to which they organize the actors' cathexes. Following the above classification of objects, we may distinguish (1) the appreciative symbolization of responses to nature, such as landscape art and appreciation; (2) the appreciative organization of responses to human personalities, for example the conception of the admirable or beautiful person; (3) the appreciative organization of responses to collectivities, for instance

---

[10] This classification of the principal foci of cognitive orientation resembles in some respects and is indebted to Dr. Florence Kluckhohn's, in her "Dominant and Substitute Profiles of Cultural Orientations: Their Significance for the Analysis of Social Stratification," *Social Forces*, May 1950.

a conception of "good company"; (4) the appreciative orientation to cultural objects, for example, a poem or a mathematical demonstration.[11]

EVALUATIVE SYMBOLS

A system of evaluative symbols comprises: (1) a subsystem of standards for solving cognitive problems, (2) a subsystem of standards for solving cathectic or appreciative problems, and (3) a subsystem of "moral" standards for the over-all integration of the various units of the system, the various processes of the system, and the various other standards involved into a single unified system. These are collectivity-oriented or self-oriented moral values, depending on whether the system to which they have reference is a collectivity or a personality. Thus, the evaluative symbols, which are the value standards, can be subclassified, as we have said, as cognitive, appreciative, and moral. The moral standards may be considered to represent the superordinate integrative techniques of a system of action (whether they are collectivity-oriented or self-oriented). In another sense, they are ways of combining all the other ingredients of action, or recipes for the arrangement of the elements or aspects that make up concrete orientations.

The moral value standards, as we can see, are diffuse patterns of value-orientation. They are organizers which define and integrate whole systems of action (and also many subsystems). These patterns are, above all else, classifiable in terms of the pattern variables. Thus, we might say, we have thirty-two cells for the subclassification (or categorization) of the moral standards, the number of cells deriving from the cross-classification of the five pattern variables. The strategic place of the pattern variables in the analysis of action derives from the fact that they present a very general set of categories which comprise all the possible ways of relating the personality processes of cognizing, cathecting, and evaluating, with cultural standards on the one hand and social objects on the other. Thus they give us a typology, in some sense, of the moral value possibilities.[12]

---

[11] These classes of objects are likewise subject, in all cultural traditions, to evaluations which are elaborated systems of value-orientation. Thus there will be (1) normative or moral judgments which organize responses toward environmental objects (e.g., judgments of the benevolence or hostility of nature towards the realization of human ends). There will be (2) normative or moral judgments which govern responses toward personalities as systems or toward segments of personalities; these are expressed in the value-orientations which define and prescribe the good or virtuous man, or the good or virtuous action. There will be (3) normative or moral judgments governing responses toward collectivities; these judgments are expressed in conceptions of the good society or the ideal commonwealth and in prescriptions of the right social policy. Finally (4) normative or moral judgments will organize our responses toward cultural objects. Among these judgments will be found those which evaluate the goodness of the pursuit of truth in the economy of human life, or which judge the moral status of aesthetic or expressive activities.

[12] The pattern variables do seem to define, above all, ways of integrating all the ingredients of action into systems. Thus they present a classification of the moral value standards of persons and collectivities. On the other hand, the moral standards of a culture,

We shall begin the analysis of the systems of moral standards by calling attention to a certain congruence with the functional problems of systems of action. This congruence resides in the fact that there is a certain range of *problems* of orientation which are inherent in the structure of systems of action and that an orientation to each of the problems is a functional imperative of action. These are problems which are produced by the very nature of action — by the very nature of orientations to objects — and particular moral values may be regarded as pragmatic solutions of these problems. Since the problems have a determinate form arising from the nature of action, the number and logical relations of the types of alternative solutions is also determinate. Each of the pattern variables states a set of possibilities of selective response to the alternatives presented by the situation of action. We have enumerated five such pattern variables and we have given reasons for believing that it is legitimate to consider them an exhaustive set. The exhaustive character of the classification of pattern variables has far-reaching implications for the analysis of systems of moral standards; it provides a determinate range of variability and it allows only a number of combinations of alternatives which — on this level of generality at least — is sufficiently small to permit analysis with the resources we possess at present. There has been a tendency, under the impact of insight into the wider range of differences among cultures to think, implicitly at least, of a limitlessly pluralistic value-universe. In its extreme form, the proponents of this view have even asserted that every moral standard is necessarily unique. There is much aesthetic sensibility underlying and justifying this contention, but it is neither convincing logically nor fruitful scientifically. If carried to its logical conclusions, it denies the possibility of systematic analysis of cultural values.

In fact, of course, all patterns of moral standards are interdependent with all the other factors which operate in the determination of action. They will, as systems, inevitably fall short of "perfect integration" *which in the case of cultural pattern systems must be interpreted to mean consistency of pattern.* At the same time the imperative of approximating consistency of pattern arising from the need to minimize the strain of conflict within a system of action is so strong that it is improbable that the actual ranges of variation of systems of moral standards will coincide with the range of possible combinations of orientations to different classes of objects.

Moral standards are not logical deductions from systems of beliefs or manifestations of systems of expressive symbols, nor do they derive from

---

which govern the integration of the other standards (and particular moral standards themselves) into action systems, color the other standards (and the other symbols and need-dispositions, too, for that matter). That is, cognitive and cathectic standards tend to differ depending on the kind of moral standards which control their integration into action. Therefore, the pattern variables can be seen as presenting a typology of all evaluative symbols (of all value-orientation patterns) owing to the fact that they primarily present a classification of various types of moral standards.

cognitive or appreciative standards. They depend in part on such systems, but they draw on all the elements of cognitive, cathectic, and evaluative selection from the alternatives of action. The important alternatives (which define the problems of action) emerge for the actor only when he, armed with his cognitive and cathectic symbols and standards, directly confronts the relevant situation with all its functional exigencies. As he develops general methods for making choices among these alternatives, he thereby gains a new set of superordinate standards. These are moral value standards.

The pattern variables are crucial here because they *are* the alternatives of action and provide the problems of the actor, the problems which are solved by reference to moral standards. These problems of action are (1) the basis of choice (or treatment) of the object to which an orientation applies (ascription-achievement), (2) the appropriateness or inappropriateness of immediate gratification through expressive action in the particular context (effectivity-neutrality), (3) the scope of interest in and obligation toward the object (specificity-diffuseness), (4) the type of norm governing the orientation toward it (universalism-particularism) and (5) the relevance or irrelevance of collective obligations in the immediate context (self-collective orientation).

Whatever may prove to be the most useful way of classifying the elements and types of systems of moral standards the resultant classification will enumerate those choices among pattern-variable alternatives to which, in the context of commitments to action, they predispose the actor.

A concrete orientation of action cannot be confronted just by any one or two of these pairs of alternatives; it must explicitly or implicitly confront all five and accept commitments in all five directions. If the pattern variables are to be used to characterize concrete systems of moral standards, rather than specially abstracted aspects of them, all five variables must be explicitly included. The consistency of pattern of such a system will exist to the extent to which the same combination of value judgments formulated in these terms runs consistently throughout the actors' responses to different situations; that is, to different classes of objects, different objects in the same class, and the same objects on different occasions. A type of moral system then will be characterized by the *dominance* in all major types of situation of a particular pattern-variable combination, that is, the content of a cell or group of cells in, for instance, Figs. 3 and 4 (Chapter I), or a particular *integration* of two or more such combinations of the values of pattern variables.

PATTERN CONSISTENCY AND SOURCES OF STRAIN

Complete consistency of pattern is an ideal type. The moral standards which are actually held and acted upon by a concrete personality or social system cannot possess complete consistency of pattern; it is indeed probable that complete empirical pattern consistency is impossible. The inconsistency of pattern which we frequently observe is engendered by the adjustive problems which arise from the difficulties of articulation of value-orientation systems with personality or social systems. It is an empirical problem, growing up from the relation between cultural systems and systems of action and from the coexistence of a plurality of cultural subsystems in the same society or personality.

The evaluation of all the strategically significant categories of the object world is a *functional imperative* of a system of moral standards. It is imposed by the nature of human action. Another principal imperative, which is not necessarily harmonious with the first, is the maximization of the consistency of pattern.[13]

Evaluative orientation confronts situational events which may be both "reinterpreted" and creatively transformed, but only within limits. The recalcitrance of events, particularly the foci of man's organic nature and the scarcity of means or resources, imposes certain functional imperatives on action. There is no necessity, and certainly little likelihood, that all the facts of a situation which in a pragmatic sense must be faced can be dealt with by the actor in accordance with all the canons of a given value system. The various value systems will be differentially selective as to which facts fit and which do not, and how well or how badly, but there will always be some facts [14] that will be *problematical* for every value system. They can be dealt with only on the basis of standards that will be inconsistent with the principal standards of the actor, whatever these may be.

In one sense the *facts* of the system of social objects are more malleable than the other classes. They are, to an important degree, themselves a product of the cultural system prevailing in the action system. Thus both a man and a society *are* in some measure what they believe. A favorable response from alter never strains ego's own values; the interacting plurality of individuals which share common values therefore stands in a sense united in defense against threats to those values. However, there are definite limits to the effectiveness of such common defense if the values in question conflict seriously with functional imperatives of systems of action, which must be dealt

---

[13] Systems of action are functional systems; cultural systems are symbolic systems in which the components have logical or meaningful rather than functional relationships with one another. Hence the imperatives which are characteristic of the two classes of systems are different. In systems of action the imperatives which impose certain adaptations on the components result from the empirical possibilities or necessities of coexistence which we designate *as scarcity*, and from the properties of the actor as an organism; in cultural systems the internal imperatives are independent of the compatibilities or incompatibilities of coexistence. In cultural systems the systemic feature is *coherence*; the components of the cultural system are either *logically consistent* or meaningfully *congruous*.

[14] *Problematical* facts in the present sense are those which it is functionally imperative to face and which necessitate reactions with value implications incompatible with the actor's paramount value system.

with. *Some* of these functional imperatives make it most improbable that the actual concrete structure of *any* concrete action system will permit the realization of full consistency of the various parts of *any* value system. There must therefore be some sort of adjustment or accommodation between them. One mode of adjustment is the tendency to "force" the structure of the system of social objects into conformity with the value system, at the cost of increased strain. Another mode of adjustment is to tolerate and in varying degrees to institutionalize into the social system or to internalize in the personality system value patterns which are not in harmony with the major emphases of the dominant value system. The inconsistencies of value patterns are intra-individually adjusted through the mechanisms of defense, and interindividually adjusted through such social control mechanisms as isolation and segregation.

It is impossible for a functionally important sector of the social system to be organized and stabilized without some degree of institutionalization, and for a correspondingly important sector of the personality to be organized and stabilized without internalization of values. In those sectors of the system of action which are out of harmony with the dominant value-system, "adaptive institutionalization" will tend to occur. There will be a special mode of integration into the action system of that sector of the value-orientation system which is more or less in conflict with the main value-orientation system and its related institutions. There will consequently exist more or less fully institutionalized value-patterns, at variance with the paramount value system; these are "endemic" in the social system, and on occasion may become important foci for structural change.

An example may be drawn from American social structure. In our value system the "individualistic achievement complex" is dominant. It is most fully institutionalized in the occupational system, but penetrates very far into the rest of society. One of the systems, however, in which it is most difficult to institutionalize is kinship, since occupation is predominantly universalistic, specific, and oriented toward achievement, while kinship is much more particularistic, diffuse, and necessarily contains elements of ascription. Although our kinship system is less incompatible with the complex of individualistic achievement than are most, there still remains a significant amount of strain between the dominant value-orientations and that contained in the kinship system. The balance between them is consequently not always stable. Occasionally, the type of value-orientation characteristic of kinship may become dominant; for example, in situations in which kinship or ethnic group membership becomes the decisive criterion in allocation of roles and rewards.

Where this order of strain exists, the accommodation will often be facilitated by "rationalization" or ideological "masking" of the conflict. This reduces awareness of the existence of a conflict and its extent and ramifications. Mechanisms of defense in the personality and mechanism of social control in the social system operate in these areas of strain to bring the system into equilibrium. Their inadequacy to reëstablish such an equilibrium constitutes a source of change.

Inconsistencies within the value system result in strain in the system of action, personal and social. Such inconsistencies often originate through historical circumstances which resulted in exposure to inconsistent value-orientation patterns so that two or more sets may have been internalized or institutionalized in some sector of the system. This source of strain, however, can only add to the original sources of strain inherent in the nature of systems of action. This original source of strain lies in the fact that *no* fully integrated internally consistent system of value-orientation can be adequate to the functional needs of any concrete system of action. Given the inevitability of strain, there must therefore be adaptive value-integrations in the sectors in which the dominant value-integration is least adequate and which compensate for these inadequacies. Were it not for this basis of malintegration in the nature of action in a system, historical malintegrations would certainly not be either severe or persistent.

Alongside the tendency for inconsistencies in the value system to engender strains in the system of action and vice versa, there is a tendency of systems of action to build up and maintain levels of consistency as high as the exigencies of action will permit. The basis of this tendency rests in the functional need for order which underlies *any* action system, and which entails the need for integration of its cultural components. The need for order is seen in its simplest and most elementary form in the complementarity of role expectations. Without stability and consequently predictability, which is the essence of order, ego and alter could not respond to one another's expectations in a mutually gratifying way. Correspondingly the need-dispositions within a personality system must be organized into a stable pattern as a condition of avoiding frustration and holding down anxiety. The recognition of this need for order in systems of action is the central reason for our introduction of evaluation as one of the few most fundamental categories. The fundamental need for order in a system is the root of the strain which appears when an inconsistent value system is translated into action.

In relatively stable systems of action there are then the two tendencies to build consistent systems of value-orientation and the contrary tendency to generate and to tolerate inconsistent subsystems with the strain which they produce. There will be a delicate dynamic equilibrium between the two maintained by a wide variety of accommodating mechanisms. Empirically the value-orientation is not autonomous except in the sense that it may be treated as an independent variable, interdependent with other variables in a system. Among the basic components of an action system, there is no causal priority of any factor as the initiator of change. Change may come from any source in the system. The outcome will depend on the balance of forces in the system at the time.

THE INTEGRATION OF SYSTEMS OF VALUE-ORIENTATIONS
IN THE SOCIAL SYSTEM

Although a set of *dominant themes* or an *ethos* may be preëminent in the
concrete value system prevailing in a given society, still there will in addition
be many lesser themes representing some or all of the possible pattern-variable
combinations to be found in it. They will have functions homologous to the
adjustive mechanisms of the personality (see Chapter II). For this reason,
the "emanationist" hypothesis which asserts that action is simply a consequence of the prevailing value system cannot be accepted. A further deficiency
of this view is its assertion that all sectors of the value system are explicable
by logical derivation from the central themes or premises. It is on this account that it is necessary to conceive of both a *functional integration* of value-
orientations and a *pattern integration*. The latter refers to the extent to which
a given pattern or theme of orientation is *consistently* manifested in the specific evaluative attitudes of the actors throughout the social system. Functional integration refers to the integration of values with systems of action
and it therefore involves priorities and allocations of diverse value components among proper occasions and relationships. This is one of the principal aspects of the structure of social systems, and it is by these mechanisms
that standards which are not integrated with respect to their patterns are
brought into a measure of functional integration sufficient to allow the social
system to operate.

If we examine the list of pattern variables and the list of components of
a society described in Chapter II and Fig. 9, we will see that each possible
variant of the value patterns will find a situation in which it has primacy. In
general, without some affective expression no personality and hence no society could function, but neither could it function without the institutionalization of discipline over otherwise spontaneous affective expression. Conversely, the complete absorption of personality, or of subgroup interest into
the larger collectivity, would involve a rigidity of social control incompatible
with the functional conditions of a society as well as with the inevitable need
of human beings for some expressive spontaneity. Some amount of subordination of private interests or expression remains, however, indispensable
for the operation of a society. Particularistic ties and solidarities, such as
those of kinship, are found in every society, but at the same time universalistic
criteria of skill, efficiency, and classificatory qualities are never entirely
ignored by any of these societies. Certain ascriptive qualities of social objects
are given and are not and cannot be subordinated in all situations to performances, but performance is so crucial in some situations for all societies
that ascriptive qualities do not and cannot always take precedence. The segregation of certain significance-contexts of objects such as the instrumental
seems to be essential at times, but many social relationships are of such a

character that the diffuse type of significance — for instance, in a parent-child relation — also inevitably develops.

The functional imperatives (which arise from the nature of the organism and the pressures of scarcity of time, opportunity and resources in the object situation) are unevenly distributed within any given social system. The kinship cluster imposes a strong tendency toward particularistic, diffuse, and ascriptive commitments. The nature of the personality system and the nature of the roles of the child-parent relationship make affective expression more likely in the kinship situation than elsewhere. Hence there is an irreducible minimum of commitments to that combination of pattern variables within the kinship sphere. At the same time, however, beyond this irreducible minimum, values institutionalized in the actual role structure of kinship systems may vary very considerably, in accordance with the value-orientations dominant throughout the society. Thus classical Chinese kinship has a strong preponderance of particularistic emphasis, placing kinship loyalties very high in the general priority scale of social values. The American kinship system, on the other hand, while granting a place to particularistic commitments, tends to restrict them even within kinship. It tends, as far as possible, to accept a commitment to reward universalistically judged classificatory qualities, such as intelligence and the kinds of performances which are assessed by universalistic criteria rather than particularistically judged qualities such as blood ties. Even obligation to a parent comes to be measured to a considerable degree by the extent to which the parent is considered "worthy" in universalistic terms. For example, the definition of a son's gratitude and hence his obligation toward his mother, is based less on the biological *fact* of the relationship than on her services and attitudes on his behalf.

Integration, both within an individual's value system and within the value system prevailing in a society is a compromise between the functional imperatives of the situation and the dominant value-orientation patterns of the society. Every society is of necessity shot through with such compromises. Therefore it may be well briefly to review the main elements of such a value system insofar as they are relevant to integration of different value patterns within the social system.

The leading element in the real interindividual or systemic integration is the major value-orientation pattern dominant in the system (*ethos*). The basic standards of the social system are, as we have seen, characterized by the two variables of universalism-particularism and ascription-achievement. Each of the four basic types will be further differentiated by admixtures of elements from the other three types. The second element is the sub-orientations, which are described by the combinations of the two basic pattern variables with the other three. Thirdly, there are adaptive value-orientations such as authoritarianism, traditionalism, and so forth, which often come to play a part in the concrete value system.

The ethos will tend to be relatively fully institutionalized in some sectors of the social system, less fully in others, and not at all in still others. The main mechanism of accommodation is the *priority scale* which is implicit in the existence of a *dominant* value-orientation. This may vary in character from the prescription of a rather loose hierarchy to the virtual exclusion of any alternative values; in extremely authoritarian cultures, for example, evaluations which are in any way critical of authority are suppressed. Short of this extreme there will be various degrees of tolerance toward alternative value patterns.

Allocation of conflicting standards between different sectors of the social system is another of the mechanisms of accommodation. Values which are not consistent with the dominant ethos may be confined to special contexts and roles. Thus even in a highly universalistic system, particularism may still be sanctioned in kinship and friendship. Affective expression will be allowed a place even though the general trend toward discipline is dominant. Such allocated subvalues are usually integrated in a certain way with the main system. Their position is not merely permitted; conformity with them is often enjoined upon those in the relevant roles.

Freedom is another of the mechanisms of accommodation of unintegrated patterns of moral standards. Varying widely in scope and distribution within different societies, spheres exist within which persons or collectivities may act freely within limits. The area of freedom in this sense is not necessarily identical with the area of self-orientation in the *institutionalized* pattern-variable sense. In the area of self-orientation there may be, apart from direct obligations to a collectivity or to several collectivities including the society as a whole, an obligation to act autonomously, which may entail an obligation to pursue certain types of private self-interest. The particular content of the actions in such cases is not institutionally prescribed, but some important elements of the choice may be; for example, self-interest and universalism. Even there however the specific content of the goals to be pursued by self-interest might be limited by expectations of pecuniary gain and the procedures will be limited too by the prohibition of violence. Freedom, however, need not entail so much prescription, and may accordingly allow more tolerance. There is, for example, no approval in the current American ethos for certain ethnic value patterns, such as the immanent-perfection ideal of the Spanish Americans. Within limits, however, tolerance is institutionalized in America so that usually there is felt to be an obligation to allow a minority to live its own life, although its principal value patterns do not conform with those of the dominant sector of the society. Similarly, some of the values held among the intelligentsia in Western society since the French Revolution have deviated widely from the prevailing ethos, but the mechanism of toleration has held in check what under other conditions would have been severe conflict and repression.

Openly tolerated patterns of divergence from the ethos shade into those which are not tolerated and which, if they exist at all, have to be protected by a mechanism of withdrawal or isolation. There are certain activities and their associated values which manage to exist alongside the prevailing ethos by the operation of the mechanisms of withdrawal or isolation which separate the bearers of the divergent value-orientations from one another, thus reducing the possibility of conflict. In most social systems considerable sections of the borderline between conformity and deviance are indistinct. This has great functional significance. The ambiguity of the standards or expectations and the legitimately divergent interpretability may also allow diverse value patterns to coexist by holding frustration and conflict in restraint.

The functional inevitability of imperfections of value integration in the social system does not, as we have seen, necessarily destroy the social system, because a set of mechanisms, which are homologous with the mechanisms of defense in the personality, limit the disintegratedness and confine its repercussions. These mechanisms render possible the continued operation of the social system; that is, the interdependent coexistence of the various parts of the system. These mechanisms moreover may even render possible a measure of limited collaboration between the sectors of the society committed in other respects to incompatible values. Just as in the personality certain defense mechanisms keep dangerous impulses below the level of consciousness, thus keeping down the level of anxiety and conflict, so in the social system certain accommodative mechanisms permit contradictory patterns to coexist by allocating them to different situations and groups within the society. The extreme rationalist or the doctrinaire who takes a system of institutionalized values as something to be rigorously and consistently applied in all situations can for this reason be a seriously disturbing influence in a social system.

Social systems and especially large-scale societies are inescapably caught in a very fundamental dilemma. On the one hand they can only live by a system of institutionalized values, to which the members must be seriously committed and to which they must adhere in their actions. On the other hand, they must be able to accept compromises and accommodations, tolerating many actions which from the point of view of their own dominant values are wrong. Their failure to do so precipitates rebellion and withdrawal and endangers the continuation of the system even at the level of integration which it has hitherto achieved. In this paradox lies a principal source of strain and instability in social systems, and many of the most important seeds of social change.[15]

---

[15] At the same time this situation is, from the theoretical point of view, the main reason for refusing to regard the problems of the integration of systems of cultural value-orientations and of social systems as homologous. It is also the predominant reason why the type of analysis of value-orientation associated particularly with the name of the late Ruth Benedict cannot serve as the sole or even primary basis for an analysis of the dynamic processes of the social system.

We have been considering largely the integration of moral standards into social systems. It is equally relevant to examine some of the problems arising in connection with the integration of these standards into the personality system. In certain respects, the considerations which were relevant above are equally valid here. It is in the combinations of the values of the pattern variables that variability of moral values is to be sought. The system of moral standards of the individual actor will have its elements of consistency and inconsistency, developing from the history of the individual personality, from its genetic processes of development, and from the various influences to which it has been exposed in its course. Where there is imperfect integration of pattern, as to some degree there always must be, there will also be strain, which can within the limits imposed by the nature of the inconsistency be ameliorated by the mechanisms of defense.

The relation between social and personal systems of values cannot, however, be wholly symmetrical. We have seen that culture as a system of symbolic meanings inherently embodies the generalized or interpersonalized aspects of the organization of action. What is commonly referred to as a culture cannot therefore be limited to the sector incorporated in a single personality. The latter is in some sense a particularized variant of emphases and selections from the major combination of themes which in the social system is generalized for many personalities. The culture of a personality, so far as it is more than a microcosm of a set of generalized patterns, is a particularized version, selected from a more comprehensive total pattern. Adding usually something of its own through interpretation and adaptation, it consists of the elements which are relevant and congenial to the particular actor in the light of his particular situations.

Order — peaceful coexistence under conditions of scarcity — is one of the very first of the functional imperatives of *social systems*. A social system has no independent source of motivation of its own; this comes only from the component individuals. The personality is in a sense a motivational "engine"; the structure and direction of its motives are derived from the modifications imposed on the innate structure by social interaction and culture. Gratification — the most general concept for the fulfillment of its motives — is the primary functional need of personality.

The personality has been treated as an organized complex of need-dispositions. The combinations of the pattern variables, as we have shown in Chapter I, describe in one sense the fundamental types of need-disposition organizations. From the exigencies confronting the need-dispositions in the external situation and in relations to each other, the further elements which we have called mechanisms of defense and adjustment are developed. The problems of the appropriate occasions for gratification or its renunciation, of diffuse attachment to an object or the specific limitation of its cathectic significance are the primary orientational dilemmas. Problems of the character of norms and of the modalities of objects are less immediately crucial and hence their solutions are more likely to be imposed by situational factors.

The generality of the values of the larger culture which are institutionalized in the social system gives them a greater share in the creation of this framework of imposed order. The range of variability available to the values of particular personalities is fixed primarily by the limits which are part of this framework.

From these considerations it becomes evident that there are *two* primary ranges of variability of personal moral patterns. First, like social value systems, personal value systems are constituted by the choices from the alternatives represented in the pattern variables. In addition, however, the existing institutionalized value system of the society must always be an independent point of reference. Regardless of its content, by virtue of his membership in the society, the individual is confronted with the problem of the degrees and modes of his acceptance or rejection of these values. Unless the social system approaches a state of extreme disorganization, the personal consequences of radical deviance are always serious.

Some of the most subtle problems of the relations of personality and culture arise in this context. Personalities as systems are thoroughly permeated by culture — the very composition of the need-dispositions which are constitutive of personality is a fusion of organic energy into a framework made up of commitments to the alternatives of value-orientation. Even after the personality has become a relatively stabilized system of need-dispositions allocated among various occasions for gratification and integrated into some approximation to a working unity, it is still continuously confronting the cultural patterns as situational objects of orientation. Even in a simple society, the cultural pattern presented as a situational object will be richer in content, more varied in scope, and of course, more contradictory than a single personality system, with its functional imperative of integration as a basic gratification, can incorporate.

The personality system will therefore tend to select particular elements from the available cultural pattern which will then become parts of the orientation system of the actor. It is certainly not permissible to assert that the actor chooses only those elements of the pattern (as a situational object) which are identical with his existing need-dispositions. If that were so, there could be no changes in the behavior of actors through their exposure to different culture patterns in the course of their lifetime. Nor is the selection a random one. There must therefore be some correspondence in general orientation between the need-disposition system of the personality and the elements selected from the available cultural patterns; that is, the pattern elements which become incorporated into the actor's orientation must still permit an adequate balance of the gratification of the various need-dispositions. The cognitive orientations accepted must have some congruity or consistency with the cognitive orientations already operative in the personality system. But it certainly need not be and is extremely unlikely to be a very detailed identity.

The reasons for this relative looseness of fit between personality systems and the selection of cultural orientations from situational cultural patterns are numerous. There seem to be two main reasons. First, need-dispositions are relatively generalized orientations in the personality system and the cultural object system is also relatively generalized, but they cannot exactly coincide. Hence in confrontation with concrete situations, the need-dispositions must become particularized and integrated with a correspondingly particularized interpretation of the relevant sector of the culture. Their balance undergoes a momentary change in accordance with the pressure of the circumstances, and the capacity of the generalized orientation to guide behavior gratifyingly is inadequate. Hence some more differentiated or particularized orientation pattern must be added to the actor's orientation system to increase his ability to maintain the level of gratification. The second reason lies on a different plane. In the first instance we spoke of the substantive content of culture patterns and their potency in providing gratifying orientations; but there is another selective factor at work: the conformity-alienation need-disposition, which in some magnitude or direction is operative in every personality. Hence there is a factor at work in the selection of cultural patterns which is independent of their content and which is determined primarily by the strength and direction of the conformity-alienation need-disposition. Cultural patterns which in their general content are quite contradictory to the value-orientation of the other need-dispositions in the personality system might well be accepted if their acceptance gratifies the conformity-alienation need-disposition. There need not necessarily be a conflict between these two criteria of selection of elements from the cultural object situation. They might well coincide and often do.

What has been said here about selection is true also of the creation of new value patterns in the personality. This occurs not only through selection but also through integration and adaptation. Here the strength of the need-dispositions and their consequent potentiality for resisting the pressure of expectations — independently of alienative need-dispositions — might be said to be one of the most important factors in determining a creative variant of an available cultural pattern. Creativity here refers to the production of new patterns of personal value-orientation which diverge significantly from any of the available cultural patterns. The newly created pattern will probably stand in closer correspondence substantively or formally to the need-dispositions of the personality than in the case of selection from situationally available patterns. But here too it is not merely a matter of finding a correspondence with the value-orientations implicit in the need-dispositions. It is the creation of a new pattern which adds to the existing body of orientations in the cultural pattern. It extends to new objects or new relations among them; it entails new patterns of cognition, expression, or value-orientation. Some important aspects of the newly created pattern will always reveal its continuity, even though remote and complex, with the elaborated need-disposition system which makes up the personality.

The personal creation of new cultural orientations might itself be a function of the selection of certain specific cultural patterns in the situation. The personal pattern of orientation toward creativity on the part of the scientist or poet, with its high evaluation of new truths and new images, is greatly promoted by the presence in the cultural orientation system of a positive pattern which highly evaluates creativity in the search for truth without requiring the acceptance of any particular substantive truths.

The differentiation of personal value systems with respect to their degree of creativity or its absence must not be confused with that of need-dispositions to conform with or be alienated from institutionalized culture patterns. These two sets of categories cut across each other. The scientist within a culture which highly values scientific creation might be much more creative than the revolutionary or the religious prophet who stands in rebellion against the prevailing patterns of his culture. Creativity is not identical with rebellion; while conformity with existing patterns may be the result of an orientation toward its mere existence or toward its content.

THE PROBLEM OF CLASSIFICATION OF VALUE SYSTEMS

Our previous discussion has assumed the possibility of a systematic classification of types of moral standards. The task however still remains to be done. It should of course be placed in the context of the larger problem of classification of cultural orientations in general. This could not, however, be undertaken within the limits of this monograph.[16]

Variations in the structure of these standards may be described systematically by the various possible combinations of the values of the pattern variables. Of the five pattern variables, it was asserted in Chapter I that one, self- versus collectivity-orientation, can be omitted from the more basic treatment of the structural *variability* of the two kinds of systems of action. The reason for this is that it refers to the integration of action systems which is *equally* a functional problem to *both* types of system. The form and scope of integration depends on the nature of the elements to be integrated, and not the other way around. This should not be understood to imply that there is no significant variation with *respect* to this variable; the variation, however, is primarily a resultant of the problems of the functional integration of the system and it is not constituent of that type of system.

[16] A tentative attempt in this direction has been made in Talcott Parsons, *The Social System*, chaps. viii and ix.

Attention may now again be directed to what was called in Chapter I (pp. 88, ff.) the "symmetrical asymmetry" of the relations among the remaining four pattern variables. Two of them, affectivity-neutrality and specificity-diffuseness, are, as we saw, peculiarly applicable to personality systems; the other two, universalism-particularism and ascription-achievement are primarily applicable to social systems.

The *primary* significance of the two pattern variables more closely related to personality lies in their organization of orientation in relative independence of the type of situation; the two pattern variables more closely related to social systems have their primary significance in the organization of the situation in relative independence of the type of orientation. Both pairs are very important in each type of action system, but their position is not the same in each.

Proceeding from this assumption, the four main types in the four cells in Fig. 4 (page 251), further elaborated in terms of their cultural significance as Fig. 10, provide the basic framework for the classification of systems of values for the social system. This classification will give us the systems of common values which are, in relation to the situational factors, the primary focus of the main institutional structure of the social system. The types in Fig. 3 (page 249) provide the corresponding framework for value systems of the personality. Of the two classifications, however, the social value-orientations (Fig. 4) have greater significance for the analysis of cultures. Cultures, being shared by many actors, comprise the values which define the common elements in the situations in which they act. (Fig. 10 is on page 258.)

The best correspondence between these major types of value patterns and social systems will be found in the more comprehensive or macroscopic kinds of comparative analysis. They will also be found in those sectors of the social system which are freest for variability, as a result of being least determined by certain of the more specific functional imperatives. For example, governmental structures and those centering about the stratification subsystem should show on the whole closer correspondence with dominant value patterns than kinship, which is bound to the relatively more specific functional conditions of man's biological nature. Kinship systems therefore do not vary as widely in terms of pattern variables,[17] and they are also less likely to fit the dominant value-orientation than are the larger governmental and stratification subsystems. Thus an increase in size introduces new functional imperatives which tend to shift the balance in the direction of universalism, specificity, etc.

A complete survey of the variability of social value systems is out of the question here; only a few illustrations can be provided. The universalism-achievement combination (Fig. 10, cell 1) approximates the dominant Amer-

---

[17] They do, of course, vary widely in terms of their composition and relations among the constituent solidary groupings.

ican "achievement complex." The particularism-achievement combination (cell 2) fits the classical Chinese value system rather closely. Universalism-ascription (cell 3) fits the pre-Nazi German value system, and finally, particularism-ascription (cell 4) seems to correspond to the Spanish American pattern.[18]

Fig. 10a further elaborates these four main types of logically possible value systems. Fig. 11 classifies each of the four main types of value patterns by each of the six classes of situational objects distinguished in Fig. 6 (page 254). For the sake of refinement and completeness, three foci of orientation are distinguished within each object class: (1) the significance of the object for the actor's symbol system (i.e., the diagnostic definition of the object with reference to which the actor prepares to act); (2) the types of striving toward a goal which, in terms of the value-orientation, it will be appropriate for the actor to undertake; and (3) the principal locus of strain in relation to the object. The third aspect is particularly important in the analysis of the integration of a system of moral standards into an empirical action system.

If the present approach is consistently adhered to, each subtype of each of the four main types of value-orientation system may be further differentiated by confrontation with each main object class. A sample of such a classification for sixteen subtypes, omitting the self-collectivity variable and confining the elaboration to three selected object classes, is presented in Fig. 12.[19]

The general theory of action points to important determinate interrelations between the cultural standards institutionalized in the social system and the distribution of personal standards among its population. Within any social system, even within any particular status within it, there will tend to be a variety of personality types. (We use the term *personality type* here to refer to a personality system characterized by its dominant complex of need-dispositions.) In principle all of the possible personality types may appear in the same society, but the nature of the relations between personality and social structure is such that their distribution cannot vary at random in any given society. In view of the special pertinence of the variables of affectivity-neutrality and specificity-diffuseness to personality, the cells within the main types of Fig. 11, in addition to defining subtypes of cultural values of the

---

[18] These assertions would of course have to be justified by more detailed discussion than is possible here, and they are in any case acknowledged to be only first approximations.

[19] For instance, within the transcendent-achievement pattern, the most significant variations lie perhaps between the subtypes distinguished by affectivity and discipline. The commitment to the transcendent-achievement pattern precludes a prominent position for diffuse obligations. The disciplined alternative more nearly characterizes the American value system with its strong emphasis on *instrumental* achievement and the puritanical attitude toward pleasure which prevailed until recently; it might be suggested very tentatively that the affective alternative comes close to certain aspects of the French with their greater emphasis on the style of life with its refined patterns for affective expression in consumption, convivial relations, etc.

social system, may also define the personality types most likely to be produced in, or at least to be necessary for the functioning of, a society with
a major value system oriented in terms of one of the main cultural types.

This possibility may be illustrated with respect to the universalistic-
achievement orientation which is rather characteristic of important tendencies
in American culture. In Fig. 3 the four major need-disposition types are designated as the *segmental gratification* value-orientation (affectivity-specific-
ity), *approval* (neutrality-specificity), *love* (affectivity-diffuseness) and
esteem (neutrality-diffuseness). The high evaluation of approval is perhaps
most peculiarly American. In one direction, this fuses with the hedonistic
(*segmental gratification*) value-orientation producing an orientation toward
achievement, with an inclination toward immediate gratifications. This is
certainly one of the directions of the break-down of Puritan discipline in
American society in recent decades. Hence such orientations may be deviant,
and thus likely to be in conflict with the predominant value system. A second
direction of deviance is from orientation toward *specific* performances assessed by universalistic standards to a *diffuseness* leading to the "esteem"
orientation. This too finds its counterpart in American culture in recent years
and is enhanced by the growth of mass communications. The personality types
that seek to be the center of attention, who are not content with specific
achievements and the corresponding approval by themselves and others, and
who must be recognized as *generally* superior, would fall into this category.
In American culture, this type has tended to be defined as somewhat deviant
— although perhaps less so now than a half-century ago — and certain attendant strains have thereby been produced. Perhaps the least common of the four
orientations in American society is the "love" pattern. Quite understandably
it is more likely to be found among women than men because women have
been excluded from the achievement complex and they have a special role in
the kinship structure. But it is by no means necessarily confined to women.
Even though not frequently found as a dominant orientation among men, it
frequently is a very important counterfoil as a partial orientation pattern in
such contexts as the romantic-love complex, where it represents a segregated
revolt against some of the other tendencies of the culture.

These remarks are at best intended only to be suggestive of the possibilities
of analysis through the use of these categories.

Both the major orientations and the subtypes are *ideal types* and there is
no reason why any concrete and in particular any dominant value-orientation
should conform exactly to any one of them. There are undoubtedly many significant marginal cases. Because of this ideal-typical character, this scheme
is highly formal and can be only a first step in the analysis of actual or historical systems of value-orientation. Much more would have to be added
before the scheme could be used for detailed concrete analysis. For instance,
our treatment of the universalistic-achievement pattern of orientation does

not specify which particular classes of achievements are valued. These might be scientific, technological, artistic, military, and so on, and concrete cultural orientations certainly do differ markedly in these respects. Moreover, the pattern-variable scheme, at this stage of the logical construction of the categories of cultural orientations, dos not explicitly formulate the types of value-orientations which are embodied in unequal but complementary social relations such as dominance-submission. The value-orientations implicit in these social relationships are to be analyzed as adaptive mechanisms mediating between major cultural patterns and the exigencies of social situations.[20]

This formal quality, although a limitation, is not in principle a deficiency of the scheme. The enormous empirical complexity of concrete value-orientation systems is not subject to question. *Any* conceptual scheme which attempted to take account of all this complexity at one stroke would be scientifically useless in the present stage of development of social science because it would be far too cumbersome to handle systematically without mathematical techniques, which, for a variety of reasons, cannot yet be applied to the relevant social science concepts. The question is not, therefore, whether the pattern-variable scheme, by being formal, "oversimplifies" empirical reality; any analytical scheme would do so. The question is whether the *selection* of variables incorporated in this scheme is more or less useful than an alternative selection. There are two kinds of criteria of the usefulness of such a selection. One is its fruitfulness in research. This test is still to be made. The other is the relationship of the chosen set of variables to other variables in a highly generalized conceptual scheme, which in its various parts has already proved itself useful in research. From this source the pattern-variable scheme draws strong support. It employs analytical concepts which have been derived from the basic categories of action, which themselves in more concrete versions have been applied with success to the study of cultures as various as ancient Israel, China, India, and modern Christendom.

The derivability of a variety of concepts from the major categories of the definition of action merits further consideration. In Chapter II, principal need-disposition orientations were derived from the general orientation scheme, through the pattern variables by means of certain techniques of conceptual derivation. The same can be done for systems of cultural orientation. A value system which appraises authority very highly is, for instance, conceptually homologous to the need for dominance in the personality and to a high degree of concentration of authority in the social system and it seems, similarly, to derive from combinations of the pattern variables.

Concretely, the type of value-orientation toward authority which will develop will depend on the combination of pattern-variable values which is associated with it. Thus in the universalism-achievement orientation author-

---

[20] A similar limitation in the use of the most elementary pattern-variable combinations in concrete description was observed in our discussion of personality.

ity will be linked to status based on achievement. At the opposite pole, in the particularism-ascription orientation, there will be a tendency to acknowledge the authority exercised by persons with an ascribed status within a particularistic structure.[21]

By similar techniques other aspects of orientations toward authority can be derived from *combinations* of the pattern variables within given cultural and social contexts without making orientation toward authority itself *one* of the basic types of value-orientation. In the present conceptual scheme, orientations toward authority belong on a derivative level of concreteness in the classification of systems of value-orientations. They are not a fundamental type. What is true of the place of the evaluation of authority would also be true of adherence to tradition or of other differentiated concepts such as the evaluation of prudence, or of adventurousness, or even the evaluation of the things of this world as distinguished from those of the "next." [22]

The different pattern-variable combinations, when integrated into action systems, will of course predispose the actors toward those derivative patterns of value-orientation which are consistent with them. Thus the universalism-ascription pattern has a tendency to authoritarianism, because the authoritarian "ideal state" involves *allocation according to qualities* and the implication that this "ideal state" should be *acknowledged by everyone.* Given the likelihood of deviant tendencies in all systems the resort to authoritarian enforcement in universalistic-ascriptively oriented culture is highly probable. Similarly, in a culture with a predominantly particularistic value-orientation, a universalistic orientation is enabled to exist only if it is "projected" into an "other worldly" sphere, thereby reducing the strain which it would otherwise cause. Thus the attainment of Nirvana in Buddhism is very strictly a universalistic-achievement value, which has been enabled to flourish in the particularistically organized social structures of Oriental societies only by virtue of its other-worldliness. Such inferences, however, must be drawn with caution; and the concrete orientations will be a resultant of many factors ranging from the functional imperatives imposed by the organism and the situation and the general value-orientations involved.

This chapter has presented an exceedingly sketchy treatment of a very complicated subject. Its aim has not been to produce a complete analysis but to indicate the main lines along which the general analysis of action presented in Chapter I could be developed in the study of value-orientations. Compared to other current modes of analysis, it possesses two distinctive features which may be regarded as significant. First, by showing the relation between cultural value-orientations and the pattern-variable scheme, it

[21] This is the predominant feature of what Weber called "traditional authority."

[22] It may be noted incidentally that the distinction between transcendence and immanence of *reference*, which is involved in th universalism-particularism variable, is not the same as the distinction between worldly and other-worldly orientations.

relates the former directly to the constitutive structural elements of personality and social systems in a way which is theoretically both generalized and systematic. For purposes of theory construction, it makes the place of cultural orientations in systems of action much clearer, and helps greatly to clear away some of the confusions involved in many current controversies in the field. It gives a general theoretical demonstration of why the analysis of value-orientations on the cultural level is of such crucial importance in the theory of action and in all its special branches. It also shows that the interpretation of concrete action exclusively in categories of value-orientation is not admissible, except as a special case. The second distinctive feature of this analysis is that it provides points of departure for a systematic classification of systems of value-orientation. This leads into the systematic classification of types of systems of action themselves as wholes and of their component parts. In both fields there has been a great need for a better basis of such systematic classification. It is hoped that the present scheme might provide the ground work for a more fundamental solution of the problem.

However, the formidable nature of the task of elaborating in detail the implications of such a scheme in relation to the infinitely various nuances of empirical differentiations should not be underestimated. We are under no illusion that more has been done here than to indicate certain fundamental starting points for such a process of elaboration.

4

The Social System

The social system is made up of the actions of individuals. The actions which constitute the social system are also the same actions which make up the personality systems of the individual actors. The two systems are, however, analytically discrete entitites, despite this identity of their basic components.

The difference lies in their *foci of organization* as systems and hence in the substantive functional problems of their operation as systems. The "individual" actor as a concrete system of action is not usually the most important unit of a social system. For most purposes *the conceptual unit of the social system is the role*. The role is a sector of the individual actor's total system of action. It is the point of contact between the system of action of the individual actor and the social system. The individual then becomes a unity in the sense that he is a composite of various action units which in turn are roles in the relationships in which he is involved. But this composite of roles is *not* the same abstraction as personality as a system. It is a special type of abstraction from the concrete totality of ego's system of action, with a highly selective inclusion of the dynamic processes and mechanisms, the selection being made on the basis of an interest in ego as a composite of action units relevant to various collectivities, no longer on the basis of an interest in ego as an action system *per se*. These distinctions, segregating the individual actor as a system, his unit of action and the role to which it corresponds, and the social system, are a precondition of any fruitful empirical analysis of social order and change, as well as of personality adjustment and cultural change.

The primary ingredient of the role is the role-expectation. Role-expectations are patterns of evaluation; their primary constituents are analytically derivable from the pattern-variable combinations and from derivatives of the pattern variables when these are combined with the specific types of situations. Role-expectations organize (in accordance with general value-orientations) the reciprocities, expectations, and responses to those expectations in the specific interaction systems of ego and one or more alters. This reciprocal aspect must always be borne in mind since the expectations of an ego *always* imply the expectations of one or more alters. It is in this reciprocity or complementarity that sanctions enter and acquire their place in systems of action. What an actor is expected to do in a given situation both by himself and by others constitutes the expectations of that role. What the relevant alters are expected to do, contingent on ego's action, constitute the sanctions.[1] Role expectations and sanctions are, therefore, in terms of the content of action, the *reciprocal of each other*. What are sanctions to ego are also role-expectations to alter, and vice versa. However, the content of ego's and alter's expectations concerning ego's action need not be identical with the content of the expectations of alter and ego regarding alter's action in response to ego's.

It may further be noted that each actor is involved in the interaction process in a dual capacity. On the one hand, he is an actor who as ego is *oriented* to alter as an object. This aspect may be called his *orientation role*. On the other hand he *is* an object of alter's orientation (and in certain circumstances of his own). This is his *object role*. When, for instance, he is *categorized* relative to others, it is as object; but when he imposes on himself the renunciation of an affective orientation in favor of a neutral one, he is acting in his orientation role.

In a social system, roles vary in the degree of their institutionalization. By institutionalization we mean the integration of the complementary role-expectation and sanction patterns with a generalized value system *common* to the members of the more inclusive collectivity, of which the system of complementary role-actions may be a part. Insofar as ego's set of role-expectations is institutionalized, the sanctions which express the role-expectations of the other actors will tend to reinforce his own need-dispositions to conform with these expectations by rewarding it and by punishing deviance.

The sanctions will be rewards when they facilitate the realization of the goals which are part of his action or when they add further gratifications upon the completion of the action at certain levels of proficiency; they will be punishments when they hinder his realization of the goals which are part of his action or when they add further deprivations during or after the execution of the action. Conformity on the part of alter with ego's expectations is a condition of ego's goal realization. In addition to the conformity or divergence of alter's actions with respect to ego's expectations, alter's attitudes of approval or disapproval toward ego's behavior are also positive or negative sanctions. In addition to these two immediate types of reward and punishment, there should be mentioned alter's supplementary granting of gratifications for ego's conformity with expectations or transcendence of them and alter's supplementary infliction of deprivations for deficiencies.

Thus far we have been treating the social system only in its most elemen-

---

[1] *Sanctions* is used here to indicate both positive and negative responses by alter to ego's response; i.e., to ego's conformity with or deviation from alter's expectations.

tary form; namely, as the interaction in which the actions of the incumbents of each role are regulated by the double contingency of expectations. Concrete social sytems are, however, more than the simple interaction of two or more individual actors with a common system of values. Social systems give rise to, and often themselves constitute, collective actors in the sense that the individual members interact with one another and with members of other social systems for the achievement of shared collective goals. By collective goals we mean (1) those which are either prescribed by persons acting in a legitimate position of authority and in which the goal is expected to involve gratifications for members other than but including the particular actor, or (2) those goals which, without being specifically prescribed by authority, have the same content as regards the recipients of their gratifications. Shared collective goals are goals which, having the content described in the preceding sentence, have the further property of being simultaneously pursued by a plurality of persons in the same system of interaction.

A social system having the three properties of collective goals, shared goals, and of being a single system of interaction with boundaries defined by incumbency in the roles constituting the system, will be called a *collectivity*.[2] The action of the collectivity may be viewed as the *action in concert* of a plurality of individual actors. Collectivities may act in concert toward their own members or toward objects outside themselves. In the latter case, complementarity of expectations and the associated shared value system exist among the actors within the collectivity but it will not exist *to the same extent* with the actors who are part of another social system. In the case of the former, complementarity of expectations and the shared value system might well exist among all the actors in the situation, with all reorganization of the action of the members being in accordance with shared general value-orientations and with specifically complementary expectations. Even in this case, there will always be involved some orientation toward social and/or nonsocial objects which are outside the collectivity.

The concept of boundary is of crucial significance in the definition of a collectivity. The boundary of a collectivity is that criterion whereby some persons are included as members and others are excluded as nonmembers. The inclusion or exclusion of a person depends on whether or not he has a membership role in the collectivity. Thus all persons who have such roles are members; they are within the boundary. Thus, the boundary is defined in terms of membership roles.

The location of the boundary of a collectivity will vary from situation to situation. Accordingly, the "concerted action" criterion must be interpreted with regard to a defined system of action; that is, a limited range of action.

---

[2] A collectivity may be defined as the integration of its members with a common value system. This integration implies that the members of the collectivity will, under appropriate circumstances, act in "defense" of the shared values.

It is only in a *given situation* that a specific role-expectation becomes the focus of the orientation of behavior. The solidarity of a collectivity may, therefore, be latent as long as certain types of situation which would activate them fail to arise. In other words, the boundary may be latent or temporarily inoperative. Thus, certain obligations to more distant kin might be activated only if such a kinsman were in danger and the actor knew it. Here the boundary of the kinship collectivity would be activated; otherwise it would not be operative. The solidarity of a collectivity might operate frequently and in a variety of situations, and conversely, the situations in which a given plurality's actions are concerted and thus solidary might be of infrequent occurrence. An aggregate of persons might be continuously solidary; that is, whenever they are in a common situation, they will act in concert, but the types of actions in which they are solidary might change continuously: for example, a military unit which has been solidary from the beginning of basic training, through combat, to the state of demobilized civilian life. To meet the definitional requirement of a collectivity, however, an aggregate of persons need not be continuously solidary; they need be solidary only when they are objects to one another in a common situation and when the situation is one which is defined by the value patterns and more specifically by the system of role-expectations as falling within the range of interest of the collectivity.

The criterion of action in concert, then, is another way of formulating the concept of the primacy of collectivity-orientation over self-orientation or private interest. It may be a purely negative, contingent solidarity, which consists in the avoidance of actions that would, in their consequence, damage the other members of the collectivity. Here, too, there is common value orientation, a conforming response to the expectation of other collectivity members.

A *collectivity*, as the term is used here, should be clearly distinguished from two other types of social aggregates. The first is a *category* of persons who have some attribute or complex of attributes in common, such as age, sex, education, which do not involve "action in concert." It is true, of course, that such categories enter into the definitions of roles and thus affect action in concert. But a number of elements must be added before such a category of persons becomes a collectivity. The second type of social aggregate is a plurality of persons who are merely interdependent with one another ecologically. The participants in an ideally perfect competitive market, as that concept is used in pure economic theory, represent an ecologically interdependent aggregate.

A collectivity differs from both these pluralities in being characterized by the *solidarity* of its members. Solidarity is characterized by the institutionalization of shared value-orientations; the values being, of course, oriented toward collective gratifications. Acceptance of common value patterns permits the more differentiated institutionalization of the action of the members of the collectivity in a wide range of specific situations. The range may be broad or narrow, but in each specific situation institutionalization exists when each actor in the situation does, and believes he should do, what the other actors whom he confronts believe he should do. Thus institutionalization is an articulation or integration of the actions of a plurality of actors in a specific type of situation in which the various actors accept jointly a set of harmonious rules regarding goals and procedures. The concrete content of these rules will differ, in the same situation, from actor to actor and from role to role. But the rules, if followed in such a situation of full institutionalization, will lead to perfectly articulated, conflictless action on the part of the several actors. These rules possess their harmonious character by virtue of their derivation, by deliberation and less conscious processes, from common value-orientations which are the same for all members of the institution or the set of institutions in the collectivity. These value-orientations contain general standards in accordance with which objects of various classes are judged, evaluated, and classified as worthy of various types of response of rewards and punishments. Specific institutional situations are differentiated by the concrete state of the objects which each actor confronts and hence by the specific rules which are appropriate in acting toward those objects. In institutionally highly integrated collectivities, situations in which uncertainty prevails about the appropriate action can in principle be clarified by closer scrutiny of the objects and more careful study of the implications of the common value-orientation. (In reality, however, new situations, because they are not always subject to this treatment and because previous cognitive orientations prove inadequate, are dealt with in a variety of ways.) Those, therefore, who share common value-orientations as commitments to action patterns in roles, constitute a collectivity.

Some additional clarification of this definition is necessary. First, with respect to the relationship of the collectivity to the properties of aggregates (sexual qualities, beauty, etc.) : insofar as certain sexual qualities become the foci of roles and thus become institutionalized in a society, the relevant value patterns defining and regulating sexual roles, along with other value patterns, are part of the constitution of a collectivity. But within this larger collectivity, those characterized by the same sexual characteristics do not necessarily act as a collectivity with a preponderant focus on sexual qualities or activities in all or even in any situation. Sex, among many other object characteristics which serve as criteria of admission and which evoke certain role-expectations, plays a constitutive part in many collectivities. An example would be a combat unit in the armed forces; but even though the demonstration of manliness is here an important goal, it is not the chief goal on which the unit is focused. There are few collectivities in which ascription by sex does not figure to some extent in the determination of admission to membership roles and in providing the chief focus of the appropriate expectations. The extent however to which any given object quality, such as sex, ethnic membership, or beauty, will perform these functions varies.

Second, some further remarks on the boundaries of collectivities are in order. Sub-collectivities within a larger inclusive collectivity may be: (1) independent of one another in the sense of having no overlapping members and having either no contact with one another or being in contact with one another only as collectivities; or (2) they may overlap in the sense that they share certain members but not all; or (3) they may be inclusive in the sense that one of the collectivities may be smaller than the other and thus all of its members be in the latter. The inclusive type of collectivity is not, however, distinguished merely by its relative size and the plural memberships of the members of the smaller, included collectivity. The smaller collectivity may be constituted by role-expectations and actions which are specifically differenti-ated versions of the general value-orientation of the larger inclusive collec-tivity. They may be oriented toward more specific goals within the general class of goals pursued by the inclusive collectivity. They may be confronted by a special class of objects within the general classes of objects with which the inclusive collectivity is constitutively concerned, including other parts of the inclusive collectivity. The role structure of the members of the smaller collectivity within the inclusive collectivity will, figuratively speaking, be onion-like in shape. One role will fit within another and so on. Thus a par-ticular professor in a university department who is a member of a depart-mental research group is simultaneously fulfilling, by a given set of actions, three roles: (1) his membership in the research group is part of (2) his role as professor, and his role as professor of a certain subject is part of (3) his role as a member of the university. The latter role may include cognate roles such as service on committees, service in representative roles, and so forth, which have nothing to do with the content of his research role, but all of which fall within the common value system and within the system of solidarity of the university as a collectivity.

The same is true of the market. Common values define general roles for participation in market relations in our society. But it is only when there are common values defining specific rights and obligations vis-à-vis other collec-tive units or persons that, *within* the market system, a collectivity would exist. The members of a cartel are not merely interdependent, they constitute a collectivity, with shared collective goals and concerted action within bound-aries which define the types of rights and obligations which are to be effective. The members of the cartel follow a set of expectations vis-à-vis one another which are different from those which they direct toward persons outside the boundaries. But both sets are in the main derived from or subsumable under the general expectations characteristic of the market as a social system.

A social system, then, is a system of interaction of a plurality of actors, in which the action is oriented by rules which are complexes of complemen-tary expectations concerning roles and sanctions. *As a system*, it has deter-minate internal organization and determinate patterns of structural change. It has, furthermore, as a system, a variety of mechanisms of adaptation to changes in the external environment. Those mechanisms function to create one of the important properties of a system; namely, the tendency to maintain boundaries. A total social system which, for practical purposes, may be treated as self-subsistent — which, in other words, contains within approximately the boundaries defined by membership all the functional mechanisms required for its maintenance as a system — is here called a *society*. Any other is a *subsystem* of a society. It is of the greatest importance in connection with any specific problem to place the subsystem in question explicitly in the context of those parts of the total society which are outside the subsystem for the purposes at hand.[3]

The social system of which roles [4] are the elementary units will of necessity involve the differentiation and allocation of roles. The different individual actors participating in the social sytem will each have different roles, and they will accordingly differ in their specific goals and cognitive orientations. Role-expectations bring into specific focus patterns of generalized orientation. They sharpen the edges of commitments and they impose further disciplines upon the individual. They can do so only as long as the conditions are present in the personality and the social system which enable human beings to *live up to these kinds of expectations*, which diminish or absorb the strains to which people are subjected, including both the "internal strains" connected with difficulty in fulfilling internalized norms and the strains which are associated with divergence from expectation.

Motivational orientations within the personality system might vary among different individuals who conform equally with the same set of expectations. But in the analysis of the social system, particularly in its descriptive analysis, we need be concerned only with the motivational orientation toward the specific set of role-expectations and toward the role itself — and may tentatively disregard the "rootedness" and repercussions of this orientation in the rest of the personality system of the actors involved. Of course, these motivational orientations will not vary at random with respect to the types of personality systems in association with which they are found, but for certain types of important problems, this aspect may be passed over. There will be for each social system, and for social systems in general, certain types of motivational orientations which are preconditions of the working of the system.

The motivational prerequisites of a social system, then, are the patterns

---

[3] It is probable that the sociologist who deals with modern large-scale societies is more frequently called upon to deal with partial systems than is the social anthropologist, who studies smaller societies, or the psychologist, who in his analysis of personality more frequently deals with the system as an integral unit.

[4] Roles are differentiated (1) with respect to value-orientation patterns and (2) with respect to specific functional content. The latter can vary over considerable ranges independently of patterns of value-orientation.

made up of the more elementary components of motivation — those which permit fulfillment to an "adequate" degree of the role-expectations characteristic of the social system in question. These necessary motivational patterns will not be the same for the different parts of the social system, and they must therefore be properly distributed in accordance with the role structure of the social system in question.

THE FOCI OF ORGANIZATION

A social system is a system of the actions of individuals, the principal units of which are roles and constellations of roles. It is a system of differentiated actions, organized into a system of differentiated roles. Internal differentiation, which is a fundamental property of all systems, requires integration. It is a condition of the existence of the system that the differentiated roles must be coördinated either negatively, in the sense of the avoidance of disruptive interference with each other, or positively, in the sense of contributing to the realization of certain shared collective goals through collaborated activity.

When a plurality of individual actors are each oriented in a situation to gratify sets of need-dispositions, certain resultant phenomena are inevitable. By virtue of the primordial fact that the objects — social and nonsocial — which are instrumentally useful or intrinsically valuable are scarce in relation to the amount required for the full gratification of the need-dispositions of every actor, there arises a problem of allocation: the problem of who is to get what, who is to do what, and the manner and conditions under which it is to be done. This is the fundamental problem which arises from the interaction of two or more actors.

As a result of the scarcity of the social and nonsocial objects of need-dispositions, the mutual incompatibility of claims might extend theoretically in the extreme case to the "state of nature." It would be the war of "each against all" in its Hobbesian formulation. The function of allocation of roles, facilities, and rewards does not, however, have to contend with this extreme possibility. The process of socialization in the family, school, and play groups, and in the community focuses need-dispositions in such a way that the degree of incompatibility of the active aspirations and claims for social and nonsocial objects is reduced, in "normal conditions," to the usually executable task of making allocations among sectors of the population, most of whose claims will not too greatly exceed what they are receiving. Without a solution of this problem, there can be no social system. It is indeed one of the functions which makes the social system. It arises in every social system, and though the solutions can vary within limits which from the standpoint of ethical values might be very wide apart, yet every allocative process must have certain properties which are common to all of them. Where the allocative process is not carried out successfully — where the allocative process either interferes with effective collaboration or is not regarded as sufficiently legitimate — the social system in question will tend to disintegrate and to give way to another social system.

The term *allocation* should not be interpreted anthropomorphically. Allocation is a resultant that is only in part a product of deliberate decision; the total allocation in a social system especially may be the product of many processes that culminate in a distribution which no individual or collective actor in the system has sought.

A social system must possess a minimum degree of integration; there must be, that is, a sufficient complementarity of roles and clusters of roles for collective and private goals to be effectively pursued. Although conflict can exist within a social system and, in fact, always does, there are limits beyond which it cannot go and still permit a social system to exist. By definition the complementarity of expectations which is associated with the complementarity of roles is destroyed by conflict. Consequently, when conflict becomes so far reaching as to negate the complementarity of expectations, there the social system has ceased to exist. Hence, for conflict among individuals and groups to be kept within bounds, the roles and role clusters must be brought into appropriately complementary relations with one another.

It is highly important to what follows to distinguish here two functional problems of social systems: (1) *What* roles are to be institutionalized in the social system? (2) *Who* is to perform these roles? Every social system has certain tasks imposed on it by the fact that its members are mortal physiological organisms, with physiological and social needs, existing in a physical environment together with other like organisms. Some variability is possible regarding the tasks which are considered as worthy of being undertaken (in the light of the prevailing value-orientations and the external situation of the social system). This selection of tasks or functions may be phrased as an answer to the question "what should be done with the existing resources of the society?" in the sense of what *jobs* are to be done.

The first allocative function of a social system, therefore, is the allocation of human capacities and human resources among tasks. In addition to a distribution of resources among tasks or functions which can be performed only by a complex of roles, each social system, inasmuch as its members are not born genetically destined to particular functional roles, must allocate its members among those roles. Also, since tasks change, and with them the roles by which they can be met, reallocation is a necessity quite in addition to that imposed by man's birth, plasticity and mortality. One of the ways in which this is done in some social systems is by definition of the criteria of eligibility for incumbency of the role by membership in solidary groups, thus regulating the flow of persons into such roles. In all social systems access to roles is regulated by the possession of qualifications which might be, but are not always necessarily, memberships or qualities.

A closely related allocative problem in the social system concerns the allocation of *facilities* for the performance of roles. The concept of role has been defined as a complementary set of expectations and the actions to be performed in accordance with these expectations. It includes as part of the expectations the rights to certain types of reaction which the actor is entitled to expect from others and the obligations to perform certain types of action which the actor believes others are entitled to expect from him. It is convenient to distinguish *facilities* from the other components in the definition of role. The term refers to those features of the situation, outside the actual actions entailed in the performance of role itself, which are instrumentally important to the actor in the fulfillment of the expectations concerning his role. Thus one cannot be a scholar without the use of books or a farmer without the use of the land for cultivation.

Facilities thus are objects of orientation which are actually or potentially of instrumental significance in the fulfillment of role-expectations. They *may* consist of physical objects, but not necessarily. The physical objects may, to varying degrees, be "natural" objects or manmade objects, such as buildings or tools. They may be the physical embodiments of cultural objects, such as books. The cultural objects may be accessible not through a physical but through a human agent; we may cite as an illustration of such a facility the type of knowledge which must be secured orally from another human being.

In the same sense that we speak of the *rights* to the *action of others* and the *obligations* to perform the *actions expected by others*, the facilities which are necessary roles are likewise the objects of rights and obligations. When the facility is a social object — that is, the action of another person — it becomes identical with the action to which one has a right and concerning which one has certain obligations. It should, however, be stressed that not all the complementary responses of alter are classifiable as facilities. Only those which ego has the right to use in an instrumental manner, without *specific* [5] regulation by a shared and collective value-orientation, are to be designated as facilities. When a social object, either an individual or a collective action system, is a facility, it may be called an opportunity; privileges are unequally distributed opportunities.

The regulation of the relationship between the incumbent of a role or the "possessor" of a facility and actual or potential claimants to displace that possessor is part of the allocation problem. This is of course a major aspect of the institution of "property." The allocation of facilities, as of roles, is made on the basis of the actor's possession of qualities or his manifestation of performances. Rights of access to facilities may, for example, be contingent

[5] The specificity with respect to the concrete situation of action is important here. In nearly all cases short of the limits of extreme brutality, instrumental use of the actors of others occurs within the framework of a *generalized* shared collective value-orientation, which, though not necessarily always conscious, sets limits to the right of instrumental use while leaving an area of freedom for the possessor of the right within those limits.

on the possession of a membership "quality" or on certain performances. The peasant may own his own land by virtue of his membership in a family; the factory worker does not himself own his machine, and his access to it is dependent on his fulfillment of certain performances specified in the "contract of employment" with the company in which ownership is vested, and whose claims are protected by the power of the state and the general value-orientation prevailing in the culture.

The allocation of facilities in a social system may be viewed as an aspect of the allocation of power. There are two senses in which this is so. First is the fact that, while the particular facilities appropriate to the attainment of particular goals may have many singular characteristics, the widespread competition for facilities (which are used to reward collaborators) gives an especially high value to those facilities which have the generalized property of enabling more specific facilities to be acquired. A facility is often such that it can be used to pursue quite a wide variety of goals that might themselves be facilities or substantive goals. This generalized potency is enormously enhanced by the development of money, which is a general medium of exchange, so that "having the price" becomes in effect equivalent to having the concrete facility on the more general level. To have the power to command by virtue of the possession of money or any other qualification is equivalent to having the concrete facility, since the latter can be purchased with the former.

Second, the achievement of goals is often possible in a social system only through collaboration in complementary role situations. One of the means of ensuring collaboration in the pursuit of goals is to control the actions of others in the relevant respects — positively by commanding their services or negatively by at least being in a position to prevent their interference. Therefore the degrees to which and the ways in which an actor (individual or collective) is enabled to control the action of others in the same social system is dependent on the facilities which have been allocated to it (or him). Facilities are powers over objects, social and nonsocial. Power, by its very nature, is a relatively scarce object; its possession by one actor in a relationship is a restriction of the other actor's power. Its intrinsic scarcity and its generalized instrumental status make it into one of the most avidly and vigorously competed for of all objects — we pass over here its very great importance as a direct cathectic object for the immediate gratification of a variety of derivative need-dispositions. It is therefore of the greatest urgency for the determinate allocation of power and the derivative allocations of other facilities to be established and generally accepted in a society. Unless this allocation is well integrated internally and with the value system so that its legitimacy is widely acknowledged, the amount of conflict within the social system may very well rise to the point of disintegration.

THE ALLOCATION OF REWARDS

The allocation of rewards is the systematic outcome of the gratification-orientation of action. It is in the nature of action for gratifications to be sought. Here as much as in the preceding categories of allocation, the objects which gratify need-dispositions [6] are scarcer than would be necessary to satisfy the demand — indeed, in the allocation of rewards, it is sometimes its very scarcity which gives an object its function of gratifying a need-disposition, that is, makes it into a reward. In a system of interaction each of the actors will strive for rewards, the attainment of which might not only be reciprocally contingent, but they might indeed actually come from the same source. The amount one actor gets will affect the amounts other actors get. The resultant, in most societies, is a distribution of rewards that is deliberately controlled only to a restricted extent. It is a resultant of the prior distribution of facilities and is effected by allocative mechanisms which work within the framework of a system of value-orientation.

In the social system the allocation of rewards has the dual function of maintaining or modifying motivation and of affecting the allocation of facilities. Where allocations of rewards diverge too widely from what is thought by the aspirant to be his right in the light of his qualifications, his motivation for the performance of his role will be affected. The effects might range from the inhibition of the need-disposition underlying the previous action to fixation and intensification of the attachment to the gratification object, to the point of disregarding the obligations usually associated with the rights to the object. The maintenance or change of object-attachment is influenced not only by the degree of congruity or discrepancy between expected (entitled) and received rewards but also by the actor's beliefs about the prevailing congruities and discrepancies between entitled and received rewards in the social system at large. Hence, as a cognitive and cathectic-evaluative object, the distribution of rewards plays a large independent part in the motivation of action and particularly in the motivation of conformity and alienation vis-à-vis general value-orientations and specific role-expectations.

The distinction between rewards and facilities is by and large not one between the "intrinsic" properties of the relevant objects, but concerns rather their functional relation in sytems of action. A facility has instrumental significance; it is desired for the uses to which it can be put. A reward, on the other hand, is an object desired for its own sake. The same concrete object may be, and indeed often is, *both* facility and reward to an actor. Not only may an object which is useful as a facility be accepted as a reward, but objects which have a high significance as rewards might also be facilities leading to

---

[6] The interdependence of the need-dispositions is one of the factors accounting for this expansiveness of human demands. The gratification of one need-disposition sets other need-dispositions into action, and inhibition of one sets up a tendency to seek alternative gratifications.

further rewards. Also, in the motivational system of the actor, there is a tendency for particular facilities to acquire reward value. Hence an object which is useful as a facility comes to be cathected directly so that its possession is also interpreted by the actor and by others as a reward. Nevertheless, it is proper to distinguish these two phases of the allocative problem of the social system.

Just as the problem of the allocation of facilities raises the problem of the allocation of power, so the allocation of rewards raises the problem of the allocation of *prestige*, and for similar reasons. Specific rewards, like specific facilities, may have highly specific relations with certain actions which they reward. But the very fact that they become the objects of competing claims — which is, of course, the fact from which the "problem" of allocation derives — is in part evidence of their generalizability to cover the claims of different individuals and to reward the different types of performance. This generalizability intensifies the concentrations of reward value on certain classes of valued objects: especially income, power, and prestige. To possess this generalized quality, each class of rewards must, in some sense, constitute a single scale rendering equivalent different qualifications for the reward. There will also tend to be a common evaluative scale cutting across the different classes of rewards; for example, a scale which enables income to be roughly equated to prestige. This evaluative scale, of course, is seldom explicitly invoked.

It should be made somewhat clearer in just what senses income and power are to be treated as rewards and not as facilities. Their *generalized* character is of significance to *both* functions. But the way in which income and power are integrated into systems of instrumental orientation makes it inevitable that they should be valued; the possession of *anything* valued — the more so if comparison with others is, as it must be, involved — is a source of prestige. Their acquisition, then, can become a goal of action and success in acquisition a *measure* of achievement. Finally, the man with money or power is valued not only for what he has done but for what he *can do*, because possession of generalized facilities widens the range of capacity for achievement. Thus the status of money and power as rewards goes back fundamentally to the valuation of achievement and to their acceptance as *symbols* of achievement, whether actual or potential.

The allocation of power in a society is the allocation of access to or control over the means of attaining goals, whatever they may be. The allocation of prestige, correspondingly, is the allocation of one of the most generalized gratifications which is, at the same time, a very generalized qualification for access to facilities and thus to further and other rewards.

THE INTEGRATION OF THE SOCIAL SYSTEM

This brings us to the consideration of the integrative problems of the social system. From the present point of view, the primary integration of the social system is based on an integrated system of generalized patterns of value-orientation. These patterns of value-orientation are to be described in the categories of the pattern variables. The pattern variables and the derivative patterns of value-orientation can, however, never by themselves adequately define the specific role-expectations which govern behavior in particular situations. Orientation to specific features of the situation in particular ways must be developed in any social system. These will be elaborations and concrete specifications of the values derived from the pattern variables.

A system or a subsystem of concerted action which (1) is governed by a *common* value-orientation and in which (2) the common values are motivationally integrated in action is, as we have said, a collectivity. It is this integration by common values, manifested in the action of solidary groups or collectivities, which characterizes the partial or total integrations of social systems.

Social integration, however much it depends on internalized norms, cannot be achieved by these alone. It requires also some supplementary coördination provided by explicit prescriptive or prohibitory role-expectations (e.g., laws) enunciated by actors in specially differentiated roles to which is attached "responsibility" in collective terms. *Responsibility* in this sense may be subdivided into two types: first, responsibility for the allocative functions in the social systems themselves, the definition and enforcement of the norms governing the allocative processes; second, responsibility for the conduct of communal affairs, for the performance of positive functions on behalf of the collectivity, especially vis-à-vis "foreign" social systems or subsystems. Insofar as such roles of responsibility are institutionally defined, they always involve a collective orientation on the part of their incumbents as one of their fundamental components.[7]

The word institutionalization means both the internalization of common values by the members of a collectivity, and also the enunciation of prescriptive or prohibitory role expectations by occupants of responsible roles.

The institutionalization of value-orientation patterns thus constitutes, in the most general sense, the mechanism of integration for social systems. However, social integration does not require a single uniform set of value-orientations equally and universally distributed throughout the social system. Social integration may well include a whole series of subsystems of common value-orientations varying around a basic pattern. Institutionally, this brings us before the integrative problem of partial integrations or collectivities within the larger social system, on the one hand, and the total collectivity as an integrated entity, on the other.

---

[7] It should go without saying that these considerations apply to any collectivity, no matter how small a part of a total society it forms. This fundamental structural homology between the total society and sub-collectivities within it is one of the most important aspects of the structure of social systems.

The role-expectations in all these situations are focused by the pattern variable of self- and collective-orientation. Every social system will have institutionalized definitions of the spheres within which a collective subunit or an individual is legitimately permitted to go its own way without specific reference to the interests of a larger collectivity, or to specific obligations toward it. On the other hand, there will be institutionalized spheres of direct obligation to the larger collectivity. This usually will be latent and will be active only discontinuously when situations arise in which the objects are threatened or in which conflict occurs. In the first case, negative sanctions apply only when the limits of permission are exceeded; in the second, they apply whenever the positive obligations fail to be fulfilled. Social systems, of course, will vary greatly with respect to the points at which this line is drawn. Only the solidary group in which there are positive collective obligations would, in a specific sense, be called an integrated social system.

There is a final point to be made in connection with social integration and nonintegration. No social system can be completely integrated; there will, for many reasons, always be some discrepancies between role-expectations and performances of roles. Similarly, at the other extreme, there is never likely to be a completely disintegrated society. The mere fact that the human beings who live in a social system are socialized to some extent gives them many need-dispositions which can be gratified only by conformity with the expectations of others and which make them responsive to the expectations of others. Even societies ridden with *anomie* (for example, extreme class conflict to the point of civil war) still possess within themselves considerable zones of solidarity. No society ever "disintegrates completely"; the "state of nature" depicted by Hobbes is never reached by any real society. Complete disintegration is a limiting case toward which social systems might sometimes move, especially in cerain sectors of the structure, but they never arrive there. A particular social system might, of course, lose its identity, or it might be transformed into one which is drastically different and can become absorbed into another social system. It might split into several social systems where the main cleavages follow territorial lines. But dissolution into the "state of nature" is impossible.

CLASSIFICATION OF SOCIAL SYSTEMS AND THEIR COMPONENTS: STRUCTURAL TYPES

The foregoing analysis of the foci of organization of social systems is a first step toward the comparative analysis of the structural variations of social systems. The beginning of such an analysis is classification. It is, however, only after the logically requisite and empirically significant invariant points of reference have been defined and the range of variability explored that the problem of classification can be seriously approached.

The construction of a classification of types of social systems is much too large a task to attempt to carry very far within the limits of the present work. A few remarks on the nature of the problem may, however, be made, and a few starting points indicated.

The principal obstacle has been the enormous variety of structural variables. The possible combinations of these are so numerous that anything approaching a determinate and manageable classification has been out of the question. Furthermore, we have hitherto lacked systematic theoretical criteria by which to select the most significant of these variables. Progress therefore depends on the selection of a limted number of criteria of strategic significance. It is the aim of the present analysis, with its point of departure in the most elementary features of the frame of reference of the theory of action and its purpose to build step by step from these features to the conception of a complex social system, to provide the required criteria.

The elements of this conceptual scheme are numerous: three modes of motivational orientation, three of value-orientation, two object modalities, six classes of objects, three allocative foci, five pattern variables, and so forth. It is not, however, necessary to treat all the conceptual elements which enter the scheme as of equal significance, or as completely independent of each other. Selection can be made, in terms of strategic significance, for the purpose. Our conceptual scheme itself yields the criteria of selection which enable us to reduce the degree of complexity.

In the first place, the basic distinctions in the structure of the object world may be eliminated as a source of further complication. They need appear only in the distinction between the modalities of quality and performance, which is, of course, included in the pattern-variable scheme. Since the three modes of motivational orientation and the three modes of value-orientation are already included in the pattern variables, the construction of the basic patterns of orientation in social relationships can proceed from the combinations of the pattern variables. The resultant combinations may then be used for the description of the structures through which the allocative and integrative functions are performed.

We may begin with the allocative problems. It is possible here to treat the three categories of allocation of personnel, facilities, and rewards together. They constitute the process of "circular flow" which may occur within a social system that is in equilibrium, without being accompanied by a change in the essential structure of the system itself. They may therefore be treated independently of the resultant substantive distribution, at least preliminarily. Further analyses will have to relate the properties of the allocative process to the distributions which they bring about.

Social systems will vary, in this range, according to whether these allocative processes are organized and controlled in terms of ascriptive or performance object properties. In different social sytems, different object properties are adjudged relevant in allocative decisions. The evaluative standards which are primarily embodied in allocative decisions, therefore, are those of ascription and achievement. Individual actors may be granted roles, facilities, or rewards in accordance with their possession of certain classificatory qualities, such as sex, age, physique, personality traits (without regard for their value for the prediction of achievement), or in accordance with their possession of certain relational qualities such as biological (kinship or ethnic) relationships, territorial location, memberships in associations, wealth, and status. On the other hand, they might be granted roles, facilities, or rewards in accordance with their past or prospective achievements, such as instances of their physical strength, performance in examinations or past roles, their power in present roles (i.e., their capacity to gratify or deprive) within a collectivity or among collectivities. Naturally it is not always easy to disentangle these various properties on the basis of which allocations are made (and acknowledged), since they often operate jointly. Indeed, a given characteristic might have several functions simultaneously; for example, take the case of proximity to the exercise of power. Individuals whose occupational roles bring them close to those who exercise great power might receive prestige and other valued objects, both because of the relationship itself and because of the potentiality which these individuals possess of influencing the direction and content of the power and thus themselves gratifying or depriving.

It is at this point relevant to recall that a concrete allocation, once made, cannot be expected to be settled indefinitely. The first and basic reason is the finiteness of life and the continual process of change of need-dispositions and situations during its passage. For a social system to function over a period extending beyond the life span of a generation, there must be a continuous recruitment of new personnel into roles, and naturally, the recruiting must be regulated by some standards of evaluation.

In addition to this fundamental source of the need for continuous allocation, many facilities and rewards are not indefinitely durable but are "consumed" or "wear out" in the course of time, and tasks change, of course, with the consequent change in roles to which there must be new allocations. Therefore, there must also be a continuous flow of replacements in these categories. Incumbency in some roles is much longer than in others, and some facilities and rewards are more durable than others; these differences in "life span" are of prime significance for many empirical problems. But here the essential point is the relative impermanence of all three classes of elements of the system; hence the functional necessity of a continuous flow of replacement and of the regulation of the process. Along side of all this, and only analytically separable from it, there are changes in the substantive content of the expectations governing roles and the organization of the roles about tasks. These changes of content are empirically intimately related to the allocative flow. Indeed, strains arising from the working of the allocative mechanisms may constitute some of the most important sources of changes in the content of roles and the mode of their organization.

As a first approximation, we may distinguish three types of mechanism by which the allocative flow can be regulated. The first is allocation by a process of deliberate selective decision by an authoritative agency and according to an established policy in which either qualities or achievements may be the chief criteria. The second is the institutionalization of some automatically applied rules of allocation, in which the chief criteria of allocation are qualities, especially memberships. The third is allocation as a resultant of a process of individual competitive or emulative achievement, or promise of achievement, whereby the "winners" automatically secure the roles, facilities, and rewards which, according to the prevailing systems of values, are the most desirable.[8] Perhaps the emulative aspect is prominent only in some cases; the most essential criterion in the third type is that the outcome is free from determination either by a fixed automatic rule or by the decision of an authority. The first type, as distinguished from the second and third, tends to be more centralized, and the actor who grants the role, facility, or reward is less likely to make his decision on the basis of a formalized examination established primarily as a recruitment device. Of course, different mechanisms may operate in different parts of the social system and in some parts there may be combinations of any two or of all three types. But variability with respect to the incidence and distribution of these types of mechanisms, which are distinguished by (1) the type of criteria (concerning objects) which they employ and (2) the extent to which organized authority makes the selective decisions, constitutes one major range of variability of social structures.

The relation to the pattern variables, and hence to the system of value-orientations, may be treated briefly. It is with special reference to its bearing on these mechanisms that the ascription-achievement variable is of primary significance, especially in the allocation of personnel. In all societies the ascriptive criteria of sex and age at least limit the eligibilities for participation in different roles, and hence memberships in collectivities. Beside these, the ascrption of roles on the basis of the criteria of biological relationship and territorial location of residence plays some significant part in all societies, by virtue of the fact that all have kinship systems and that kinship units are units of residence. But, of course, the range of allocative results determined by these ascriptive criteria varies enormously in different societies. The maximum application of the "hereditary principle" — in, for example an Australian tribe or the Indian caste system — represents one extreme of variation in this respect. Our own society is considerably removed in the opposite direction.

[8] Even in the case of a system of allocation by individual competition, much of the allocation will be by virtue of qualities such as membership and particularly membership in a kinship group. The winner in individual competition usually shares the prizes with his family.

However widely complexes of qualities may operate as determinants in a social system in which there is a competitive allocative process, they set limits to, rather than serve as a constitutive part of that process. Such a system therefore accords primacy to criteria of performance and increases the range of roles which can be entered through achievement. It is noteworthy in this connection that ascriptive criteria may, and often do, include memberships in collectivities — for example, by virtue of birth — but criteria of achievement cannot do so, as far as the allocation of personnel is concerned. In this context, therefore, an orientation toward achievement is inherently "individualistic." Of course, the same basic schema may be applied to the relationships of collectivities, such as those of business firms.

With respect to the ascription-achievement variable, allocation by authoritative decision is, as we have said, neutral; it may lean either way or combine both types of criteria. Indeed, it may facilitate the adjustment of the two types of processes to each other. However, the more widely ascriptive criteria are applied in allocation, the less necessary specific authoritative decision becomes for routine cases. There is thus a definite relationship between such a situation and traditionalism. There are, however, almost always small openings left by ascriptively oriented allocative processes, and these tend to be regulated by authoritative decision.

Allocation by authoritative decision quite often serves as a mechanism for the universalistic application of an achievement-oriented system of allocation. In the Chinese bureaucracy the allocation of personnel by appointment, on the basis of achievement in examinations, made access to bureaucratic roles more dependent on achievement than it probably would have been if it had been left to open emulative competition under the conditions then prevailing in Chinese society.

In short, the variability of social structures with respect to the incidence of these various types of allocative mechanisms seems capable of empirical establishment and is, as well, of central theoretical importance.

THE CONTENT OF ROLES

The allocative process does not determine the role structure of the social system or the content of the roles. It is necessary, therefore, to develop categories which make possible the analysis of the variability of the social system with respect to the content and organization of roles. We will take up role contents first, and the structural integration of roles later.

Role contents can be classified according to three sets of invariant points of reference. That is, there are three separate classes of problems that must be solved by all role occupants; if we classify the solutions to these problems generally enough, we will thereby have, in some sense, a classification of role contents. The three sets of problems (or invariant points of reference) are

(1) problems of instrumental interaction, (2) problems of expressive interaction, and (3) integrative problems.[9]

Problems of instrumental interaction concern relationships with alters
which ego engages in, not primarily for their own sake, but for the sake of
goals other than the immediate and direct gratification experienced in contact with the object. The social elaboration of instrumentally significant
activities is what, in economic theory and its utilitarian philosophical background, has come to be called the division of labor. Problems of expressive
interaction concern relationships with alters which ego engages in primarily
for the immediate direct gratification they provide. Integrative problems are
problems of a somewhat different order. They are the problems which arise
when one would maintain proper relationships between roles with an eye to
the structural integration of the social system. We will take up in the following pages, first, problems of instrumental interaction as bases for classification
of role contents, and second, problems of expressive interaction as bases for
classification of role contents. Then we will go on to discuss problems of
structural integration.

A system of instrumentally interdependent roles has a basic structure
which, throughout the variability of the substantive goals which are being
instrumentally sought, may be treated as constant. There are a limited number
of functional problems arising in ego's instrumental relations with others,
problems which have to be solved if the system is to persist. These problems
are constant in all systems of instrumental interaction although some of them
are logically appropriate to higher degrees of differentiation of the instrumental system, and thus need not be considered at the more elementary
levels. These problems provide a set of invariant points of reference or comparative categories for the analysis of the structure and content of roles in
systems of instrumental allocation.

It is inherent in the nature of human action that some goals should be
sought instrumentally. It is consequently inherent in the nature of social
systems that their members should perform certain mutually significant
functions on the instrumental level — functions which require disciplined
activity and in which the actor's interest in direct and immediate expression
of gratification will not have primacy. But it is equally a precondition of the
functioning of social systems that they should provide a minimum of essential
gratifications direct and indirect to their members (i.e., to a sufficient proportion of them a sufficient proportion of the time). These direct gratifications of need-dispositions are so organized into a system of relationships that
the structure of that system is just as vital to the actor's interest in expressive

---

[9] So far as problems of instrumental and affective interaction are concerned, it seems
fair to treat complex societies and smaller units (e.g., the conjugal families) of which it is
composed as homologous. They will differ, of course, with respect to their structural
integration.

gratification as the structure of the instrumental system is to their instrumental interests. Moreover, the systems of gratification and instrumentality are intertwined in the same concrete system of social roles, and many of the factors that cause change emerge from this intertwining.

If we take the instrumental system first, we find there are four fundamental problems. The first derives from the fact that, given the division of labor,[10] one or more alters must be the *beneficiaries* of ego's activities. In the terminology of economics, they must be the consumers of his product. In addition to the *technical* problem, then, of how ego is to organize his own resources, including his actions to produce the service or commodity, there is the further problem of determining the terms on which alter is allowed to become the beneficiary. This is a special case of the problem of the terms of exchange; specifically it is the problem of the terms of disposal. Thus, the problem of disposal is the first problem of instrumental interaction. Secondly, insofar as ego specializes in a particular type of instrumentally significant activity, he becomes dependent on the output of one or more alters for meeting his own needs. These may or may not be the same alters involved in the former relationship of disposal — in a complex economy they usually are not. At any rate there is an exchange problem here, too, growing out of the functional need, as it may be called, for ego to receive *remuneration* for his activities. Thus, the problem of remuneration is the second problem of instrumental interaction.

Problem of access to facilities (alters as *suppliers* of facilities)		Disposal problem (alters as *consumers*)
	Technical instrumental goal-orientation of ego	
Problem of collaboration (alters as *collaborators*)		Remuneration problem (alters as *sources* of income)

Third, only in a limiting case will all the facilities that ego needs to perform his instrumental functions be spontaneously available to him. It will be necessary for him to acquire or secure access to some of them through arrangement with one or more alters, involving still a third set of exchange relations and the associated standard incorporated into the terms of exchange. This third instrumental problem is that of access to facilities. Fourth, the product may not be capable of production by ego through his own unaided efforts. In this case he is dependent on still a fourth set of alters for collaboration in the joint instrumental process. The process requires organization

[10] Individual self-sufficiency is of no interest here because it does not entail interdependence.

in which ego and alters collaborate to produce a unitary result which is the object of instrumental significance. Thus, the fourth instrumental problem is the problem of coöperation or collaboration. These relations are set forth in the accompanying diagram.

In each of these relationships of ego and the alters, there is a problem of exchange, the solution of which is the settlement of the terms on which ego enters into mutually acceptable relations with the relevant alters. The settlement of the terms of exchange is a basic functional problem inherent in the allocative process of social systems. It was not directly taken account of in our discussion of the institutionalization of roles, but it must be treated in a more differentiated analysis. In our analysis of institutionalization we treated the evaluative content of the expectations of the actors toward themselves and others as unproblematical. In actuality, however, each expectation contains or is associated with an evaluation of the action of the actor in its relation to the value of the complementary action of the alter.[11] All human interaction contains a scale of evaluative equivalence. In instrumental relationships this scale of evaluative equivalence tends to be determinate, specific, and explicit. In diffuse affective attachments the equivalences are much broader and less determinate and much less explicit, as well. The standards of the terms of exchange not only become imbedded in the expectations of instrumental orientations; they also become institutionalized, as do the processes for establishing them when they are not spontaneously and automatically effective. The institutionalization of the processes and standards by which the terms of exchange come to be settled constitutes one essential component of social structures.

In addition to this, *exchange* implies a thing which changes hands. This entity may be called a *possession* and analysis will show that *possession* is always reducible to *rights*. Physical objects are significant insofar as one actor (individual or collective) has various types of control — acknowledged as legitimate — over them while others do not. The terms on which possessions are held, used, controlled, and disposed of is another focus of the functional problems of allocation: *property*.

We turn now to a somewhat different problem, also derivative from the division of labor. A most important range of variability occurs along the continuum of *fusion* and *segregation* of roles in instrumental relationships. The role allocated to ego may be confined to a technical instrumental content, such as the arrangement of the facililties through his own resources while assigning the "responsibility" for the execution of all four of the essential conditions of that role to the incumbents of the other roles. Such a *technical*

---

[11] The notion here is this: when ego acts with respect to alter, his action is seen as having some ("evaluative") value to alter. That is, it gratifies alter, or helps alter along the road toward gratification. When ego acts in such a fashion, alter is expected to return the favor by acting with respect to ego with an action of similar value.

role would be the extreme of segregation. This is the typical case of the functionally specific (specialized) roles within large-scale organizations in modern society. At the other extreme, is the type of role in which the incumbent has not only the responsibility for the technical performance but for all four associated functions — as in the case of the medieval craftsman, or the ideal type of independent general practitioner in medicine. This may be called the artisan [12] role.

The larger and more differentiated an instrumental system the more essential management or managed coördination becomes to keep the organization going as a functioning concern. With this, there emerge *executive* or managerial roles. In the executive role is centered the responsibility for the specification of roles to be performed, the recruitment of personnel to perform the roles, the organization and regulation of the collaborative relations among the roles, the remuneration of the incumbents for their performances, the provision of facilities for performance of the roles, and the disposal of the product. The organization of an instrumental complex into a corporate body which exists in a context of other individual actors and corporate bodies involves also the management of "foreign relations." Here rearrangements of the internal organization and the use of the power to gratify or deprive which the corporate body has at its disposal are available to the manager (as well as the invocation and interpretation of the common value-orientations which are shared with the "foreign" body).

Thus social systems may be further characterized by the extent to which they are made up of fused or segregated roles in an instrumental context or, more concretely, of technical, of artisan, and of executive roles.[13]

Up to this point, our discussion has entirely passed over that aspect of the system of relationships which is oriented primarily by interests in direct and immediate gratification.[14] Within such a system of relationships oriented toward direct and immediate gratification the basic functional categories are homologous with those of the instrumental complex. In the first place, direct gratification in relation to a cathected social object is a relation to that ob-

[12] The independent professional role is then defined as a special subtype in which the technical competence of the incumbent includes the mastery of a generalized intellectual orientation. The professional role, too, is subject to a fairly high degree of segregation of its component elements, although some limits are imposed by the generalized intellectual orientation.

[13] The executive or managerial function itself might be fused or segregated. The more segregated it is, however, the more functionally necessary is some type of integrative mechanism which will perform the function of fusion at this level.

[14] Here gratifications which do not involve social relationships with a cultural component may be ignored. In the context of the present discussion, we are using the terms *gratification interests* and *expressive interests* more or less interchangeably. By expressive orientation we mean a type of action orientation parallel to the instrumental through its inclusion of a cultural component. It is gratification *within* a pattern of appreciative standards.

ject as a "consumer" of the impulse. It is not enough to have the need-disposition. An object must be available which is both "appropriate" for the gratification and "receptive." Alter must allow himself to be an object and not resist or withdraw.

Second, there is also a parallel to remuneration in the dependence of ego, not merely on the receptiveness but on what may be called the *response* of alter. Alter does not merely allow ego to *express* or gratify his need-disposition in the relationship; alter is also expected to act positively in such a way that ego will be the receptive object. These two types of functional preconditions for the gratification of need-dispositions are not always fulfilled by the same objects — where they are we may speak of a symmetrical attachment.

Third, gratification needs not merely an object but is also dependent on the set of circumstances referred to in Chapter II as occasions, which appear, in certain respects, to have functions homologous with those of facilities in the instrumental relationship. Occasions often center around relations to third parties, both because of the necessity of ego's distribution of his expressive orientations among the different objects in a system and be-

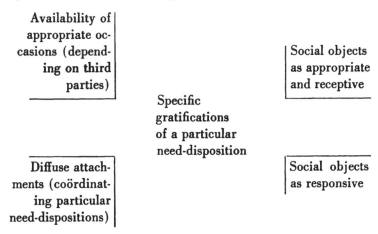

cause the prerequisite of giving gratification to and receiving it from certain actors in a system is a certain relationship with all other actors in the system.

Finally, if we take the need-disposition for gratification and not the object relation as the unit, there is an important functional parallel with coöperation in the instrumental complex. Some need-dispositions, like some technical performances, may be segregated into a separate object relation. But for reasons which have already been discussed, there is a strong tendency for ego to become attached to particular objects for the gratifications of a variety of different need-dispositions. We have called this kind of object relationship a diffuse "attachment." Such an attachment organizes need-disposition gratifications into a "coöperative" system. Putting these various elements together we derive the accompanying homologous paradigm of the structure of the system of relationships of direct and immediate gratifications or expressions. This paradigm analyzes the elementary structure of a social relationship system relevant to the actor's needs for direct gratification or expression. For n actors to participate in the same social system, the relationships involved in this paradigm must be organized and controlled, generally through institutionalization. There is in each case a problem of the settlement of the terms on which the gratifications in question can be attained, or in other terms, of the reciprocal rights and obligations to receive and to give various types and degrees of gratification, which is directly homologous with the problem of the settlement of the terms of exchange.

There is, furthermore, in the expressive system an important homologue to possessions in the instrumental system, since there are entities which can "change hands." The actor can acquire them from someone else or grant them to someone else and he can have, acquire, or relinquish rights in them. In the focal case where alter is the cathected object, this must mean the establishment of rights vis-à-vis the *action* of alter, that is, of a situation where ego can *count* on alter's actions. This will include expectations of alter's overt behavior, but for the reasons which have already been discussed, the central interest will be in alter's *attitudes*. Such a right to a given attitude on alter's part may be called a relational possession. Relational possession in this sense constitutes the core of the reward system of a society and thus of its stratification, centering above all on the distribution of rights to response, love, approval, and esteem. (This also means that there will be an equivalent in the expressive system to the "terms of exchange.")

The expressive system of an actor will therefore, to a highly important degree, have to be organized in a system of relationships with other actors in appropriate roles. This system will regulate choice of objects, occasions — and what is primarily at issue in the present discussion — which objects have segmental significance, gratifying only one need-disposition at a time, and which other objects have diffuse significance, gratifying many need-dispositions at the same time. Here the two most obvious types of role would be on the one hand, segregated or specific gratification roles; on the other, diffuse attachment roles. A diffuse attachment then would involve gratification of a plurality of need-dispositions; it would place each object in both receptive and responsive roles and would involve the actor in a more or less continuous complex of appropriate occasions.

The instrumental complex and the complex of direct gratifications or expressions are both aspects of the total allocative mechanism of a concrete social system. The next step in our analysis then, is to see how they both work in a single system. Once again the concepts of fusion and segregation are pertinent. Instrumental and expressive functions may be segregated from each other, each being performed by distinctly separate objects in distinct roles, or they may be fused in the same objects and roles. Where there is segregation of the instrumental and need-gratifying roles and orientations toward objects, it does not necessarily mean that the need-dispositions are always frustrated. It means that the roles and objects which are instrumentally defined may be either neutral or negative as far as their capacity for the gratification of direct need-dispositions is concerned. There certainly can be and very frequently are cases of conflict where segregation is imperfect and positive fusion is impossible. In these cases there must be either frustration of the immediate and direct gratification of need-dispositions or the instrumental complex will be distorted because the instrumentally necessary actions will not be performed in accordance with instrumental role-expectations. In the total economy of the personality, however, adequate motivation of instrumental activities becomes impossible if the performance of instrumental roles imposes too heavy a sacrifice of the larger gratification interests of the personality.

It would be possible to carry out the classification of the possible combinations in this sphere to a high degree of elaboration. For our present purposes, however, it is sufficient to distinguish six major types of combination which are particularly relevant to the broader differentiations of role types. They are the following:

1. The segregation of specific expressive interests from instrumental expectations; for example, the role of a casual spectator at an entertainment.

2. The segregation of a diffuse object attachment from instrumental expectations; for example, the pure type of romantic love role.

3. The fusion of a specific expressive or gratificatory interest with a specific instrumental performance; for example, the spectator at a commercialized entertainment.

4. The fusion of a diffuse attachment with diffuse expectations of instrumental performances; for example, kinship roles.

5. The segregation of specific instrumental performances, both from specific expressive interests and attachments and from other components of the instrumental complex; for example, technical roles.

6. The fusion of a plurality of instrumental functions in a complex which is segregated from immediate expressive interests; for example, "artisan" and "executive" roles.

This classification has been constructed by taking the cases of fusion and segregation of the instrumental and direct gratification complexes and, within each of the segregated role orientations, distinguishing the segregation of role components from the fusion of role complexes. The technical role (5) and the executive role (6) are the two possibilities of segregation and fusion in the instrumental complex when it is segregated from the direct gratification complex. The role of casual spectator (1) and the romantic love role (2) are the two possibilities of segregation and fusion of the direct gratification complex when it has been segregated from the instrumental complex. There is a fusion of the two complexes in roles (3) and (4). In the role of the paying spectator there is segregation both in the direct gratification and in the instrumental orientation; in the role of member of a kinship group there is fusion of all role components in each orientation. (See Fig. 13, p. 273.)

Before proceeding to examine the dynamic implications of this scheme and its closely connected relevance to the comparative analysis of social systems, we shall reformulate it in terms of the pattern-variable scheme in order to show its derivation from the basic categories of the theory of action.[15]

Three pattern variables are involved: affectivity-neutrality, universalism-particularism, and specificity-diffuseness. Primacy of direct and immediate gratification interests implies affectivity. Neutrality is expected in the orientation which is central in the instrumental complex. Where instrumental considerations have primacy, the discipline is institutionalized. Neutrality is not, however, to be found only in institutionalized instrumental orientations.

The pattern variable of specificity underlies the segregation of role components. Specificity consists in this sphere in the segregation of an instrumental performance or of an expressive interest from *responsibility* for its context of preconditions or repercussions so that no evaluative adaptations in this area are required of the actor. Diffuseness unites the particular component with the other components which make up its relational context. From a certain point of view, therefore, the institutionalization of diffuse orientations into fused roles and relationships constitutes a highly important mechanism of social control, in that it binds together empirically the potentially independent elements of a system of relationships. When, on the other hand, diffuseness breaks down and specificity emerges so that roles become segregated into their components and the complexes become segregated too, certain additional problems of control, particularly the promulgation and the regulation of the terms of exchange and of the maintenance of rights to possession and of motivation — emerge with it.

A further subdivision is introduced by the pattern variable particularism-universalism. Whereas affectivity-neutrality refers to an orientation toward objects focused on the mode of their appropriateness for gratification, particularism-universalism refers to an orientation toward objects focused on their membership or quality *in relation to* the actor as a member of a collectivity or an ecological complex. To the extent that the *relationship* (of common membership) to the actor is disregarded we have a universalistic orientation, the object being then judged by its properties in relation to objects other than the actor. Thus, a segregated specific expressive interest is compatible with a universalistic orientation so long as a *class* of objects defined by general properties is appropriate to the gratification and ap-

---

[15] Owing to the rather difficult and technical nature of this derivation, those satisfied of its possibility might be advised to pass over the next four paragraphs.

propriateness is not confined to members of a class already in a special relation to the actor. Therefore, roles 1 and 3 *may* be universally institutionalized. Particularism, on the other hand, though it *may* be involved in specific gratifications, is much more fundamental to diffuse attachments. Therefore, any role in which the element of attachment has primacy is almost necessarily particularistic.[16]

When the possible combinations of these three pattern variables are considered, all of our six types are found, in addition to one other which we did not mention; one which combines universalism, diffuseness, and affectivity.[17] Since a diffuse-affective orientation has been specifically defined as an attachment, we must inquire into the possibility of an attachment without particularity of object. As an empirical phenomenon in a social system, it is a marginal case. It corresponds to "universal love" in a religious sense, which is certainly a value-orientation of great importance. Perhaps it might be desirable to add it as a seventh type. In any case, the difficulties of its institutionalization are obvious.

With respect to their composition in terms of role contents, then, social systems should be susceptible to classification with respect to the functional importance and frequency in different parts of the system of the above enumerated six (or seven) types of role. As far as major societies are concerned, by far the most prominent are the fourth, fifth, and sixth types. The grounds for this lead us into some important dynamic considerations.

In social systems, because of the dependence of ego's gratifications on the responses — actions and attitudes — of alter, there tends to be a primacy of functional interest in performance of roles. The gratifications the actors receive are, therefore, in a sense secondary and instrumental to this interest; the performance of a role in accordance with expectations — i.e., in conformity with standards of obligation and efficiency — becomes established as an intrinsic good. Moreover, in the major role structure of the social system, a particular functional importance tends to fall to those role patterns which perform functions other than gratifying direct expressive interests. When conflict arises between functional role performance in accordance with obligations and direct gratifications, there is always a strong tendency, although not always a successful one, for the former to be given priority. In a secondary sense, however, types one, two, and three are both widespread and functionally very important in most social systems in the reduction of strains created by instrumental roles and sometimes in the disruption of institutions. But only where it is directly integrated with instrumental expectations in the

---

[16] This connection of particularism with diffuse attachments is explicitly limited to the present context. When patterns of value-orientation are taken into consideration, other bases of particularism might be found, notably, the orientation to solidarity based on value-integration.

[17] See Fig. 14

context of diffuse attachment is direct expressive orientation prominently institutionalized in the wider social structure.

Furthermore, these considerations point toward a very important set of dynamic relations between the social system and the personality. All action in roles is motivated and hence must bear some relation to the need-disposition system of the actor. A given need-disposition can be best gratified in certain types of roles, and the balance of the system of need-dispositions in the personality will have much to do with the probable "adjustment" of ego to different types of role. Generally speaking, the need-dispositions for specific gratifications (cell 1, Fig. 14, p. 274) will be best fitted to roles one and three. Since these roles are usually functionally peripheral to the organization and working of the social structure, a person in whom these need-dispositions are especially strong will probably have a difficulty in adjustment in most societies. The need for love, on the other hand, will fit best with roles two and four. There may, however, be a problem engendered by the instrumental expectations and hence the elements of discipline necessitated by adjustment to role four. Finally, roles five and six would seem most effectively to gratify, other things being equal, the need-disposition for approval and esteem, when there is no necessity for either diffuse or specific immediate gratifications or expressions.

The fourth type of role would probably be the stablest, inasmuch as it offers the possibility of directly gratifying the need-dispositions and enhances stability through the effect of diffuseness in both instrumental and expressive systems.

The relative strength of the different classes of need-dispositions will, of course, vary with different personality types and hence with different types of socialization experience. However, there is likely to be a certain minimum strength of each of these need-dispositions although some might undergo pronounced transformations through the mechanisms of defense and adjustment. A society which makes the institutionalization of roles five and six very widespread must have, if it is to continue more or less stable, some compensatory mechanisms for the gratification of need-dispositions for immediate gratification. The emphasis in the American kinship system on affectivity, especially the prominence of romantic love and the emergence of various types of relatively undisciplined hedonism in our society such as commercialized entertainment, drinking, and the literature and films of violence, might be among the adjustive consequences of the institutional emphasis. These might be regarded as a balancing of the "one-sidedness" of roles five and six through compensating outlets allowed by roles two and three. The interrelationships are, however, neither immediate nor direct and many other factors are involved.

INTEGRATION: CONSENSUS AND POWER

The foregoing discussion has been concerned with the allocative organization of social systems. Variability will also be found in structures which are primarily of integrative significance. Of these, two classes are especially important. They are the systems of value-orientation, which are institutionalized in the social system and define the scope and depth of solidarities among its members, and the adaptive structure through which the system achieves sufficient integration to keep going as a system.

We have already discussed systems of value-orientation in general in the last chapter. Systems of value-orientation defined (in the categories of the pattern variables) the main outlines of the expectations governing roles. But even though there is a relatively definite "ethos" in the value system of the culture, the roles in a social system are not uniform. The distribution of the different types of roles within the social system cannot be explained merely by reference to this ethos, for reasons which have been reviewed already. Hence there will not be one internally consistent system of values in a society. Even in a highly integrated society, there will be at best a heterogeneous combination of variants of the main theme of the ethos, with numerous elements of compromise and inhibition of the consistent application of the system of values which is generally acknowledged as legitimate.

The fifth pattern variable, self-orientation–collective-orientation, is especially important in the analysis of solidarity. This pattern variable defines the scope of the obligations to the collectivity and consequently the areas of permissiveness which are left open to private goals, whether they be sought instrumentally or as objects of immediate and direct gratification. The private goals may be those of individuals or of collectivities vis-à-vis other collectivities. Social systems vary greatly in the ways and in the scope which they allow the sphere of permissiveness. Although no society is entirely without a sphere of permissiveness, just as no society is without a high degree of regulation, yet the differences both in magnitude and qualitative incidence may be extremely significant from both an ethical and a scientific standpoint.

Thus the patterns of value-orientation, as defined in pattern variable terms, can be seen to define the scope and depth of solidary groupings in the social system. The functions of all solidary groupings are largely, although by no means entirely, allocative, as we have seen. The value patterns may, like the ascription-achievement variable, be particularly relevant to the regulation of the allocative flow of personnel, facilities, and rewards among roles and incumbents of roles; or, like affectivity-neutrality, universalism-particularism, and specificity-diffuseness, they may describe the roles and systems of roles within which this flow takes place. Or, finally, like self-orientation–collective-orientation, their relevance may lie in defining the boundaries of the obligations of solidarity and the areas of permissiveness which these leave open. In doing this, they have a large share in the settlement of the terms of exchange.

Where the terms of exchange are not arrived at spontaneously and simultaneously by the partners to the exchange relationship, some type of adjudication or settlement becomes necessary. The bargaining or discussion by which they arrive at a settlement might be simply the result of the coercive power [18] of one of the actors over the other. Usually, however, it will not be; for no social system could persist through time and meet most of the functional problems which arise in it if the terms of exchange in its instrumental complex — both economic and political — were exclusively or even predominantly settled by coercion. The threat of coercion certainly has an important place, and actual coercion, too, plays a marginal though very significant part. In periods of extensive disintegration, indeed, actual coercion assumes a more prominent position as a factor both in disintegration and in reintegration. But at almost all times the terms of exchange — the expectations of what will be given him on the basis of which ego acts in a given situation — have their roots in the generalized patterns of value-orientation widely shared in the society. However, there is a gap between the generalized patterns and the specific terms of exchange. Sometimes this gap can be closed by a gradual give-and-take, a trial-and-error process in the course of which a balance satisfactory to the parties immediately involved is gradually worked out. More likely is some sort of adjudication by discussion, in which the generalized patterns are invoked as legitimating specific proposals for settlement. Other forms of settlement include threats of deprivation within the sphere of permissiveness allowed by the generalized patterns and settlement through declaration or legislation by an authority whose powers are regarded as legitimate in the light of the generalized patterns of value-orientation.

Even in a society in which the consensus on the generalized patterns of value-orientation — by their nature, patterns of value-orientation must be generalized — is great, it will still be insufficient for the maintenance of order. Nor can the equally necessary specificity of role-expectation be counted upon to remedy the deficiency. Some sort of institutionalized mechanism is indispensable, and this is the function of authority. We have already mentioned the function of authority in connection with the allocation of facilities and rewards. Here we shall refer briefly to the function of authority in integration. The standard governing the terms of exchange, or the standard by which expectations are made mutual and articulated so that both ego and alter obtain the gratification which they seek in the particular situation, is an evaluative standard. It is the functional link between allocation and integra-

[18] Coercive power is the capacity to inflict deprivations despite physical resistance. Short of this extreme, coercive power is the imposition of deprivations which cannot be evaded because attempting to do so would result in other more serious deprivations.

tion. It is the measuring rod of apportionment, and its acceptance by the recipients is the foundation of an integrative social system of social order.

THE ANALYSIS OF SOCIAL STRUCTURE

We may now try to deal more synthetically with the various components
and functional processes of the social system. The object orientations and
processes which we have treated constitute characteristic *trait complexes* of
the social system as a whole. They are found throughout the system, although they are particularly prominent in some section of it; and they may
be regarded as resultants of all the factors hitherto explicitly dealt with,
including the specific situation of the social system and its history.

They may be most conveniently classified in the categories of Fig. 15
(p. 275). First, all social systems will, in these terms, have certain relatively
general patterns of categorization of their units, both individual actors and
collectivities. All societies, for example, evaluate individuals by their age and
sex, although the particular evaluations will vary from society to society.

In the second place, all social systems have characteristic patterns of role
orientation to which both individual and collective actors adhere. The
basic variations are, as we have seen, definable in terms of combinations of the
pattern variables. But in consequence of adaptation to the exigencies of situational and motivational conditions — societies will vary with respect to the
distribution of these patterns throughout their respective structures. Thus
a role exercising authority may, as we saw in the last chapter, be defined
in relatively sharp authoritarian terms; or a role placing emphasis on individual responsibility may receive a strong anti-authoritarian emphasis. The
sources of these adaptive reorganizations of the fundamental role-expectations
(conceptually derived from the pattern variables) are essentially those analyzed in the last chapter in connection with the integration of value-orientation patterns in the social system. With reference to the dominant ethos of
the society, they give rise to such broad traits as are usually called "indvidual-
ism," "collectivism," "traditionalism."

With regard to our third category, we need do no more than refer briefly
to the division of labor, since it has already been dealt with earlier in this
chapter. No attempt was made above to characterize types of the division of
labor as a whole; for example, with respect to the degree of differentiation
of functions or the points at which the fusions and segregations occur. These
tasks still remain. In respect to our fourth category, we have dealt with the
system of social stratification, which is the reward system integrated about
the allocation of prestige. This is a major structural aspect of all social systems, and produces extremely far-reaching functional consequences. Finally,
the fifth category comprises the specifically integrative structures of collectivities, with the society as a whole regarded as the most important of these
collectivities. These integrative structures include the modes cf organization

and regulation of the power system and the ways in which orientation to a paramount focus of values, as in religion, are organized. These integrations take the form of state and church, insofar as differentiation has made them distinctive structures. It is here that differentiated roles with integrative functions on behalf of the social system as a whole will be found. The components which enter into them will, however, be those already discussed.

Whatever success we have in the development of categories which will be useful in describing the ranges of variability of social structures will prepare us to approach those really important problems for which classification is not the solution. One of the foremost of these is the problem of the discovery and explanation of certain empirical clusters among the formally possible structural clusters. Thus in kinship, for example, although there is nothing intrinsic to either the socialization of the child or the regulation of sex relations which makes it necessary that these two functions should be handled by the same institution; yet they do both tend to be accomplished by one institution, usually the family. Their thoroughgoing separation, where it has been attempted, has not lasted long. Similarly, the distributions of prestige and power do not vary independently of one another, even though intrinsically the two are quite discrete. A wide discrepancy between the distribution of power and prestige limits the degree of integration and creates a disequilibrium; the discrepancy cannot last long unless special mechanisms reduce the strains and reinforce the capacity of the system to withstand them. Otherwise the system will have to undergo marked modifications before an equilibrium is reestablished.

The existence of such empirical clusters simplifies the ultimate problem of classification and helps us to formulate more systematically the problems of dynamic analysis. It reduces the variety of types which must be taken into consideration, and it more sharply defines the problem of explanation by presenting for any variable both those categories or series with which it is highly correlated and those with which it has a low correlation. An adequate explanation should account for both. Thus this method of classification enables us to perceive problems in relationships which had previously been regarded as scientifically unproblematical, and it enables us to trace out more sharply the particularly dynamic property of certain of the variables which we use.

It is by no means necessary to suspend all comparative structural analyses pending the emergence of a comprehensive systematic classification of types of society. Work of the highest order can be done in particular areas of social subsystems, and although it might have to be reformulated in the light of general theory, its intrinsic value is indisputable. As the general theory of social systems and particularly of societies develops, the nature of the situation in which subsystems operate can be clarified. Gradually the analysis of such subsystems may be expected to merge into the general theory. At the same time, the development of the general theory of social systems needs to be carried on with special attention to the task of elaboration toward the more specific, more concrete subsystems.

Our own analysis is thus very far from a classification of actual structural types of social systems. But it does present, we feel, a systematic approach to the problem, which is capable of further development into the very heart of substantive theory. It delineates all the principal components — the elements of orientation and the functional problems which it will be necessary to incorporate into such a classification — and works out some of their relations to each other.

MOTIVATION AND THE DYNAMICS OF SOCIAL PROCESS

The preceding section has led us necessarily to the border of the dynamic problems of the stability and change of social systems.[19] It is a measure of the validity of our conceptual scheme that it should have done so since it may be regarded as evidence that our categories even in their most elementary form were defined so as to include dynamic properties. A cursory retrospect of all our categories will show that they were from the very start directed, not just toward classificatory or taxonomic description, but toward the explanation of why various structures endure or change. The employment of motivational categories in our description of action meant that we had made the first preliminary step toward the analysis of the conditions of persistence and change. The categories of cognitive, cathectic, and evaluative orientation carried in them the possibilities of the redirection of action with changes in internal or external conditions. The introduction of the concepts of gratification-deprivation balance and of the optimum of gratification provided a first approximation to the formulation of hypotheses about the direction of modifications where these occur, and of the continuation of a given pattern of

[19] Only in a very specifically qualified sense is the problem here one of "psychology." It is not sufficient to take over the theoretical genralizations held to be established in psychology and apply them without further ado to the analysis of the behavior of many individuals interacting as a social system. "Psychologism" is inadequate for our task because we must study dynamic problems in the context of a social system and the social system and the personality system are of course not identical. The social roles in which the actor is implicated become constituents of the structure of his personality. They become such through identifications and the internalization of the value-orientations of alters, which are thus part of the shared value-orientations of the members of a collectivity. Without categories which permit the analysis of the significance of relations to social objects, and hence of sensitivity to sanctions, "dynamic psychology" (i.e., the study of personality within the action frame of reference) would be impossible.

Likewise, without the basic constituents of personality, without the elements of motivational orientation, the organization of orientations to objects and so on, action in the role structure of the social system could not be successfully analyzed. The dynamic processes involved in the maintenance and change of institutional structures could not be treated without a basic understanding of personalities as well as of culture. But the analysis of the dynamics of social process is *not* simply an application of the theory of personality.

action. The categories of value standards — cognitive, appreciative, and moral — were again constructed with reference to the persistent possibilities of change which are present when alternative paths of action must be discriminated and selected in the light of standards. The object classification had the same function of preparing our scheme for use in dynamic analysis — it was a further step in the delineation of the fundamental alternatives in confrontation with which either persistence or change may result. The pattern variables carried in themselves the same dynamic properties which were present in the more elementary categories from which they were constructed. This could most clearly be seen in our analysis of the personality system where a direct line runs from cathexis through attachment and the dependence on positive attitudinal response to identification, and it could be seen in the concept of need-dispositions as well. When we placed the individual actor in the context of the social system, the dynamic implications became even more apparent. The concept of functionally necessary tasks, the performance of which in certain ways is a condition of the maintenance of social order, and the concept of strain which is a systemic concept, referring to the problems arising from the coexistence of different entities in the same system, brought us into the very midst of the problems of dynamic analysis.

We have argued above that there is no point-for-point articulation between the performance of a role and the personality of its incumbent and that the social structure could not be described from knowledge, however detailed, concerning the personality systems of its members. This should not, however, be interpreted to mean that social process can be analyzed in any other than motivational categories or that the analysis of the processes of its maintenance or change can proceed at any stage without referring to components and mechanisms of personalities.

Thus, although a close correspondence is impossible, it is equally impossible that personality structure and the structure of role-expectations should vary at random with respect to each other. In the first place, the mere existence of an internalized common culture as a component of personality precludes this and so, although in different ways, does the existence of the same basic object system, which is equally a target of evaluation for both personality and social systems.

The core of the personality system may be treated in great measure as a product of socialization, both through learning and by adjustments and defenses against threats introduced in the course of the socialization process. It is also a product of the expressive and instrumental involvement of the individual, in the course of life, in his various statuses within the social system. These connect the personality with the primary patterns of value-orientation. There is no doubt of the influence of these components in the personality and consequently of the great part which the personality system plays in the maintenance of certain generalized orientations.

There has, however, been a strong tendency in some of the recent discussions of "personality and culture" to assume an altogether too simple relationship between personality structure and social action. The proponents of these views have tended to impute too much rigidity to behavior, and they have also overestimated the uniformity of behavior within a given society and even within a subsystem. They have overgeneralized their often penetrating observations of some uniformities into a nearly complete uniformity. They have tended to regard most adult social behavior as little more than the "acting out" of the need-dispositions of a typical character structure, as if the actor were incapable of reality-testing, discipline, and evaluation when confronting particular situations with their own particular tasks.

Of course the individual's character structure has much to do with his response to a situation. It influences his cognition and expectations and the selections which he makes from the various aspects of the situation. Nonetheless, nothing approaching absolute uniformity, even for those individuals who have been socialized in relatively specific and uniform statuses, can be legitimately assumed. Both the constitutional endowment and the concrete practices of child training will vary from individual to individual — though within limits and certainly not randomly. The internal variations of socialization practices within the same society contribute further to the heterogeneity of personality types in a given society.

There is also no reason to believe that all personality structures are equally rigid. They do undergo change, again within limits imposed by preexisting structures, but the constellation of need-dispositions, reality-testing capacities, and disciplinary capacities can change through action in situations (even in situations which are not specifically therapeutic).[20] In the study of the bearing of personality on social processes, however, the overwhelmingly important point is that behavior is not uniform in different situations. If behavior were merely the acting out of personality qualities, it would be uniform in different types of situations. It would show no adaptability to variations in the situation. Once it is acknowledged that personality systems do have a reality-testing function which explores situations and contributes to the guidance of behavior, then it follows that the situation as a set of opportunities for direct expressive or instrumental gratification and of possible threats of deprivation must be regarded as a co-determinant of behavior in the *here and now*. Only when the structure of opportunities can be treated as constant can interindividual differences of concrete behavior be attributed *exclusively* to the factor of personality structure. And even then such propositions would be methodologically and substantively defective.

[20] This phenomenon has not been sufficiently appreciated in contemporary analysis — partly bcause of the difficulties of intensive and accurate biographical studies, partly because the source of much of our insight into personality, psychoanalytic theory, has grown up in a context in which the uniformities of the personality system through quite long periods of life of an individual have been selected for concentrated scrutiny.

These strictures on the explanation of social behavior simply by reference to personality are directed only against certain exaggerations. Personality variables *are* obviously in the first rank among the factors which are continuously operating in behavior at all times. The attention given earlier to the importance of the gratification-deprivation balance and the optimum of gratification, the sensitivity of the actor to the approval and disapproval of alter, the need-disposition scheme, and the concept of attachment is an indication of the large place allowed to personality in the working of social systems. Social systems work through their impact on the motivational systems of individuals, and the intra-individual complications and elaborations of motivation into systems lead back into the social system. The destination to which it is led back, however, is determined by the situation. The role in which the individual is expected by others to act, and in which he will act when there is a correspondence between his own expectations and the expectations of the others who surround him, was not the product of his personality. In any concrete situation it is given to his personality as a set of alternatives. His action is limited to the alternatives, and his choice is partly a function of his personality system, partly a function of the repercussions which may be expected by him from each of the alternatives in the way of gratifications and deprivations of various types.

Thus for the social system to continue to function as the same system, the reliable expectations of ego's gratification through the alternatives which the other actors in the situation expect him to follow will be the basis of his conformity with their expectations (regardless of whether he is motivated by a specific substantive need-disposition or by a generalized conformist need-disposition). To the extent that these expected gratifications are not forthcoming at the expected times and places in the system ego will not produce the expected actions, and the system will accordingly undergo some change. The kinds of expectations which ego will have, the selective focus of his cognitive orientation, the kinds of gratifications which he will seek, will, of course, all be integral to his personality system. The same responses of alters will not be equally gratifying to all individuals since all individuals will not all have the same system of need-dispositions.

The social system depends, then, on the extent to which it can keep the equilibrium of the personality systems of its members from varying beyond certain limits. The social system's own equilibrium is itself made up of many subequilibriums within and cutting across one another, with numerous personality systems more or less in internal equilibrium, making up different equilibrated systems such as kinship groups, social strata, churches, sects, economic enterprises, and governmental bodies. All enter into a huge moving equilibrium in which instabilities in one subsystem in the personality or social sphere are communicated simultaneously to both levels, either disequilibrating the larger system, or part of it, until either a reëquilibration takes place or the total equilibrium changes its form.

The equilibrium of social systems is maintained by a variety of processes and mechanisms, and their failure precipitates varying degrees of disequilibrium (or disintegration). The two main classes of mechanisms by which motivation is kept at the level and in the direction necessary for the continuing operation of the social system are the *mechanisms of socialization* and the *mechanisms of social control*.[21] The mechanisms of socialization are those mechanisms which form the need-dispositions making for a generalized readiness to fulfill the major patterns of role-expectation which an individual will encounter. From the personality point of view this is one essential part of the learning process, but *only* one. The mechanisms of socialization, in this sense, must not be conceived too narrowly. They include some which are relevant to the production of relatively specific orientations toward certain roles (e.g., the sex role). But they also include more general traits such as relatively generalized "adaptiveness" to the unforeseen exigencies of different roles. The latter may be particularly important in a complex and changing society.

The process of socialization operates mainly through the mechanisms of learning of which generalization, imitation, and identification are perhaps particularly important. The motivational processes which are involved in the learning mechanisms become organized as part of the mechanisms of socialization through the incorporation of the child into a system of complementary role-expectations. Two main levels may be distinguished. First, mainly in the identifications formed through the attachments of early childhood, the primary patterns of value-orientation in the institutionalized role-system become internalized as part of the child's own personality. Second, at a later stage, on the foundations thus laid, the child acquires orientations to more specific roles and role complexes and learns the definitions of the situation for incumbents of these roles, the goals which are appropriate to them according to the prevailing value-orientations, the procedures which are appropriate according to the same standards, and the symbolic structure of the rewards associated with them.

The first type of process forms what is sometimes called the basic char-

---

[21] This classification of the mechanisms of the social system rests on the fact that all motivational processes of action, hence all mechanisms, are processes *in the individual personality*. It is individuals who are socialized and whose tendencies to deviant behavior are controlled. There is no motivation of a collectivity *as such*. Cutting across this classification of the social mechanisms, however, is a set of distinctions relative to the locus of functional significance for the social system of a given motivational mechanism. This significance may center in (*a*) its bearing on the adequacy of motivation of individuals to the performance of their social roles, i.e., their gratification-deprivation balances; (*b*) its bearing on the allocative processes of the social system; or (*c*) its bearing on the integration of the social system. Mechanisms either of socialization or of social control may have any one or any combination of these types of significance.

acter or personality structure of the individual. But the orientations on this level are too general to constitute adequate motivation for the fulfillment of specific role-expectations. Furthermore, although there are undoubtedly modal types of such character orientation within a given social system, the product cannot be uniform; there will always be considerable variability about such modal types. For both these reasons the second level of the socialization process, which may be called the situational specification of role-orientations, is vital to the development of adequate social motivation. The mechanisms of socialization thus prepare the actor on a fairly broad level of generalizazion for the various roles in which he is likely to be placed subsequently in his career. Some of these roles may be uniform through time, subsequent to childhood; others might vary according to the various qualities and performance propensities which he possesses. The mechanisms of socialization will not prepare him for these roles in detail, but they will, insofar as they function effectively, give him the general orientations and expectations which will enable him to add the rest by further learning and adjustment. This preparation in advance makes the inevitable occurrence of succession less disruptive of equilibrium than it might otherwise be. Where the socialization mechanisms have not provided the oncoming generation or the native-born or immigrants with the requisite generalized orientation, a disequilibration will be very likely to occur.[22]

Failure of the mechanisms of socialization to motivate conformity with expectations creates tendencies to deviant behavior which, beyond certain critical points, would be disruptive of the social order or equilibrium. It is the function of the mechanisms of social control to maintain the social system in a state of stable or moving equilibrium; and insofar as they fail to do so, as has often happened in history, more drastic disequilibration will take place before equilibrium is reëstablished; that is, there will be changes in the structure of the social system.

It is not possible to draw a rigid line between socialization and social control. But the rough delimitation of the former would be given by the conception of those mechanisms necessary to maintain a stable and institutionally integrated social system through the formation of a given set of appropriate personality systems and the specification of their role-orientation with the assumption that there would be no serious endogenous tendencies to alienation from these institutionalized role-expectations, no serious role-conflict, and a constant measure of institutionalized flexibility. Such a social system is of course the concept of a limiting case like that of a frictionless machine and does not exist in reality. But the function of the mechanisms of social

---

[22] The proportion of the population whose major need-dispositions are left ungratified is less important than the cruciality of their position in the social system and the magnitude of the discrepancy between needs and expectations on the one hand and fulfillments on the other.

control is indicated by the extent to which actual social systems fail to achieve the above order of integration through socialization.

In the first place, the generalized patterns of orientation which are formed through socialization need constantly to be reinforced through the continuing presence of the symbolic equivalents of the expectations, both generalized and specific, which were effective at earlier stages in the socialization process. The orientations which have become the shared collective and private goals must be reinforced against the perpetual pressures toward disruption in the personality system and in the social system. The mechanisms for the maintenance of the consensus on value-orientations will have different functions depending on the type of social system in which they are operating. A social system with a very high degree of consensus covering most spheres of life and most types of activities and allowing little area to freely selected modes of behavior will have different problems of maintaining equilibrium than a system which allows large areas of individual freedom — and their mechanisms of control will also be different.

Even if the strains which come from inadequate socialization and from changes in the situation of the social system in relation to nature or to other social systems were eliminated, the problems of control would still persist. Tendencies toward alienation are endogenous in any social system. The arguments adduced in the preceding chapter concerning the impossibility of the complete cultural value-integration of a social system bear directly on these endogenous alienation tendencies. There cannot be a society in which some of the members are not exposed to a conflict of values; hence personality strains with resultant pressures against the expectation-system of the society are inevitable. Another basic source of conflict is constitutional variability and the consequent difficulties in the socialization of the different constitutional types. It is impossible for the *distribution* of the various constitutional endowments to correspond exactly to the distribution of initial or subsequent roles and statuses in the social system, and the misfits produce strains and possibly alienation. What is more, the allocative process always produces serious strains by denying to some members of the society what they think they are entitled to, sometimes exacerbating their demands so that they overreach themselves and infringe on the rights of others. Sometimes denial deadens the motivation of actors to role fulfillment and causes their apathetic withdrawal from the roles which they occupy. Where the sense of deprivation is associated with an identification with a collectivity or a class of individuals who come to identify themselves as similarly deprived in the allocation of roles, facilities, and rewards, the tasks of the control mechanism, and the strains on the system, become heavy indeed.

We cannot undertake here the construction of a systematic classification of the mechanisms of social control. All that we will offer will be illustrations of some of them.

One of the most prominent and functionally most significant of them is the artificial identification of interests through the manipulation of rewards and deprivations. This is the exercise of authority in its integrative function. When alienation exists because of ineffective socialization, character-determined rebelliousness, conflicting value-orientation, or apathy, the incumbent of a role endowed with the power to manipulate the allocation of facilities, roles, and rewards can redirect the motivational orientation of others by offering them objects which are more readily cathected, or by threatening to take away objects or remove opportunities. Much of the integration in the instrumental institutional complex is achieved through this artificial identification of interests, which usually works in the context of a consensus concerning general value-orientations. The weaker the consensus, however, and the larger the social system, the greater the share borne by these mechanisms in the maintenance of some measure of integration.

Among the other mechanisms of social control, insulation has an important part. Certain types of deviant behavior which do occur are sealed off, and thereby their disruptive potentialities are restricted, since in their isolation they cannot have much direct effect on the behavior of the other members of the society. On the individual level, this mechanism operates with both the criminal and the ill. On the collective level, it operates in the case of deviant and "interstitial" "subcultures" or collectivities which are not positively fully integrated with the main social system, and which are more or less cut off from widespread contact with the dominant sector of the social system — a contact which, if it did occur, would engender conflict. Segregation is the spatial consequence of the operation of the mechanism of insulation.

Another type of mechanism of social control is contingent reintegration; the care of the ill in modern medicine is a good example of this in certain respects. The medical profession exposes the sick person, so far as his illness constitutes "deviant behavior," to a situation where the motivation to his deviance is weakened and the positive motivations to conformity are strengthened. What is, from the viewpoint of the individual personality, conscious or unconscious psychotherapy, is from the viewpoint of the social system a mechanism of social control.

These examples should give the reader a general idea of what is meant by the control mechanisms of the social system which have their efficacy through their effect on motivation.

The Problem of Social Change

The present theory of the social system is, like all theories involving causal or functional explanation, concerned equally with the conditions of stability and the conditions of change. It is equally concerned with slow cumulative change and with sudden or fluctuating change, and the categories and the variables which have been presented are equally applicable to stable or rapidly or slowly changing systems.

The state of a system at a point in time or at a series of points in time is a fundamental referent for the analysis of social systems. It is also the fundamental referent for the analysis of change from that state to other states of the system. The theoretical scheme here presented offers a number of categories and hypotheses by which possibilities of change may be described and analyzed.

We have given prominence in earlier phases of our analysis to the integration of motivational elements into patterns of conformity with role-expectations, to the general category of alienation and the conditions of its emergence, and to the part played by the mechanisms of social control. The entire discussion of motivation and its relation to the mechanisms of socialization and control in the section immediately preceding was directly addressed to the problems of stability *and* change. If analyzed in these terms, the maintenance of any existing status, insofar as it is maintained at all, is clearly a relatively contingent matter. The obverse of the analysis of the mechanisms by which it is maintained is the analysis of the forces which tend to alter it. *It is impossible to study one without the other.* A fundamental potentiality of instability, an endemic possibility of change, is inherent in this approach to the analysis of social systems. Empirically, of course, the degree of instability, and hence the likelihood of actual change, will vary both with the character of the social system and of the situation in which it is placed. But in principle, propositions about the factors making for maintenance of the system are at the same time propositions about those making for change. The difference is only one of concrete descriptive emphasis. There is no difference on the analytical level.

A basic hypothesis in this type of analysis asserts the imperfect integration of all actual social systems. No one system of value-orientation with perfect consistency in its patterns can be fully institutionalized in a concrete society. There will be uneven distributions among the different parts of the society. There will be value conflicts and role conflicts. The consequence of such imperfect integration is in the nature of the case a certain instability, and hence a susceptibility to change if the balance of these forces, which is often extremely delicate, is shifted at some strategic point. Thus, change might result not only from open deviation from unequivocally institutionalized patterns but also from a shift in the balance between two or more positively institutionalized patterns, with an invasion of part of the sphere of one by another. The loopholes in the institutionalized system are one of the main channels through which such shifts often take place. Hence, in the combination of the inherent tendencies to deviation and the imperfections of the integration of value-orientations, there are in every social system inherent possibilities of change.

In addition to these two major sources, positively institutionalized sources of change are particularly prominent in some social systems. The most prominent type of case seems to be the institutionalized commitment to a cultural configuration, in Kroeber's sense, so that there is an endogenous process of development of the possibilities of that configuration. Where the cultural orientation gives a prominent place to achievement and universalistic orientation, this endogenous tendency toward change may be very pronounced. The obvious example is modern science, with its technological applications. Scientific knowledge is by its nature open to development — otherwise the activities concerned could not be called scientific investigation. When made into the object of concern by scientific institutions — universities and research organizations — there is an institutionalized motivation to unfold this possibility. There are, furthermore, powerful tendencies, once the ethos of science is institutionalized in a society sufficiently for an important scientific movement to flourish, to render it impossible to isolate scentific investigation so that it will have no technological application. Such applications in turn will have repercussions on the whole system of social relationships. Hence a society in which science is institutionalized and is also assigned a strategic position cannot be a static society.

What is very conspicuously true of science is also true of the consequences of many religious movements, once certain processes of internal development have started. The value-orientations of modern capitalistic enterprise are similarly endogenously productive of change. Any society in which the value standards, as in a legal code (even though it is not in their formal nature to undergo development), are capable of reinterpretation will also tend toward change. Any society in which the allocations create or maintain dissatisfaction will be open to change; especially when the cultural standards and the allocations combine to intensify need-dispositions, change will be a certainty.

Changes in the external situation of a social system, either in its environmental conditions (as in the case of the depletion or discovery of some natural resource), changes in its technology which are not autonomous, changes in the social situation of the system (as in its foreign relations), may be cited as the chief exogenous factors in change. Inspection of the paradigm for the analysis of social systems will show that these variables can be fully taken into account in this scheme of analysis (see Fig. 15).

There is no suggestion that these sources of social change exhaust the list, but they will suffice for the present. The possibility of doing empirical justice to all of them is certainly present in the treatment of social systems in terms of the theory of action. Furthermore, this type of analysis puts us in possession of important canons for the criticism of other theories of social change. It would seem, for instance, that there is no inherent reason why the "motive force" of social change *in general* has to be sought in any one sector of the social system or its culture. The impetus to a given process of change may come from an evolution of "ideas." It may come from secular changes in climate which profoundly alter the conditions of subsistence. It may center in shifts in the distribution of power or in technological developments which permit some needs to be satisfied in ways that change the conditions and the level of satisfaction of the needs of other actors in the sytsem. The theoretical generalization of change will in all probability not take the form of a "predominant factor theory," such as an economic or an ideological interpretation, but of an analysis of the modes of interdependence of different parts of the social system. From such hypotheses it should be possible to predict that a certain type of change, initiated at any given point, will, given the main facts about the system, have specifiable types of consequences at other points.

To avoid confusion, one final point should be mentioned. The analysis of social change is not to be confused with the analysis of the dynamics of action in the theory of action. There is much dynamic process in action, including change in the structure of personalities, *within a stable social system.* Indeed it is inherent in the frame of reference that *all* action is a dynamic process. The emphasis of this work on the organization of action is not to be taken to imply that organization has some sort of ontological priority over dynamic process. They are the two aspects of the same phenomenon. It has been more convenient to stress the organizational aspect since it provides certain relatively definite and manageable reference points, which make possible a more incisive and rigorous analysis of certain problems in the process of action.[23]

[23] As noted in the Introduction, a greatly expanded treatment of the subject-matter of this chapter will be found in Talcott Parsons, *The Social System* (Glencoe, Illinois: The Free Press, 1951).

5

Conclusion

We have now set forth the main conceptual scheme of the theory of action and its elaboration in each of the three areas of systemic organization. In conclusion we shall summarize briefly, underscore a few specific features of the scheme, and indicate some of the problems toward which future effort might be directed.

Logically the scheme is founded on certain categories of behavior psychology. These contain by implication the main categories of the frame of reference of the theory of action. The implications, however, have not heretofore been drawn in a manner which would be adequate to the study of human personality, cultural, and social systems, although the categories developed previously by Tolman in his study of animal behavior have brought these implications within reaching distance.

The present analysis began with the set of fundamental definitions which constitute the frame of reference for the analysis of the structure of human action. The dynamic properties of this frame of reference have not been treated with the same degree of explicitness as the more descriptive aspects. We have devoted more attention to the derivation of complex concepts descriptive of structure than we have to the formulation of the dynamic hypotheses implicit in some of these concepts. However, it seems to us that a whole system of dynamic hypotheses is implicit in our conceptual scheme and that these hypotheses are susceptible of treatment by the same kind of systematic deductive procedure which has been used in constructing the descriptive side of the scheme. We have regarded it, however, as more urgent to develop the descriptive side first.

The basic frame of reference deals with action as a process of striving for the attainment of states of gratification or goals within a situation. The polarity of gratification and deprivation, and hence of the two fundamental tendencies of action — seeking and avoidance — are inherent in this conception. So also is the reference to the future, which is formulated in the concept of expectations. Finally, the selective nature of the orientations of action, which is formulated in the concept of the pattern variables, is similarly logically inherent in the basic conception of action.

In our construction of the categories of the theory of action, we distinguished three major modal aspects of the frame of reference which have been called motivational orientation, value-orientation, and the structure of the situation. These are *all* elements of the "orientation" of an actor to a situation; *each* of them is involved in *any* action whatever. Only when objects are both cognized and cathected does "drive" or "need" become motivation in action. But the completely isolated elementary "unit action" is an abstraction. Actions occur only in systems which necessitate evaluations of alternative paths of action and commitments to those alternatives which have been chosen. Selection or choice is an essential component of action as we view it. Selectivity is a function both of the goal-orientedness of the actor and the differentiation of the object situation. Selectivity in orientation moreover entails simultaneous orientation toward criteria of the validity of the substantive selections. There thus seems to be no doubt of the fundamental independent significance of value standards, and this justifies the granting to value-orientation a conceptually independent place in the frame of reference.

Moreover, it is of the first importance that the structure of the situation be analyzed not only in terms of the classes of concrete objects, but of the modalities of objects, especially of the quality and performance modalities. The modality classification, already widely applied in more concrete studies, has crucial theoretical significance in the analysis of the role-expectations, cultural orientations, and need-dispositions.

The basic frame of reference is in principle applicable to the hypothetically isolated actor in a nonsocial situation. In a situation in which a plurality of actors are in interaction, the scheme must be further differentiated to take into account the fact of complementarity of expectations — but this involves no modification in the basic frame of reference, merely a more elaborate deductive treatment. It is through the complementarity of expectations in interaction that the symbols essential to human action are built up, that communication on the humanly significant levels, and therefore culture, become possible. It is with analysis of action on these levels of complexity that the scheme is primarily concerned.

Following the delineation of the fundamentals of the frame of reference in terms of the three major aspects of action, the first major *theoretical* step was taken with the derivation from that frame of reference of a systematic scheme for defining and interrelating the choice-alternatives toward which there is evaluative orientation of action. The alternatives toward which the evaluative orientation is focused are called the *pattern variables*. It is clear that the pattern-variable elements could not have been derived if the independent significance of value-orientation had not been established beforehand. But the pattern variables are not a product solely of value-orientations;

they involve relations among the different components of the frame of reference.

The pattern variables had previously been developed in a less systematic fashion in connection with the analysis of certain concrete problems of social structure. They were not originally devised for the analysis of personality and cultural systems. However, in attempting to develop the analysis of personality systems in the framework of the action scheme, it became clear that if personality is to be analyzed in terms of the action schema at all, the pattern variables must also be relevant to the analysis of personality. The further pursuit of that line of inquiry showed that the need-dispositions which had previously been classified largely in an *ad hoc* clinical way, could be defined in terms of the pattern variables with results which showed a remarkable correspondence with the results of clinical observation. Finally, it became apparent that they constituted principal categories for the description of value-orientations, and not only of the empirical action systems in which value-orientations are involved. After all, role-expectations, which are the essential element of institutionalized behavior, are drawn in general from the same general dispositions as cultural value-orientations. The perception of this relationship provides a most important means for clarifying the conceptual relations between cultural orientations on the one hand and personality and social systems on the other, and for preparing the way for the study of their empirical interrelations.

Preliminary consideration of the pattern-variable scheme in relation to these two types of system also revealed the symmetrical asymmetry of its application to personalities and to social systems.

The definition of the main terms of the action frame of reference, and the derivation of the pattern variables from the frame of reference have thus provided a point of departure for the analysis of the three types of system into which the elements of the action scheme are organized. (Of course, the "fundamentals of behavior psychology" are assumed in the definition of the elements of action and the derivations into which they enter.)

But the concepts thus constructed are insufficient in that particular form for the analysis of systems of action. The problem of constructive systemic concepts was first dealt with in connection with personality in Chapter II. It is essentially a matter of the conditions and consequences of the differentiation of action elements and their integration into a system. The types of differentiation which are logically conceivable can, in the nature of the case, be realized only in a highly selective manner. There are definite imperatives imposed by the conditions of empirical coexistence in the same system. The further conceptual differentiation, to be added to the elements considered in Chapter I, is presented in the paradigm of the "functioning system" of a personality. The structure of such a system is constituted by the interrelations of the elements of action (formulated in the categories of the action frame of reference), their elaboration in the pattern-variable scheme. The structure is complicated by the derivation of the origins and place in the system of certain "adjustive" mechanisms (such as needs for dominance or for aggression) and defensive mechanisms.

It is particularly important that motivational factors should be viewed with reference to their functional significance for personality as a system. The concept of mechanism was introduced because it provides a conceptual tool for the analysis of motivational factors in just this light.

In the social system too the concept of mechanism is introduced because of its relevance in dealing with the dynamic aspects of *systemic* problems, particularly the problems of allocation and integration. In consequence of the fundamental difference in the locus of personality systems on the one hand and social systems on the other, the functional mechanisms which operate in both systems may be regarded as homologous only to a limited extent. Only when these differences are clarified is it possible to make progress in the analysis of the nature of the empirical articulations between them. In the persent monograph only a few initial considerations could be presented concerning this very complicated set of problems.

Systems of value-orientation (discussed in Chapter III) do not entail the existence of functional mechanisms because they are not empirical action systems, and hence do not have either motivational processes or the *same kinds* of allocative and integrative problems. After a discussion of their place in the general structure of culture, the problem of the consistency of systems of value-orientation was explored through relating the major combinations of the pattern variables to certain features of the situation.

The model of the system of value-orientation with a fully consistent pattern, however important for theoretical purposes, can serve only as a point of departure for the analysis of empirical value systems, as they operate in personality and in social systems. The pattern-consistent system is both formal and elementary. In systems of action, the system of value-orientation takes rather different directions, but they could not be fully treated here. In particular, the complications arising from orientation to many of the "adaptive" problems, such as authority or freedom from control, have not been included; they must be worked out in relation to the more concrete action structure and situation. A further limitation on the empirical utility of the concept of the completely pattern-consistent system of value-orientation is that concrete systems of action are not oriented toward such pattern-consistent value systems. The exigencies of the empirical action system are such that there will be areas of strain and even of sheer impossibility of full integration of a consistent value-orientation. Where these areas of strain and incompatibility are located and how they are organized and responded to will depend on the dominant value system and on the structure of the particular situation.

This means that the study of concrete systems of value-orientation should be related to the study of empirical systems of action. The purely "cultural" type of analysis, though indispensable as a first step, can only carry us a certain distance. Even when we are concerned with the cultural value orientation, in order to account for its inconsistencies and heterogeneities, we must consider the interdependence of that system with the motivational and situational components of personality and with the functional problems of social systems. Of course, even when the theory of personality is the prime object of our interest, we cannot do without the cultural analysis of value-orientations.

Finally, from the point of view of the general anthropological student of culture, the treatment of cultural problems in this monograph must appear highly selective if not one-sided. We have intentionally placed primary emphasis on value-orientations because they constitute the strategically crucial *point of articulation* between culture and the structure of personalities and of social systems. In the introductory section of Chapter III we attempted to place value-orientations in relation to the other elements of cultural systems as a whole. But this brief treatment did not attempt to do justice to the intricacy of the problems and their implications for action — for example, the role of ideas or belief systems or the role of expressive symbols. Also the complex interdependencies between the internalized culture and culture as an accumulation of objects other than value-orientations have merely been suggested, not analyzed.

Can any general statement be made about the significance of what has been achieved in this monograph? In the first place it should be quite clear that nearly all the concepts which have here been brought together have been current in various forms and on various levels of concreteness in the social sciences in the twentieth century. Whatever originality exists here can be found only in the way in which the concepts have been related to one another.

It may well be that an equally comprehensive or even more comprehensive synthesis could have been made from a different point of view, with different emphases and combinations. But even if this is so, it might be fairly claimed that the present scheme offers the basis of an important advance toward the construction of a unified theory of social science. It perhaps may be said to put together more elements, in a more systematic way, than any other attempt yet made on this level of abstraction. We also think that it has been sufficiently differentiated here to show that it can be useful in the analysis of empirical problems in an open, undogmatic way. It should thus contribute substantially to the development of a common way of looking at the phenomena of human conduct.

Nothing could be more certain than that any such attempt is tentative in its definitions and in their particular derivations and combinations; it is thus destined to all manner of modifications. A critic may well be able to find serious difficulties, or may simply prefer, for good reasons of his own, to use a different scheme. But the whole course of development of work in the social

sciences to which this monograph has sought to give a more systematic theoretical formulation is such that it is scarcely conceivable that such a large
measure of conceptual ordering which connects with so much empirical
knowledge should be completely "off the rails." It seems therefore that however great the modifications which will have to be introduced by empirical
application and theoretical refinement and reformulation, the permanently
valid precipitate will prove to be substantial.

In very general terms, one of the achievements of this undertaking is the
clarification of the relations between what have been called the "levels" of
action. The doctrine of "tandem emergence," most recently and fully stated by
Kroeber, seems to be definitely untenable. The idea that personality is emergent from the biological level of the organism, social systems are emergent
from personality, and culture from social systems, which this view puts forth,
has been shown to be wrong. In place of this we have put forward the view
that personality, culture, and social system are analytically coequal, that each
of the three implies the other two. If there is anything like emergence, it is
action as the category embracing all three which is emergent from the organic
world. One of the general implications of this contention is that the analysis
of social systems and of culture is not a derivation of the theory of personality.
Nor can there be "sociology" which is precultural or independent of culture,
whether it be conceived as "applied psychology" or as a Durkheimian "theory
of social facts." Finally, culture cannot stand in isolation, as something self-
sufficient and self-developing. Culture is theoretically implicated with action
in general, and thus with both personalities and social systems. Indeed
the only prerequisites of any essential part of the theory of action are the
organic and situational prerequisites of action in general, and not any one
subsystem.

This conception of the relations of the three system-levels to each other is
not in its most general form original. But in the current discussion of these
problems there has been a large amount of uncertainty and vacillation about
these matters. There has been a tendency for the proponents of each of the
three disciplines concerned to attempt to close their own systems, and to
declare their theoretical independence of the others. At the same time, even
among those who asserted the interdependence of the three fields, it has tended
to be done in an *ad hoc,* fragmentary manner, without regard to the methodological and theoretical bases of such interdependence. The present scheme
may claim to have resolved in large part both of these difficulties.

One of the major difficulties in relating culture to social structure has
been uncertainty about the meaning of the institutionalization of culture
patterns. In the light of the present analysis, this uncertainty can be seen to
derive from the fact that the meaning of institutionalization is different for
the different parts of a cultural system. A set of beliefs, of expressive symbols, or of instrumental patterns may be institutionalized in the sense that

conformity with the standards in question may become a role-expectation for members of certain collectivities, as is the case, for example, when there is a high valuation of abstract art in a certain circle. But only patterns of value-orientation — that is, in our terms, pattern-variable combinations — become directly constitutive of the main structure of alternative types of social relationships which is the central structural focus of social systems. This is the set of primary institutions of a social system. The others are structurally secondary. This differentiated analysis of the relations between culture and systems of action makes it possible to overcome the "emanationist" fallacy which has plagued idealistic social theory. If culture as a system is treated as closed and either conceptually or empirically independent of social structure and personality, then it follows that culture patterns "realize themselves" in personality or social structure without the intervention of motivation. The proponents of one view invoke only a few "obvious" mechanisms connected with child training in order to explain the personality which becomes the recipient and bearer of culture. This theory, although it alleges to show the "human element" in the great impersonal patterns of culture, assumes, quite unjustifiably, that there *is* in concrete reality a cultural orientation system, given separately from the system of action. This is the exact counterpart of the view that there is a human nature independent of society and culture. In both cases, the procedure has been to determine what the system is, and then to analyze how it affects the other systems. The correct procedure is to treat the cultural orientation system as an integral *part* of the real system of action, which can be separated from it *only analytically*. Culture in the anthropological sense is a condition, component, and product of action systems.

Similarly, the pattern variables seem to provide a crucial clue to the relation between personality and culture. The distinction between cultural objects (accumulation) and cultural orientations, which has been followed in the present analysis, turns psychologically on the internalization of values and other elements of culture. Insofar as a value pattern becomes internalized, it ceases to be an object and becomes directly constitutive of the personality. It is "transferred" from one side of the "action equation" to the other. (It is this transferability of cultural factors which in the last analysis makes it necessary to treat them as an independent range of variation in the basic paradigm of action.) Internalization of values in the personality is thus the direct counterpart of their institutionalization in the social system. Indeed, as we have seen, they are really two sides of the same thing. This institutionalization and internalization of value patterns, a connection independently and from different points of view discovered by Freud and by Durkheim, is the focus of many of the central theoretical problems of action theory. Many elements in action, both organic and situational, are causally independent of role-value structure. But only through their *relation* to this problem, can they be systematically analyzed in terms of the theory of action.

A second and closely related accomplishment of the present analysis is the clarification of the functional problems of the theory of action in the analysis of systems. Incompatibilities among the component actions and actors in the several systems result from their coexistence in the same situation or the same personality. Insofar as the system remains a system, some mechanisms must come into play for reducing these incompatibilities to the point where coexistence in the system becomes possible. (These mechanisms do of course change the character of the system but they allow it to function as a system.)

Now these mechanisms cannot be derived simply from the theory of motivation in general. Some conception of *functional imperatives* — that is, constituent conditions and empirically necessary preconditions of on-going systems, set by the facts of scarcity in the object situation, the nature of the organism, and the realities of coexistence — are necessary.

We have stressed that these mechanisms are to be defined by the systemic conditions which give rise to them and the systemic consequences or functions which are effected by their operation. There are, of course, certain dangers in the use of such functional analysis. The overtones of teleology must be guarded against particularly in dealing with the social system. There are dangers of hypostatization of the "system" and its "needs" which can be insured against only by bearing constantly in mind that the system is a system of individual actors and their roles but that needs in the systemic sense are not the same as the need-dispositions of the actors or even homologous with them — although there are complicated empirical interrelations among them. Systemic needs can never be reduced to need-dispositions although systemic needs are the resultant of the coexistence in determinate relationships in a situation of a plurality of actors each of whom has a system of need-dispositions. If it is remembered that the mechanisms which are the systemic modes of responding to the "needs of the system" are empirical generalizations about motivational processes — a sort of shorthand for the description of complex processes which we do not yet fully understand — we may feel free to employ functional analysis without involvement either in metaphysical teleology or in hidden political and ethical preferences. Neither of these is in any way *logically* entailed in the kind of functional analysis which we have presented here.

In addition to the two general directions in which we believe progress has been made, there have been a good many categories and hypotheses of a more specific sort which have emerged or which have been reformulated in the course of this analysis. Rather than attempt a summary of these, however, we will conclude with a brief suggestion of three general lines of development along which it might be fruitful to move in the formulation of general social science theory.

One field which is basic to our work here and development of which is necessary for further progress deals with the nature and role of symbols in action. The present monograph has not specifically dealt with these problems. But symbolism has emerged as almost a kind of counterpoint theme throughout the discussion and requires much more explicit attention than it has received. There are many points at which such an analysis could begin. It should not center so much in the "origins" of symbols as in their actual role in the interactive processes which have been central to this analysis. A central problem will be the relation among the symbolic elements in cognitive and in cathectic orientations. Every one of the psychological mechanisms discussed operates through responses to symbols. For instance, the mechanism of generalization which operates when ego comes to attribute significance to alter's attitudes as distinguished from his "overt acts" is possible only through a process of symbolization. There is probably no problem in the analysis of action systems which would not be greatly clarified by a better understanding of symbolism. Motivation in particular will be better understood as a knowledge of symbolism advances. Indeed, there is much to be said for the view that the importance of culture is almost synonomous with the importance of what in motivational terms are sometimes called "symbolic processes." There is at the very least an intimate connection.

Second, it is important to press forward with systematic structural classification of types and their component elements, in all three types of system. The bearing of this task on the structural-functional character of the theory of action should be clear. Our dynamic generalizations have to be formulated relative to their structural setting. The present state of knowledge does not allow the establishment of dynamic generalizations which both cut across many different social and personality structures and are sufficiently concrete to be very helpful in the solution of concrete problems. Thus we may say that "in the long run only behavior which is adequately rewarded will tend to persist," but if we do not concretely know what the reward structure and its relation to the value and role structure of the requisite social system are, this helps us very little. Indeed it may get us into a great deal of trouble if we tacitly assume that the concrete rewards of our society will exist in another society. Only when we know what the concrete reward system is does the generalization become useful. We cannot rest content with a pure *ad hoc* empiricism in this respect.

We must try to systematize the relations between different types of reward systems which means systematizing the classification of the cultures and social structures within which the rewards are given. This is the most promising path to the extension of the empirical relevance of generalizations from the one structural case to families of structural cases. It is the way to transcend the "structural particularism" of the particular personality, the particular culture, or the particular social structure. We think that some of the procedures we have proposed provide starting points for such classificatory systematization, and that further work in this direction is likely to be productive.

The development of a classification of types of structures is necessary particularly for the elaboration of *middle principles*, that is, propositions of lower ranges of generality (and consequently greater concreteness). The working out of a typology of structures will enable us to know what we are holding constant in our concrete investigations into *middle principles*. And it will also make much more feasible the absolutely indispensable unification of theory of the present level of generality and theory on the level of middle principles.

Finally, the last direction of development has been emphasized so often that it does not need to be extensively discussed again. This is the dynamic analysis of the role or role-constellation where value pattern, social structure, and personality come together. This, without doubt, is the most strategic point at which to attempt to extend dynamic knowledge in such a way that it will promise a maximum of fruitful general results for the theory of action. The establishment of the crucially strategic place of this complex should not, however, lead one to underestimate the difficulty of the theoretical problems surrounding it.

It has repeatedly been pointed out that this difficulty above all derives from the undoubted fact that in spite of the basic structural homology of personalities and social systems, the two are not directly, reciprocally translatable. This translation can be accomplished only through certain "transformation equations," of which unfortunately many constituents are still unknown. The basic grounds of this difficulty have been explored at various points in the course of the foregoing analysis. Among other things this analysis provides canons of criticism of the various oversimplified solutions of the problem which are current. But in addition to attaining critical vantage points, real progress has been made in defining the nature of the problems, and here and there is a glimmer of positive insight. It may confidently be hoped that intensive and competent work toward pushing forward this frontier of our knowledge should yield results of some value. Here, above all, the resources of modern social science can be mobilized for the task of extending and ordering our knowledge of human conduct.

FIGURES 1-15

Accompanying Part II

Fig. 1 COMPONENTS OF THE ACTION FRAME OF REFERENCE

THE SUBJECT	THE OBJECT
1. An actor-subject: the actor whose orientation of action is being analyzed. (In an interaction situation, this actor is called "ego.")	2. Objects: those objects to which the actor-subject is oriented. These are (i) social objects and (ii) nonsocial objects.
The actor-subject is sometimes called simply the "actor" and is always an "action system." Thus the actor-subject is either:	i. Social objects are actors (i.e., action systems) but here they are objects rather than subjects in a given analysis. (In an interaction situation, these actors are called "alters.") Social objects are:
a. A personality. b. A social system.	a. Personalities. b. Social systems.

Personalities and Social systems fit together in the following fashion whether they are subjects or objects.

	Personality A	Personality B	Personality C
Social system 1	Role 1-A* Motivational aspects Value aspects	Role 1-B Motivational aspects Value aspects	Role 1-C Motivational aspects Value aspects
Social system 2	Role 2-A Motivational aspects Value aspects	Role 2-B Motivational aspects Value aspects	Role 2-C Motivational aspects Value aspects
Social system 3	Role 3-A Motivational aspects Value aspects	Role 3-B Motivational aspects Value aspects	Role 3-C Motivational aspects Value aspects

ii. Nonsocial objects may be:

    a. Physical objects
    b. Cultural objects (i.e., symbols or symbol systems).

Cultural Systems

Cultural systems are the common values, beliefs, and tastes of the actors (as either subjects or objects) interacting with symbol systems (as objects). Thus the underlined components above show the abstraction of cultural systems from the action frame of reference.

*Each of these roles is a subsystem of orientations. This subsystem can be analyzed with respect to either (i) the personality's motives, of which the orientations are a function, or (ii) the values which the personality respects in this specific social system. Thus roles are divided into motivational aspects and value aspects.

Fig. 2 DERIVATION OF THE PATTERN VARIABLES

SUBJECT

Orientation of the Actor-Subject	Three Pattern Variables Derivable from the Orientation

The actor-subject is analyzed with respect to the modes of his orientation. (These orientations, taken in constellations, make up the "roles" in Fig. 1.)

A. Motivational orientation
  1. Cognitive
  2. Cathectic (Inseparable modes)
  3. Evaluative: brings in thought for consequences and can invoke value standards.

No. 1

Affectivity: cognitive-cathectic modes determine behavior without evaluation.

Affective neutrality: behavior does not occur until after evaluation has occurred (and thus, usually, some of the value-orientation standards invoked). (Cognitive-cathectic modes of course, are also active.)

No. 3

B. Value-orientation
  1. Cognitive standards ⟶
  2. Appreciative standards ⟶

Universalism: whether or not moral standards have primacy in an evaluative situation, cognitive standards have primacy over appreciative.
Particularism: whether or not moral standards have primacy, appreciative standards have primacy over cognitive ones.

  3. Moral standards
    a. ego-integrative

    b. collectivity-integrative

No. 2

Self-orientation: whether or not evaluation occurs, the actor does not give primacy to collective moral standards, but instead to cognitive or appreciative or ego-integrative moral standards, or no standards are invoked.
Collectivity-orientation: evaluation occurs and the actor gives primacy to collective moral standards.

OBJECT

Alternatives within the Class of Social Objects	Two Pattern Variables from these Alternatives

Only the class of social objects is relevant here, since all pattern variables are in one sense modes of relationship between people. Two distinctions which cross-cut each other can be applied to the category of social objects:

A. The quality-performance distinction
  1. A social object may be a complex of qualities.

  2. A social object may be a complex of performances.

No. 4

Ascription: the actor chooses to see a social object as a complex of qualities.

Achievement: the actor chooses to see a social object as a complex of performances.

B. The scope-of-significance distinction
  1. A social object may have diffuse significance.

  2. A social object may have specific or segmental significance.

No. 5

Diffuseness: the actor chooses to grant a social object all requests that do not interfere with other obligations.
Specificity: the actor grants a social object only such rights as are explicitly defined in the definition of the relationship between them.

Fig. 3 VALUE COMPONENTS OF NEED-DISPOSITIONS

	AFFECTIVITY	AFFECTIVE NEUTRALITY
SPECIFICITY	I. Segmental Gratification The need-disposition to find a receptive and/or responsive social object and to be responsive vis-á-vis that object, in a context of direct gratifications and specific qualifications without regard to responsibilities beyond it.	II. Approval The need-disposition for such approval and its reciprocation in a relation with a social object with respect to value standards governing specific types of quality or performance and without regard to responsibilities outside the specific context.
DIFFUSENESS	III. Love The need-disposition for a relationship with a social object characterized by reciprocal attitudes of diffuse love, without regard to any particular content of specific gratifications or specific qualifications.	IV. Esteem The need-disposition to be esteemed and to reciprocate this attitude in a relation to a social object in a diffuse way, without regard to a particular context of specific qualities or performances, but with regard to the standard by which the person as a whole is the object of esteem.

Fig. 3a TYPES OF VALUE COMPONENTS OF NEED-DISPOSITIONS

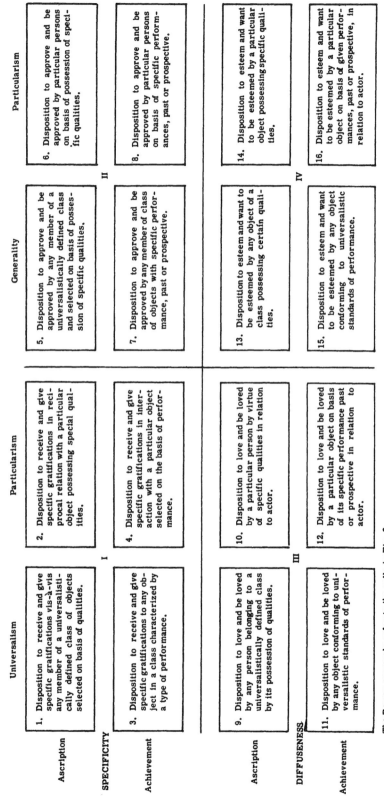

The Roman numerals refer to the cells in Fig. 3.

Fig. 4 VALUE COMPONENTS OF ROLE-EXPECTATIONS

	UNIVERSALISM	PARTICULARISM
ASCRIPTION	I. Expectation of conformity with universal norms. The orientation of action to an expectation of conformity with a universalistic standard governing the conduct of actors possessing certain qualities (classificatory or relational) universalistically assessed.	II. Expectation of orientation by virtue of particular prior relationship. The orientation of action to an expectation of conformity with a standard governing the conduct of actors possessing certain qualities (classificatory or relational) assessed in the light of their particular relationship to the actor.
ACHIEVEMENT	III. Expectation of successful accomplishment. The orientation of action to an expectation of achievement in accordance with a universalistic standard of attainment of a minimum level of satisfactory achievement or a requisite degree of excellence above that minimum.	IV. Expectation of obligations of particular relationship or membership. The orientation of action to the expectation of performance in conformity with a standard of achievement appropriate to a particular membership in a class or relationship independent of universalistically defined standards of performances.

Fig. 4a TYPES OF VALUE COMPONENTS OF ROLE-EXPECTATION

	UNIVERSALISM		PARTICULARISM	
	Affectivity	**Neutrality**	**Affectivity**	**Neutrality**
ASCRIPTION **Specificity**	1. Orientation toward an expectation of specific affective expression on basis of qualities toward class of objects defined by universalistic standards.	2. Orientation toward an expectation of specific disciplined action on basis of qualities toward class of objects defined by universalistic standards.	5. Orientation toward an expectation of specific affective expression toward object on basis of qualities in particularistic relation to actor.	6. Orientation toward an expectation of specific disciplined action.toward object on basis of qualities in particularistic relation to ego.
Diffuseness	3. Orientation toward an expectation of diffuse affective expression on basis of qualities toward class of objects defined by universalistic standards.	4. Orientation toward an expectation of generalized disciplined action on basis of qualities toward class of objects defined by universalistic standards.	7. Orientation toward an expectation of diffuse affective expression toward object on basis of qualities in particularistic relation to actor.	8. Orientation toward an expectation of generalized disciplined action toward object on basis of qualities in particularistic relation to actor.
ACHIEVEMENT **Specificity**	9. Orientation toward an expectation of specific affective expressions toward class of objects designated on basis of achievement defined by universalistic standards.	10. Orientation toward an expectation of specific disciplined action in relation to a class of objects designated on basis of achievement defined by universalistic standards.	13. Expectation of specific affective expression vis-à-vis an object on the basis of its achievements in a particular relation with the actor.	14. Expectation of specific disciplined action toward an object on basis of performances in particularistic relation to actor.
Diffuseness	11. Orientation toward an expectation of diffuse affective expression toward classes of objects on basis of achievement defined by universalistic standards.	12.. Orientation toward an expectation of generalized disciplined action toward classes of objects on basis of achievement, defined by universalistic standards.	15. Orientation toward an expectation of diffuse affective expression toward object on basis of performance in particularistic relation to actor.	16. Orientation toward an expectation of generalized disciplined action toward object on basis of performance in particularistic relation to actor.

Quadrant labels: I (Universalism–Ascription), II (Particularism–Ascription), III (Universalism–Achievement), IV (Particularism–Achievement).

The Roman numerals refer to the cells of Fig. 4.

Fig. 5 GROUPING OF CHOICE PATTERN VARIABLES

Value-Orientation

Focus of Social Value Systems

Universalism-Particularism   Ascription-Achievement

Collective-Self-Orientation

Diffuseness-Specificity   Neutrality-Affectivity

Focus of Personal Value Systems

Motivation-Orientation

Fig. 6 ACTION RELEVANT STRUCTURE OF THE OBJECT SYSTEM

Objects as Units	Social Objects		Cultural Objects	Physical Objects	
	QUALITY COMPLEXES	PERFORMANCE COMPLEXES		QUALITY COMPLEXES	PERFORMANCE COMPLEXES
Self (ego as personality)	Classificatory: Personality traits Relational: Memberships, possessions	Classificatory: Performance propensities Relational: Roles in relationship systems	Cognitive and cathectic field and instrumental means, conditions and obstacles, and symbols		
Alter (as personality)	Classificatory: Personality traits Relational: Memberships, possessions	Classificatory: Performance propensities Relational: Roles in relationship systems	Cognitive and cathectic field and instrumental means, conditions and obstacles, and. symbols		
Collectivity	Classificatory:. Group characteristics plus size, status structure, membership composition. Relational: Memberships, possessions plus membership status, internal and external.	Classificatory: Performance propensities plus scope of collective activity Relational: Roles in relationship systems plus propensities of role in collective relationship systems	Cognitive and cathectic field and instrumental means, conditions and obstacles, and symbols		
Organisms (ego's own and alter's)			Cultural Objects as conditions of organic functioning and survival	Classificatory: Sex, age, physical qualities Relational: Biological relatedness, territorial location	Organic capacities, skills, etc.
Other Environmental Objects			Cognitive and cathectic field and instrumental means, conditions and obstacles - objects as traits of ego's object world	Cognitive and cathectic field and instrumental means, conditions, obstacles, etc.	
Symbols, Belief Systems, Standards, etc.			Cognitive and cathectic field and instrumental means, conditions and obstacles - objects as traits of ego's object world	Cognitive and cathectic field and instrumental means, conditions, obstacles, etc.	

Fig. 7 CLASSIFICATION OF THE MECHANISMS

Type of Problem	Learning Processes *	Performance Processes †

FOR SOLVING EXTERNAL PROBLEMS ‡

Type of Problem	Learning Processes *	Performance Processes †

Integrative §	1. Mechanisms of congnitive learning
	
	2. Reality testing
		1. Reality testing
		2. Dependency
		   a. dominance
		   b. submission
		3. Compulsive independence
		   a. agressiveness
		   b. withdrawal

Allocative	1. Substitution (2. Displacement) (3. Fixation) 4. Mechanisms of cathectic learning	1. Allocation of attention to different objects. 2. Allocation of cathexes to different means and goals

FOR SOLVING INTERNAL PROBLEMS

Type of Problem	Learning Processes *	Performance Processes †
Integrative //	1. Learned inhibition 2. Learned evaluation patterns of functioning with an eye to prevention of conflicts.	1. Rationalization 2. Isolation 3. Displacement 4. Fixation 5. Repression 6. Reaction-formation 7. Projection
Allocative	1. Allocation of functions to various need-dispositions 2. Changes of evaluation patterns with an eye to maintaining the system.	1. Allocation of "action-time" to various need-dispositions.

*Changes in structure.

†Changes without changes in structure.

‡The terms "external" and "internal" refer to the phenomenological place of the problems.

§The mechanisms which solve external integrative problems are the mechanisms of adjustment. Specifically, the "performance" mechanisms here are the ones traditionally attributed to adjustment.

//The mechanisms which solve internal integrative problems—specifically those listed under performance processes—are the mechanisms of defense.

Fig. 8 CLASSIFICATION OF THE PRIMARY
MECHANISMS OF ADJUSTMENT

	Retention (Dependency)	Relinquishment (Compulsive independence)
Active Alternative	Dominance	Aggressiveness
Passive Alternative	Submission	Withdrawal

Fig. 9 POINTS OF RELATION BETWEEN SOCIAL SYSTEMS AND PERSONALITY SYSTEMS

Social Systems	Personality Systems
1. Categorization of object units (individuals and collectivities) in terms of ascriptive qualities and performance capacities.	1. Cognition and cathexis of self and alters in terms of qualities and/or performance (and more or less stable need–dispositions to cognize and cathect in certain ways).

2. Role definitions including:
  a. Who shall occupy role (in terms of qualities and performance).
  b. What he shall do.
  c. The relation of roles to one another.
	2. Ego's several roles (which are superordinate need–dispositions within his character structure) and his role-expectancies (which are need-dispositions to get certain responses from alters).

3. The allocation of functions and facilities to roles.	3. Ego's orientation (and need–dispositions which control them) to various alters (and to the specific attitudes and actions of alters) as means to ego's ulterior goals. Alters are seen as consumers, sources of income, collaborators.
4. The allocation of sanctions and rewards (especially prestige and status).	4. Ego's orientation (and the need–dispositions which control it) to various alters as objects of gratification, attachment and identification, and to nonsocial reward objects.
5. Integrative structure of the social system: sub-collectivities, the inclusive collectivity, and internal roles with integrative functions.	5. Ego's superego organization (which has the status of a superordinate need–disposition) including the organization of the adjustive mechanisms.

Fig. 10 MAJOR TYPES OF SOCIAL VALUE-ORIENTATION

	UNIVERSALISM	PARTICULARISM
ACHIEVEMENT	1. The Transcendent Achievement Ideal The valuation of directional activity toward the achievement of universalistically defined goals, and the requisite performance propensities.	2. The Immanent Achievement Ideal Valuation of a harmonious system achieved by effort and maintained or restored by it. Emphasis on responsibility in this context.
ASCRIPTION	3. The Transcendent Quality-Perfection Ideal Valuation of a set of ideal qualities of action system or collectivity and of action oriented to their realization and maintenance. Absolutism of an ideal state and dualism of contrast to the evil state.	4. The Immanent Quality-Perfection Ideal Valuation of the harmonious and accepting adaptation to the given situation, "making the most" of it as an expressive opportunity.

| | | UNIVERSALISM | |
		Affectivity	Neutrality
ACHIEVEMENT	**SPECIFIC** — Self	Valuation of specific affective expression to class of persons designated on basis of achievement (e.g., expectation of respect from others on basis of specific achievement).	Valuation of specific disciplined action in relation to a class of persons designated on basis of achievement (e.g., readiness to collaborate with technically qualified persons).
	SPECIFIC — Collectivity	Valuation of specific affective expression on behalf of a class of persons designated on basis of achievement (e.g., loyalty to professional group which is recruited on basis of standards of specific performance).	Valuation of specific disciplined action with obligation to a class of persons designated on basis of achievement (e.g., professional relation to client).
	DIFFUSE — Self	Valuation of general affective expression toward classes of persons or groups on basis of achievement (e.g., expectation of esteem on part of the successful).	Valuation of general disciplined action toward classes of persons or groups on basis of achievement (e.g., generalized readiness to collaborate, in equal or subordinate role, with persons who are esteemed on a basis of achievement.
	DIFFUSE — Collectivity	Valuation of general affective expression and action on behalf of class of persons on basis of their specific or diffuse achievement (e.g., general prestige of achievement group; rationalistic social engineering enthusiasm on part of scientists; general prestige of the versatile person with diffuse achievements).	Valuation of general disciplined action on behalf of a class of persons on basis of their achievement (e.g., obligations of "citizenship" within an achievement collectivity).

PARTICULARISM

		Affectivity	Neutrality
ACHIEVEMENT	SPECIFIC — Self	Valuation of action constituting self-gratification in accordance with a conception of right and appropriate relations in a specific situation vis-à-vis particularistically designated persons or classes of persons (e.g., expectation of rightfulness of abusing Negroes under certain conditions.)	Valuation of disciplined action, in conforming with a differentiated standard, leading toward self-gratification in a specific situation (e.g., the behavior of the head of a long-established business enterprise).
	SPECIFIC — Collectivity	Valuation of specific affective action as on behalf of one's particular collectivity (e.g., expectation of devoted defense for one's collectivity in a conflict situation in accordance with a general code of responsibility appropriate to the situation).	Valuation of disciplined action on behalf of one's particular collectivity in conforming with a differentiated standard in a specific situation (e.g., expectation of father as provider for family in a stable family system).
	DIFFUSE — Self	Valuation of action constituting self-gratification in a wide variety of situations vis-à-vis particular persons (e.g., in romantic love: selection of partner; friendship selection).	Valuation of disciplined action in conforming with a differentiated standard leading toward self-gratification in a wide variety of situations vis-à-vis particular persons (e.g., status behavior of arrived and parvenu classes in a "status" oriented society).
	DIFFUSE — Collectivity	Valuation of action involving affective expression in a variety of situations on behalf of a particular collectivity or on behalf of a particular person (e.g., charismatic leadership and followership in a situation in which such behavior is considered to be appropriate).	Valuation of disciplined action in a variety of situations on behalf of a particular collectivity (e.g., traditionalistic authority and responsibility).

		UNIVERSALISM	
		Affectivity	Neutrality
ASCRIPTION	**SPECIFIC** — Self	Valuation of specific emotional gratifications in specific types of situations or with specific types of ascriptively designated persons (e.g., affective expression permitted under certain convivial conditions).	Valuation of specific style patterns appropriate to specific situations or with specific types of ascriptively selected persons (e.g., modes of dress appropriate to weddings).
	SPECIFIC — Collectivity	Valuation of certain kinds of affective action in specific types of situations or with specific types of persons; the action is an obligatory one toward ascriptively selected persons (e.g., condolence, congratulations on birthday, etc.) organized deference behavior.	Valuation of certain kinds of disciplined action in specific types of situations or with specific types of persons ascriptively designated (e.g., bureaucratic etiquette in official capacity; organized deference behavior in hierarchies).
	DIFFUSE — Self	Valuation of general affective expression (or receptiveness) with classes of persons ascriptively selected (e.g., expectations regarding appropriate types of affectivity in male and female relationships).	Valuation of a general discipline or style of life, either individually of within a group, with action toward classes of persons and objects in accordance with their ascribed qualities (e.g., expectation of behavior in accordance with a differentiated "style of life" which stresses appropriateness of various types of action for various situations).
	DIFFUSE — Collectivity	Valuation of a general affective obligation toward ascriptively selected classes of persons (e.g., expectation of completely selfless absorption into a community insofar as the process represents some high ethical ideal).	Valuation of a general discipline which imposes obligations toward classes of persons and according to classes of situations (e.g., aristocratic code of honor; Kantian ethics).

		PARTICULARISM	
		Affectivity	Neutrality
ASCRIPTION	**SPECIFIC** Self	Valuation of specific affective expression toward particular (ascriptively designated) persons (e.g., expectation of anxiety or pleasure of a particular sort from presence and activities of certain individuals or groups).	Valuation of disciplined utilization of particular persons or groups in a specific way (e.g., conformity with a specific renunciatory pattern of behavior in relations with a particular group member selected by his qualities).
	Collectivity	Valuation of specific affective expression and action toward particular persons or groups ascriptively designated (e.g., expectation of anxiety or pleasure of a particular sort from participation in collective undertakings such as ceremonials).	Valuation of disciplined action on behalf of particular persons in performance of specific actions (e.g., expectation of conformity with code of behavior in such collective activities as agricultural cooperatives even though conformity involves renunciation of pleasures).
	DIFFUSE Self	Valuation of general affective action in relation to ascriptively designated particular persons or groups (e.g., generalized gratification expectation in connection with individuals or groups having certain qualities and having a particularistic relation to ego).	Valuation of general disciplined action in relation to particular persons ascriptively designated (e.g., hostile or suspicious attitudes and action vis-à-vis ethnic outgroups).
	Collectivity	Valuation of general affective action in relation to an ascriptively designated particular person or group (e.g., expectation of anxiety or pleasure of a general sort from membership in a particular collectivity independently of the actions undertaken).	Valuation of general disciplined action in relation to an ascriptively designated particular person or group (e.g., Chinese kinship system; obligations of citizenship to a particular country or group.

Fig. 11 TYPES OF SOCIAL VALUE-ORIENTATION IN RELATION TO
CLASSES OF OBJECTS

ORGANISMS

Object Focus	Transcendent Achievement Pattern 1	Immanent Achievement Pattern 2	Transcendent Quality-Perfection Pattern 3	Immanent Quality-Perfection Pattern 4
Problem of object-significance (diagnosis)	Ego's, alter's and collectivity's utilization of bodily qualities and impulse forces so far as possible in a performance context for positive achievements; warding off and controlling threats to the achievement.	Ego's and alter's bodies as capable of being fitted into a harmonious system by requisite control of impulses and cultivation of qualities.	Sharply dualistic problem of whether impulses and bodily qualities do or do not fit the perfection ideal.	Impulses and bodily qualities as "God given," or as possible threats to the perfection of the ideal system.
Type of goal-striving in relation to object	Realization of valued goals without reference to ultimate terminal point; utilization and requisite control of bodily capacities in goal interest, not suppression of them as intrinsically evil.	Attempt to control impulses and to shape them and bodily qualities in interest of a harmony ideal.	Attempt to shape impulses and make the most of bodily uniformity with ideal, but to master or eliminate everything deviant.	Attempt to make the most of the given gratification capacities of the body and appreciate bodily qualities.
Locus of strain	Danger that body will not be adequate or its needs or propensities will interfere with achievement goals.	Those impulse factors and bodily qualities which cannot be made to "fit," or only with difficulty.	The right-wrong duality: what to "do about" impulses and bodily qualities that are not right.	The danger that impulse forces and bodily qualities will not fit—one will be aggressive or lack beauty.

Fig. 11 (Cont.)

EGO AS ROLE PERSONALITY

	1	2	3	4
Problem	Ego's capacities, including "will power," for valued achievements.	The "fitting" of ego, as personality, into the harmonious system. Can he be "educated" to his role?	Suitability of ego as a personality for his perfection destiny.	Personality as "in tune" with the expressive opportunities.
Type of goal-striving	To "try hard" in the right kind and direction of activity, universalistically valued.	To try to "do the right thing" in order to fit oneself into a harmonious order.	To achieve the ideal state without regard to cost.	To take advantage of the situation in accord with an appreciative standard, but avoid disturbing order.
Locus of strain	Problem of adequacy relative to the more particularized achievement contexts: "Can I do it?"	Possibility of discrepancy — a personality which fails to fit the requirements of role-achievement expectations.	Conflict between commitment to the ideal and deviant need-dispositions.	Possible incompatibility with conditions of a given system: "Am I out of tune?"

Fig. 11 (Cont.)

ALTER AS ROLE PERSONALITY

	1	2	3	4
Problem	Alter as the kind of person who can be expected to "pull his oar," or at least not to "gum the works." Respect for his point of view, his interests and commitments.	Definition of alter's complementary role of co-responsibility for the harmonious system: "Where does he fit?"	Do alter and I "belong together"? Is he "worthy" to be a comrade or fellow-disciple?	Does alter "belong" and can I have satisfactory reciprocity with him within the given system? Will he conform or "rock the boat"?
Type of ego's goal-striving	To facilitate securing alter's co-operation — if irrelevant — to respect his "rights."	To "do his part" in specific reciprocation with alter's, properly respecting alter's status (not rights).	To live up to the imperative of comradeship or to bring alter up to it; if hopeless to do so, to "treat him as he deserves."	Reciprocal gratification and appreciation. To take care not to let him step out of line.
Locus of strain	Alter's "reliability" as pulling his oar or respecting ego's rights to "go about his job his own way."	The possibility of the breakdown of reciprocities from either side; failure of responsibility.	Ego's or alter's worthiness with respect to the perfection ideal; danger of either or both "backsliding."	Possibility of alter's "not fitting," "stepping out of line," and becoming a disturbing element.

Fig. 11 (Cont.)

<table>
<tr><th></th><th colspan="4">COLLECTIVITY</th></tr>
<tr><th></th><th>1</th><th>2</th><th>3</th><th>4</th></tr>
<tr>
<td>Problem</td>
<td>Is the collectivity a cooperative system within which ego can play his achievement role — or at least a "free country" where he can count on non-interference?</td>
<td>Does the collectivity measure up to the ideal of a cooperative achievement system? How can this be maintained or restored?</td>
<td>Is the collectivity an embodiment of the ideal or an evil countertype? Which?</td>
<td>Suitability of the collectivity as a stage for expressive activity.</td>
</tr>
<tr>
<td>Type of ego's goal-striving</td>
<td>To "do his job" within the system, to take advantage of its opportunities and to combat features threatening to interfere with either.</td>
<td>To "take responsibility" according to his status for his share of maintenance or restoration of the immanent pattern.</td>
<td>To help realize the ideal social order and combat the evil countertypes.</td>
<td>To combat threats to its integrity —otherwise indifference.</td>
</tr>
<tr>
<td>Locus of strain</td>
<td>General basis of difficulties of "securing cooperation" or of securing freedoms and opportunities.</td>
<td>Tendencies for the ideal order to "break up" and the collectivity to fail into disharmony; need for continual effort to maintain it.</td>
<td>The precariousness of maintenance of the ideal and imminence of the threat of its subversion; the "lurking enemy."</td>
<td>Instability of the established taken-for-granted order.</td>
</tr>
</table>

Fig. 11 (Cont.)

PHYSICAL ENVIRONMENT

	1	2	3	4
Problem	The environment's utility as a set of resources and conditions relative to achievement goals: What can ego do with it?	How to shape and fit the environment into a harmonious pattern — the cultivated world.	Is nature part of the ideal state or inimical to it?	Discrimination of "God given" nature and its threatening aspects.
Type of ego's goal-striving	To make the most effective use of resources and progressively to overcome obstacles.	Adaptation of nature to man, and vice versa, into a harmonious system.	Enjoyment of idealized aspects and attempts to master inimical aspects.	Enjoyment of good part; warding-off of threats.
Locus of strain	Recalcitrance of nature to being used effectively by men.	Threats of disorderliness and disruption of harmonious system.	The struggle against the inimical aspects; transitoriness and instability of the ideal aspects.	Instability of the natural conditions of immanent perfection.

CULTURAL ACCUMULATION OBJECTS

Fig. 11 (Cont.)

	1	2	3	4
Problem	"Knowledge for what?" Cultural tradition as means of achievement.	How actively to fit cultural elements into a harmonious pattern; utility but in an aesthetic setting.	Is cultural element good or bad? Expression of ideal, or of evil.	Discrimination of the elements that belong and those that do not.
Type of ego's goal-striving	Attempts to make the most of available cultural resources; to overcome "ignorance" and other limitations.	Attempts to construct actively harmonized cultural system; active aestheticism.	Attempts to create idealistic art and to attain perfection of knowledge; search for an absolute.	Enjoyment and acceptance of a given culture and aesthetic patterns. Avoidance of what does not fit.
Locus of strain	Problem of adequacy of cultural resources to "do the job."	Elements of cultural disharmony which cannot be organized.	Uncertainty about perfection of cultural possessions.	Threats to the given perfection of the culture.

Fig. 12 TRANSCENDENT ACHIEVEMENT

Types of ego's goal-striving toward classes of objects	Affectivity-Specificity 1	Affectivity-Diffuseness 2	Neutrality-Specificity 3	Neutrality-Diffuseness 4
Ego's body	Striving to achieve specific types of bodily enjoyment or gratifying performances: e.g., food, sex, pleasurable motor activity in sports.	Striving to achieve diffuse bodily well-being and to exercise bodily capacities: cult of "enjoyment of health."	Striving to achieve specific types of bodily efficiency and discipline, such as athletic prowess. Specific instrumental uses of body.	Striving for a diffuse state of bodily efficiency and discipline—be "in training." General instrumental utilization of body.
Alter as personality	Striving to achieve specific gratification from alter, reciprocally or otherwise.	Striving to achieve and utilize a diffuse affective attachment to alter, for mutual gratification: romantic love, "winning" the object.	Striving to win and utilize alter as a cooperator or exchange partner in achieving specific goals, or to "get something out of him" for a specific goal.	Striving to bring alter into a diffuse relation of solidarity in the interest of general achievement orientation.
Physical environment	Striving to secure or control specifically enjoyable resources: foods, beautiful locations, etc.	Striving to secure diffuse gratifications from nature by earning or winning them.	Striving to control requisite resources for specific achievements and to shape them accordingly.	Striving to attain diffuse control over nature to be available for any goal.

Fig. 12 (Cont.)

IMMANENT ACHIEVEMENT

	1	2	3	4
Ego's body	Striving to maintain strict limitation on gratifications through use of body by allotting special times, places to such activities. Constant concern not to allow pattern or harmony to be broken.	Striving to maintain a diffuse state of bodily gratification in accordance with an established pattern of harmony among bodily and other pleasures and among various bodily pleasures.	Striving to maintain specific types of discipline as part of a general pattern in which body is controlled: carriage, physical fortitude, etc.	Striving to maintain a general state of discipline as part of a pattern in which body is controlled but not repressed. Valuing discipline without stressing its repressive function.
Alter as personality	Restricted stylized enjoyment of relations with alter according to an established pattern, with carefully structured expectations as to limits of the relationship.	General stylized enjoyment of relations with alter according to an established pattern covering many relationships with same persons, each of which is regulated by a standard of propriety.	Striving to maintain a restrained disciplined relationship strictly bound by limits of propriety and in right proportion to other relationships and activities.	Striving to maintain a generally disciplined set of relationships extending to all spheres and not differentiated by context. A generalized respectability.
Physical environment	Enjoyment of specific resources – food, beautiful locations, etc. – within context of an established pattern.	Striving to maintain general enjoyment of nature in its various aspects with concern to keep a proper balance between these enjoyments and other activities.	Striving to maintain natural environment in an ordered differentiated pattern relevant to specific activities; e.g., gardening.	Striving to maintain nature in a generally ordered state conforming to a pattern in which gentle wildness and cultivation might be intermixed.

Fig. 12 (Cont.)

TRANSCENDENT QUALITY-PERFECTION

	1	2	3	4
Ego's body	Striving to conform with an ideal which allows certain bodily gratifications and strictly represses others.	Striving to achieve some state of ideal beauty or euphoria; horror of ugliness.	Striving to conform with an ideal which imposes specific deprivations and repressions which are highly evaluated.	Striving to conform with a generally repressive ideal in which the repressive element is highly evaluated as such.
Alter as personality	Intense specific demands on alter to achieve ideal relationship in a particular activity.	Striving to achieve an ideal of complete fusion of love or comradeship; fear of anything less.	Striving to achieve an ideal of proper fulfillment of specific obligations in relations with others; e.g., bureaucratic fulfillment of obligation (formal justice).	Striving to achieve a repressive relationship in all spheres vis-à-vis others as fulfillment of an ideal of manly or paternal authority.
Physical environment	Striving to achieve some enjoyment in a specific activity; e.g., reaching a particular landscape or mountain peak.	Striving to achieve an ideal state through contact with nature as such or Reality.	Striving to achieve some specific discipline or deprivation by extreme exertion vis-à-vis nature, the end being the performance of the action itself.	Striving to achieve an ideal state in which all of nature is fully under control, with nothing left to nature's own operations (but not for instrumental purposes).

Fig. 12 (Cont.)

IMMANENT QUALITY-PERFECTION

	1	2	3	4
Ego's body	Acceptance of opportunities for specific gratifications along already established channels. No substitutibility of one mode of gratification for another.	Acceptance of opportunities for any gratification as they occur or as need emerges. No attachment to specific objects or modes of gratification.	Acceptance of specific deprivations as imposed by object situation. (Not ethically required to accept them but absence of feasible alternatives renders it necessary.)	Acceptance of deprivations in general on grounds that they are imposed by the situation.
Alter as personality	Acceptance of a specific alter as a satisfactory partner for enjoyment of a specific gratification. No joint exertion with alter to achieve hitherto unrealized goals.	Acceptance of any alter as a satisfactory partner for enjoyment of any gratification as needs arise and as opportunities occur. No joint exertion with alter to achieve hitherto unrealized goals.	Acceptance of a specific alter as imposing deprivations which are not to be avoided since they are part of the situation.	Acceptance of other persons in general as agents of deprivations which are not to be avoided since they are part of the situation.
Physical environment	Acceptance of available opportunities for specific gratifications afforded by environment and some effort to ward off loss of these opportunities without, however, effort to extend range of opportunities for gratification or to guarantee them.	Acceptance of available opportunities for any kind of gratifications as they occur and as need arises. Efforts to ward off losses taken only with respect to most immediately enjoyed gratification opportunity but in view of wide substitutibility of gratification objects.	Acceptance of specific environment deprivations as they occur with little effort to avoid them in the future, looking upon them as given by the situation.	Acceptance of environment as generally deprivational without alternatives and hence with little effort to avoid them.

Fig. 13

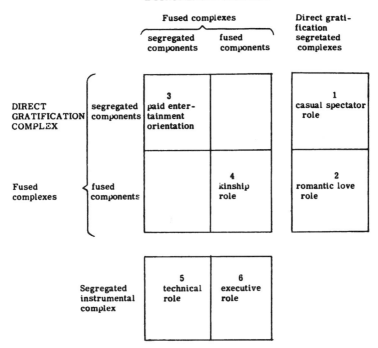

INSTRUMENTAL COMPLEX

Fig. 14

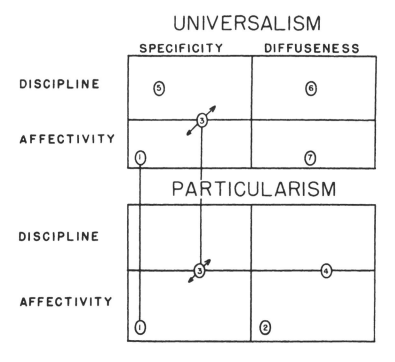

Fig. 15 POINTS OF CORRESPONDENCE BETWEEN SOCIAL SYSTEMS
AND PERSONALITY SYSTEMS

Social Systems	Personality Systems
1. Categorization of object units (individual actors and collectivities) in terms of ascriptive qualities and performance capacities.	1. Categorization of self as object in relation to alters—as possessing qualities and performance capacities.
2. Distribution types of role-orientation pattern—of individuals and collectivities—in the social system.	2. Ego's different types of role-orientations as an interdependent system.
3. The economy of instrumental orientations (division of labor) in ecological complexes and in organizations.	3. The relational complex of ego's instrumental orientations to alters as consumers, sources of income, facilities, collaborators.
4. The economy of expressive orientations in attachment patterns and the corresponding symbolic reward system.	4. The relational complex of ego's expressive orientations to alters as objects of gratification, attachment, and identification.
5. Integrative structures of the social system; sub-collectivities, the over-all collectivity, and internal role of differentiation relative to collective responsibility.	5. Ego's integration with social system in terms of superego-integration, including the organization of adjustive mechanisms relative to collective obligations.

Index

elementary form, 16; ethos of, 169, 176, 178, 219; and pattern variables, 79-88, 105, 186-189, 236; and value-orientation, 159-167. *See also* Orientation, cultural; Symbolic systems; Value-orientation

Culture patterns, 8, 21, 98; consistency of, 21, 167, 172; and need-dispositions, 115; systems of expressive symbols, 21, 24, 162, 169-170; systems of ideas, 20-21, 24, 162, 167, 169; systems of value-orientation, 21, 24, 163, 170-172; and value-orientations, 165, 159-189. *See also* Internalization; Institutionalization

Defense, mechanisms of, 19, 133-137, 157, 237
Dependency, 140
Deprivation, 9, 68, 106, 121, 134, 138, 169; anxiety, 13, 134, 140; expectation of, 13, 134, 140
Deviance, 151, 156-158, 179, 231
Dichotomies of action, see Pattern variables Diffusion, transmission of culture, 159
Discipline, 84
Displacement, 136
Division of labor, see Allocative processes; Instrumental action
Dominance, 89, 140. *See also* Mechanisms of integration
Drive, 5, 110, 112, 235; and action, 114; as component of a need disposition, 113.
See also Need-dispositions; Needs
Durkheim, Emile, 52, 74, 239
Dysphoria, 121, 142

Economic processes, see Allocative processes; Instrumental action
Economic theory, 28
Ego, reference Point, 15, 56, 67, 87, 100, 103; individuality of, 156; instrumental relations of, 209-212; relations to alter, 105, 140, 153

Ego structure; integration of, 144; organization of, 85. *See also* Personality
Environment, 31
Equilibrium, 107, 113, 120, 142; and disequilibrium, 168; of personality, 226; of social system, 226, 228; and value systems, 175
Ethos, 169, 176, 178, 219. *See also* Modal matrix
Evaluation, 5, 11, 70, 163, 175
Evaluative symbols, see Culture patterns; Value-orientation
Expectancy, aspect of orientation, 68
Expectations, 11, 64, 113; anxiety, 13, 134, 142; activity-passivity reaction, 11; complementarity of, 15, 64, 105, 115, 153, 191, 235; systems of, 20.
See also Beliefs, means-end; Choice; Normative orientation; Role-expectations

Facilities, 199
Fear, 133, 138, 142
Fixation, 136
Frank, Philipp, 34
Freud, Sigmund, 52, 67, 85, 102, 118, 240
Function, in social system, 25
Functional approach, 35
Functional autonomy, 97, 143
Functional imperatives, 173, 177, 241
Functional problems, 25, 76, 198, 211. *See* also Structural-functional theory
Fusion, 214, 221

Gemeinschaft and Gesellschaft, 49
Generalization, 106, 126, 130, 161
Goals, 5, 53, 68. *See also* Objects
Gratification, 10, 68, 80, 106, 113, 114, 118, 120, 123, 169, 201; immediate, 211-214
Guilt, 142, 157